MostUsedWords.com presents

Dutch Frequency Dictionary

Essential Vocabulary

2500 Most Common Dutch Words

Book 1

First Printing, 2019

MostUsedWords.com
10685-B Hazelhurst Dr. # 22933
HOUSTON, TX 77043
United States

www.MostUsedWords.com

Contents

Why This Book?

Hello, dear reader.

Thank you for purchasing this book. We hope it serves you well on your language learning journey.

Not all words are created equal. The purpose of this frequency dictionary is to list the most common Dutch words in descending order, so you can learn this language as fast and efficiently as possible.

First, we would like to illustrate the value of a frequency dictionary. For the purpose of example, we have combined frequency data from various languages (mainly Romance, Slavic and Dutchic languages) and made it into a single chart.

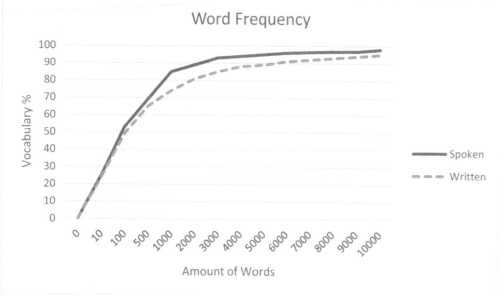

The sweet spots, according to the data seem to be:

Amount of Words	Spoken	Written
• 100	53%	49%
• 1.000	85%	74%
• 2.500	92%	82%
• 5.000	95%	89%
• 7.500	97%	93%
• 10.000	98%	95%

Above data corresponds with Pareto's law. Pareto's law, also known as the 80/20 rule, states that, for many events, roughly 80% of the effects come from 20% of the causes.

In language learning, this principle seems to be on steroids. It seems that just 20% of the 20% (95/5) of the most used words in a language account for roughly all the vocabulary you need.

To put this further in perspective: The authorative Algemeen Nederlands Woordenboek of the Dutch Institute of Language lists over 255.000 references in current use. You will only need to know 1.96% (5000 words) to achieve 95% and 89% fluency in speaking and writing respectively. Knowing the most common 10.000 words, or just 3.92%, will net you 98% fluency in spoken language and 95% fluency in written texts.

Keeping this in mind, the value of a frequency dictionary is immense. Study the most frequent words, build your vocabulary and progress quickly.

One more frequently asked question needs to be answered: how many words do I need to know for varying levels of fluency?

While it's important to note that it is impossible to pin down these numbers and statistics with 100% accuracy, these are a global average of multiple sources.

According to research, this is the amount of vocabulary needed for varying levels of fluency.

1. 250 words: the essential core of a language. Without these words, you cannot construct any meaningful sentences.
2. 750 words: are used every single day by every person who speaks the language.
3. 2500 words: should enable you to express everything you could possibly want to say, although some creativity might be required.
4. 5000 words: the active vocabulary of native speakers without higher education.
5. 10,000 words: the active vocabulary of native speakers with higher education.
6. 20,000 words: the amount you need to be able to recognize passively to read, understand, and enjoy a work of literature such as a novel by a notable author.

Caveats & Limitations.

1. A frequency list is never "The Definite Frequency List."

Creating an accurate frequency list is more complicated than it seems. Depending on the source material analyzed, you will get different frequency lists. A corpus on spoken word differs from source texts based on a written language. That is why we chose subtitles as our source, because, according to science, subtitles cover the best of both worlds: they correlate with both spoken and written language.

The frequency list is based on an analysis of huge amount of Dutch subtitles. If you were to read the source text used for this book, it would take you around 100 years of non-stop reading. A large base text is absolutely vital in order to develop an accurate frequency list. The raw data included abit over 1 million entries, or different "words". The raw data has been lemmatized; words are given in their dictionary form.

Lemmatization and correct classification does come with its own complications. We list the most common issues in the following list. The examples below are given in different languages, but they are applicable to Dutch as well.

2. Homographs

Let's begin with homographs. Put quite simply, a homograph is a group (usually a pair) of words that are spelled the same way. In example:

- **Advocate** (verb) can mean "to speak or write in support of"
- **Advocate** (noun) can also and refer to a person who supports or pleads the cause of another.

Since a dictionary does not list separate entries for the same word, we did not splice Dutch homographs in ours. Because homographs are quite rare, we kindly ask you to use your common sense while using this dictionary. If you think a particular translation of a homograph is not used fairly often, then just skip learning it.

3. Inflections, Declensions and Conjugations

In grammar, inflection is the modification of a word to express different grammatical categories such as tense, case, voice, aspect, person, number, gender, and mood. It is found in many, but not all languages. The inflection of verbs is also called conjugation, and one can refer to the inflection of nouns, adjectives, adverbs, pronouns, determiners, participles, prepositions, postpositions, numerals, articles etc., as declension. How do these modifications create difficulties in establishing reliable frequency lists?

Some inflections can be classified as multiple parts of speech. Take for example the Spanish word **dicho**. It originally ranked somewhere around the 147th most common Spanish word.

As a conjugated verb, **dicho** is the past participle of "**decir** - to say" and translates as "said", while as a noun it means "saying, expression".

No way, José, that "saying, expression" is the most 147th most used Spanish word. As previously stated, our words are lemmatized, and **decir** is already listed at place 77. Turns out that the noun **dicho** is around the 11.000th most common words, and thus beyond the scope of our dictionary series.

4. Nouns

We tried our best to keep out proper nouns, such as "**James**, **Ryan**, **Alice** as well as "**Rome**, **Washington**" or "the **Louvre**". Names of countries are an exception to the rule, and are included.

Some common proper nouns have multiple translations. Take for example "**Jack**" in our English frequency list. "**Jack**" is a very common first name, but also a noun (a jack to lift up a vehicle) and a verb (to steal something). So is the word "**can**" It is a conjugation of the verb "to be able" as well as a noun (a tin can, or a can of soft drink).

5. This word doesn't belong there!

Some entries you might find odd in their respective frequency rankings. We were surprised a couple of times ourselves while creating this series. Keep in mind that the frequency list is compiled from a large amount of text, and may include words you wouldn't use yourself. But you might very well encounter them.

In our opinion, it is important you do know these words. Store them somewhere in your passive vocabulary, instead of trying to integrate them into your active vocabulary. But in the end, it's up to you whether you think you should learn a word, or skip it. We provide the data, it is up to you to select and learn relevant vocabulary.

6. This is not a Dutch word!

You might find non-Dutch loanwords in this dictionary. We decided to include them, because if they're being used in subtitle translation, it is safe to assume the word has been integrated into the Dutch general vocabulary.

7. Vulgarities

We also decided to keep out most vulgarities, even though these are rather common in daily speech. We wanted to keep this book appropriate for readers of all ages. We tried to imagine what a modern-day midwestern American woman would take offense to, and drew the line there.

At the same time, some words absolutely needed to be clarified. In rare occasions, the usage of vocabulary items can differ severely various locales. It could lead to pretty awkward situations if you were not aware of these differences.

These words have been censored in a way that one can still deduce their meaning, if one is already in the know.. Let's take the Spanish word **coger** as an example: "**coger**-*vb* - to take, f*ck (LA)" In Europe, **coger** is pretty innocent. But in Latin-America, it has a whole different meaning.

8. Parallel text example sentences

Example sentences are great, because they show you Dutch word usage in context. You get to learn extra vocabulary from the sentences, since they're in parallel text format. And since you'll encounter important, common words over and over again, you will ingrain those words faster.

Some sentences are easy, some are more difficult. Some are a direct translation, some are more loosely translated. Some mimic spoken language, some mimic written language. Some are more high-brow, some are more colloquial. In short, we tried to include a mix of different types of language, just like you would encounter in real life. The first book in the series generally contains easier sentences than the 2nd, 3rd and 4th book.

9. A dictionary for learners.

This book is made for learners of Dutch vocabulary. We tried to keep the translations as direct and concise as possible. Sometimes words can be used in a multitude of ways, but for the sake of facilitating learning, we tried to keep it as short and direct as possible. If you are more advanced and do require a more thorough dictionary, we suggest investing in an orthographic dictionary.

10. Final thoughts

We are pretty confident that our frequency ranking is pretty solid, while keeping above pitfalls in mind. Still, this frequency list includes 25 extra words to compensate for any irregularities you might encounter. Or you might disagree with the addition of non-Dutch loanwords, or whatever it is that irks you. So instead of the 2500 most common words, you actually get the 2525 most common words. #winning.

And one more thing.

The big secret to learning language is this: build your vocabulary, learn basic grammar and go out there and speak. Make mistakes, have a laugh and then learn from your mistakes. Wash, rinse, repeat..

We hope you enjoy this frequency dictionary and that it helps you in your journey of learning Dutch.

How To Use This Dictionary

abbreviation	*abr*	phrase	*phr*
adjective	*adj*	prefix	*pfx*
adverb	*adv*	preposition	*prp*
article	*art*	pronoun	*prn*
auxiliary verb	*av*	suffix	*sfx*
conjunction	*con*	verb	*vb*
contraction	*cntr*	singular	*sg*
interjection	*i*	plural	*pl*
noun	*de*	colloquial language	*(coll)*
	het	formal language	*(fml)*
numeral	*nu*		
particle	*prt*		

Word Order

Different parts of speech are divided by the semicolon ";".

Translations

We made the decision to give the most common translation(s) of a word, and respectively the most common part(s) of speech. It does, however, not mean that this is the only possible translations or the only part of speech the word can be used for. This is a dictionary for learners, and not an ortographic dictionary.

International Phonetic Alphabet (IPA)

The pronunciation of foreign vocabulary can be tricky. To help you get it right, we added IPA entries for each entry. If you already have a base understanding of the pronunciation, you will find the IPA pronunciation straightforward. For more information, please visit www.internationalphoneticalphabet.org

Dutch English Frequency Dictionary

Rank	Dutch	English Equivalent
	Part of Speech	Dutch Sentence
	IPA	-English Sentence
1	**je**	**you**
	prn	Kun je dat per e-mail sturen?
	[jə]	-Could you send that by e-mail?
2	**het**	**the; it**
	art; prn	Het is het lot van de mens om te lijden.
	[hɛt/ət]	-It is man's destiny to suffer.
3	**de**	**the**
	art	De hemel is bezaaid met sterren.
	[də]	-The sky is full of stars.
4	**ik**	**I**
	prn	Ik kom zo bij je!
	[ɪk]	-I will be right with you!
5	**zijn**	**his, its; be**
	prn; vb	De voetnoten zijn aangeduid met een sterretje.
	[zɛin]	-The footnotes are marked with an asterisk.
6	**dat**	**that; that**
	con; prn	Dat is geen mening, het is een feit.
	[dɑt]	-That's not an opinion, it's a fact.
7	**een**	**a; one; any**
	art; nu; prn	Heb je een aansteker?
	[en]	-Have you got a lighter?
8	**niet**	**not**
	adv	Ik heb mijn haar niet gewassen.
	[nit]	-I haven't washed my hair.
9	**en**	**and**
	con	John en Jane gingen naar het oogstfeest.
	[ɛn]	-John and Jane went to the harvest festival.
10	**wat**	**what; what; few**
	con; prn; adv	Wat was er aan de hand met de oude?
	[wɑt]	-What was wrong with the old one?
11	**van**	**of, from**
	prp	Één van mijn kinderen is ziek
	[vɑn]	-One of my children is sick.
12	**we**	**we**
	prn	Het enige wat we weten, is dat John schuldig is.
	[wə]	-All we know is that John is guilty.
13	**in**	**in**
	prp	John stopt Jane in bed.
	[ɪn]	-John puts Jane into bed.
14	**ze**	**she, they**
	prn	Ze ving een glimp van hem op terwijl hij door de menigte liep.
	[zɛ]	-She glimpsed him walking through the crowd.
15	**op**	**on, up, at; on, up; spent**
	prp; adv; adj	Ik werk op de ambassade.
	[ɔp]	-I work at the embassy.

16 te
adv; prp
[tə]

too, to; in
Het is heel moeilijk hem te verstaan.
-It's very difficult to understand him.

17 hij
prn
[hɛi]

he
Voor zover ik kon zien, was hij aan het experimenteren met nieuwe methodes.
-As far as I could make out, he was experimenting with new methods.

18 er
adv
[ɛr]

there
Er staan auto's in de straat.
-There are cars in the street.

19 maar
adv; con
[mar]

however, just; but
"Maar dat is belachelijk!" protesteerde John. "Ik heb er maar twee opgegeten!"
-"But that's ridiculous!" John protested. "I only ate two!"

20 me
prn
[mə]

me
De leraar vroeg me of ik klaar was en voegde eraan toe dat iedereen bij de schoolpoort op me wachtte.
-The teacher asked me if I was ready, adding that everybody was waiting for me at the school gate.

21 die
prn; con
[di]

that; which
Ik heb hoofdpijn gekregen van drie baby's die onophoudelijk huilden.
-Three babies crying incessantly gave me a headache.

22 hebben
av; vb
['hɛbə(n)]

have; have
We hebben een afwijking in uw röntgenfoto ontdekt.
-We have detected an abnormality on your x-ray.

23 voor
prp; adv; con
[vor]

for; before; ere
Voor de oorlog zijn we naar Londen verhuisd.
-We moved to London before the war.

24 met
prp; adv
[mɛt]

with; along with
Denk je dat hij de fout met opzet gemaakt heeft?
-Do you think he made that mistake on purpose?

25 als
adv; con; prp
[als]

as; as; like
Bovendien beschouwt China kernenergie als hernieuwbare energie.
-Moreover, China refers to nuclear power as a form of renewable energy.

26 mijn
prn
[mɛin]

my, mine
Mijn oom heeft drie kinderen.
-My uncle has three children.

27 u
prn
[y]

you
Ik wens u een goede reis.
-I wish you a pleasant voyage.

28 dit
prn
[dɪt]

this
Wat is dit? Dit is een grap.
-What is this? This is a joke.

29 aan
prp; adj
[an]

to, on; on
Aan wie ging je het verkopen?
-Who were you going to sell it to?

30 hier
adv
[hir]

here
Hier is de keuken.
-The kitchen is here.

31 om
prp; adv
[ɔm]

to, for; about
Om de kerk ligt een grindpad.
-There is a gravel path around the church.

32 naar

to, for; along; awful

	prp; adv; adj	Hij gaat zelden naar de kerk.
	[nar]	-He seldom goes to church.
33	**dan**	**than; then**
	con; adv	Hij is groter dan ik ben.
	[dɑn]	-He is bigger than I am.
34	**jij**	**you**
	prn	Hou jij van chocolademelk?
	[jɛi]	-Do you like chocolate milk?
35	**weten**	**know**
	vb	Ik weet niet zeker wanneer hij zal aankomen.
	['wetə(n)]	-I don't know for certain when he will arrive.
36	**ja**	**yes**
	prt	Ja of nee… wat wordt het?
	[ja]	-Yes or no.. what will it be?
37	**kunnen**	**can**
	vb	Vanaf morgen kunnen we samen naar het werk gaan.
	['kʏnə(n)]	-From tomorrow on we can go to work together.
38	**geen**	**not one, no; no; no; none**
	art; adj; adv; prn; nu	John heeft geen zussen.
	[xen]	-John has no sisters.
39	**zo**	**so, that; if**
	adv; con;	We zijn zo door dat gat naar de overkant gekropen
	[zo:]	-We have crawled through that hole to the other side.
40	**nog**	**yet, still**
	adv	Nog één! Hoeveel nog?
	[nɔx]	-Still one more! How many left?
41	**willen**	**want**
	vb	Zou je graag willen weten wie zij is?
	['wɪlə(n)]	-Would you like to know who she is?
42	**wel**	**well; alright; as many as**
	adv; adj; con	Ik mag hem wel.
	[wɛl]	-I think he is alright.
43	**moeten**	**must, need; should**
	vb; av	Je moet je vermogen niet onderschatten.
	['mutə(n)]	-You must not underestimate your abilities.
44	**goed**	**good, correct; well; estate**
	adj; adv; het	Dat is goed, nietwaar?
	[xut]	-That's good, isn't it?
45	**hem**	**him**
	prn	Heb je hem in de universiteit ontmoet?
	[hɛm]	-Did you meet him at the university?
46	**nee**	**no**
	prt	O nee! Wat doen we nu?
	[ne]	-Oh no! What do we do now?
47	**waar**	**where; where; true; merchandise**
	adv; con; adj; de	Waar woont hij?
	[war]	-Where does he live?
48	**nu**	**now; now**
	adv; con	Ik moet nu even boodschappen doen.
	[ny]	-I have to do some grocery shopping now.
49	**hoe**	**how; how**

	adv; prn [hu]	Hoe oud is hij? -How old is he?
50	**gaan** *vb; av* [xan]	**go, work; shall** Laten we met de bus gaan. -Let's go by bus.
51	**komen** *vb* ['komə(n)]	**come, come to** Wij allen proberen minstens een keer per jaar bijeen te komen. -We all try to get together at least once a year.
52	**uit** *prp; adv; adj* [œyt]	**from; out; off** Ik kom uit Amsterdam. -I am from Amsterdam.
53	**haar** *prn; het* [har]	**her; hair** Ze heeft haar kinderen in de steek gelaten. -She abandoned her children.
54	**doen** *vb; het* [dun]	**do, perform; doing** Ik wou dat ik dat kon doen, maar ik kan het niet. -I wish I could do that, but I can't.
55	**ook** *adv* [ok]	**also, as well** Hij studeert ook Chinees. -He studies Chinese as well.
56	**mij** *prn* [mɛi]	**me** Geef mij een stuk papier. -Give me a piece of paper.
57	**over** *prp; adv* ['ovər]	**about; over** Het lijkt dat u veel over mij weet. -You seem to know a lot about me.
58	**of** *con* [ɔf]	**or, whether** Het valt te betwijfelen of deze methode zal werken. -It is doubtful whether this method will work.
59	**daar** *adv; con* [dar]	**there; as** Wie maakt zich daar druk over? -Who cares about that?
60	**zullen** *vb; av* ['zʏlə(n)]	**will; shall** We zullen zien. -We shall see.
61	**al** *adv; het; con* [ɑl]	**already; all; though** Heb je al gegeten deze middag? -Have you had dinner already?
62	**jullie** *prn* ['jʏli]	**you** Kan ik jullie hamer lenen? -Can I borrow your hammer?
63	**bij** *prp; de; adv* [bɛi]	**at; bee; up to date** Ik was niet bij zijn begrafenis. -I didn't attend his funeral.
64	**ons** *prn; het/de* [ɔns]	**us; ounce** Ze is erg aardig tegen ons. -She is very kind to us.
65	**meer** *adj; adv; het* [mer]	**more; more; lake** Ik eet geen rijst meer. -I don't eat rice anymore.
66	**waarom**	**why; why**

	adv; con		Waarom ging ze weg?
	[war'ɔm]		-Why did she leave?
67	**iets**		**something; some**
	prn; adv		Wil je iets te drinken?
	[its]		-Would you like something to drink?
68	**laten**		**let, leave**
	vb		Iedereen heeft donkere zijde die hij nooit aan iemand laat zien.
	['latə(n)]		-Everyone has a dark side which he never shows to anybody.
69	**deze**		**this**
	prn		Deze mevrouw zal alles betalen.
	['dezə]		-This lady will pay for everything.
70	**wie**		**who; who**
	con; prn		De man met wie ze gaat trouwen is een astronaut.
	[wi]		-The man she's going to marry is an astronaut.
71	**jou**		**you**
	prn		Dit is een geschenk voor jou.
	[jɑu]		-This a gift for you.
72	**alles**		**all, everything**
	prn		John doet alles.
	['ɑləs]		-John does everything.
73	**denken**		**think, think of**
	vb		Ik denk dat je dit nodig zal hebben.
	['dɛŋkə(n)]		-I suppose you'll be needing this.
74	**eens**		**once; agree**
	adv; adj		Je hebt jezelf weer eens overtroffen.
	[ens]		-Once again you've managed to top yourself.
75	**echt**		**really; real**
	adv; adj		Ik heb echt een baan nodig.
	[ɛxt]		-I really need a job.
76	**man**		**man**
	de		Hij is een man van nobel bloed.
	[mɑn]		-He is a man of noble blood.
77	**weg**		**road; away, gone**
	de; adv		Toen ik terugkwam was mijn auto weg.
	[wɛx]		-When I came back, my car was gone.
78	**toch**		**yet, so, right; nevertheless**
	adv; con		John nam toch meer dan één foto?
	[tɔx]		-John took more than one picture, right?
79	**zien**		**see, look**
	vb		We zien wat we verwachten te zien.
	[zin]		-We see what we expect to see.
80	**alleen**		**only, merely; only; alone**
	adv; con; adj		Ik moet met hem alleen spreken.
	[ɑ'len]		-I need to speak with him alone.
81	**nou**		**now**
	adv		Wat kan er nou misgaan?
	[nɑu]		-Now what could go wrong?
82	**dus**		**so, consequently; therefore**
	adv; con		Dus, wat gaat het worden?
	[dʏs]		-So, what's it gonna be?
83	**nooit**		**never, no way**

	adv	Ik heb dat nooit gezegd!
	[nojt]	-I have never said that!
84	**terug**	**back, again**
	adv	Als je terug wilt komen, zal ik het begrijpen.
	[teˈrʏx]	-If you want to come back, I'll understand.
85	**mee**	**also, with**
	adv	Hij heeft er weinig mee bereikt.
	[me]	-He has accomplished very little with it.
86	**houden**	**keep, hold**
	vb	Houd je niet van zwemmen?
	[ˈhɑudə(n)]	-Don't you like swimming?
87	**even**	**momentarily; even**
	adv; adj	Mag ik even rondkijken?
	[ˈevə(n)]	-Can I take a quick look around?
88	**niets**	**nothing; nothing; none**
	het; prn; adv	Hij kocht helemaal niets.
	[nits]	-He bought nothing at all.
89	**zeggen**	**say**
	vb	Ik zei iets tegen hem.
	[ˈzɛxə(n)]	-I said something to him.
90	**misschien**	**maybe**
	adv	Misschien zou ze er echt niet zijn?
	[mɪsˈxin]	-Maybe she really won't be there?
91	**iemand**	**someone; person**
	prn	Het doet er niet toe hoe iemand sterft, maar hoe hij leeft.
	[ˈimɑnt]	-It matters not how anybody dies, but how he lives.
92	**kijken**	**look**
	vb	Kijk naar de sterren.
	[ˈkɛikə(n)]	-Look at the stars.
93	**tot**	**to; until**
	prp; con	Ze verkozen haar tot burgemeester.
	[tɔt]	-They elected her to be the mayor.
94	**veel**	**much, a lot**
	adv	Veel mensen reizen graag.
	[vel]	-Many people like to travel.
95	**worden**	**will be, become**
	vb	Het gaat vrij koud worden.
	[ˈwɔrdə(n)]	-It is going to be quite cold.
96	**mens**	**human**
	het	De mens als een biologisch wezen hoort tot de dierenwereld.
	[mɛns]	-Human as a biological being belongs to the animal world.
97	**onze**	**our**
	prn	Hij is zonder twijfel de beste atleet van onze school.
	[ˈɔnzə]	-He is beyond doubt the best athlete in our school.
98	**leven**	**life; live**
	het; vb	Mensen die vroeg naar bed gaan en vroeg opstaan, leven lang.
	[ˈlevə(n)]	-People who go to bed early and get up early live a long time.
99	**gewoon**	**just, plainly; ordinary**
	adv; adj	Ik haat jou gewoon.
	[xəˈwon]	-I just hate you.
100	**weer**	**weather; again**

het; adv   We hebben goed weer gehad de afgelopen tijd.
[wer]   -We've been having good weather.

101   nodig   **necessary, required**
adj   John heeft kleding nodig.
['nodəx]   -John needs clothes.

102   wij   **we**
prn   Wij zijn tweelingen.
[wɛi]   -We are twins.

103   twee   **two**
nu   De thee kost twee euro.
[twe]   -The tea costs two euros.

104   tijd   **time**
de   Het is tijd om te gaan.
[tɛit]   -It is time to go.

105   uw   **your**
prn   Ik heb uw vriend ontmoet.
[yw]   -I met your friend.

106   tegen   **against**
prp; adv   De plant leunt tegen de muur.
['texə(n)]   -The plant leans against the wall.

107   toen   **when; then**
con; adv   Hij woonde in Engeland toen de oorlog uitbrak.
[tun]   -He was living in England when the war broke out.

108   zitten   **sit**
vb   Hij zit op een stoel.
['zɪtə(n)]   -He sits on a chair.

109   net   **just; net; elegant**
adv; het; adj   Ik ben net klaar.
[nɛt]   -I just finished.

110   heel   **very, whole**
adj; adv   Het is een heel moeilijke tongbreker.
[hel]   -It's a very difficult tongue-twister.

111   maken   **make**
vb   Zij maakte een zandkasteel.
['makə(n)]   -She made a sandcastle.

112   mogen   **may, like**
vb   Mogen kinderen jou?
['moxə(n)]   -Do kids like you?

113   dood   **death; dead**
de; adj   Ik weet niet of hij dood is of leeft.
[dot]   -I don't know if he's dead or alive.

114   altijd   **always**
adv   Ze glimlacht altijd.
['altɛit]   -She is always smiling.

115   af   **off; ready**
adv; adj   Het alarm gaat af.
[af]   -The alarm is going off.

116   wachten   **wait**
vb   Ik kan niet wachten.
['waxtə(n)]   -I can't wait.

117   geven   **give**

vb	Een kado geven aan iemand.
['xevə(n)]	-To give a present to someone.
118 omdat	**because**
con	Wij zijn anders dan dieren omdat wij kunnen spreken.
[ɔm'dat]	-We are different from animals in that we can speak.
119 dag	**day; bye**
de; int	Ik zou ooit op een dag in Europa willen wonen.
[dɑx]	-I'd like to live in Europe someday.
120 zeker	**confident; sure**
adj; adv	Ik zal ze zeker missen.
['zekər]	-I will surely miss them.
121 allemaal	**everything, everybody**
prn	Men zal jullie allemaal nog honderden jaren herinneren.
['ɑləmal]	-All you people will be remembered for hundreds of years.
122 danken	**thank**
vb	Dank je wel jullie beiden!
['dɑŋkə(n)]	-Thanks to both of you.
123 huis	**house**
het	Breng hem alsjeblieft naar zijn huis.
[hœys]	-Please take him to his house.
124 oh	**oh**
int	Oh, okee John. Ouwe zeikerd.
[oː]	-Oh, okay John. You old bugger.
125 zij	**she, they; side**
prn; de	Zij zal weldra trouwen.
[zɛi]	-She'll get married soon.
126 jaar	**year**
het	Ik ben van plan naar Frankrijk te gaan volgend jaar.
[jar]	-I plan to go to France next year.
127 vader	**father**
de	Mijn vader zei altijd dat geld niet alles is.
['vadər]	-My father used to say that money is not everything.
128 jouw	**your**
prn	Was zij niet jouw vriendin?
[jɑu]	-Wasn't she your girlfriend?
129 geld	**money, cash**
het	We hebben geld nodig.
[xɛlt]	-We need money.
130 vrouw	**woman, wife**
de	Deze vrouw is knap.
[vrɑu]	-This woman is pretty.
131 zoals	**as; as; such as; like**
adv; con; adj; prp	Ik verzeker je dat een fout zoals deze nooit meer zal voorkomen.
[zoˈɑls]	-I assure you that an error like this will never happen again.
132 hun	**their**
prn	De dieven verdeelden hun buit.
[hʏn]	-The thieves divided their booty.
133 god	**god**
de	Haar geloof in God is erg sterk.
[ɣɔt]	-Her belief in God is very firm.
134 keer	**time**

	de	Is dit uw eerste keer in Korea?
	[ker]	-Is this your first time in Korea?
135	**erg**	**very; terrible**
	adv; adj	We zijn allemaal erg trots op John.
	[ɛrx]	-We're all very proud of John.
136	**anders**	**different, else; otherwise**
	adv; con	Misschien wil je later wat anders.
	['andərs]	-Maybe later on you want something else.
137	**bedanken**	**thank**
	vb	Ik kan hem niet genoeg bedanken.
	[bə'daŋkə(n)]	-I cannot thank him enough.
138	**iedereen**	**everyone**
	prn	Iedereen moet dansen!
	['idəren]	-Everybody has to dance!
139	**niemand**	**nobody**
	prn	Ik zag niemand.
	['nimant]	-I saw nobody.
140	**ander**	**other; other**
	adj; prn	Deze heeft een andere kleur.
	['andər]	-This one has a different color.
141	**niks**	**nothing; none**
	prn; adv	Heb je hem niks gezegd?
	[nɪks]	-You didn't tell him anything?
142	**binnen**	**within; inside**
	adv; prp	John zette het raam open en liet frisse lucht binnen.
	['bɪnə(n)]	-John opened the window and let in some fresh air.
143	**spijt**	**regret**
	de	Het spijt me dat ik je aan het huilen heb gemaakt.
	[spɛit]	-I regret making you cry.
144	**beter**	**better; superior**
	adv; adj	John is beter in skiën dan ik.
	['betər]	-John is better at skiing than me.
145	**hallo**	**hello**
	int	Hallo, hoe heet je?
	['halo]	-Hello, what's your name?
146	**nemen**	**take**
	vb	Neem je dingen mee!
	['nemə(n)]	-Take your things with you!
147	**vinden**	**find**
	vb	We moeten de sleutel vinden.
	['vɪndə(n)]	-We've got to find the key.
148	**staan**	**stand**
	vb	Ik zit liever dan dat ik sta.
	[stan]	-I like sitting better than standing
149	**werk**	**work**
	het	Alleen mijn werk beheers ik volkomen.
	[wɛrk]	-Work is the only thing I have complete control over.
150	**zich**	**himself**
	prn	Hij waste zich onder de douche
	[zɪx]	-He washed himself in the shower.
151	**moeder**	**mother**

	de	Alleen mijn moeder begrijpt me echt.
	['mudər]	-Only my mother really understands me.
152	**praten**	**talk**
	vb	Waarom wil ze met Jane praten?
	['pratə(n)]	-Why does she want to talk to Jane?
153	**bedoelen**	**mean**
	vb	Wat bedoel je?
	[bə'dulə(n)]	-What do you mean?
154	**meneer**	**mister**
	de	Meneer John, er is telefoon voor u.
	[mə'ner]	-Mister John, you are wanted on the phone.
155	**genoeg**	**enough; enough**
	adj; adv	Ik er genoeg van.
	[xə'nux]	-I have had enough.
156	**klaar**	**ready, finished; clear**
	adj; adv	Deze is klaar voor verwijdering.
	[klar]	-This one is ready for deletion.
157	**leuk**	**nice, fun**
	adj	Jij hebt een leuke persoonlijkheid.
	[løk]	-You have a nice personality.
158	**mooi**	**beautiful, pretty**
	adj	Je bent zo mooi als een kersenbloesem.
	[moj]	-You are pretty like a cherry blossom.
159	**luisteren**	**listen**
	vb	Je had naar mij moeten luisteren.
	['lœystərə(n)]	-You should have listened to me.
160	**uur**	**hour**
	het	Ik heb twaalf uur in de trein doorgebracht.
	[yr]	-I spent twelve hours on the train.
161	**na**	**after; post**
	prp; adv	Ze zijn na de film in slaap gevallen.
	[na]	-They fell asleep after the movie.
162	**drie**	**three**
	nu	De drie musketiers.
	[dri]	-The three musketeers.
163	**toe**	**to; towards**
	prp; adv	Ik moest naar huis toe gaan.
	[tu]	-I needed to go home.
164	**alsjeblieft**	**please (coll)**
	int	Alsjeblieft! Kom naar ons huis.
	[ˌalʃə'blift]	-Please! Come to our house.
165	**elkaar**	**each other; each other**
	adv; prn	We vinden elkaar aardig.
	[ɛl'kar]	-We like each other.
166	**sorry**	**sorry**
	int	Maar ik herinner het me niet, sorry!
	['sɔri]	-But I don't remember, I'm sorry!
167	**blijven**	**stay**
	vb	Hoelang gaat u hier blijven?
	['blɛivə(n)]	-How long will you be staying here?
168	**verdomme**	**damn**

	int		Verdomme, ik heb mijn voet bezeerd.
	[vərdɔmə]		-Damn, I hurt my foot.
169	**alle**		**every, all**
	prn		Zijn alle kroegen gesloten?
	['ɑlə]		-Are all the bars closed?
170	**gek**		**crazy; fool; fool**
	adj; de; adv		John is een beetje gek.
	[xɛk]		-John is a little crazy.
171	**helpen**		**help**
	vb;		We moeten iets doen om te helpen.
	['hɛlpə(n)]		-We must do something to help.
172	**groot**		**large, big**
	adj		Je kunt zoiets groots niet geheim houden.
	[xrot]		-You can't keep something that big a secret.
173	**lang**		**long, tall; long**
	adj; adv		Zijn nek is lang.
	[lɑŋ]		-He has a long neck.
174	**wissen**		**wipe**
	vb		Het dreigt het hele systeem te wissen.
	['wɪsə(n)]		-It's threatening to wipe out the entire system.
175	**graag**		**gladly, willingly**
	adv		Ik zou graag in New York willen wonen.
	[xrax]		-I'd gladly live in New York.
176	**ding**		**thing, object**
	het		De beste dingen in het leven zijn duur.
	[dɪŋ]		-The best things in life are expensive.
177	**eerste**		**first; initial**
	de; adv		John was de eerste die de paal heeft bereikt.
	['erstə]		-John was the first to reach the pole.
178	**krijgen**		**get**
	vb		Ik zou een ongeluk kunnen krijgen!
	['krɛixə(n)]		-I might have an accident!
179	**zonder**		**without**
	prp		Hij zit al een maand zonder werk.
	['zɔndər]		-He has been without employment for a month.
180	**vriend**		**friend**
	de		Ik heb veel vrienden.
	[vrint]		-I have many friends.
181	**naam**		**name**
	de		Mijn naam is John.
	[nam]		-My name is John.
182	**jongen**		**boy**
	de		Jane kuste de jongen op zijn wang.
	['jɔŋə(n)]		-Jane kissed the boy on his cheek.
183	**steeds**		**always, still**
	adv		Deze truc werkt nog steeds.
	[stets]		-This trick still works.
184	**beetje**		**bit; little**
	het; adj		Een beetje suiker, alstublieft.
	['becə]		-A little bit of sugar, please.
185	**achter**		**behind; behind**

	adv; prp	Hij verstopt zich achter de kast.
	['ɑxtər]	-He is hiding behind the closet.
186	**snel**	**fast; quick**
	adv; adj	De kat is snel.
	[snɛl]	-The cat is quick.
187	**kind**	**child**
	het	Ze koopt een stuk speelgoed voor haar kind.
	[kɪnt]	-She is buying a toy for her child.
188	**ooit**	**ever**
	adv	Jij bent het beste wat me ooit overkomen is.
	[ojt]	-You're the best thing that's ever happened to me.
189	**wanneer**	**when; when**
	adv; con	Wanneer is het bosbessenseizoen?
	['wa'ner]	-When is the blueberry season?
190	**onder**	**under, underneath; under**
	adv; prp	Je hebt wallen onder je ogen.
	['ɔndər]	-You've got bags under your eyes.
191	**bang**	**afraid, scared; anxious**
	adj; adv	Ben je bang om te sterven?
	[bɛŋ]	-Are you afraid to die?
192	**hand**	**hand**
	de	John had een hamer in zijn hand.
	[hɑnt]	-John had a hammer in his hand.
193	**vertellen**	**tell**
	vb	Ik zal je meer vertellen over Japan.
	[vər'tɛlə(n)]	-I will tell you more about Japan.
194	**eten**	**eat; food**
	vb; het	Ik wil lekker eten eten want ik heb honger.
	['etə(n)]	-I want to eat yummy food because I'm hungry.
195	**horen**	**hear**
	vb	Ik hoor voetstappen buiten.
	['horə(n)]	-I hear footsteps outside.
196	**auto**	**car**
	de	John wilde een nieuwe auto kopen.
	['ɑuto, 'oto]	-John wanted to buy a new car.
197	**idee**	**idea, notion**
	het	Het was mijn idee.
	[i'de]	-It was my idea.
198	**paar**	**couple**
	het	Ik zal een paar vrijwilligers nodig hebben.
	[par]	-I'm going to need a couple of volunteers.
199	**zorgen**	**care, worry**
	vb	Het feit dat ze ziek is, maakt me echt zorgen.
	[zorxə(n)]	-The fact that she's sick really worries me.
200	**geweldig**	**great, awesome**
	adj	Je bent een geweldige vriendin!
	[xə'wɛldəx]	-You're a wonderful friend.
201	**wereld**	**world**
	de	Mumbai is één van grootste steden van de wereld.
	['werəlt]	-Mumbai is one of the biggest cities in the world.
202	**vraag**	**question**

	de		Het is een interessante en moeilijke vraag.
	[vrax]		-It's an interesting and difficult question.
203	**gebeuren**		**happen**
	vb		Je zei dat dit zou gebeuren.
	[xəˈbørə(n)]		-You said this was going to happen.
204	**nieuw**		**new, novel**
	adj		Ik wil een nieuwe televisie.
	[niw]		-I want a new television.
205	**morgen**		**tomorrow, morning**
	de		Ik ga hem morgen zien.
	[ˈmɔrxə(n)]		-I'm going to see him tomorrow.
206	**vragen**		**ask**
	vb		Ik zou twee vragen willen stellen.
	[ˈvraxə(n)]		-I would like to ask two questions.
207	**laatst**		**last, latest; lately**
	adj; adv		Ze is als laatste gekomen.
	[latst]		-She came last.
208	**lijken**		**seem, resemble; cadavers**
	vb; de		Ze lijken zich goed te amuseren.
	[ˈlɛikə(n)]		-They seem to be having fun.
209	**vandaag**		**today**
	adv		John heeft het vandaag druk.
	[vanˈdax]		-John is busy today.
210	**want**		**because; mitten**
	con; de		Het kind weent, want het wil eten.
	[want]		-The child is crying, because it wants to eat.
211	**zelf**		**self**
	prn		Ik heb de aanvraag zelf ingediend.
	[zɛlf]		-I submitted the application myself.
212	**best**		**best; sufficiently**
	adj; adv		Doe wat u het beste lijkt.
	[bɛst]		-Do what you think is best.
213	**heen**		**there, away**
	adv		Heen en weer. En weer terug
	[hen]		-There and back. And back again.
214	**meisje**		**girl**
	het		Het meisje met de blauwe jas is mijn dochter.
	[ˈmɛiʃə]		-The girl in the blue coat is my daughter.
215	**kennen**		**know**
	vb		Waar kennen jullie elkaar van?
	[ˈkɛnə(n)]		-How do you know each other?
216	**zelfs**		**even**
	adv		Ik kan zelfs niet één stap salsa dansen.
	[zɛlfs]		-I cannot even dance one single step of Salsa.
217	**rustig**		**calm; quietly**
	adj; adv		Rustig aan. Denk aan je hart!
	[ˈrʏstəx]		-Calm down. Think of you heart!
218	**enig**		**any; solely; single**
	adv; adj; prn		Heb je enig goed nieuws?
	[ˈenəx]		-Do you have any good news?
219	**thuis**		**home**

	adv [tœys]	Wat doe je hier? Waarom ben je niet thuis? -What are you doing here? Why aren't you home?
220	**buiten** *adv; prp* ['bœytə(n)]	**outside, out; outside** Ik hoor voetstappen buiten. -I hear footsteps outside.
221	**klein** *adj* [klɛin]	**small, little** Holland is een klein land. -Holland is a small country.
222	**geloof** *het* [xə'lof]	**faith, belief** Geloof jij in God? -Do you believe in God?
223	**eerst** *adj; adv* [erst]	**first, primary; first** Ik dacht eerst ook hetzelfde. -At first, I thought the same thing.
224	**samen** *adv* ['samə(n)]	**together** Pizza en bier gaan goed samen. -Pizza and beer go together well.
225	**halen** *vb* ['halə(n)]	**get, fetch** Ga haar medicijnen halen en een glas water. -Go get her medicine and a glass of water.
226	**eigen** *adj* ['ɛixə(n)]	**own** Estland heeft zijn eigen volkslied. -Estonia has its own national anthem.
227	**hen** *prn; de* [hɛn]	**them; hen** Heeft de gevangenis hen veranderd? -Has prison changed them?
228	**hopen** *vb* ['hopə(n)]	**hope** Ik hoop dat we niet al te lang hoeven wachten. -I hope we don't have to wait for too long.
229	**zoon** *de* [zon]	**son** Hij heeft nog een zoon. -He has another son.
230	**open** *adj; adv* ['opə(n)]	**open, overt; overtly** Ik vroeg John het raam te openen. -I asked John to open the window.
231	**probleem** *het* [pro'blem]	**problem** John heeft problemen met het zicht. -John has eyesight problems.
232	**elk** *prn; adj; adv* [ɛlk]	**each, any; every** Dit gebeurde elke herfst. -This was happening every autumn.
233	**geleden** *adv; adj* [xə'ledə(n)]	**ago; past** Vier jaar geleden heb ik deze fiets gekocht. -I bought this bike four years ago.
234	**orde** *de* ['ɔrdə]	**order, discipline** Ik wil dat je de kamer vlug in orde brengt. -I want you to put the room in order quickly.
235	**bijna** *adv* ['bɛina]	**almost** Bijna alles is verbeterd. -Almost everything has been improved.
236	**kant**	**side, lace**

	de	Aan de andere kant.
	[kɑnt]	-At the other side.
237	**begrijpen**	**understand, grasp**
	vb	Ik begrijp geen woord van wat hij zegt.
	[bəˈxrɛipə(n)]	-I don't understand a word of what he says.
238	**gelijk**	**equal, similar; right**
	adj; het	John had gelijk.
	[xəˈlɛik]	-John was right.
239	**politie**	**police**
	de	De politie beschouwt hem als de voornaamste verdachte.
	[poˈli(t)si]	-He is considered the prime suspect by the police.
240	**soms**	**sometimes**
	adv	Hij praatte soms met de soldaten.
	[sɔms]	-He would sometimes talk with the soldiers.
241	**eigenlijk**	**really; actually**
	adv; adj	Ze lijkt jong maar eigenlijk is ze ouder dan jij.
	[ˈɛixə(n)lək]	-She looks young, but actually she's older than you are.
242	**hoofd**	**head, principal**
	het	Mijn hoofd doet pijn.
	[hoft]	-My head hurts.
243	**vanavond**	**tonight**
	adv	Wat dacht je ervan om vanavond uit eten te gaan?
	[vanˈavɔnt]	-How about going out to eat tonight?
244	**alsof**	**like; as if**
	con; adv	Ken praat alsof hij alles weet.
	[ɑlsˈɔf]	-Ken talks as if he knew everything.
245	**zetten**	**put, place**
	vb	Zet alsjeblieft wat kaarsen op de verjaardagstaart.
	[ˈzɛtə(n)]	-Please put some candles on the birthday cake.
246	**voelen**	**feel**
	vb	Ik voel dat ik vrij ben.
	[ˈvulə(n)]	-I feel that I am free.
247	**precies**	**exactly, precise; exact**
	adv; adj	Het onderscheid is niet altijd precies.
	[prəˈsis]	-The distinction is not always precise.
248	**heet**	**hot, warm**
	adj;	De thee is erg heet.
	[het]	-The tea is very hot.
249	**proberen**	**try, attempt**
	vb	Ik probeer Engels te leren.
	[proˈberə(n)]	-I am trying to learn English.
250	**verder**	**further; moreover**
	adj; adv	Verdere stappen in de onderhandelingen.
	[ˈvɛrdər]	-Further steps in negotiations.
251	**pas**	**just now; pass**
	adv; de	John en ik zijn pas verloofd.
	[pɑs]	-John and I got engaged only recently.
252	**werken**	**work**
	vb	Ik werk om te kunnen leven, maar ik leef niet om te kunnen werken.
	[ˈwɛrkə(n)]	-I work to live, but I don't live to work.
253	**familie**	**family**

	de	Ik woon met mijn familie in Australië.
	[faˈmili]	-I live in Australia with my family.
254	**volgen**	**follow, track**
	vb	Ik kan je niet goed volgen.
	[ˈvɔlxə(n)]	-I don't quite follow you.
255	**bellen**	**dial**
	vb	Ik zal je morgen bellen.
	[ˈbɛlə(n)]	-I'll give you a call tomorrow.
256	**eruit**	**out**
	adv	Mijn voortand viel eruit.
	[ɛrˈœyt]	-My front tooth fell out.
257	**vijf**	**five**
	nu	Ik studeer het al vijf jaar.
	[vɛif]	-I have been studying it for five years.
258	**vermoorden**	**murder, assassinate**
	vb	Mijn vader gaat me vermoorden.
	[vərˈmordə(n)]	-My father's going to murder me.
259	**oud**	**old**
	adj	De oude vrouw leent geld.
	[aut]	-The old woman lends money.
260	**schieten**	**shoot, fire**
	vb	Schiet op! Anders ga ik schieten met m'n geweer.
	[ˈsxitə(n)]	-Hurry up. Or else I'm shooting you with my rifle.
261	**stad**	**city**
	de	Het is de derde grootste stad van Servië.
	[stat]	-It's the third biggest city in Serbia.
262	**hoeveel**	**how much; what**
	nu	Hoeveel personages zijn er in je verhaal?
	[ˈhuvel]	-How many characters are there in your story?
263	**oog**	**eye**
	het	Oog om oog en tand om tand.
	[ox]	-An eye for an eye, a tooth for a tooth.
264	**plaats**	**place, location**
	de	Wat zou jij doen in mijn plaats?
	[plats]	-What would you do if you were in my place?
265	**manier**	**way, how**
	de	Dit probleem kan op verschillende manieren opgelost worden.
	[maˈnir]	-This problem may be solved in a variety of ways.
266	**zoeken**	**search**
	vb	Hulpdiensten zoeken nog in het puin naar overlevenden.
	[ˈzukə(n)]	-Emergency services are still searching through the rubble for survivors.
267	**jezelf**	**yourself**
	prn	Druk jezelf zo duidelijk mogelijk uit.
	[jəˈzɛlf]	-Express yourself as clearly as you can.
268	**daarom**	**therefore; hence**
	con; adv	Hij zei dat hij moe was en zou daarom vroeger naar huis willen.
	[ˈdarɔm]	-He said that he was tired and therefore he'd like to go home earlier.
269	**minuut**	**minute**
	de	Ik wil over 20 minuten iedereen op mijn kantoor hebben.
	[miˈnyt]	-I want everyone in my office in 20 minutes.
270	**school**	**school**

	de	Onthou goed wat je op school leert.
	[sxol]	-Remember well what you learn at school.
271	**geloven**	**believe, think**
	vb	Je moet me geloven.
	[xəˈlovə(n)]	-You have to believe me.
272	**spelen**	**play, game**
	vb	Wij spelen dikwijls schaak.
	[ˈspelə(n)]	-We often play chess.
273	**slecht**	**bad, evil; badly**
	adj; adv	Wat een slechte film!
	[slɛxt]	-What a bad movie!
274	**moment**	**moment**
	het	Aardbevingen kunnen zich op elk moment voordoen.
	[moˈmɛnt]	-Earthquakes may occur at any moment.
275	**pijn**	**pain**
	de	John wilde niemand pijn doen.
	[pɛin]	-John didn't want to hurt anyone.
276	**dollar**	**dollar**
	de	Ik heb ongeveer vijftig dollar betaald.
	[ˈdɔlar]	-I paid about 50 bucks.
277	**kamer**	**room, chamber**
	de	Ik versier graag mijn kamer met bloemen.
	[ˈkamər]	-I like to adorn my room with flowers.
278	**welk**	**which; which**
	con; prn	Welk historisch figuur zou je willen ontmoeten als je de kans had?
	[wɛlk]	-Which historical figure would you want to meet if you could?
279	**blij**	**happy, joyous; glad**
	adj; adv	Mijn vrouw zal ook blij zijn u te zien.
	[blɛi]	-My wife will be glad to see you, too.
280	**vier**	**four**
	nu	Nadat John vier keer een verkeerde pincode had ingegeven, slikte de geldautomaat zijn kaart in.
	[vir]	-After John had entered four wrong PIN numbers, the ATM swallowed his card.
281	**schat**	**treasure, honey**
	de	We schatten zijn verliezen op 100 dollar.
	[sxat]	-We estimated his losses at 100 dollars.
282	**water**	**water**
	het	Waarom is er geen warm water?
	[ˈwatər]	-Why is there no hot water?
283	**kans**	**chance**
	de	Ik kan niet weggaan, en dat wil ik ook niet.
	[kɑns]	-I can't go, nor do I want to.
284	**deur**	**door**
	de	Ik wil de deur sluiten.
	[dør]	-I want to close the door.
285	**land**	**land, earth, country**
	het	In rijke landen verhongeren weinig mensen.
	[lɑnt]	-In rich countries, few people starve.
286	**vooruit**	**forward, ahead**
	adv	Hij zond zijn bagage vooruit.

[vor'œyt] -He sent his luggage in advance.

287 brengen
vb
['brɛŋə(n)]

bring
Ik breng haar achteraf naar huis.
 -I'm bringing her home afterwards.

288 broer
de
[brur]

brother
Ik heb acht broers.
 -I have eight brothers.

289 lekker
adj; adv
['lɛkər]

tasty, nice; deliciously
Dat parfum ruikt lekker.
 -That perfume smells nice.

290 later
adv; adj
['latər]

later, hereafter; after
We zullen er later over spreken.
 -We'll talk about it later.

291 volgens
adv
['vɔlxə(n)s]

according to
Volgens de krant was er gisteren een grote brand.
 -According to the newspaper, there was a big fire last night.

292 boven
adv; prp
['bovə(n)]

above, over; above
Ons vliegtuig vloog boven de wolken.
 -Our plane was flying above the clouds.

293 ergens
adv; prn
['ɛrxə(n)s]

somewhere; someplace
Als de bal je ergens anders dan op je hoofd of je handen raakt, ben je af.
 -If the ball hits you somewhere else than on the head or hands, you're out.

294 liggen
vb
['lɪxə(n)]

lie
Ik wil dat u een paar uur stil blijft liggen.
 -I want you to lie still for a few hours.

295 juist
adj; adv
[jœyst]

just, correct; just
Dat was de juiste beslissing.
 -That was the right thing to do.

296 spreken
vb
['sprekə(n)]

speak
Ik spreek geen Ests.
 -I don't speak Estonian.

297 prima
adj;adv
['prima]

great, fine
Alles ziet er prima uit.
 -Everything looks fine.

298 papa
de
['papa]

dad
Papa heeft boeken voor me gekocht.
 -My dad bought me books.

299 tussen
prp
['tʏsə(n)]

between
John weet het verschil niet tussen God en de Duivel.
 -John doesn't know the difference between God and the Devil.

300 zoveel
adv
[zo'vel]

so many, so much
Ik moet je nog zoveel vertellen.
 -I've got so much more to tell you.

301 week
de; adj
[we:k]

week; soft
Hij won vorige week de prijs.
 -He won the prize last week.

302 soort
de
[sort]

kind
Wat voor soort muziek hou je van?
 -What kind of music do you like?

303 hulp
de

help, assistance
Wij hebben hulp nodig.

[hʏlp]   -We need help.

304 **vergeten**   **forget**
vb   Ik zal je nooit vergeten.
[vərˈxetə(n)]   -I'll never forget you.

305 **pakken**   **grab**
vb   Pak een ticket voor me.
[ˈpɑkə(n)]   -Grab a ticket for me.

306 **plan**   **plan, scheme**
het   Ben je van plan die auto te kopen?
[plɑn]   -Do you plan on buying that car?

307 **dokter**   **doctor**
de   Ik ben geen dokter, maar een leraar.
[ˈdɔktər]   -I am not a doctor, but a teacher.

308 **betekenen**   **mean**
vb   Het zou zoveel betekenen voor iedereen.
[bəˈtekənə(n)]   -It would mean a lot to everybody.

309 **hoi**   **hi**
int   Hoi allemaal. Mijn naam is John en ik ben alcoholist.
[hɔj]   -Hi everybody. My name is John and I'm an alcoholic.

310 **kloppen**   **knock, beat**
vb   Sommige mensen kloppen niet eens aan.
[ˈklɔpə(n)]   -Some people won't even knock on a door.

311 **kop**   **head, cup**
de   Ik trek je kop eraf.
[kɔp]   -I will rip your head off.

312 **beginnen**   **start, begin**
vb   Ik ga beginnen.
[bəˈxɪnə(n)]   -I'm going to start.

313 **mevrouw**   **lady**
de   Deze mevrouw zal alles betalen.
[məˈvrɑu]   -This lady will pay for everything.

314 **nacht**   **night**
de   De maan schijnt 's nachts.
[nɑxt]   -The moon shines at night.

315 **bed**   **bed**
het   Mijn moeder was zo moe, dat ze vroeg naar bed is gegaan.
[bɛt]   -My mother was so tired that she went to bed early.

316 **lopen**   **walk**
vb   Ik ben moe van het lopen.
[ˈlopə(n)]   -I am tired of walking.

317 **mama**   **mom**
de   Mama, John heeft mijn koekje opgegeten!
[ˈmɑmɑ]   -Mom, John ate my cookie.

318 **stoppen**   **stop, cease**
vb   Als ze eenmaal begint te praten, is ze niet te stoppen.
[ˈstɔpə(n)]   -Once she starts talking, there is no stopping her.

319 **vrij**   **free, clear; free**
adj; adv   We zijn nog niet vrij.
[vrɛi]   -We're not free yet.

320 **zorg**   **care, worry**
de   Ondertussen verlenen we zorg, zo goedkoop mogelijk.

[zɔrx] -In the meantime, we provide care as inexpensively as possible.

321 **zaak** **case, matter**
de Indien mogelijk zou ik graag nieuwe informatie over deze zaak ontvangen.
[zak] -If possible, I'd like to receive new information about this case.

322 **gebruiken** **use**
vb Ik had een condoom moeten gebruiken.
[xəˈbrœykə(n)] -I should have used a condom.

323 **liefde** **love**
de Liefde is gewoon een tijdelijke hormonale onevenwichtigheid.
[ˈlivdə] -Love is simply a temporary hormonal imbalance.

324 **ervan** **from it**
prn Ik schrok me dood ervan.
[ɛrˈvan] -It scared me to death.

325 **los** **loose; loose**
adj; adv Toen brak de hel los
[lɔs] -And then all hell broke loose.

326 **mis** **wrong, erroneous; wrong; mass**
adj; adv; de Wat is er mis met je?
[mɪs] -What is wrong with you?

327 **tien** **ten**
nu De bushalte is hier tien minuten lopen vandaan.
[tin] -It's a ten-minute walk to the bus stop.

328 **beneden** **down, below; below**
adv; prp Het is beneden haar waardigheid om zoiets te zeggen.
[bəˈnedə(n)] -It's below her to say such a thing.

329 **hart** **heart**
het Het hart dient om bloed te pompen.
[hart] -The heart serves to pump blood.

330 **verhaal** **story, redress**
het Zijn verhaal was de eenvoud zelve.
[vərˈhal] -His story was simplicity itself.

331 **wakker** **awake**
adj Ze zijn altijd vroeg wakker, zelfs op zondag.
[ˈwakər] -They always wake up early, even on Sundays.

332 **voordat** **prior to; ere**
prp; con Je moet deze brief tekenen voordat ik hem kan opsturen.
[ˈvorˈdat] -I need your signature on the letter before I can mail it.

333 **voorbij** **gone; past; beyond**
adj; adv; prp We zijn er voorbij.
[vorˈbɛi] -We have are past it.

334 **leren** **learn; teach**
vb; adj Hoe kan ik gemakkelijk Engels leren?
[ˈlerə(n)] -How can I learn English easily?

335 **nummer** **number, digit**
het Ik heb het nummer van de auto niet kunnen noteren.
[ˈnʏmər] -I was unable to write down the number of the car.

336 **neer** **down**
adv Het ging op en neer.
[ner] -It went up and down.

337 **vol** **full, crowded; full**
adj; adv Nee, het is genoeg. Ik zit vol.

[vɔl]	-No, it is enough. I am full.

338 zodat — **so that**
con
[zoˈdɑt]
Geef me alsjeblieft een foto van je, zodat ik niet vergeet hoe je eruitziet.
-Please give me your picture so that I don't forget how you look.

339 hoeven — **need, have to**
av
[ˈhuvə(n)]
Ze had niet naar de vergadering hoeven komen.
-She needn't have come to the meeting.

340 slapen — **sleep**
vb
[ˈslapə(n)]
"Ik kan niet slapen." "Ik ook niet."
-"I can't sleep." "Me neither."

341 Jezus — **Jesus**
de
[ˈje.zʏs]
Moslims geloven dat Jezus een boodschapper van God was.
-Muslims believe that Jesus was one of God's messengers.

342 druk — **pressure; busy; busily**
de; adj; adv
[drʏk]
Ze is zeker druk bezig.
-She must be very busy.

343 dicht — **close, closed; densely**
adj; adv
[dɪxt]
Doe de deur achter je dicht.
-Close the door behind you.

344 dochter — **daughter**
de
[ˈdɔxtər]
Ik kijk tv met mijn dochter.
-I watch television with my daughter.

345 snappen — **understand, get**
vb
[ˈsnɑpə(n)]
We snappen dat het moeilijk was.
-We understand you were in a difficult position.

346 zoiets — **such a thing**
adj
[zoˈits]
Zoiets heb ik nog nooit in mijn leven gezien, niet één keer!
-I've never seen such a thing in my life, not once!

347 gelukkig — **happy**
adj
[xəˈlʏkəx]
John leek gelukkig.
-John seemed happy.

348 gezicht — **face, sight**
het
[xəˈzɪxt]
Ik kan er niet toe komen te geloven dat John me in mijn gezicht gelogen heeft over wat er gebeurd is.
-I can't believe John lied to my face about what happened.

349 zes — **six**
nu
[zɛs]
Ze is zes jaar ouder dan ik.
-She's six years older than me.

350 meteen — **immediately**
adv
[məˈten]
Als we meteen vertrekken, lukt het misschien.
-If we set off immediately, maybe we'll make it.

351 moeilijk — **difficult, tough**
adj
[ˈmujlək]
Wiskunde is moeilijk voor mij.
-Mathematics is difficult for me.

352 stel — **set, bunch, couple**
het
[stɛl]
We zijn net een getrouwd stel.
-We're like a married couple.

353 sinds — **since; since**
adv; con
[sɪn(t)s]
Ik woon hier sinds 1990.
-I have lived here since 1990.

354 plek — **place, spot**

	de	Ik kan me geen plek bedenken waar ik liever zou zijn.
	[plɛk]	-I can't think of any place I'd rather be.
355	**begin**	**beginning, start**
	het	In het begin wist ik niet wat te doen.
	[bəˈxɪn]	-In the beginning, I didn't know what to do.
356	**drinken**	**drink**
	vb	Ik wil iets kouds om te drinken.
	[ˈdrɪŋkə(n)]	-I want something cold to drink.
357	**hetzelfde**	**same; ditto; ditto**
	prn; adj; adv	Het werkt hetzelfde in elk land.
	[hɛtˈsɛlfdə]	-It works the same way in every country.
358	**per**	**by**
	prp	We gaan per trein.
	[pɛr]	-We'll go by train.
359	**bezig**	**busy**
	adj	Mijn moeder is bezig het avondeten te koken.
	[ˈbezəx]	-My mother is busy cooking supper.
360	**ver**	**far, remote; far**
	adj; adv	Het is niet ver van Parijs.
	[vɛr]	-It is not far from Paris.
361	**eerder**	**earlier, rather**
	adj	Mijn kennis van Japans is eerder zwak.
	[ˈerdər]	-My knowledge of Japanese is rather poor.
362	**eraan**	**with it**
	adv	Wat is eraan te doen?
	[ɛrˈan]	-What is to be done about it?
363	**baas**	**boss**
	de	Ik ben uw baas.
	[bas]	-I'm your boss.
364	**baby**	**baby, nursling**
	de	De baby kan lopen.
	[ˈbebi]	-The baby is able to walk.
365	**agent**	**agent, policeman**
	de	Hij is een agent van het FBI.
	[aˈxɛnt]	-He is an FBI agent.
366	**film**	**film**
	de	Als het om films gaat, vind ik alles leuk, als het maar geen horror is.
	[fɪlm]	-When it comes to movies I like anything, as long as it's not horror.
367	**mond**	**mouth**
	de	Je hoort niet te praten met je mond vol.
	[mɔnt]	-You shouldn't speak with your mouth full.
368	**waarschijnlijk**	**probably, presumably; likely**
	adv; adj	John is waarschijnlijk ook dood.
	[warˈsxɛinlək]	-John is probably dead, too.
369	**vent**	**fellow, geezer, guy**
	de	Denk je dat hij de vent is die het raam heeft gebroken?
	[vɛnt]	-Do you think he is the guy that broke the window?
370	**vallen**	**fall, drop**
	vb	Hij liet zijn potlood vallen.
	[ˈvalə(n)]	-He dropped his pencil.
371	**oorlog**	**war**

de	Niemand houdt van oorlog.
[ˈɔrlɔx]	-Nobody likes war.

372 rusten — **rest, lie**
vb
[ˈrʏstə(n)]
Moge hij rusten in vrede!
-May he rest in peace!

373 sterven — **die**
vb
[ˈstɛrvə(n)]
Mensen wonende in dit gebied sterven aan een gebrek aan water.
-People living in this area are dying because of the lack of water.

374 hond — **dog**
de
[hɔnt]
De kinderen solden met de hond.
-The children were messing around with the dog.

375 waarheid — **truth**
de
[ˈwarhɛit]
Vroeg of laat komt de waarheid boven tafel.
-Sooner or later the truth will come out.

376 geluk — **happiness, luck**
het
[xəˈlʏk]
Alles waar je goed in bent draagt bij aan geluk.
-Anything you're good at contributes to happiness.

377 heer — **lord, gentleman**
de
[her]
Dames en heren, we zijn net geland op de internationale luchthaven van Tokio.
-Ladies and Gentlemen, we have now landed at Tokyo International Airport.

378 rond — **around; round**
adv; adj
[rɔnt]
Vraag rond. Of google het.
-Ask around. Or google it.

379 avond — **evening, night**
de
[ˈavɔnt]
Het was een waar genoegen de avond met een slim, grappig en mooi meisje als jou door te brengen.
-It was a pleasure to spend the evening with a smart, funny and beautiful girl like you.

380 zeer — **very, highly; very; sore**
adj; adv; het
[zer]
Ik was zeer blij toen ik dat nieuws vernam.
-I was very happy when I heard that news.

381 welkom — **welcome, appreciated**
int, adj
[ˈwɛlkɔm]
Welkom in ons restaurant!
-Welcome to our restaurant!

382 nieuws — **news, novelty**
het
[niws]
Dat soort nieuws is toch onbetaalbaar.
-You can't put a price on that kind of news.

383 terwijl — **while, whereas**
con
[tɛrˈwɛil]
Sommige mensen houden van klassieke muziek, terwijl anderen van populaire muziek houden.
-Some people like classical music, while others like popular music.

384 veilig — **safe, sure; safely**
adj; adv
[ˈvɛiləx]
Is het daar veilig?
-Is it safe in there?

385 stuk — **piece, part; broken**
het; adj
[stʏk]
De curryvisballetjes zijn één dollar per stuk.
-The curry fish balls are one dollar each.

386 aardig — **nice, pretty; nicely**
adj; adv
[ˈardəx]
Ze waren erg aardig voor me.
-They were very kind to me.

387 maand — **month**
de
De president van Frankrijk zal volgende maand Japan bezoeken.

[mant] -The French president is to visit Japan next month.

388 **fijn** **fine, nice; delicately**
adj; adv We hebben een fijn huis.
[fɛin] -We have a nice house.

389 **bloed** **blood**
het Zij geeft haar bloed om haar zus te redden.
[blut] -She's giving blood to save her sister.

390 **mogelijk** **possible, eventual; possibly**
adj; adv Hoe is het mogelijk?
[ˈmoxələk] -How is this possible?

391 **mam** **mom**
de Mam, ik wil dit niet aantrekken.
[mɑm] -Mom, I don't want to wear this.

392 **redden** **save, rescue**
vb Je moet haar redden.
[ˈrɛdə(n)] -You must save her.

393 **rest** **rest, remainder**
de Je kunt de rest van de taart opeten als je wilt.
[rɛst] -It's okay to eat the rest of the cake if you want.

394 **eerlijk** **honest, straight; honestly**
adj; adv En ik ben eerlijk tegen mezelf gebleven.
[ˈerlək] -And I've remained honest to myself.

395 **langs** **along; along**
adv; prp Langs het strand lopen.
[lɑŋs] -Walking along the beach.

396 **stil** **quiet, still; quietly**
adj; adv Stil blijven, alstublieft.
[stɪl] -Please be quiet.

397 **vriendin** **girlfriend**
de Is dat John zijn vriendin?
[vrinˈdɪn] -Is that John's girlfriend?

398 **schuld** **debt, blame**
de Hij heeft veel schulden.
[sxʏlt] -He has a lot of debts.

399 **betalen** **pay**
vb Ik doe het als ze me betalen.
[bəˈtalə(n)] -I'll do it if they pay me.

400 **buurt** **neighborhood, district**
de Deze buurt is een stuk veiliger zonder die sneeuwscooter.
[byrt] -This neighborhood will be a lot safer without that snowmobile around.

401 **kerel** **guy, fellow**
de Ze werden verliefd op dezelfde kerel.
[ˈkerəl] -They fell in love with the same guy.

402 **ouder** **older, senior; parent**
adj; de Ik zou graag mijn ouders zien.
[ˈaudər] -I'd like to see my parents.

403 **recht** **right; right; right**
adj; adv; het We moeten er zeker van zijn dat we het bij het rechte eind hebben.
[rɛxt] -We have to be sure we're right.

404 **vandaan** **from**
prp Hij woont zes huizen van me vandaan.

[vanˈdan]   -He lives six houses from my house.

405 ermee   **with it**
adv   Of je het ermee eens bent of niet, ik ga het toch doen.
[ɛrˈme]   -Whether you agree with it or not, I'm going to do it.

406 rede   **reason, speech**
de   Dat is degene die de rede heeft gemaakt.
[ˈredə]   -That's the one who made the speech.

407 overal   **everywhere**
adv   Mijn hond gaat overal met me mee.
[ovərˈal]   -My dog goes everywhere with me.

408 belangrijk   **important**
adj   Het is belangrijk.
[bəˈlaŋrɛik]   -It's important.

409 fout   **error, mistake; wrong**
de; adj   Ik maak te veel fouten.
[faut]   -I'm making too many mistakes.

410 telefoon   **phone**
de   Is er ergens een telefoon?
[teləˈfon]   -Is there a telephone anywhere?

411 hard   **hard, loud; hard**
adj; adv   Ik heb jouw hulp hard nodig.
[hart]   -I am badly in need of your help.

412 mezelf   **myself**
prn   Als ik eenmaal begin met schoonmaken, kan ik mezelf niet meer tegenhouden.
[məˈzɛlf]   -Once I start cleaning, I can't stop myself.

413 duidelijk   **clear, obvious; clearly**
adj; adv   John is duidelijk uit vorm.
[ˈdœydələk]   -John is clearly out of practice.

414 baan   **job, track**
de   De enige baan die John ooit had is degene die hij nu heeft.
[ban]   -The only job John has ever had is the one he has now.

415 boek   **book**
het   Ik heb een uur naar het boek gezocht.
[buk]   -I looked for the book for an hour.

416 straks   **soon, later**
adv   Ik denk dat het straks gaat regenen.
[straks]   -My guess is that it will rain soon.

417 klinken   **sound, ring; clink**
vb; het   Je begint als een echtgenoot te klinken.
[ˈklɪŋkə(n)]   -You're beginning to sound just like a husband.

418 prachtig   **wonderful, magnificent**
adj; adv   Haar haar is lang en prachtig.
[ˈpraxtəx]   -Her hair is long and beautiful.

419 woord   **word**
het   Dit woord komt uit het Grieks.
[ʋoːrt]   -This word is derived from Greek.

420 kapitein   **captain**
de   De kapiteins zijn verantwoordelijk voor schip en bemanning.
[kapiˈtɛin]   -Captains have responsibility for ship and crew.

421 vaak   **often, regularly**
adv   Jane spreekt vaak in raadselen.

[vak] -Jane often speaks in riddles.

422 **haten** **hate**
vb Ik haat sneeuw!
['hatə(n)] -I hate snow!

423 **erop** **on**
adv Ongelofelijk dat ze die stickers erop deden.
[ɛr'ɔp] -I can't believe they put those stickers on.

424 **pa** **dad**
de Mijn pa belde net.
[pa] -My dad just called.

425 **zin** **sentence**
de Dat is geen goede Engelse zin.
[zɪn] -That is not a proper English sentence.

426 **deel** **part, segment**
het Welk deel van de pizza wil jij?
[del] -Which part of the pizza do you want?

427 **vanaf** **from**
prp Studeer vanaf nu harder.
[van'af] -Study harder from now on.

428 **rijden** **ride, drive**
vb Deze kameel is zo tam dat iedereen erop kan rijden.
['rɛidə(n)] -This camel is so tame that anyone can ride it.

429 **team** **team**
het John is de aanvoerder van het team.
[ti:m] -John is the team's captain.

430 **miljoen** **million**
nu De verliezen zullen oplopen tot miljoenen dollars.
[mɪl'jun] -Losses will run into millions of dollars.

431 **lieverd** **darling, honey**
de Ik ga wat pakken om dat schoon te maken, lieverd.
['livərt] -I'm going to go get something to clean that up, darling.

432 **voorzichtig** **careful, cautious; carefully**
adj; adv Wees voorzichtig als je de weg oversteekt.
[vor'zɪxtəx] -Be careful when you cross the street.

433 **geval** **case**
het Gebruik niet de lift in geval van brand.
[xə'val] -In case of fire, do not use the lift.

434 **licht** **light, mild; light; slightly**
adj; het; adv Zijn mening werpt nieuw licht op de kwestie.
[lɪxt] -His opinion adds a new light to the question.

435 **enkel** **only, single; only; ankle**
adj; adv; de John brak zijn enkel.
['ɛŋkəl] -John broke his ankle.

436 **dezelfde** **same**
prn John en Jane vertrokken in dezelfde richting.
[də'zɛlvdə] -John and Jane headed off in the same direction.

437 **lief** **lovable, nice; sweet**
adj; adv Als je geliefd wilt zijn, heb dan lief!
[lif] -If you want to be loved, love!

438 **tweede** **second**
nu De heren shirts bevinden zich op de tweede verdieping.

['twedə]   -Men's shirts are on the second floor.

439 erin   **in it**
adv   Het water is warm genoeg om erin te zwemmen.
[ɛr'ɪn]   -The water's warm enough to swim in it.

440 president   **president**
de   George Washington was de eerste president van de Verenigde Staten van Amerika.
[prezi'dɛnt]   -George Washington was the first President of the United States of America.

441 ontmoeten   **meet**
vb   Ik kon je niet ontmoeten op het vliegveld.
[ɔnt'mutə(n)]   -I could not meet you at the airport.

442 noemen   **call, mention**
vb   Hoe noem je deze vogel?
['numə(n)]   -What do you call this bird?

443 vechten   **fight, battle**
vb   Ik kan je leren vechten.
['vɛxtə(n)]   -I can teach you how to fight.

444 trouwen   **marry**
vb   Ik zal je nooit dwingen om met hem te trouwen.
['trɑuwə(n)]   -I will never force you to marry him.

445 lichaam   **body**
het   John heeft een prachtig lichaam.
['lɪxam]   -John has a fantastic body.

446 inderdaad   **indeed, actually**
adv   Inderdaad, Japans snoep gaat goed samen met Japanse thee.
[ɪndər'dat]   -Indeed, Japanese sweets go well with Japanese tea.

447 kwaad   **evil, angry; evil**
adj; het   Mijn oom is kwaad.
[kwat]   -My uncle is angry.

448 verliezen   **loss; lose**
het; vb   Je gezondheid verliezen is erger dan geld te verliezen.
[vər'lizə(n)]   -Losing one's health is worse than losing money.

449 nergens   **nowhere**
adv   De ring kon nergens gevonden worden.
['nɛrxəns]   -The ring was nowhere to be found.

450 antwoord   **answer**
het   Als antwoord sloeg hij mij op mijn hoofd.
['ɑntwort]   -His answer was to strike me on the head.

451 veranderen   **change**
vb   We moeten ons plan veranderen.
[vər'ɑndərə(n)]   -We have to change our plan.

452 grappig   **funny**
adj   John heeft een grappige manier van lachen, niet?
['xrɑpəx]   -John has a funny way of laughing, doesn't he?

453 wapen   **weapon**
het   Geduld is soms het meest effectieve wapen.
['wapə(n)]   -Patience is sometimes the most effective weapon.

454 verdommen   **refuse**
het   John verdomt het.
[vər'dɔmə(n)]   -John refuses to do it.

455 idioot   **idiot; idiotic**

	de; adj		John is ofwel een idioot ofwel een genie.
	[idiˈjot]		-John is either an idiot or a genius.
456	**stap**	**step, move**	
	de		Ik stap uit op het volgende station.
	[stɑp]		-I am getting off at the next station.
457	**einde**	**end**	
	het		Tegen het eind van de maand is John meestal helemaal blut.
	[ˈɛində]		-John is usually broke by the end of the month.
458	**tijdens**	**during**	
	prp		De vogelverschrikker in de achtertuin viel om tijdens de orkaan.
	[ˈtɛidəns]		-The scarecrow in the backyard fell over during the hurricane.
459	**kwijt**	**lost**	
	adj		Ik ben mijn kaartje kwijt.
	[kwɛit]		-I've lost my ticket.
460	**vertrouwen**	**confidence, faith; trust**	
	het; vb		Vertrouw John, en niet zijn zuster.
	[vərˈtrɑuwə(n)]		-Trust John, and not his sister.
461	**daarna**	**then, after; whereupon**	
	adv; con		Jij spreekt eerst, daarna spreek ik.
	[darˈna]		-You speak first, I will speak after.
462	**plezier**	**fun**	
	het		Ik wil tegenwoordig meer plezier maken.
	[pləˈzir]		-I'm trying to have more fun these days.
463	**pap**	**dad**	
	de		Is pap in de keuken?
	[pɑp]		-Is dad in the kitchen?
464	**naartoe**	**there**	
	adv		Wij gingen daar naartoe.
	[narˈtu]		-We went there.
465	**kopen**	**buy**	
	vb		Normaal koop ik geen dingen online.
	[ˈkopə(n)]		-I usually don't buy things online.
466	**koning**	**king**	
	de		Lang leve de koning!
	[ˈkonɪŋ]		-Long live the king!
467	**spel**	**game**	
	het		Dit is mijn favoriete spel.
	[spɛl]		-This is my favorite game.
468	**koffie**	**coffee**	
	de		Deze koffie is koud.
	[ˈkɔfi]		-This coffee is cold.
469	**omhoog**	**up**	
	adv		Ze keek omhoog naar het plafond.
	[ɔmˈhox]		-She looked up at the ceiling.
470	**gevoel**	**feeling**	
	het		Ik heb het gevoel dat ze vandaag zal komen.
	[xəˈvul]		-I have a feeling that she will come today.
471	**ervoor**	**for it**	
	adv		Vraag hem hoeveel ik ervoor krijg.
	[ɛrˈvor]		-Ask him how much I'll get for it.
472	**achten**	**deem**	

	vb	John doet wat hij goed acht.
	[ˈɑxtə(n)]	-John does what he deems to be right.
473	**ziek**	**sick**
	adj	Je bent ziek! Maar je ziet er wel lekker uit.
	[zik]	-You're sick! But you're still looking good.
474	**gang**	**corridor, hallway**
	de	De wc is aan het einde van de gang.
	[xɑŋ]	-The bathroom is at the end of the hall.
475	**trek**	**pull**
	de	U moet de knoop strakker trekken.
	[trɛk]	-You must tighten the knot.
476	**lucht**	**air, sky**
	de	Lucht is lichter dan water.
	[lʏxt]	-Air is lighter than water.
477	**meid**	**girl**
	de	Die meiden zijn aangekomen.
	[mɛit]	-Those girls arrived.
478	**zichzelf**	**himself**
	prn	Johnd heeft zichzelf duidelijk overtroffen.
	[zɪxˈsɛlf]	-Clearly, John has outdone himself this time.
479	**leggen**	**lay, put**
	vb	Leg de krant op de tafel.
	[ˈlɛxə(n)]	-Put the newspaper on the table.
480	**fantastisch**	**fantastic**
	adj	John is fantastisch.
	[fɑnˈtɑstis]	-John is fantastic.
481	**winnen**	**win**
	vb	Laat mij ook eens een keertje winnen.
	[ˈwɪnə(n)]	-Let me win for once.
482	**zeven**	**seven**
	nu	Gulzigheid is een van de zeven hoofdzonden.
	[ˈzevə(n)]	-Gluttony is one of the seven deadly sins.
483	**zus**	**sister**
	de	Ze had haar zus die dag minstens honderd keer gebeld.
	[zʏs]	-She made at least a hundred phone calls to her sister that day.
484	**onzin**	**nonsense, rubbish**
	de	Praat geen onzin, je weet dat dat onmogelijk is.
	[ˈɔnzɪn]	-Don't talk nonsense, you know that's impossible.
485	**gisteren**	**yesterday**
	adv	Het voorstel dat hij gisteren heeft gemaakt, is nu in overweging.
	[ˈxɪstərə(n)]	-The proposal he made yesterday is now under consideration.
486	**muziek**	**music**
	de	Zijn muziek is te luid.
	[myˈzik]	-His music is too noisy.
487	**men**	**people, one**
	prn	Wiens brood men eet, diens woord men spreekt.
	[mɛn]	-Whose ever bread one eats, his language one speaks.
488	**eindelijk**	**finally**
	adv	God zij dank regent het eindelijk!
	[ˈɛindələk]	-Thank God, it is finally raining.
489	**normaal**	**normal**

	adj	Dit is niet normaal.
	[nɔr'mal]	-This isn't normal.
490	**oom**	**uncle**
	de	De auto van mijn oom is sneller dan de mijne.
	[om]	-My uncle's car is faster than mine.
491	**vreemd**	**strange; strangely**
	adj; adv	Hij heeft vreemde ideeën.
	[vremt]	-He has strange ideas.
492	**daarmee**	**therewith, with that**
	adv	Ben je het daarmee eens of niet?
	[dar'me]	-Do you agree with that or not?
493	**herinneren**	**remember**
	vb	Ze zijn neven, als ik het me goed herinner.
	[ɦɛr.'ɪ.nə.rə(n)]	-They are cousins, if I remember rightly.
494	**pardon**	**pardon, excuse me**
	het	Pardon, waar is de taxistandplaats?
	[par'dɔn]	-Excuse me, where is the taxi stand?
495	**nogal**	**rather; pretty**
	adv; adj	John leek nogal dronken.
	[nɔ'xɑl]	-John seemed to be rather drunk.
496	**minder**	**less; less, fewer**
	adj; adv	Zijn oom bezit niet minder dan tien huizen.
	['mɪndər]	-His uncle owns no fewer than ten houses.
497	**verwachten**	**expect**
	vb	Jane verwacht dat er vreemde dingen gebeuren
	[vər'wɑxtə(n)]	-Jane expects strange things to happen.
498	**grond**	**ground**
	de	De grond was koud.
	[xrɔnt]	-The ground was cold.
499	**nietwaar**	**is(n't) it**
	int	Spijtig dat een biljarttafel niet kan vliegen, nietwaar?
	[nit'war]	-Regrettable that one can't fly a billiard table, isn't it?
500	**menen**	**mean**
	verb	Laten we de eersten zijn die het echt menen.
	['menə(n)]	-Let's be the first to really mean it.
501	**beloven**	**promise**
	vb	Je moet me alleen één ding beloven.
	[bə'lovə(n)]	-You just have to promise me one thing.
502	**verkeerd**	**wrong; wrong**
	adj; adv	Je bent op de verkeerde weg.
	[vər'kert]	-You're on the wrong road.
503	**kantoor**	**office**
	het	Waar is mijn kantoor?
	[kan'tor]	-Where is my office?
504	**droom**	**dream**
	de	Ze had een aangename droom.
	[drom]	-She had a pleasant dream.
505	**hoezo**	**why; why**
	adv; con	Hoezo wil je in het buitenland studeren?
	[hu'zo]	-Why do you want to study abroad?
506	**allebei**	**both**

adj	John en Jane zijn allebei vegetariër.
[alə'bɛi]	-John and Jane are both vegetarians.
507 **hemel**	**sky, heaven**
de	Nee, de hemel zal niet op ons hoofd vallen.
['heməl]	-No, the sky won't fall on our heads.
508 **foto**	**photo**
de	Ik houd van deze foto.
['foto]	-I love this photo.
509 **perfect**	**perfect**
adj	Het ruimteschip heeft een perfecte landing gemaakt.
[pɛr'fɛkt]	-The spaceship made a perfect landing.
510 **waard**	**worth**
adj	Is biologisch eten wel zijn geld waard?
[ʋaːrt]	-Is eating organic food worth the money?
511 **erbij**	**at, with, there**
adv	Jane was erbij.
[ɛr'bɛi]	-Jane was there.
512 **zomaar**	**just**
adv	Hij ging zomaar weg.
['zomar]	-He just left.
513 **gebruik**	**use**
het	Gebruik je het?
[xə'brœyk]	-Do you use it?
514 **half**	**half; semi**
het; adv	Mexico telt half zo veel mensen als Japan.
[halff]	-Mexico has half as many people as Japan.
515 **vroeger**	**earlier; former**
adv; adj	Je moet vroeger opstaan.
['vruxər]	-You have to wake up earlier.
516 **sturen**	**send, steer**
vb	Ik weet niet zeker of John degene is die we naar Boston moeten sturen.
['styrə(n)]	-I'm not certain John is the one we should send to Boston.
517 **trots**	**pride; proud**
de; adj	Ik ben trots op dit land.
[trɔts]	-I'm proud of this country.
518 **aarde**	**earth**
de	Aarde, wind en vuur.
['ardə]	-Earth, wind and fire.
519 **vuur**	**fire**
het	Het huis staat in de brand.
[vyr]	-The house is on fire.
520 **gevangenis**	**prison**
de(f)	John werd tot vijf maanden gevangenis veroordeeld.
[xə'vaŋənɪs]	-John was sentenced to five months in prison.
521 **hierheen**	**here; hither**
adv; adj	Kom hierheen, Heather!
[hiːrheːjn]	-Come hither, Heather!
522 **leger**	**army**
het	Hoe lang zat je bij het leger?
['lexər]	-How long did you serve in the army?
523 **persoon**	**person**

	de	Jij bent hier een heilig persoon.
	[pɛrˈson]	-You are a sacred person here.
524	**opnieuw**	**again**
	adv	Kan je dat opnieuw doen?
	[ɔpˈniw]	-Can you do that again?
525	**kracht**	**force**
	de	Ze heeft speciale krachten.
	[krɑxt]	-She has special powers.
526	**serieus**	**serious**
	adj	John klinkt serieus.
	[seriˈjøs]	-John looks serious.
527	**ziekenhuis**	**hospital**
	het	John vroeg Jane hem naar het ziekenhuis te brengen.
	[ˈzikə(n)hœys]	-John asked Jane to take him to the hospital.
528	**moord**	**murder**
	de	Jullie zijn schuldig aan moord.
	[mort]	-You are guilty of murder.
529	**verlaten**	**leave; abandoned**
	vb; adj	Waarom wilt u Boston verlaten?
	[vərˈlatə(n)]	-Why do you want to leave Boston?
530	**lezen**	**read**
	vb	Ik had de gebruiksaanwijzing moeten lezen.
	[ˈlezə(n)]	-I should've read the instructions.
531	**dansen**	**dance**
	verb	Zij wil dansen.
	[ˈdɑnsə(n)]	-She wants to dance.
532	**tv**	**TV**
	abr	Het drama op tv was zo populair dat het de interesse van de mensen opwekte.
	[teˈve]	-The drama on TV was so popular that it stirred up people's interest.
533	**stom**	**stupid**
	adj	Mijn broer is stom.
	[stɔm]	-My brother is stupid.
534	**slim**	**smart**
	adj	Waarom zijn jullie zo slim?
	[slɪm]	-Why are you so smart?
535	**vertrek**	**departure, room**
	het	Ik vertrek uit het vertrek.
	[vərˈtrɛk]	-I am leaving the room.
536	**ongeveer**	**about, approximately**
	adv	John werkt al ongeveer drie jaar voor ons.
	[ɔnxəˈver]	-John has been working for us for about three years.
537	**punt**	**point**
	het	Het punt is dat ze honger hebben.
	[pʏnt]	-The point is that they are hungry.
538	**stellen**	**suppose, put**
	vb	Stel dat ik wil vertrekken
	[ˈstɛlə(n)]	-Suppose that I want to leave.
539	**eentje**	**alone, by yourself**
	prn	Ik kan niet geloven dat je dit in je eentje gedaan hebt.
	[ˈencə]	-I can't believe you did this by yourself.
540	**pistool**	**pistol**

	het		Leg het pistool op de tafel.
	[pi'stɔl]		-Put the pistol on the table.
541	**straat**		**street**
	de		Jullie staken de straat over.
	[strat]		-You crossed the street.
542	**toekomst**		**future**
	de		Ons land heeft geen toekomst.
	['tukɔmst]		-Our country has no future.
543	**zwart**		**black**
	adj		Ik hou van de kleur zwart.
	[zwɑrt]		-I like the color black.
544	**sommige**		**some; some**
	adj; prn		In sommige landen is abortus illegaal.
	['sɔməxə]		-In some countries, abortion is illegal.
545	**bank**		**bank; couch**
	de		De bank ligt naast het postkantoor.
	[bɑŋk]		-The bank is next to the post office.
546	**degene**		**the one, those**
	prn		In veel oude films is de heldin altijd degene die doodgaat.
	[də'genə]		-In many old movies the heroine is always the one to die.
547	**spul**		**stuff**
	het		Deze video is echt goed spul.
	[spʏl]		-This video is the good stuff.
548	**schrijven**		**write**
	vb		Ik ben van plan om Jane een brief te schrijven.
	['sxrɛivə(n)]		-I plan to write Jane a letter.
549	**vliegtuig**		**airplane**
	het		Het is warm in het vliegtuig.
	['vlixtœyx]		-It is hot on the airplane.
550	**verliefd**		**in love**
	adj		Ze werd verliefd op een man uit de sportschool.
	[vər'lift]		-She fell in love with a guy from the gym.
551	**ieder**		**each; every**
	prn; adj		Ik vond het nodig om iedere morgen vroeg op te staan.
	['idər]		-I found it necessary to get up early every morning.
552	**informatie**		**information**
	de		Klopt deze informatie?
	[ɪnfɔr'ma(t)si]		-Is this information right?
553	**tenminste**		**at least**
	adv		Mijn broer is zeer belangrijk. Dat denkt hij tenminste.
	[tən'mɪnstə]		-My brother is very important. At least he thinks he is.
554	**slechts**		**only**
	adv		Het is slechts een modegril.
	[slɛx(t)s]		-It's just a fad.
555	**makkelijk**		**easy; easy**
	adj; adv		Het is makkelijk voor mij om te zwemmen.
	['mɑkələk]		-It is easy for me to swim.
556	**boos**		**angry; angrily**
	adj; adv		Maak me niet boos.
	[bos]		-Don't make me angry.
557	**slaan**		**beat, hit**

	vb	Natuurlijk wou ik je niet slaan.
	[slan]	-Of course I didn't mean to hit you.
558	**generaal**	**general**
	de	De generaal inspecteerde de soldaten.
	[xenəˈral]	-The general inspected the soldiers.
559	**boot**	**boat**
	de	Onze boot volgde een school vissen.
	[bot]	-Our boat followed a school of fish.
560	**succes**	**success**
	het	We streven allemaal naar succes.
	[sʏkˈsɛs]	-We all strive for success.
561	**feest**	**party**
	het	Wie heeft je uitgenodigd voor het feest?
	[fest]	-Who invited you to the party?
562	**trouwens**	**by the way**
	adv	Trouwens, ik heb je iets te vertellen.
	[ˈtrɑuwəns]	-By the way, I have something to tell you.
563	**vliegen**	**fly**
	vb	Een struisvogel kan niet vliegen.
	[ˈvlixə(n)]	-An ostrich can't fly.
564	**geest**	**spirit, ghost**
	de	Ik dacht dat ik een geest zag.
	[xest]	-I thought I saw a ghost.
565	**ongeluk**	**accident**
	het	Dat ging per ongeluk!
	[ˈɔnxəlʏk]	-I didn't mean to!
566	**ter**	**to**
	prp	De beschuldigde werd ter dood veroordeeld.
	[tɛr]	-The defendant was sentenced to death.
567	**kleren**	**clothes**
	de	In mijn koffer was niets op vuile kleren na.
	[ˈklerə(n)]	-The suitcase contained nothing but dirty clothes.
568	**koud**	**cold**
	adj	Het is zo koud vanavond.
	[kɑut]	-It's so cold tonight.
569	**liefje**	**sweetheart**
	het	Morgen, liefje! Heb je goed geslapen?
	[ˈlifjə]	-Good morning, sweetheart! Did you sleep well?
570	**weinig**	**little, few**
	adj	Deze jurk laat weinig aan de verbeelding over.
	[ˈwɛinəx]	-This dress leaves little to the imagination.
571	**jawel**	**yes, sure enough**
	int	Jawel, je moet!
	[jaˈwɛl]	-Yes, you have to!
572	**onderzoek**	**research, study**
	het	Dat is een interessant onderzoek.
	[ˈɔndərzuk]	-That's an interesting study.
573	**honger**	**hunger**
	de	Ik heb liever honger dan dat ik dit eet.
	[ˈhɔŋər]	-I'd rather go hungry than eat this.
574	**vreselijk**	**terrible; terribly**

	adj; adv		De luier stinkt vreselijk.
	['vresələk]		-The nappy smells very dirty.
575	**hotel**	**hotel**	
	het		We overnachtten in een goedkoop hotel.
	[hoˈtɛl]		-We spent the night in a cheap hotel.
576	**bal**	**ball**	
	het		Deze zeeleeuw kan een bal op zijn neus balanceren.
	[bɑl]		-This sea lion can balance a ball on its nose.
577	**behalve**	**except**	
	prp		Ieder van ons, behalve hij, ging.
	[bəˈhɑlvə]		-All of us, except him, went.
578	**controle**	**control**	
	de		Het lawaai was snel onder controle.
	[kɔnˈtrɔːlə]		-The noise was quickly brought under control.
579	**zak**	**bag**	
	de		Adem gewoon eventjes in een zak.
	[zɑk]		-Just breathe into a bag for a while.
580	**wonen**	**live**	
	vb		Wil je in Mumbai wonen?
	[wonə(n)]		-Do you want to live in Mumbai?
581	**contact**	**contact**	
	het		Hoe kan ik contact opnemen met een Japans sprekende dokter?
	[kɔnˈtakt]		-How can I contact a Japanese-speaking doctor?
582	**meter**	**meter**	
	de		Het gebouw is honderd meter hoog.
	['metər]		-The building is one hundred meters high.
583	**schip**	**ship**	
	het		John ontdekte een fout in het ontwerp van het schip.
	[sxɪp]		-John discovered a flaw in the ship's design.
584	**sterk**	**strong**	
	adj		Hij is niet zo sterk als eerst.
	[stɛrk]		-He's not as strong as before.
585	**verkopen**	**sell**	
	vb		Verkopen ze schriften in die winkel?
	[vərˈkopə(n)]		-Do they sell notebooks at that store?
586	**show**	**show**	
	de		De show was spannend.
	[ʃo]		-The show was exciting.
587	**geheim**	**secret; secret**	
	adj; het		Een geheim bewaren heb ik nooit gekund.
	[xəˈhɛim]		-I never could keep a secret.
588	**rot**	**rot; rotten**	
	het; adj		De helft van de appels is rot.
	[rɔt]		-Half of the apples are rotten.
589	**doden**	**kill**	
	vb		Je moet ze uiteindelijk allemaal doden.
	['dodə(n)]		-You must kill every one of them eventually.
590	**absoluut**	**absolutely; absolute**	
	adv; adj		Het is absoluut fantastisch.
	[ɑpsoˈlyt]		-It's absolutely fantastic.
591	**zolang**	**as long as**	

	con	Je mag hier blijven zolang je rustig bent.
	[zoˈlɑŋ]	-As long as you keep quiet, you can stay here.

592 dienst
de
[dinst]

service
Buiten het uitlenen van boeken bieden bibliotheken verschillende andere diensten aan.
-Besides lending books, libraries offer various other services.

593 wegwezen
vb
['wɛxwezə(n)]

get out
Wegwezen! Of ik bel de politie!
-Get out! Or else I'm calling the cops!

594 rug
de
[rʏx]

back
Ik heb mijn rug gebroken.
-I broke my back.

595 advocaat
de
[ɑtfoˈkat]

lawyer
We zullen een andere advocaat zoeken.
-We'll find another lawyer.

596 afgelopen
adj; adv
[ˈɑfxəlopə(n)]

over, last; out
Ze is afgelopen jaar geboren.
-She was born last year.

597 moe
adj
[mu]

tired
Ik heb het gehad voor vandaag. Ik ben te moe.
-I've had it for today. I'm too tired.

598 geboren
adj
[xəˈborə(n)]

born
John is niet blind geboren.
-John was not born blind.

599 meester
de
['mestər]

master, teacher
Het schilderij is het werk van een Nederlandse meester.
-The painting is the work of a Dutch master.

600 jong
adj; het
[jɔŋ]

young; cub
John is te jong om auto te rijden.
-John is too young to drive a car.

601 naast
adj; prp
[nast]

near; next to
Nee, de stoelen zijn naast de tafel.
-No, the chairs are next to the table.

602 beschermen
vb
[bəˈsxɛrmə(n)]

protect
We zijn hier om u te beschermen.
-We're here to protect you.

603 bestaan
het; vb
[bəˈstan]

existence; exist
Niet alles krijgt een kans om te bestaan.
-Not everything gets a chance to exist.

604 erover
adv
[ɛrˈovər]

about
Ik zal je erover vertellen.
-I'll tell you about it.

605 bewijs
het
[bəˈwɛis]

proof
Het is zo voor de hand liggend dat er geen bewijs vereist is.
-It's so obvious we don't need proof.

606 lachen
vb
[ˈlɑxə(n)]

laugh
Haar lach galmde door het huis.
-Her laughter echoed through the house.

607 reis
de
[rɛis]

travel
Ik zal mijn reis naar Schotland uitstellen tot het warmer is.
-I will postpone my trip to Scotland until it is warmer.

608	**afspraak**	**appointment**
	de	Ik wil je er aan herinneren dat je om half drie een afspraak hebt.
	[ˈɑfsprak]	-I want to remind you that you have a 2:30 appointment.
609	**rij**	**row**
	de	Ja! Ik heb twee keer op een rij gewonnen!
	[rɛi]	-Yes! I won twice in a row!
610	**voorstellen**	**propose**
	vb	De methode die wij voorstellen, heeft twee belangrijke voordelen.
	[ˈvorstɛlə(n)]	-The method we propose has two major advantages.
611	**raken**	**hit, touch**
	vb	Raak mijn auto niet aan.
	[ˈrakə(n)]	-Don't touch my car.
612	**kont**	**buttocks, bum**
	de	Ik wil niet dat ze mijn kont zien.
	[kɔnt]	-Because l don't like people to see my bum.
613	**schelen**	**differ, care**
	vb	Kan het ons wat schelen?
	[ˈsxelə(n)]	-Do we care?
614	**lukken**	**succeed**
	vb	Misschien zal het je lukken.
	[ˈlʏkə(n)]	-Maybe you'll succeed.
615	**seks**	**sex**
	de	Seks is goed. Net zoals pizza.
	[sɛks]	-Sex is good. Just like pizza.
616	**dame**	**lady**
	de	Hij begroette de dame.
	[ˈdamə]	-He greeted the lady.
617	**prijs**	**price, prize**
	de	Elk van de drie jongens hebben een prijs gewonnen.
	[prɛis]	-Each of the three boys won a prize.
618	**trekken**	**pull; draft**
	vb; het	Trek aan mijn arm.
	[ˈtrɛkə(n)]	-Pull my arm.
619	**stelen**	**steal**
	vb	Ze wilden de auto stelen.
	[ˈstelə(n)]	-They wanted to steal the car.
620	**dragen**	**wear, carry**
	vb;	Waarom draag jij mijn jurk?
	[ˈdraxə(n)]	-Why are you wearing my dress?
621	**gevaarlijk**	**dangerous; hazardous**
	adj; adv	Dat is gevaarlijk!
	[xeˈvarlək]	-That's dangerous!
622	**maat**	**size, buddy**
	de	Weet u welke maat u hebt?
	[mat]	-Do you know your size?
623	**hel**	**hell; bright; glaringly**
	de; adj; adv	Tussen hemel en hel.
	[hɛl]	-Between heaven and hell.
624	**rennen**	**run**
	vb	Blijf rennen en kijk niet achterom.
	[ˈrɛnə(n)]	-Keep running and don't look back.

625	**seconde**	**second**
	de	Na elf seconden kunnen ze de straat oversteken.
	[səˈkɔndə]	-After eleven seconds they can cross the street.
626	**regel**	**rule**
	de	Spelers moeten zich houden aan de regels van het spel.
	[ˈrexəl]	-Players must adhere to the rules of the game.
627	**sla**	**lettuce**
	de	John voederde sla aan de slakken.
	[sla]	-John fed the snails lettuce.
628	**jammer**	**unfortunate; unfortunately**
	adj; adv	Dat is jammer. Voor jou dan.
	[ˈjamər]	-That's unfortunate. Well.. for you.
629	**missen**	**miss**
	vb	Je vrienden zullen je missen.
	[ˈmɪsə(n)]	-You'll be missed by your friends.
630	**doel**	**purpose, goal**
	het	Het doel is toegankelijkheid.
	[dul]	-The goal is accessibility.
631	**raar**	**strange; strangely**
	adj; adv	Dat was raar, maar wel opwindend.
	[rar]	-That was strange, but still pretty exciting.
632	**stem**	**vote, voice**
	de	Ze spreekt tegen hem altijd met luide stem.
	[stɛm]	-She always speaks to him in a loud voice.
633	**zweren**	**swear**
	verb	Ik zweer bij God dat ik niets gedaan heb.
	[ˈzwerə(n)]	-I swear to God I didn't do anything.
634	**gevaar**	**danger**
	het	Atoombommen zijn een gevaar voor de mensheid.
	[xeˈvar]	-Atomic bombs are a danger to the human race.
635	**bekend**	**known**
	adj	Hij maakte het bekend waar de president naartoe was.
	[bəˈkɛnt]	-He made it known where the president had gone.
636	**arm**	**arm; poor**
	de; adj	Ik heb mijn arm gebroken.
	[arm]	-I broke my arm.
637	**derde**	**third**
	nu	Hij is de derde persoon.
	[ˈdɛrdə]	-He is the third person.
638	**kolonel**	**colonel**
	de	Ik ben zenuwachtig omdat kolonel John komt.
	[koloˈnɛl]	-Right. I'm just so nervous about Colonel John coming.
639	**paard**	**horse**
	het	Waar is jouw paard?
	[part]	-Where's your horse?
640	**tafel**	**table**
	de	Ik zit aan tafel.
	[ˈtafəl]	-I am sitting at the table.
641	**totdat**	**until**
	con	Ik was kalm totdat ik de spuit zag.
	[tɔˈdat]	-I was calm until I saw the syringe.

642	**groep**	**group**
	de	Een group mensen.
	[xrup]	-A group of people.
643	**wedstrijd**	**match, game**
	de	Ons team heeft alle wedstrijden verloren.
	['wɛtstrɛit]	-Our team lost all its games.
644	**dom**	**stupid**
	adj;	Ze zijn niet dom.
	[dɔm]	-They aren't stupid.
645	**wagen**	**car; risk**
	de; vb	Ik wil een tweede poging wagen.
	['waxə(n)]	-I want to try again.
646	**grap**	**joke**
	de	Het was maar een grap.
	[xrɑp]	-It was just a joke.
647	**gat**	**hole**
	het	Er is een gat in de weg.
	[xɑt]	-There's a hole in the road.
648	**via**	**via**
	prp	Dit dorp is niet te bereiken, behalve via de rivier.
	['vija]	-This village cannot be reached except via the river.
649	**raden**	**guess**
	vb	Raad eens hoe ik heet.
	[ˈrɑdə(n)]	-Guess what my name is.
650	**band**	**tire, band**
	de	Ik moest mijn fiets duwen omdat ik een platte band had.
	[bɑnt]	-I had to push my bicycle because I had a flat tire.
651	**nadat**	**after**
	con	Hij bloosde nadat de meisjes naar hem floten op straat.
	[naˈdɑt]	-He blushed after the girls whistled at him in the street.
652	**moordenaar**	**killer, murderer**
	de	De moordenaar verstopte zich in de bergen.
	['mordənar]	-The murderer hid in the mountains.
653	**ma**	**mom**
	de	Ma, ik heb honger.
	[ma]	-Mom, I'm hungry.
654	**kaart**	**map**
	de	Heb je een kaart van Boston?
	[kart]	-Do you have a map of Boston?
655	**zover**	**as far as**
	adv	Voor zover ik weet, is hij schuldig.
	['zɔvər]	-As far as I know, he's guilty.
656	**kerk**	**church**
	de	Daar staat een prachtige kerk op de heuvel.
	[kɛrk]	-There stands a beautiful church on the hill.
657	**rijk**	**rich; empire**
	adj; het	Hij is rijk genoeg om twee auto's te kopen.
	[rɛik]	-He is rich enough to buy two cars.
658	**macht**	**power**
	de	Macht en geld zijn onafscheidelijk.
	[mɑxt]	-Power and money are inseparable.

659	**vluchten**	**flee**
	vb	Als de verdachte probeert te vluchten.
	['vlʏxtə(n)]	-When the suspect intends to flee.
660	**schuldig**	**guilty**
	adj	Ik geloof dat John niet schuldig is.
	['sxʏldəx]	-I believe that John is not guilty.
661	**zwaar**	**heavy**
	adj	Dat boek is zwaar.
	[zwar]	-This book is heavy.
662	**ruimte**	**space**
	de	Hij stapte in mijn ruimte.
	['rœymtə]	-He stepped into my space.
663	**zodra**	**once, as soon as**
	con	Ik ben zo moe dat ik naar bed ga zodra ik thuiskom.
	[zo'dra]	-I'm so tired that I'm going to bed as soon as I get home.
664	**negen**	**nine**
	nu	Ik kocht negen bloemen.
	['nexə(n)]	-I bought nine flowers.
665	**vanuit**	**from**
	prp	Je kunt vanuit het raam de schoorstenen van de fabriek zien.
	[van'œyt]	-You can see the smokestacks of the factory from the window.
666	**vooral**	**especially, above all**
	adv	Pas vooral op voor zakkenrollers.
	[vor'al]	-Above all, beware of pickpockets.
667	**vorig**	**last**
	adj	Waar was je de vorige nacht?
	['vorəx]	-Where were you last night?
668	**brief**	**letter**
	de	Ik zal John een brief schrijven.
	[brif]	-I'll write John a letter.
669	**gedachte**	**thought**
	de	Uiteindelijk is hij van gedachten veranderd.
	[xə'daxtə]	-Eventually, he changed his mind.
670	**zuster**	**sister**
	de	Mijn zuster is drie jaar oud.
	['zʏstər]	-My sister is three years old.
671	**gooien**	**throw**
	vb	Gooi dit tijdschrift niet weg.
	['xojə(n)]	-Don't throw away this magazine.
672	**wet**	**law**
	de	De lange arm van de wet.
	[wɛt]	-The long arm of the law.
673	**dronken**	**drunk**
	adj	John was dronken.
	['drɔŋkə(n)]	-John was drunk.
674	**ziel**	**soul**
	de	Zijn ziel was in de hemel.
	[zil]	-His soul was in heaven.
675	**drug**	**drug**
	de	Uw dochter is aan de drugs.
	['drʏg]	-Your daughter's on drugs.

676	**kapot**	**broken; to pieces**
	adj; adv	Ze sloeg de spiegel kapot met een hamer.
	[ka'pɔt]	-She shattered the mirror with a hammer.
677	**sleutel**	**key**
	de	Ik ben mijn sleutel verloren.
	['sløtəl]	-I lost my key.
678	**haast**	**hurry; almost**
	de; adv	Hij ging in alle haast weg.
	[hast]	-He went away in a hurry.
679	**eind**	**end**
	het	Tegen het einde van de excursie hadden we al erg veel dorst.
	[ɛint]	-By the end of the trip we were very thirsty.
680	**duren**	**last, take**
	vb	Het duurt lang.
	['dyrə(n)]	-It takes very long.
681	**eer**	**honor; ere**
	de; con	Met wie heb ik de eer te spreken?
	[er]	-With whom do I have the honor to speak?
682	**zee**	**sea**
	de	Vele mannen stierven op zee.
	[ze]	-Many men died at sea.
683	**onmogelijk**	**impossible; impossibly**
	adj; adv	Ik kan het je onmogelijk uitleggen.
	[ɔn'moxələk]	-It's impossible for me to explain it to you.
684	**lijn**	**line**
	de	Ik heb een lijn overgeslagen bij het lezen.
	[lɛin]	-I skipped a line when I was reading.
685	**teken**	**sign**
	het	Ik leef, zelfs al geef ik geen teken van leven.
	['tekə(n)]	-I am alive even though I am not giving any sign of life.
686	**links**	**left**
	adj	Hij keek naar links en rechts.
	[lɪŋks]	-He looked left and right.
687	**gast**	**guest, man**
	de	De gastheer sneed de kalkoen aan voor de gasten.
	[xɑst]	-The host cut the turkey for the guests.
688	**situatie**	**situation**
	de	Ik hoop dat de situatie zich zal verbeteren.
	[sity'wa(t)si]	-I hope things will get better.
689	**wit**	**white**
	adj	De vogel was bedekt met witte veren.
	[wɪt]	-The bird was covered with white feathers.
690	**warm**	**warm**
	adj	Het was warm gisternacht.
	[wɑrm]	-It was hot last night.
691	**vanwege**	**because of**
	prp	Dat meisje is arrogant vanwege haar schoonheid.
	[vɑn'wexə]	-That girl is arrogant because of her beauty.
692	**zon**	**sun**
	de	De zon en de maan.
	[zɔn]	-The sun and the moon.

693	**trein**	**train**
	de	Laten we de trein nemen.
	[trɛin]	-Let's go by train.
694	**daarvoor**	**therefor, for that**
	adv	De voornaamste reden daarvoor was dat hij te weinig tijd ervoor had.
	[dar'vor]	-The main reason for this was that he had too little time.
695	**gebouw**	**building**
	het	Ik ben de eigenaar van dit gebouw.
	[xə'bɑu]	-I'm the owner of this building.
696	**delen**	**share**
	vb	Vanaf nu zullen jullie ons lijden delen.
	['delə(n)]	-From now on, you will share our suffering.
697	**huwelijk**	**wedding**
	het	Ze hadden besloten het huwelijk uit te stellen tot haar broer terug was gekomen uit het buitenland.
	['hywələk]	-They had decided to put the wedding off until her brother came home from abroad.
698	**draai**	**turn**
	de	Draai ik naar links bij het eerste verkeerslicht?
	[draj]	-Do I turn left at the first stoplight?
699	**oma**	**grandmother**
	de	Ook de ooms, tantes, opa's en oma's zijn daar.
	['oma]	-The uncles, aunts, granddads and grandmas are there as well.
700	**schoen**	**shoe**
	de	Jane deed haar schoenen en sokken uit.
	[sxun]	-Jane took off her shoes and socks.
701	**bus**	**bus**
	de	Ik wilde een bus huren.
	[bʏs]	-I wanted to rent a bus.
702	**bedrijf**	**business, company**
	het	Zijn bedrijf groeit snel.
	[bə'drɛif]	-His business is growing rapidly.
703	**bewegen**	**move**
	vb	Lawines bewegen sneller dan overstromingen.
	[bə'wexə(n)]	-Avalanches move faster than floods.
704	**diep**	**deep; deep**
	adj; adv	Die vijver is drie meter diep.
	[dip]	-The pond is three meters deep.
705	**respect**	**respect**
	het	Met alle respect, ik denk dat zij beiden valide punten hadden.
	[rɛ'spɛkt]	-With all due respect, I think they both had valid points.
706	**direct**	**directly; direct**
	adv; adj	Je had me direct moeten bellen.
	[di'rɛkt]	-You should've phoned me right away.
707	**vannacht**	**tonight**
	adv	Er is vannacht een feestje bij John thuis.
	[vɑ'nɑxt]	-There's a party at John's house tonight.
708	**kalm**	**calm; calmly**
	adj; adv	Blijf kalm. Je zult morgen je beloning krijgen.
	[kɑlm]	-Stay calm. You'll have your reward tomorrow.
709	**muur**	**wall**

de	John klauterde over de muur.
[myr]	-John climbed over the wall.
710 breken	**break**
vb	Je kan geen omelet maken zonder eieren te breken.
['brekə(n)]	-You cannot make omelets without breaking eggs.
711 waarvoor	**for what**
adv	Waarvoor heb je dat geld nodig?
[war'vor]	-What do you need the money for?
712 angst	**fear**
de	Ze kon haar angst voor de duisternis niet overwinnen.
[ɑŋst]	-She could not get over her fear of the dark.
713 been	**leg**
het	Breek een been!
[ben]	-Break a leg!
714 keuze	**choice**
de	Ik had geen keuze.
['køzə]	-I had no choice.
715 broek	**pants, trousers**
de	Dat is mijn broek.
[bruk]	-Those are my trousers.
716 regelen	**arrange**
vb	Dat zal ik voor je regelen.
['rexələ(n)]	-I'll arrange that for you.
717 sergeant	**sergeant**
de	Alles lijkt in orde, sergeant.
[sɛr'ʒɑnt]	-Everything seems to be okay here, Sergeant.
718 gisteravond	**last night**
adj	We hebben rijst met curry gegeten gisteravond.
[xɪstər'avɔnt]	-We ate curry rice last night.
719 gezin	**family**
het	Ik kom uit een groot gezin.
[xə'zɪn]	-I'm from a big family.
720 zingen	**sing**
vb	Zing je graag?
['zɪŋə(n)]	-Do you like singing?
721 onderweg	**en route, on the way**
adv	Ik ben mijn leraar tegengekomen onderweg naar het station.
[ɔndər'wɛx]	-I met my teacher on the way to the station.
722 tenzij	**unless**
con	Blijf niet in bed tenzij u geld in bed kunt verdienen.
['tɛnzɛi]	-Don't stay in bed, unless you can make money in bed.
723 weggaan	**go away, leave**
vb	Ga alsjeblieft weg.
['wɛxan]	-Please leave.
724 midden	**middle; mid; amidst**
het; adj; prp	Ik sta in het midden van het schoolplein.
['mɪdə(n)]	-I am standing in the middle of the schoolyard.
725 rood	**red**
adj	Het boek is rood.
[rot]	-The book is red.
726 beide	**both; either**

	adj; prn	Ze werken beiden.
	[ˈbɛidə]	-They both work.
727	**les**	**lesson**
	de	Ik heb een prachtige les geleerd.
	[lɛs]	-Brothers, I've learned a wonderful lesson.
728	**sluiten**	**close**
	vb	Sluit je ogen weer.
	[ˈslœytə(n)]	-Close your eyes again.
729	**brand**	**fire**
	de	Het bed staat in brand!
	[brɑnt]	-The bed is on fire!
730	**heerlijk**	**delicious; deliciously**
	adj; adv	Je taart is heerlijk.
	[ˈherlək]	-Your cake is delicious.
731	**rechts**	**right**
	adj	Draai naar rechts aan de volgende hoek.
	[rɛx(t)s]	-Turn right at the next corner.
732	**hoog**	**high; high**
	adj; adv	Hoog in de lucht.
	[hox]	-High in the sky.
733	**neus**	**nose**
	de	Uw neus bloedt.
	[nøs]	-Your nose is bleeding.
734	**verleden**	**past**
	het	John zit vast in het verleden.
	[vərˈledə(n)]	-John is stuck in the past.
735	**bericht**	**message**
	het	Zijn er berichten voor mij?
	[bəˈrixt]	-Are there any messages for me?
736	**goud**	**gold**
	het	Gezondheid is belangrijker dan goud.
	[xɑut]	-Health is more important than gold.
737	**donker**	**dark; dark**
	adj; het	Het is al donker.
	[ˈdɔŋkər]	-It is already dark.
738	**club**	**club**
	de	Die club is veel te groot.
	[klʏp]	-That club is way too big.
739	**helft**	**half**
	de	Het werk is voor de helft gedaan.
	[hɛlft]	-The job is half done.
740	**winkel**	**shop**
	de	Deze winkel heeft de beste keuze in hoeden van de stad.
	[ˈwɪŋkəl]	-This store has the best selection of hats in town.
741	**verdienen**	**earn**
	vb	We werken om geld te verdienen.
	[vərˈdinə(n)]	-We work to earn money.
742	**vuil**	**dirt; dirty; filthily**
	het; adj; adv	Ze wierp me een vuile blik toe.
	[vœyl]	-She gave me a dirty look.
743	**kwalijk**	**bad, wrong; amiss**

	adj; adv	**Het heeft kwalijke gevolgen.**
	['kwalək]	-It has bad consequences.
744	**godsnaam**	**for god's sake**
	int	Wat was je in godsnaam aan het doen?
	['xɔtsnam]	-For god's sake, what were you doing?
745	**sheriff**	**sheriff**
	de	Ik overleg dat met sheriff John.
	[ʃerif]	-I'll work that out with Sheriff John
746	**vlees**	**meat**
	het	Hij wil vlees. Echt varkensvlees.
	[vles]	-He wants meat. Real pork meat.
747	**welterusten**	**sleep well**
	int	Welterusten. Tot morgen.
	['wɛltərʏstə(n), wɛltə'rʏstə(n)]	-Sleep well! See you tomorrow.
748	**relatie**	**relation(ship)**
	de	Wat is de relatie tussen politiek en oorlog?
	[rə'la(t)si]	-What is the relationship between politics and war?
749	**zulk**	**such**
	adj	Zulke schoenen zijn mooi.
	[zʏlk]	-Such shoes are pretty.
750	**raam**	**window**
	het	Het was gisteren dat ik per ongeluk het raam brak.
	[ram]	-It was yesterday that I broke the window by mistake.
751	**partner**	**partner**
	de	Ik heb een partner nodig.
	['partnər]	-I need a partner.
752	**moeite**	**trouble, effort**
	de	Doe geen moeite.
	['mujtə]	-Don't bother.
753	**professor**	**professor**
	de	Jij bent professor.
	[pro'fɛsɔr]	-You are a professor.
754	**camera**	**camera**
	de	Houd de camera in de gaten als ik telefoneer.
	['kaməra]	-Watch the camera for me while I make a phone call.
755	**eraf**	**off**
	adv	Het was zo'n krachtige explosie dat het dak eraf geblazen werd.
	[ɛr'af]	-It was such a powerful explosion that the roof was blown off.
756	**achteruit**	**backwards; reverse**
	adv; de	Ik zou je achteruit moeten laten lopen.
	[ɑxtər'œyt]	-I ought to make you walk backward.
757	**lift**	**lift, elevator, ride**
	de	Ik heb een lift naar huis nodig.
	[lɪft]	-I need a ride home.
758	**lijst**	**list**
	de	Uw naam staat als eerste op mijn lijst.
	[lɛist]	-Your name stands first on my list.
759	**vrede**	**peace**
	de	De vrede kwam terug na drie jaar oorlog.
	['vredə]	-Peace has returned after three years of war.
760	**bereiken**	**reach**

	vb		Ik heb een mijlpaal bereikt.
	[bəˈrɛikə(n)]		-I reached a milestone.
761	**werkelijk**		**really; real**
	adv; adj		Wilt u werkelijk een week hier blijven?
	[ˈwɛrkələk]		-Do you really want to stay here for a week?
762	**geweer**		**rifle**
	het		John heeft een geweer.
	[xəˈwer]		-John has a rifle.
763	**hangen**		**hang**
	vb		Veel schilderijen hangen in kunstmusea.
	[ˈhaŋə(n)]		-Many paintings hang in art museums.
764	**tante**		**aunt**
	de		Mijn tante spreekt zowel Chinees als Engels.
	[ˈtɑntə]		-My aunt speaks Chinese as well as English.
765	**uiteindelijk**		**finally; sooner or later**
	adj; adv		Uiteindelijk komt John hier wel.
	[œytˈɛindələk]		-John will get here sooner or later.
766	**uitleggen**		**explain**
	vb		Ik kan het niet uitleggen.
	[ˈœytlɛxə(n)]		-I can't explain it.
767	**leiden**		**lead**
	vb		Alle wegen leiden naar Rome.
	[ˈlɛidə(n)]		-All roads lead to Rome.
768	**ach**		**oh, ah**
	int		Ach, sneeuw! Zolang het maar niet te koud is.
	[ɑx]		-Ah, snow! As long as it's not too cold.
769	**vijand**		**enemy**
	de		Vertrouw nooit je vijand.
	[ˈvɛijɑnt]		-Never trust your enemy.
770	**volk**		**people, folk**
	het		Het volk had de buik vol van het geweld.
	[vɔlk]		-The people were through with violence.
771	**gebied**		**area**
	het		Dit gebied is zeer afgelegen.
	[xəˈbit]		-This area is extremely isolated.
772	**dorp**		**village**
	het		Hoe heet dit dorp?
	[dɔrp]		-What's the name of this village?
773	**daarvan**		**of it**
	adv		Wat is het nut daarvan?
	[darˈvɑn]		-What's the point of doing that?
774	**bureau**		**desk**
	het		Dit is mijn bureau.
	[byˈro]		-This is my desk.
775	**gevecht**		**fight, battle**
	het		We namen beslag op de stad na een kort gevecht.
	[xəˈvɛxt]		-We seized the town after a short battle.
776	**held**		**hero**
	de		Helden komen altijd te laat.
	[hɛlt]		-Heroes always arrive late.
777	**voet**		**foot**

de	Was uw voeten. Ik ruik ze van een kilometer afstand.
[vut]	-Wash your feet. I can smell them from a mile away.
778 teveel	**excess; excess, too much**
het; adj	Hij heeft teveel vertrouwen in Holmes.
[təˈvel]	-He puts too much faith in the great detective.
779 bevel	**order**
het	Waarom heb je mijn bevel niet opgevolgd?
[bəˈvɛl]	-Why did you disobey my order?
780 extra	**extra; extra**
adj; adv	Ik vroeg om extra zout op mijn patat.
[ˈɛkstra]	-I requested extra salt on my French fries.
781 slag	**battle, stroke**
de	De slag gaat beginnen.
[slɑx]	-The battle is about to begin.
782 la	**drawer**
de	Er zit een geheime la in het bureau.
[la]	-There's a secret drawer in the desk.
783 positie	**position**
de	Hij heeft een belangrijke positie binnen het bedrijf.
[poˈsi(t)si]	-He got an important position in the company.
784 opschieten	**hurry**
vb	Schiet op, ik bevries!
[ˈɔpsxitə(n)]	-Hurry up, I'm freezing!
785 christus	**Christ**
pn	Voor Christus was er niets, behalve alles.
[ˈkristus, ˈxristus]	-Before Christ there was nothing, except everything.
786 gesprek	**conversation**
het	Extreem harde muziek onderbrak hun gesprek.
[xeˈsprɛk]	-Extremely loud music interrupted their conversation.
787 wens	**wish**
de	Ik wens jullie beiden veel geluk.
[wɛns]	-I wish you both the best of luck.
788 knap	**handsome; cleverly**
adj; adv	Dat meisje is heel knap.
[knɑp]	-That girl is very beautiful.
789 beurt	**turn**
de	Het was mijn beurt om de kamer schoon te maken.
[børt]	-It was my turn to clean the room.
790 radio	**radio**
de	Wees lief en zet de radio wat zachter.
[ˈradijo]	-Be kind and turn the radio down.
791 gewond	**injured**
adj	De soldaat was gewond aan het been.
[xəˈwɔnt]	-The soldier was wounded in the leg.
792 lot	**fate**
het	Iedereen wachtte hetzelfde lot - de dood.
[lɔt]	-Everybody was waiting for the same fate - death.
793 luitenant	**lieutenant**
de	Ik wil u spreken, luitenant.
[lœytəˈnɑnt]	-I want to speak with you Lieutenant.
794 ophouden	**stop**

vb
['ɔphɑudə(n)]

Eerst moet u ophouden met roken.
-First, you have to stop smoking.

795 boom
de
[bom]

tree
Ze zaten in de schaduw van die grote boom.
-They sat in the shade of that big tree.

796 verdwijnen
vb
[vər'dwɛinə(n)]

disappear
Mijn geld schijnt aan het eind van de maand te verdwijnen.
-My money seems to disappear by the end of the month.

797 lastig
adj
['lɑstəx]

difficult
De toets was lastig.
-The test was difficult.

798 speciaal
adj; adv
[spe'ʃal]

special; especially
Ze zijn allemaal speciaal.
-They're all special.

799 alweer
adv
[al'wer]

again
Alweer vis? Ik haat vis.
-Fish again? I hate fish.

800 verdorie
interj
[vər'dori]

shucks
Verdorie, ik heb mijn trein gemist!
-Oh shucks, I missed my train.

801 ongelooflijk
adj
[ɔnxə'loflək]

incredible, unbelievable
Het is ongelooflijk!
-It's incredible!

802 vis
de
[vɪs]

fish
Ik heb liever vis dan vlees.
-I prefer fish to meat.

803 koningin
de
[kɔnɪŋ'ɪn]

queen
Lang leve de koningin!
-Long live the Queen!

804 bezoek
het
[bə'zuk]

visit
Ze heeft mij gisteren een bezoek gebracht.
-She paid me a visit yesterday.

805 interessant
adj
[ɪntərɛ'sɑnt]

interesting
Ik heb insecten altijd erg interessant gevonden.
-I have always found insects to be very interesting.

806 tas
de
[tɑs]

bag
De sleutels zaten in mijn tas.
-The keys were in my bag.

807 rechter
adj; de
['rɛxtər]

right; judge
De gepensioneerde rechter bezocht mij vroeger.
-The retired judge used to visit me.

808 heilig
adj
['hɛiləx]

holy, sacred
In India is de koe een heilig dier.
-A cow is a sacred animal in India.

809 leeg
adj; adv
[lex]

empty; vacantly
De beker is leeg.
-The cup is empty.

810 wijn
de
[wɛin]

wine
Wil je graag witte of rode wijn?
-Would you like white wine or red?

811 verrassing

surprise

	de	John heeft een verrassing voor Jane.
	[vərˈɑsɪŋ]	-John has a surprise for Jane.
812	**belachelijk**	**ridiculous**
	adj	Wat jij zegt is gewoon belachelijk.
	[bəˈlɑxələk]	-What you say is simply ridiculous.
813	**persoonlijk**	**personal**
	adj	Alle stoelen hebben persoonlijke beeldschermen.
	[pɛrˈsonlək]	-All seats have personal screens.
814	**aandacht**	**attention**
	de	Hij wil gewoon aandacht.
	[ˈɑndɑxt]	-He just wants attention.
815	**ijs**	**ice**
	het	Jij loopt op het ijs.
	[ɛis]	-You walk on the ice.
816	**rivier**	**river**
	de	Deze rivier gaat overstromen.
	[riˈvir]	-This river is going to overflow.
817	**blijkbaar**	**apparently**
	adv	Blijkbaar vereist de wond zelf slechts een paar hechtingen.
	[ˈblɛikbar]	-Apparently the wound itself only needs a few stitches.
818	**ring**	**ring**
	de	De ring was nergens te vinden.
	[rɪŋ]	-The ring was nowhere to be found.
819	**waarop**	**when; whereupon**
	con; adv	Waarop zit je?
	[warˈɔp]	-What are you sitting on?
820	**klas**	**class**
	de	Hij is groter dan alle andere jongens in zijn klas.
	[klɑs]	-He is taller than any other boy in his class.
821	**dier**	**animal**
	het	Honden zijn mijn favoriete dieren.
	[dir]	-Dogs are my favorite animals.
822	**geschiedenis**	**history**
	de	John weet veel over de geschiedenis van Amerika.
	[xəˈsxidənɪs]	-John knows a lot about American history.
823	**wind**	**wind**
	de	Wat een harde wind!
	[wɪnt]	-What a strong wind!
824	**missie**	**mission**
	de	Deze missie is topgeheim en uiterst gevaarlijk.
	[ˈmɪsi]	-This mission is top-secret and extremely dangerous.
825	**bekijken**	**view, look at**
	vb	Laten we die groene plekken bekijken.
	[bəˈkɛikə(n)]	-Let's have a look at the green patches.
826	**meenemen**	**take, bring**
	vb	Je mag wie je maar wilt meenemen.
	[ˈmenemə(n)]	-You may bring whoever you like.
827	**volledig**	**full; completely**
	adj; adv	Dit kan niet volledig genezen worden.
	[vɔˈledəx]	-It cannot be completely cured.
828	**adem**	**breath**

de
[ˈadəm]
Ik houd mijn adem in.
-I am holding my breath.

829 **doorgaan**
vb
[ˈdorxan]
go on, continue
We kunnen niet doorgaan dit te doen.
-We can't continue doing this.

830 **verjaardag**
de
[vərˈjardɑx]
birthday
Het is mijn verjaardag.
-It is my birthday.

831 **weekend**
het
[ˈwikɛnt]
weekend
Ben je vrij dit weekend?
-Are you free this weekend?

832 **aantal**
het
[ˈantɑl]
number
Het aantal mensen op Facebook is groter dan de bevolking van de Verenigde Staten van Amerika.
-The amount of people on Facebook is greater than the population of the United States of America.

833 **eiland**
het
[ˈɛilɑnt]
island
Het eiland ligt ten westen van Japan.
-The island lies to the west of Japan.

834 **nek**
de
[nɛk]
neck
John gooide zijn armen om de nek van zijn broer.
-John flung his arms around his brother's neck.

835 **helaas**
adv
[heˈlas]
unfortunately, alas
Helaas ben ik maar één keer per jaar jarig.
-Unfortunately, my birthday is only once a year.

836 **rekening**
de
[ˈrekənɪŋ]
account, check
Mag ik de rekening alstublieft?
-May I have the check, please?

837 **kiezen**
vb
[ˈkizə(n)]
choose
Ik moest kiezen tussen die twee.
-I had to choose between the two.

838 **aangenaam**
adj
[ˈanxənam]
pleasant
De muziek is erg aangenaam.
-The music is very pleasant.

839 **kort**
adj
[kɔrt]
short, brief
Dat is een kort verhaal.
-That is a short story.

840 **regering**
de
[rəˈxerɪŋ]
government
De regering is corrupt!
-The government is corrupt!

841 **boodschap**
de
[ˈbotsxɑp]
message
Laat uw boodschap achter na de piep.
-Leave your message after the beep.

842 **boord**
het
[bort]
board, collar
Man over boord! Haal een touw!
-Man overboard! Get a rope!

843 **dak**
het
[dɑk]
roof
De vorm van het dak lijkt op een piramide.
-The shape of the roof looks like a pyramid.

844 **verschil**
het
difference
Het verschil tussen de twee versies is niet duidelijk.

[vərˈsxɪl]   -The difference between the two versions isn't clear.

845 bar
de; adj
[bɑr]
bar; severe
Laten we wat drinken aan de bar.
-Let's have a drink at the bar.

846 zelfmoord
de
[ˈzɛlfmort]
suicide
John pleegde zelfmoord.
-John committed suicide.

847 kennis
de
[ˈkɛnɪs]
knowledge
Ook voor mij is het aangenaam kennis te maken.
-It's nice to meet you too.

848 huilen
vb
[ˈhœylə(n)]
cry
Stop met huilen.
-Stop crying.

849 vlug
adv; adj
[vlʏx]
quickly; quick
Ik heb het zo vlug mogelijk nodig.
-I need it as quickly as possible.

850 bom
de
[bɔm]
bomb
De bom tikt.
-The bomb is ticking.

851 vakantie
de
[vaˈkan(t)si]
holiday, vacation
John is op vakantie in Spanje.
-John is on holiday in Spain.

852 meestal
adv
[ˈmestal]
usually
Welke krant lees je meestal?
-Which newspaper do you usually read?

853 knul
de
[knʏl]
young fellow
John is een aardige knul.
-John is a friendly bloke.

854 engels
adj; het
[ˈɛŋəls]
English; English
Spreek je Engels?
-Do you speak English?

855 kat
de
[kɑt]
cat
Ik haat katten.
-I hate cats.

856 soldaat
de
[sɔlˈdat]
soldier
Zonder water zouden de soldaten gestorven zijn.
-Without water, the soldiers would have died.

857 zwanger
adj
[ˈzwaŋər]
pregnant
U bent zwanger.
-You are pregnant.

858 glas
het
[xlɑs]
glass
Ik heb mezelf aan wat gebroken glas gesneden.
-I cut myself on some broken glass.

859 systeem
het
[sisˈtem]
system
Het is een kwetsbaar systeem.
-It is a vulnerable system.

860 aanval
de
[ˈanval]
attack
De aanval is de beste verdediging.
-The attack is the best form of defense.

861 opa
de
grandpa
Mijn opa was boer.

['opa] -My grandfather was a farmer.

862 **mes** **knife**
het Wij gebruiken stokjes in plaats van vork en mes.
[mɛs] -We use chopsticks in place of knives and forks.

863 **hoek** **corner**
de John zat in de hoek.
[huk] -John was sitting in the corner.

864 **begraven** **bury**
vb Hij werd begraven in dit kerkhof.
[bə'xravə(n)] -He was buried in this graveyard.

865 **stoel** **chair**
de Er zat een kat op de stoel.
[stul] -A cat was sitting on the chair.

866 **taxi** **taxi**
de Is dit een illegale taxi?
[taksi] -Is this an illegal taxi?

867 **mijnheer** **sir, mister**
de Mijnheer Smith leert mij Engels.
[mə'ner] -Mister Smith teaches me English.

868 **kus** **kiss**
de Één kus of twee?
[kʏs] -One kiss or two?

869 **krant** **newspaper**
de De krant publiceerde een biografie over haar nieuwe redacteur.
[krɑnt] -The paper published a profile of its new editor.

870 **keus** **choice**
de John heeft geen keus.
[køs] -John has no choice.

871 **ontsnappen** **escape**
vb Hij probeerde te ontsnappen.
[ɔnt'snapə(n)] -He attempted to escape.

872 **park** **park**
het Afgelopen zondag ben ik naar het park gegaan.
[pɑrk] -I went to the park last Sunday.

873 **liegen** **lie**
vb Je kunt niet gewoon tegen ons liegen.
['lixə(n)] -You can't just lie to us.

874 **adres** **address**
het Ik heb nu het adres niet.
[a'drɛs] -I don't have the address now.

875 **dichtbij** **near, nearby**
adv Is er een ziekenhuis dichtbij?
[dɪx(t)'bɛi] -Is there a hospital nearby?

876 **richting** **direction**
de De wind waait in onze richting.
['rɪxtɪŋ] -The wind is blowing in our direction.

877 **vergeven** **forgive**
vb John kan Jane niet vergeven voor wat zij heeft gedaan.
[vər'xevə(n)] -John can't forgive Jane for what she did.

878 **ruziën** **argue, fight**
vb John en Jane zijn nog steeds aan het ruziën.

['ryzijə(n)]   -John and Jane are still arguing.

879 **bier**   **beer**
het   Laten we wijn of bier drinken.
[bir]   -Let's drink wine or beer.

880 **draaien**   **turn**
vb   Draai je om! Anders zwaait er wat.
['drajə(n)]   -Turn around! Or else…

881 **beest**   **beast**
het   Het wilde beest is boos.
[best]   -The wild beast is angry.

882 **geluid**   **sound, noise**
het   Hij hoorde een geluid uit de keuken.
[xəˈlœyt]   -He heard a noise from the kitchen.

883 **gauw**   **soon, quickly**
adv   Ik hoop dat u gauw terugkomt.
[xɑu]   -I hope you'll come back soon.

884 **overleven**   **survive**
vb   John en Jane hebben het overleefd.
[ovərˈlevə(n)]   -John and Jane survived.

885 **vrijheid**   **freedom**
de   Individuele vrijheid is de ziel van de democratie.
['vrɛihɛit]   -Individual freedom is the soul of democracy.

886 **simpel**   **simple, basic**
adj   Dingen zouden zo simpel mogelijk moeten zijn.
['sımpəl]   -Things should be as simple as possible.

887 **langzaam**   **slow**
adj   De langzame schildpad liep naar het water.
['lɑŋzam]   -The slow turtle walked towards the water.

888 **prinses**   **princess**
de   De prinses heeft blond haar.
[prınˈsɛs]   -The princess has blond hair.

889 **lol**   **fun**
de   We gaan veel lol trappen.
[lɔl]   -We're going to have a lot of fun.

890 **eenmaal**   **once**
adv   Eenmaal buiten zuchtte ik diep van opluchting.
['enmal]   -Once outside, I gave a deep sigh of relief.

891 **totaal**   **total; total; totally**
adj; het; adv   In totaal ben je me dertig euro verschuldigd.
[toˈtal]   -In total you owe me thirty euro.

892 **bek**   **beak, mouth**
de   De hond hield een kip in zijn bek.
[bɛk]   -The dog was holding a chicken in his mouth.

893 **computer**   **computer**
de   Dit is mijn computer.
[kɔmˈpjutər]   -This is my computer.

894 **leer**   **leather; teaching**
het; de   John heeft een leren jack.
[ler]   -John has a leather jacket.

895 **zagen**   **saw**
vb   John en Jane zagen een houten plank doormidden.

['zaxə(n)]   -John and Jane saw a wooden plank in half.

896 hopelijk   **hopefully**
adv
['hopələk]   Hopelijk is het eiland mooi.
    -Hopefully, the island is beautiful.

897 monster   **sample, monster**
het
['mɔnstər]   Dit is geen spin, het is een monster!
    -This is not a spider, it's a monster!

898 juffrouw   **female teacher, unmarried woman**
de
['jʏfrɑu]   Juffrouw Swan is onze lerares Engels.
    -Ms. Swan is our English teacher.

899 ontslaan   **dismiss, fire**
vb
[ɔnt'slan]   De baas denkt eraan, een werknemer te ontslaan.
    -The boss is thinking of firing an employee.

900 twintig   **twenty**
nu
['twɪntəx]   Het kost twintig minuten om van het station naar school te lopen.
    -It takes twenty minutes to walk from the station to the school.

901 blauw   **blue**
adj
[blɑu]   Neem je de rode pil of de blauwe?
    -Will you take the red pill or the blue pill?

902 maan   **moon**
de
[man]   De zon is achter de maan.
    -The sun is behind the moon.

903 jurk   **gown, dress**
de
[jʏrk]   Jane droeg een donkerbruine jurk.
    -Jane wore a dark brown dress.

904 keuken   **kitchen**
de
['køkə(n)]   Moeder is in de keuken aan het koken.
    -Mother is cooking in the kitchen.

905 vanmorgen   **this morning**
adv
[vɑ'mɔrxə(n)]   Mijn grootmoeder postte de brief vanmorgen.
    -My grandmother posted the letter this morning.

906 plaatsen   **place, plant, put**
vb
['platsə(n)]   Paaltjes zijn geplaatst langs de route.
    -Poles have been placed along the route.

907 onmiddellijk   **immediate**
adj
[ɔn'mɪdələk]   Je moet onmiddellijk naar huis.
    -You need to go home immediately.

908 waarvan   **of which, whose, where from**
adv
[war'vɑn]   Ik bezoek gezinnen waarvan de kinderen ontsporen.
    -I visit families whose kids are out of control.

909 trap   **stairs**
de
[trɑp]   Ik stel voor dat we de trap nemen.
    -I suggest we take the stairs.

910 beweging   **movement**
de
[bə'wexɪŋ]   De kleinste beweging is al moeilijk.
    -It is hard to make the slightest movement.

911 kilometer   **kilometer**
de
['kilometər]   Haar huis staat een paar kilometer hiervandaan.
    -Her house is a few kilometers away from here.

912 honderd   **hundred**
nu
    In dit geval, honderd euro alstublieft.

['hɔndərt]   -In this case, one hundred euro please.

913 actie   **action**
de   Wat we nu nodig hebben is actie, niet discussie.
['aksi]   -What we need now is action, not discussion.

914 rol   **role**
de   Geluk speelt een belangrijke rol in ons leven.
[rɔl]   -Luck plays an important role in our life.

915 last   **burden, bother**
de   Op de dag van zijn examen had John heel veel last van zijn maag.
[last]   -On the day of his exam, John had a very bad stomachache.

916 hiermee   **herewith**
adv   Hiermee ben ik het met hen niet eens.
['hirme]   -I can't agree with them on this matter.

917 twaalf   **twelve**
nu   Een jaar heeft twaalf maanden.
[twalf]   -A year has twelve months.

918 hoelang   **how long**
adv   Hoelang geleden is John vertrokken?
['hulaŋ]   -How long ago did John leave?

919 jas   **coat**
de   Hangt u uw jas toch op.
[jas]   -Hang up your coat, please.

920 planeet   **planet**
de   Jupiter en Mars zijn planeten.
[pla'net]   -Jupiter and Mars are planets.

921 bouwen   **build**
vb   Ons bedrijf is van plan een nieuwe chemische fabriek te bouwen in Rusland.
['bɑuwə(n)]   -Our company is planning to build a new chemical plant in Russia.

922 neef   **cousin**
de   John is niet mijn broer maar mijn neef.
[nef]   -John is not my brother, but my cousin.

923 schoon   **clean**
adj   Willen jullie een schone vork?
[sxon]   -Do you want a clean fork?

924 indruk   **impression**
de   Wat was je eerste indruk van Londen?
['ɪndrʏk]   -What was your first impression of London?

925 betrekken   **involve**
vb   Betrek mij daar niet bij.
[bə'trɛkə(n)]   -Don't get me involved.

926 broeder   **brother**
de   Hou vol, broeder.
['brudər]   -Hold on, my brother.

927 bezorgd   **concerned, troubled**
adj   John kon zien dat Jane bezorgd was.
[bə'zɔrxt]   -John could tell Jane was troubled.

928 toestemming   **permission**
de   Dat hoor je zonder toestemming niet te doen.
['tustɛmɪŋ]   -You're not supposed to do that without permission.

929 ster   **star**
de   John is nu de ster van een realityserie.

[stɛr]
-John is now the star of a reality show.

930 **springen** — **jump**
vb
['sprɪŋə(n)]
Laten we tegelijkertijd het water in springen!
-Let's jump into the water at the same time!

931 **bos** — **forest**
het
[bɔs]
Dieren leven in het bos.
-Animals live in the forest.

932 **passen** — **suit, fit**
vb
['pasə(n)]
Het past precies.
-It suits perfectly.

933 **ontdekken** — **discover**
vb
[ɔn'dɛkə(n)]
Heeft Columbus Amerika ontdekt?
-Has Columbus discovered America?

934 **gratis** — **free**
adj
['xratəs]
Ik heb het praktisch gratis gekregen.
-I got it practically for free.

935 **mist** — **fog**
de
[mɪst]
Wij hebben niets anders dan mist gezien.
-We could see nothing but fog.

936 **brug** — **bridge**
de
[brʏx]
De nieuwe brug werd Rainbow Bridge genoemd.
-The new bridge was named Rainbow Bridge.

937 **kussen** — **pillow; kiss**
het; vb
['kʏsə(n)]
Dit kussen is oncomfortabel.
-This pillow is uncomfortable.

938 **excuus** — **excuse**
het
[ɛks'kys]
Je hebt zeker een goed excuus.
-I'm sure you have a great excuse.

939 **waarmee** — **with which**
adv
[war'me]
De pen waarmee ik schrijf is van John.
-The pen I am writing with belongs to John.

940 **ontvangen** — **receive**
vb
[ɔnt'faŋə(n)]
We hebben een e-mail ontvangen met het nieuws over de dood van John.
-We received an email with the news about John's death.

941 **rook** — **smoke**
de
[rok]
Rook steeg op uit de schoorsteen.
-Smoke rose from the chimney.

942 **procent** — **percent**
het
[pro'sɛnt]
De prijs van rijst steeg met drie procent.
-The price of rice rose by three percent.

943 **getuigen** — **testify**
vb
[xe'tœyxə(n)]
Ik kan je niet dwingen om te getuigen.
-I can't force you to testify.

944 **durven** — **dare**
vb
[dʏrfə(n)]
Hoe durf je aan mij te twijfelen!
-How dare you doubt me!

945 **trouw** — **faith; loyal**
de; adj
[trɑu]
Honden zijn trouwe dieren.
-Dogs are loyal animals.

946 **leider** — **leader**
de
Hij is mijn leider.

['lɛidər]   -He is my leader.

947 **bidden**   **pray**
vb   Ik bid ervoor dat je veel geluk zult hebben.
['bɪdə(n)]   -I pray that you will have the best of luck.

948 **leeftijd**   **age**
de   Hij is klein voor zijn leeftijd.
['leftɛit]   -He's small for his age.

949 **code**   **code**
de   De code is niet te kraken.
['kodə]   -The code cannot be cracked.

950 **feit**   **fact**
het   Deze feiten zijn zeker.
[fɛit]   -These facts are certain.

951 **hoogte**   **height**
de   Hij is van grote hoogte gevallen.
['hoxtə]   -He must have fallen from quite a height.

952 **starten**   **start**
vb   Je zou jouw eigen bedrijf kunnen starten.
['stɑrtə(n)]   -You could start your own company.

953 **homo**   **gay**
de   Zo wat als ik homo ben?
['homo]   -So what if I am gay?

954 **vieren**   **celebrate**
vb   Ik wil Kerstmis met jullie vieren.
['virə(n)]   -I want to celebrate Christmas with you.

955 **commandant**   **commander**
de   Majoor Burns wil u spreken als waarnemend commandant.
[kɔmanˈdɑnt]   -Major Burns would like to talk to you as acting commander.

956 **ervaring**   **experience**
de   John heeft geen ervaring.
[ɛrˈvariŋ]   -John lacks experience.

957 **nadenken**   **reflect, think**
vb   Ik denk dat je over de toekomst moet nadenken.
['nadɛŋkə(n)]   -I think you should think about the future.

958 **publiek**   **audience; public**
het; adj   Het publiek leek verveeld.
[pyˈblik]   -The audience appeared bored.

959 **roepen**   **call**
vb   Je ziet bleek. Moet ik een dokter roepen?
['rupə(n)]   -You look pale. Shall I call the doctor?

960 **slagen**   **succeed**
vb   Ik ben geslaagd voor mijn rijexamen.
['slaxə(n)]   -I passed my driving test.

961 **slot**   **lock**
het   De deur is op slot.
[slɔt]   -The door is locked.

962 **strijd**   **fight, competition**
de   Het lijkt erop dat de strijd tussen Microsoft en Apple nooit zal ophouden.
[strɛit]   -It seems that the battle between Microsoft and Apple will never end.

963 **verschrikkelijk**   **horrible; terrible**
adj; adv   Het vlees ruikt verschrikkelijk.

[vər'sxrɪkələk]   -The meat smells terrible.

964 duizend   **thousand**
nu   John is Jane iets meer dan een duizend dollars schuldig.
['dœyzənt]   -John owes Jane slightly over a thousand dollars.

965 test   **test**
de   Het is de ultieme test.
[tɛst]   -It's the ultimate test.

966 besluiten   **decide**
vb   Je moet besluiten wat voor persoon je wilt zijn.
[bə'slœytə(n)]   -You need to decide what kind of person you want to be.

967 opdracht   **assignment**
de   Zonder haar hulp kon ik mijn opdracht niet volbrengen.
['ɔpdrɑxt]   -Without her help, I could not finish my assignment.

968 roken   **smoke**
vb   Roken is verboden in de lift.
['rokə(n)]   -Smoking prohibited inside the elevator.

969 prins   **prince**
de   De prins leerde Engels van de Amerikaanse dame.
[prɪns]   -The prince learned English from the American lady.

970 bereid   **prepared**
adj   Je moet bereid zijn je te engageren voor het programma voor ten minste een
[bə'rɛit]   jaar.
        -You must be willing to commit to the program for at least a year.

971 storen   **disturb**
vb   Niet storen. Ik ben Chinese tekenfilmpjes aan het kijken ook al ben ik
['storə(n)]   volwassen.
        -Do not disturb. I'm watching Chinese cartoons for kids even though I'm an
        adult.

972 vernietigen   **destroy**
vb   We vernietigen ons eigen land.
[vər'nitəxə(n)]   -We're destroying our own country.

973 tand   **tooth**
de   Ik moet mijn tanden poetsen.
[tɑnt]   -I have to brush my teeth.

974 zomer   **summer**
de   Ik houd niet van de zomer.
['zomər]   -I don't like summer.

975 waarover   **about which/what**
adv   Waarover gaat de tekst?
[war'ovər]   -What's the text about?

976 duivel   **devil**
de   Jij probeert de duivel te bedriegen!
['dœyvəl]   -You are trying to cheat the devil!

977 motor   **engine**
de   De motor stopt als je op die knop drukt.
['motər]   -If you pressed that button, the engine would stop.

978 bezitten   **own**
vb   Hij heeft heel wat bezittingen.
[bə'zɪtə(n)]   -He has a great deal of property.

979 bloem   **flower**
de   Er waren overal bloemen.
[blum]   -There were flowers everywhere.

980	**operatie**	**operation**
	de	Hoe lang kostte het je om van je operatie te herstellen?
	[opəˈra(t)si]	-How long did it take you to recover from your operation?
981	**restaurant**	**restaurant**
	het	Hebt je goed gegeten in het restaurant?
	[rɛstoˈrɑnt, rɛstoˈrã]	-Did you have a good meal at that restaurant?
982	**spoor**	**track**
	het	We volgden het spoor dat het hert had achtergelaten.
	[spor]	-We followed the tracks left by the deer.
983	**inspecteur**	**inspector**
	de	John was een ervaren inspecteur.
	[ɪnspɛkˈtør]	-Dan was a seasoned investigator.
984	**binnenkort**	**shortly**
	adv	We moeten een tankstation vinden omdat deze auto binnenkort geen benzine meer zal hebben.
	[bɪnə(n)ˈkɔrt]	-We need to look for a gas station because this car will soon run out of gas.
985	**waarin**	**wherein**
	adv	John vindt het huis waarin hij woont maar niks.
	[warˈɪn]	-John doesn't like the house that he lives in.
986	**wonder**	**wonder, miracle**
	het	Ik heb een wonder nodig.
	[ˈwɔndər]	-I need a miracle.
987	**basis**	**basis, base**
	de	Een driehoek heeft een basis.
	[ˈbazɪs]	-A triangle has a base.
988	**vertaling**	**translation**
	de	Ik vond het een accurate vertaling.
	[vərˈtalɪŋ]	-I thought that was quite an accurate translation.
989	**betreffen**	**concern**
	vb	Benadrukt moet worden dat de maatregelen slechts noodhulp betreffen.
	[bəˈtrɛfə(n)]	-It should be emphasized that the measures concern emergency relief only.
990	**vlak**	**flat; surface; just**
	adj; het; adv	Hij woont in een stadje vlak bij Osaka.
	[vlɑk]	-He lives in a small town just outside Osaka.
991	**beeld**	**image, sculpture**
	het	Daar is een beeld van Cristiano Ronaldo.
	[belt]	-There is a sculpture of Cristiano Ronaldo.
992	**wijten**	**blame**
	vb	De vlek op de labjas is te wijten aan zilvernitraat.
	[wɛjtə(n)]	-The stain on the lab coat is due to silver nitrate.
993	**boel**	**a lot**
	de	Ik moet een boel wassen in het weekend.
	[bul]	-Over the weekend I have a lot to wash.
994	**enorm**	**enormous; vast**
	adj; adv	De regio is enorm, maar dunbevolkt.
	[eˈnɔrm]	-The region is enormous, but sparsely populated.
995	**veiligheid**	**safety**
	de	Jane maakt zich zorgen om uw veiligheid.
	[ˈvɛiləxhɛit]	-Jane is worrying for your safety.
996	**top**	**top, peak**
	de	De top van de berg ligt rond de 3000 meter.

['tɔp]   -The mountain´s peak lies somewhere around 3000m.

997 coach
de
[kotʃ]

coach
Guardiola is de huidige coach van Manchester City.
-Guardiola is the current coach of Manchester City.

998 gemakkelijk
adj
[xəˈmakələk]

easy
Het is helemaal niet gemakkelijk een vreemde taal onder de knie te krijgen.
-It's by no means easy to master a foreign language.

999 genieten
vb
[xəˈnitə(n)]

enjoy
Ontspan gewoon en geniet ervan.
-Just relax and enjoy yourself.

1000 blank
adj
[blaŋk]

white, blank
De verdachte is blank en heeft blauwe ogen.
-The suspect is white and has blue eyes.

1001 pad
het
[pɑt]

path
Waar leidt dit pad naartoe?
-Where does this path go?

1002 opstaan
vb
[ˈɔpstan]

stand up, rise, get up
Ik wil niet opstaan.
-I don't want to get up.

1003 tonen
vb
[ˈtonə(n)]

show
Ik zal u mijn nieuwe auto tonen.
-I will show you my new car.

1004 ontbijt
het
[ɔndˈbɛit]

breakfast
Bij het ontbijt drinkt John altijd een kop warme chocolademelk.
-At breakfast, John always drinks a cup of hot chocolate.

1005 beslissing
de
[bəˈslɪsɪŋ]

decision
Hij trof vlug een beslissing.
-He quickly made a decision.

1006 ineens
adv
[ɪnˈens]

suddenly
Toen ik mijn ogen weer open deed, stond er ineens een onbekende dame voor mijn neus.
-When I opened my eyes again, all of a sudden an unknown lady was standing right in front of me.

1007 energie
de
[enɛrˈʒi]

energy
Hij is nog steeds vol met energie.
-He is still full of energy.

1008 sexy
adj
[ˈsɛksi]

sexy
John leek heel sexy in zijn koningsblauw pak.
-John looked very sexy in his royal blue suit.

1009 zwemmen
vb
[ˈzwɛmə(n)]

swim
De jongen is met zijn vrienden aan het zwemmen.
-The boy is swimming with his friends.

1010 wezen
het; vb
[ˈwezə(n)]

being; be
Ik respecteer de bidsprinkhaan als een levend wezen!
-I respect the praying mantis as a living being.

1011 cel
de
[sɛl]

cell
En ik wil een grotere cel met betere ventilatie.
-And I want a bigger cell with better ventilation.

1012 papieren
adj; de
[paˈpirə(n)]

paper; papers
Papier brandt gemakkelijk.
-Paper burns easily.

1013	**ochtend**	**morning**
	de	In de ochtend was het erg koud.
	[ˈɔxtənt]	-In the morning it was very cold.
1014	**eeuwig**	**eternal; forever**
	adj	Mensen kunnen niet eeuwig leven.
	[ˈewəx]	-It's not possible for humans to live forever.
1015	**amerikaan**	**American**
	de	Dit is een oud Amerikaans gebruik.
	[ameriˈkan]	-That's an old American custom.
1016	**wraak**	**revenge**
	de	Na de orkaan was hun huis een wrak.
	[vrak]	-Their house was a wreck after the hurricane.
1017	**tekenen**	**draw, sign**
	vb	Jane kan goed tekenen.
	[ˈtekənə(n)]	-Jane can draw very well.
1018	**vorm**	**form**
	de	In alle vormen en maten.
	[vɔrm]	-In all forms and shapes.
1019	**verklaring**	**statement**
	de	Deze verklaring is door u ondertekend.
	[vərˈklarɪŋ]	-This statement is signed by you.
1020	**dik**	**thick, fat**
	adj	Ik ben niet dik!
	[dɪk]	-I'm not fat!
1021	**directeur**	**director**
	de	Hij handelde achter de rug van de directeur.
	[dirɛkˈtør]	-He acted behind the director's back.
1022	**volwassen**	**adult**
	adj	Word niet volwassen. Het is een valstrik!
	[vɔlˈwasə(n)]	-Don't grow up. It's a trap!
1023	**leiding**	**leadership**
	de	John heeft nu de leiding.
	[ˈlɛidɪŋ]	-John is in charge now.
1024	**zwaard**	**sword**
	het	Het zwaard van john is heel scherp.
	[zwart]	-John's sword is really sharp.
1025	**afstand**	**distance**
	de	Die afstand is moeilijk te bepalen.
	[ˈɑfstɑnt]	-It is hard to determine the distance.
1026	**oor**	**ear**
	het	Het gaat bij hem het ene oor in, het andere weer uit.
	[or]	-For him, it always goes in one ear and out the other.
1027	**lunch**	**lunch**
	de	We lunchen vaak samen.
	[lʏnʃ]	-We often eat lunch together.
1028	**toilet**	**toilet**
	het	Waar is het toilet?
	[twaˈlɛt]	-Where is the bathroom?
1029	**gemeen**	**mean**
	adj	Hé, dat is gemeen!
	[xəˈmen]	-Hey, that's mean!

1030	**ruiken**	**smell**
	vb	Zijn kleren ruiken altijd slecht.
	[ˈrœykə(n)]	-His clothes always smell bad.
1031	**programma**	**program**
	het	Dat programma is nog verre van perfect.
	[proˈxrɑmɑ]	-That program is still far from perfect.
1032	**fles**	**bottle**
	de	Waarom brengen we hem geen fles wijn?
	[flɛs]	-Why don't we bring him a bottle of wine?
1033	**behoorlijk**	**quite**
	adj	Ik ben behoorlijk rijk.
	[bəˈhorlək]	-I'm quite wealthy.
1034	**opzij**	**aside**
	het	Ze trok het gordijn opzij.
	[ɔpˈsɛi]	-She pulled the curtain aside.
1035	**verantwoordelijk**	**responsible**
	adj	Deze kleren zijn duurder, maar ze zijn op een milieuvriendelijke en
	[vərɑntˈwordələk]	verantwoorde manier gemaakt.
		-These clothes are more expensive, but they are made in an eco-friendly and responsible way.
1036	**toevallig**	**accidental**
	adj	Weet je toevallig waar ze woont?
	[tuˈvɑləx]	-Do you happen to know where she lives?
1037	**dol**	**crazy**
	adj	Ze is dol op tennissen.
	[dɔl]	-She is crazy about tennis.
1038	**gevoelens**	**feelings**
	de	Hoe langer je je gevoelens voor iemand verbergt, des te meer je voor hen zal vallen.
	[xəfuːlˈns]	-The longer you hide your feelings for someone, the more you fall for them.
1039	**nerveus**	**nervous**
	adj	Spreken in het openbaar maakt me nerveus
	[nɛrˈvøs]	-Speaking in public makes me nervous.
1040	**neerschieten**	**shoot**
	vb	Ze had mij ook kunnen neerschieten.
	[ˈnersxitə(n)]	-She could have shot me down as well.
1041	**appartement**	**apartment**
	het	Heb je hun nieuwe appartement gezien?
	[ɑpɑrtəˈmɛnt]	-Have you seen their new apartment?
1042	**universiteit**	**university**
	de	Hij studeert geschiedenis aan de universiteit.
	[ynivɛrsiˈtɛit]	-He is studying history at the university.
1043	**moed**	**courage**
	de	Zorg maar dat je de moed vindt om het hem vanavond te zeggen.
	[mut]	-You'd better find the courage to tell him tonight.
1044	**verboden**	**forbidden**
	adj	Bedelen op straat is bij wet verboden.
	[vərˈbodə(n)]	-By law, begging in the street is forbidden.
1045	**taak**	**task**
	de	Mijn eerste taak was om er ongekwalificeerde sollicitanten uit te halen.
	[tak]	-My first task was to screen out unqualified applicants.
1046	**kamp**	**camp**

	het	We moeten terug naar het kamp.
	[kɑmp]	-We have to get back to the camp.
1047	**kip**	**chicken**
	de	De kip is in de keuken.
	[kɪp]	-The chicken is in the kitchen.
1048	**onschuldig**	**innocent**
	adj	Ik denk dat John onschuldig is.
	[ɔnˈsxʏldəx]	-I think John is innocent.
1049	**dankzij**	**due to**
	prp	Dankzij zijn moeder werd hij beroemd.
	[ˈdɑŋksɛi]	-He became famous due to his mother.
1050	**vertalen**	**translate**
	vb	Ik was erg onder de indruk van jouw vertaling van Engelse zinnen in het Nederlands.
	[vərˈtalə(n)]	-I was really impressed with your translation of English sentences in Dutch.
1051	**truck**	**truck**
	de	Kijk, een truck met een trailer.
	[trʏk]	-Look, a truck with a trailer.
1052	**misdaad**	**crime**
	de	De misdaad was vanmorgen gepleegd.
	[ˈmɪsdat]	-The crime was committed this morning.
1053	**jaloers**	**jealous, envious**
	adj	Je gaat jaloers zijn.
	[jaˈlurs]	-You're going to be jealous.
1054	**tevreden**	**satisfied**
	adj	Ik ben tevreden met de uitkomst van mijn wiskundetoets.
	[təˈvredə(n)]	-I am satisfied with the result of my math test.
1055	**veld**	**field**
	het	De omgeploegde velden waren besneeuwd.
	[vɛlt]	-Snow covered the plowed fields.
1056	**sukkelen**	**struggle**
	vb	John sukkelt wat met zijn gezondheid.
	[ˈsʏkɛlə(n)]	-John is struggling a bit with regard to his health.
1057	**slachtoffer**	**victim**
	het	De forensisch onderzoeker vond kruitsporen op de hand van het slachtoffer.
	[ˈslɑxtɔfər]	-The forensic technician found gunshot residue on the victim's hand.
1058	**troep**	**flock, pack, mess**
	de	Ik wilde die troep al maanden opruimen.
	[trup]	-I've been meaning to clean out this mess for months.
1059	**drankje**	**drink**
	het	John bood Jane een drankje aan.
	[ˈdrɑŋkjə]	-John offered Jane a drink.
1060	**majesteit**	**majesty**
	de	Blij u te ontmoeten, majesteit.
	[ˈmajəstɛit]	-Glad to meet you, Your Majesty.
1061	**opeens**	**suddenly**
	adv	We moesten opeens zelf beslissingen nemen.
	[ɔpˈens]	-Suddenly we were forced to decide for ourselves.
1062	**melk**	**milk**
	de	Een koe geeft ons melk.
	[mɛlk]	-A cow gives us milk.

1063	**bijzonder** *adj; adv* [biˈzɔndər]	**extraordinary; thoroughly** Jane is een heel bijzondere vrouw. -Jane is an extraordinary woman.
1064	**post** *de* [pɔst]	**post** De post is al gebracht. -The post has been delivered.
1065	**strand** *het* [strɑnt]	**beach** Ik hou van het strand. -I like the beach.
1066	**terugkomen** *vb* [təˈrʏxkomə(n)]	**return** Als ik terugkom, wil ik dat alles voorbereid is. -When I return I want everything to be prepared.
1067	**getuige** *de* [xeˈtœyxə]	**witness** Wij waren getuigen van het ongeluk. -We were witnesses of the accident.
1068	**gaaf** *adj* [xaf]	**whole, great** Het horloge ziet er gaaf uit. -The watch looks great.
1069	**donder** *de* [ˈdɔndər]	**thunder** Omdat licht sneller reist dan geluid zien we de bliksem voordat we de donder horen. -Because light travels faster than sound we see lightning before we hear thunder.
1070	**openen** *vb* [ˈopənə(n)]	**open** Ik heb de poort open gedaan. -I opened the gate.
1071	**steen** *de* [sten]	**stone** Stenen drijven niet. -Stones don't float.
1072	**kogel** *de* [ˈkoxəl]	**bullet, ball** De politie zal jullie dwingen de kogels te vinden. -The police will get you to find the bullets.
1073	**hoed** *de* [hut]	**hat** Doe je hoed op. -Put your hat on.
1074	**chef** *de* [ʃɛf]	**chef** Vandaag is John de chef. -John is the chief today.
1075	**antwoorden** *vb* [ˈɑntwordə(n)]	**answer** Ik heb geen antwoord ontvangen. -I did not receive an answer.
1076	**gedoe** *het* [xəˈdu]	**hassle** Gisteren was er al dat gedoe. -Yesterday there was all that hassle.
1077	**terecht** *adj;adv* [təˈrɛxt]	**justified; back, found** Haar woede is volkomen terecht. -Her outrage is completely justified.
1078	**ophalen** *vb* [ˈɔphalə(n)]	**collect** Kun je helpen met het ophalen? -Can you help with collecting?
1079	**vangen**	**catch**

vb
['vaŋə(n)]

Het is voor het eerst dat ik zo'n grote vis vang!
-This is the first time I've caught such a big fish!

1080 **bedoeling**
de
[bə'dulɪŋ]

intention
Bedoel je dat je met opzet je schoonheid verbergt?
-You are saying you intentionally hide your good looks?

1081 **steken**
vb
['stekə(n)]

put, poke, stab
Steek alles in een taxi.
-Put everything in a taxi.

1082 **pond**
het
[pɔnt]

pound
John heeft drie pond bananen gekocht.
-John bought three pounds of bananas.

1083 **overleden**
adj
[oufərle:jdə]

deceased
Een vrouw wier echtgenote is overleden is een weduwe.
-A woman whose husband has died is a widow.

1084 **afmaken**
vb
['afmakə(n)]

finish
Ik zal dit werk op een of andere manier afmaken.
-I will finish this work somehow.

1085 **verslaan**
vb
[vər'slan]

defeat
Ik denk dat het onmogelijk is dat wij hem verslaan.
-I think it's impossible for us to beat him.

1086 **pak**
het
[pak]

suit, pack
Ik hoef geen pak en stropdas te dragen naar werk.
-I don't need to wear a suit and tie to work.

1087 **cent**
de
[sɛnt]

cent
Ze waren ongeveer 25 cent per pond goedkoper.
-They were about 25 cents a pound cheaper.

1088 **risico**
het
['riziko]

risk
Van hard werken is nog nooit iemand dood gegaan. Maar waarom het risico nemen?!
-Hard work never killed anyone. But why take the risk?!

1089 **schijnen**
vb
['sxɛinə(n)]

seem
Zowel John als Jane schijnen niet in staat om dat te doen.
-John and Jane both seem unable to do that.

1090 **kleur**
de
[klør]

color
Wat is jouw favoriete kleur?
-What's your favorite color?

1091 **afspreken**
vb
['afsprekə(n)]

arrange
Zij was degene die wilde afspreken.
-She's the one who wanted to meet.

1092 **berg**
de
[bɛrx]

mountain
Hij beloofde een berg van goud.
-He promised a mountain of gold.

1093 **genoegen**
het
[xə'nuxə(n)]

pleasure
Altijd een genoegen om u te zien.
-Always a pleasure to see you.

1094 **bespreken**
vb
[bə'sprekə(n)]

discuss
Het loont de moeite dit onderwerp te bespreken.
-The topic is worth discussing.

1095 **type**
het
['tipə]

type
John is het type persoon dat een kat een kat noemt.
-John is the type of person who calls a spade a spade.

1096	**stilte**	**silence**
	de	Ben je bang van de stilte?
	[ˈstɪltə]	-Are you afraid of silence?
1097	**medicijn**	**medicine**
	het	Ik moet medicijnen gebruiken.
	[mediˈsɛin]	-I have to take medicine.
1098	**mening**	**opinion**
	de	Hij dringt altijd zijn mening aan mij op.
	[ˈmenɪŋ]	-He always imposes his opinion on me.
1099	**schoonheid**	**beauty**
	de	Van een afstand gezien is ze een schoonheid.
	[ˈsxonhɛit]	-Seen from a distance, she's a beauty.
1100	**erachter**	**behind**
	adv	Hij heeft zich erachter geparkeerd.
	[ɛrˈɑxtər]	-He parked behind it.
1101	**omkeren**	**turn**
	vb	Keer je alsjeblieft om!
	[ˈɔmkerə(n)]	-Please turn around!
1102	**twijfel**	**doubt**
	de	Ik twijfel er niet aan dat hij me zal helpen.
	[ˈtwɛifəl]	-I don't doubt that he will help me.
1103	**bepalen**	**determine**
	vb	Het is niet aan mij om dat te bepalen.
	[bəˈpalə(n)]	-It's not for me to determine.
1104	**dichterbij**	**closer**
	adv	De toekomst is dichterbij dan je denkt.
	[dixtərbɛj]	-The future is closer than you think.
1105	**controleren**	**check**
	vb	Laten we Johns voorgeschiedenis controleren.
	[kɔntroˈlerə(n)]	-Let's check John's background.
1106	**tent**	**tent**
	de	Uw tent is vannacht gebruikt voor sluwe streken.
	[tɛnt]	-Your tent was used last night for some devious shenanigans.
1107	**hoop**	**hope**
	de	We zijn jullie laatste hoop.
	[ɦoːp]	-We're your last hope.
1108	**geweld**	**violence**
	het	Ik hou niet van geweld.
	[xəˈwɛlt]	-I do not like violence.
1109	**vertrekken**	**leave**
	vb	Ik moet mij scheren voor mijn vertrek.
	[vərˈtrɛkə(n)]	-I've got to shave before leaving.
1110	**officier**	**officer**
	de	Wat is het probleem officier?
	[ɔfiˈsir]	-What is the problem officer?
1111	**arresteren**	**arrest**
	vb	De politie zal je arresteren.
	[ɑrɛsˈterə(n)]	-The police will arrest you.
1112	**hartelijk**	**cordial, warm**
	adj	Hartelijk bedankt voor uw gastvrijheid.
	[ˈhɑrtələk]	-Thank you very much for your hospitality.

1113	**bevallen**	**please, give birth**
	vb	Ze is bevallen van een gezonde baby.
	[bə'valə(n)]	-She gave birth to a healthy baby.

1114	**taal**	**language**
	de	In Papoea-Nieuw-Guinea worden 850 verschillende talen door Papoea's gesproken.
	[tal]	-In Papua New Guinea, there are 850 different languages spoken by Papuans.

1115	**opnemen**	**record, take**
	vb	Laat me jullie temperatuur opnemen.
	['ɔpnemə(n)]	-Let me take your temperature.

1116	**onderzoeken**	**examine**
	vb	Ik ga het nader onderzoeken.
	[ɔndər'zukə(n)]	-I'll look into it.

1117	**klant**	**customer**
	de	Bijvoorbeeld, zij zijn niet blij om klanten in de winkel te helpen.
	[klɑnt]	-For example, they are not happy to help clients in the store.

1118	**stappen**	**step, go, stride; night out**
	het; vb	Ze zagen ons terwijl ze bezig waren uit de trein te stappen.
	['stɑpə(n)]	-They saw us as they were getting off the train.

1119	**akkoord**	**agreement**
	het	Ga je niet akkoord met dat plan?
	[a'kort]	-Don't you agree with this plan?

1120	**verdenken**	**suspect**
	vb	Waarom verdenk je John ervan het gedaan te hebben?
	[vər'dɛŋkə(n)]	-Why do you suspect it was John who did that?

1121	**gedrag**	**behavior**
	het	Je gedrag was beschamend.
	[xə'drɑx]	-Your behavior was shameful.

1122	**bedenken**	**think**
	vb	Ik kan geen ander plan bedenken.
	[bə'dɛŋkə(n)]	-I can't think of any other plan.

1123	**Vrijdag**	**Friday**
	de	Eindelijk is het vrijdag.
	['vrɛidɑx]	-Finally, it's Friday.

1124	**verstand**	**intellect, sense**
	het	Ik vertrouwde op je gezonde verstand.
	[vər'stɑnt]	-I expected some common sense on your part.

1125	**vriendelijk**	**friendly, kind**
	adj	Wil je zo vriendelijk zijn de pizza in drie stukken te verdelen?
	['vrindələk]	-Would you be so kind as to slice the pizza in three parts.

1126	**hersenen**	**brain**
	de	Zombies eten hersenen.
	['hɛrsənə(n)]	-Zombies eat brains.

1127	**raad**	**advice**
	de	John geeft Jane raad.
	[rat]	-John gives Jane advice.

1128	**vinger**	**finger**
	de	Mijn vingers zijn zo stijf van de kou dat ik geen piano kan spelen.
	['vɪŋər]	-My fingers are so numb with cold that I can't play the piano.

1129	**vaarwel**	**goodbye**
	het	Zeg vaarwel. Doe het. Nu!

[faːrvɛl]   -Say goodbye. Do it.. Now!

1130 rekenen — **calculate, count**
vb
['rekənə(n)]
U kunt altijd op ons rekenen.
-You can always count on us.

1131 toon — **tone**
de
[ton]
Dat is een scherpe toon.
-That is a sharp tone.

1132 favoriet — **favorite**
de
[faforiːt]
Was het jouw favoriet?
-Was it your favorite?

1133 heus — **real**
adj
[høs]
Maar de meiden waren heus in gevaar.
-But the threat to those girls was real.

1134 huid — **skin**
de
[hœyt]
John heeft een mooie huid.
-John has nice skin.

1135 overkomen — **happen, visit**
vb
['ovərkomə(n)]
Dat zal me niet overkomen.
-It won't happen to me.

1136 machine — **machine**
de
[ma'ʃinə]
Het menselijk lichaam is een soort machine.
-Man's body is a sort of machine.

1137 uitstekend — **excellent**
adj
[œyt'stɛkənt]
De wijn was uitstekend.
-The wine was excellent.

1138 echtgenoot — **husband**
de
['ɛxtxənot]
Ze vermoordde haar echtgenoot.
-She murdered her husband.

1139 afdeling — **department**
de
['ɑvdelɪŋ]
Ga naar de afdeling chirurgie alstublieft.
-Please go to the surgery department.

1140 grens — **border, limit**
de
[xrɛns]
Blijf zwemmen tot je aan je grens zit.
-Keep on swimming up to your limit.

1141 drank — **beverage, booze**
de
[drɑŋk]
Is John gestopt met het drinken van alcoholische dranken?
-Did John stop drinking alcoholic drinks?

1142 blik — **look, tin**
de
[blɪk]
John opende een blik tonijn.
-John opened a can of tuna fish.

1143 ho — **stop**
interj
[hoʊ]
Nou, ho, hou even op, oké?
-Well, wait, just stop, okay?

1144 burgemeester — **mayor**
de
[bʏrxə'mestər]
De burgemeester is nu niet beschikbaar.
-The mayor is not available now.

1145 rapport — **report**
het
[ra'pɔrt]
Het is zeer onwaarschijnlijk dat John dit rapport heeft geschreven.
-It's very unlikely that John wrote this report.

1146 paniek — **panic**
de
Wie raakte in paniek?

[paˈnik] -Who panicked?

1147	**begrafenis**	**funeral**
	de	John heeft de begrafenis van Jane bijgewoond.
	[bəˈxrafənɪs]	-John attended Jane's funeral.

1148	**gezelschap**	**company**
	het	Wil je wat gezelschap?
	[xəˈzɛlsxap]	-Do you want some company?

1149	**tegenhouden**	**retain, hold**
	vb	Niemand zal ons tegenhouden.
	[ˈtexə(n)haudə(n)]	-No one will hold us back.

1150	**bakken**	**bake**
	vb	Ik was cake aan het bakken.
	[ˈbakə(n)]	-I was baking a cake.

1151	**tuin**	**garden**
	de	Zijn tuin is een kunstwerk.
	[tœyn]	-His garden is a work of art.

1152	**doos**	**box**
	de	Neem die doos hier vandaan!
	[dos]	-Take that box away!

1153	**blind**	**blind**
	adj	Hij was zo lelijk. Ze werd blind.
	[blɪnt]	-He was so ugly. She went blind.

1154	**voedsel**	**food**
	het	Je eet te veel ongezond voedsel.
	[ˈvutsəl]	-You eat too much junk food.

1155	**gouden**	**golden**
	adj	De kist bevatte gouden munten.
	[ˈxaudə(n)]	-The chest contained gold coins.

1156	**bende**	**mess, gang**
	de	Het is hier echt een bende.
	[ˈbɛndə]	-It is really a mess here.

1157	**voeren**	**feed, pursue**
	vb	John voert zijn hond.
	[ˈvurə(n)]	-John feeds his dog.

1158	**hoewel**	**although**
	con	Hoewel hij moe was, hield hij niet op met werken.
	[huˈwɛl]	-Although he was tired, he would not stop working.

1159	**lijden**	**suffer**
	vb	Mensen die regelmatig in de open lucht werken, lijden niet aan slapeloosheid.
	[ˈlɛidə(n)]	-People who regularly work in the open air do not suffer from sleeplessness.

1160	**compleet**	**complete**
	adj	De schatting was een complete schok!
	[kɔmˈplet]	-The estimate was a complete shock!

1161	**talent**	**talent, gift**
	het	Zijn zoon heeft talent voor muziek.
	[taˈlɛnt]	-His son has a gift for music.

1162	**kunst**	**art**
	de	Weet je veel over kunst?
	[kʏnst]	-Do you know much about art?

| 1163 | **uitnodigen** | **invite** |
| | *vb* | John nodigde Jane uit om langs te komen. |

['œytnodəxə(n)]   -John invited Jane to come over.

1164	**bijvoorbeeld**	**for instance**
	adv	Een Fransman bijvoorbeeld kan misschien moeilijk lachen om een Russische grap.
	['bɛi'vorbelt]	-A Frenchman, for instance, might find it hard to laugh at a Russian joke.
1165	**jazeker**	**surely so**
	int	Wil je dit echt? Jazeker.
	[ja'zekər]	-Do you really want this? For sure.
1166	**tegenwoordig**	**current; currently**
	adv; adj	Ik woon tegenwoordig in Dublin.
	[texə(n)'wordəx]	-I live in Dublin right now.
1167	**elf**	**elf; eleven**
	de; nu	"Hoe laat is het?" "Het is half elf."
	[ɛlf]	-"What time is it?" "It is ten-thirty."
1168	**noorden**	**north**
	het	Mijn land ligt in Noord-Afrika, ten zuiden van de Middellandse Zee.
	['nordə(n)]	-My country is situated in North Africa, south of the Mediterranean Sea.
1169	**project**	**project**
	het	Die projecten bieden veel nieuwe en innovatieve inhoud en ideeën.
	[pro'jɛkt]	-Those projects offer a lot of new and innovative content and ideas.
1170	**advies**	**advice**
	het	We hebben je advies nodig.
	[at'fis]	-We do need your advice.
1171	**koffer**	**suitcase**
	de	Ik wacht op mijn koffer.
	['kɔfər]	-I'm waiting for my suitcase.
1172	**zwak**	**weak**
	adj	Vroeger was ik zwak en kwetsbaar.
	[zwɑk]	-I used to be weak and vulnerable.
1173	**westen**	**west**
	het	Culturen uit het Oosten en het Westen ontmoeten elkaar in dit land.
	['wɛstə(n)]	-Cultures of the East and the West meet together in this country.
1174	**vloer**	**floor**
	de	Gooi niets op de vloer.
	[vlur]	-Don't throw anything onto the floor.
1175	**zondag**	**Sunday**
	de	Zondag komt na zaterdag.
	['zɔndɑx]	-Sunday comes after Saturday.
1176	**duur**	**duration; expensive**
	de; adj	Deze laarzen zijn duur.
	[dyr]	-These boots are expensive.
1177	**vandoor**	**away**
	adv	Het is te laat om de schuurdeur te sluiten als het paard er al vandoor is.
	[fando:r]	-It's too late to shut the barn door when the horse has already run off.
1178	**vogel**	**bird**
	de	Deze vogel wordt een meeuw genoemd.
	['voxəl]	-This bird is called a seagull.
1179	**laag**	**low; layer**
	adj; de	De prijs is laag, maar de kwaliteit is niet heel goed.
	[lax]	-The price is low, but the quality isn't very good.
1180	**zonde**	**sin; too bad**

de; adj
['zɔndə]
Verwissel zonde niet met misdaad.
-Do not mistake sin with crime.

1181 papier — **paper**
het
[pa'pir]
Kunt u de benodigde papieren inleveren?
-Please hand in the necessary papers.

1182 brood — **bread**
het
[brot]
Het brood is vers.
-The bread is fresh.

1183 hemelsnaam — **heaven's name**
in
[he:jmǝlsna:m]
Wat ben je hemelsnaam aan het doen?
-What in the world do you think you're doing?

1184 interesseren — **interest**
vb
[ɪntərɛ'serə(n)]
Interesseren bloemen u?
-Are you interested in flowers?

1185 alarm — **alarm**
het
[a'lɑrm]
We hadden vandaag twee keer loos alarm.
-Today, we had two false alarms.

1186 station — **station**
het
[sta(t)s'jɔn]
Hij was zo vriendelijk om me een lift naar het station te geven.
-He kindly drove me to the station.

1187 storm — **storm**
de
[stɔrm]
De storm veroorzaakte veel schade.
-The storm caused a lot of damage.

1188 oplossing — **solution**
de
['ɔplɔsɪŋ]
U vindt de oplossingen aan het einde van deze les.
-You will find the solutions at the end of this lesson.

1189 loven — **praise**
vb
['lovə(n)]
Maar boven alles loven ze John.
-But, above all, they praise John.

1190 schot — **shot**
het
[sxɔt]
Het volgende schot is op u gericht.
-The next shot is aimed at you.

1191 menselijk — **human**
adj
['mɛnsǝlǝk]
Geld is de god van het menselijk ras.
-Money is the god of the human race.

1192 verraden — **betray**
vb
[vər'adə(n)]
Je moet mij niet verraden!
-You must not betray me!

1193 bruiloft — **wedding**
de
['brœylɔft]
Hij heeft zich bedacht als gevolg van de bruiloft.
-He changed his mind as a result of the marriage.

1194 jagen — **hunt**
vb
['jaxǝ(n)]
Vissen, jagen, wandelen en skiën zijn populair.
-Fishing, hunting, hiking and skiing are popular.

1195 vergadering — **meeting**
de
[vər'xadərɪŋ]
Ze is in een vergadering.
-She's at a meeting.

1196 zuiden — **south**
het
['zœydə(n)]
Vogels vliegen naar het Zuiden.
-Birds fly to the south.

1197 reizen — **travel**

	vb	Jullie zijn te jong om alleen te reizen.
	[ˈrɛizə(n)]	-You are too young to travel alone.
1198	**eigenaar**	**owner**
	de	Ik ben de eigenaar van dit gebouw.
	[ɛjxənaːr]	-I am the owner of this building.
1199	**contract**	**contract**
	het	Ze heeft een onbepaald contract.
	[kɔnˈtrakt]	-She has an indefinite contract.
1200	**vrolijk**	**cheerful, happy**
	adj	Vrolijk Pasen! Zo lekker paashaas braden.
	[ˈvrolək]	-Happy Easter! Let's go roast the easter bunny.
1201	**beer**	**bear**
	de	De beer is groot.
	[ber]	-The bear is big.
1202	**proces**	**process, trial**
	het	John zit in de gevangenis, in afwachting van zijn proces.
	[proˈsɛs]	-John is in jail, awaiting trial.
1203	**tong**	**tongue**
	de	Ben je je tong verloren?
	[tɔŋ]	-Cat got your tongue?
1204	**leraar**	**teacher**
	de	Ik ben een leraar, geen student.
	[ˈlerar]	-I am a teacher, not a student.
1205	**beslissen**	**decide**
	vb	Jullie beslissen.
	[bəˈslɪsə(n)]	-You decide.
1206	**wijs**	**wise; tune**
	adj; de	Niet alle mannen zijn wijs.
	[wɛis]	-Not all men are wise.
1207	**koken**	**cook**
	vb	Pasta koken is makkelijk.
	[ˈkokə(n)]	-Cooking pasta is easy.
1208	**pikken**	**steal, peck, put up with**
	vb	Ik pik dit niet!
	[ˈpɪkə(n)]	-I don't put up with this!
1209	**zwijgen**	**keep silent**
	vb	Hij kan niets doen dan zwijgen.
	[ˈzwɛixə(n)]	-He can't do anything but keep silent.
1210	**kust**	**coast**
	de	In 1942 begonnen ze de kust te versterken.
	[kʏst]	-In 1942 they had started to strengthen the coast.
1211	**tegenover**	**opposite**
	prp	Tegenover het park is er een mooie rivier.
	[texə(n)ˈovər]	-Opposite the park there is a beautiful river.
1212	**verbergen**	**hide**
	vb	Verbergen zij iets?
	[vərˈbɛrxə(n)]	-Are they hiding something?
1213	**stront**	**shit**
	de	Dit is een klomp bevroren stront.
	[strɔnt]	-This is a big frozen chunk of shit.
1214	**ei**	**egg**

	het		Thomas kookt een ei.
	[ɛi]		-John is boiling an egg.
1215	**pers**		**press, media**
	de		De pers schrijft artikelen over Jane.
	[pɛrs]		-The press writes articles about Jane.
1216	**kampioen**		**champion**
	de		Ajax zal kampioen worden van de Eredivisie.
	[kɑmpiˈjun]		-The champion of the Eredivisie will be Ajax.
1217	**bieden**		**offer**
	vb		Dit jaar bieden we dezelfde taalcursus aan als vorig jaar.
	[ˈbidə(n)]		-This year we offer the same language course as last year.
1218	**nat**		**wet**
	adj		De handdoek is nat.
	[nɑt]		-The towel is wet.
1219	**pot**		**crock, pot**
	de		Spinnen en schorpioenen hebben acht poten.
	[pɔt]		-Spiders and scorpions have eight legs.
1220	**rechercheur**		**detective**
	de		De rechercheur die vanmorgen werd neergeschoten is overleden.
	[reʃɛrˈʃør]		-The detective that got shot this morning died.
1221	**dankbaar**		**grateful**
	adj		Ik ben zeer dankbaar voor jouw hulp.
	[ˈdɑŋkbar]		-I am very grateful for your help.
1222	**ziekte**		**disease**
	de		Ik ben net beter van een ernstige ziekte.
	[ˈziktə]		-I just got over a severe illness.
1223	**kilo**		**kilo**
	de		John heeft drie kilo appels gekocht.
	[ˈkilo]		-John bought three kilograms of apples.
1224	**lid**		**member**
	het		Hij is lid van de golfclub.
	[lɪt]		-He's a member of the golf club.
1225	**kelder**		**basement**
	de		De kelder staat onder water.
	[ˈkɛldər]		-The basement is full of water.
1226	**klus**		**job**
	de		Ik zal met je meegaan als ik klaar ben met de klus.
	[klʏs]		-I'll come with you if I finish the job.
1227	**straf**		**punishment; strong**
	de; adj		Onwetendheid beschermt niet tegen straf.
	[strɑf]		-Ignorance does not protect against punishment.
1228	**super**		**super, great**
	adj		Super! Je bent nog beter dan Superman.
	[ˈsypər]		-Right on! You're even better than Superman!
1229	**senator**		**senator**
	de		Mag ik onze nieuwe senator voorstellen.
	[səˈnatɔr]		-I'd like you to meet our latest senator.
1230	**schreeuwen**		**shout**
	vb		Ze begon te schreeuwen, en ik liep weg.
	[ˈsxrewə(n)]		-She started shouting and I ran away.
1231	**verborgen**		**hidden**

adj
[vər'bɔrxə(n)]

Het verborgen bos is verborgen.
-The hidden forest is hidden.

1232 shirt
het
[ʃy:rt]

shirt
Waarom doe je dat? Je maakt mijn shirt nat!
-Why are you doing that? You're getting my shirt wet!

1233 ernstig
adj
['ɛrnstəx]

serious
We worden met een ernstige crisis geconfronteerd.
-We are facing a serious crisis.

1234 vliegveld
het
['vlixfɛlt]

airport
Ik ben nu op het vliegveld.
-I'm at the airport now.

1235 flink
adj; adv
[flɪŋk]

robust, firm; substantial
Een flinke knul.
-A robust guy.

1236 erom
adv
[ɛr'ɔm]

around it, about it
Jammer, niemand geeft erom.
-Too bad nobody cares about it.

1237 lach
de
[lɑx]

smile
John had een lach op zijn gezicht.
-John had a smile on his face.

1238 west
de
[vest]

west
Die stad kan je ten westen van Londen vinden.
-The city is found west of London.

1239 eenvoudig
adj
[en'vaudəx]

plain, simple
John draagt eenvoudige kleren.
-John wears simple clothes.

1240 aandoen
vb
['andun]

put on
Wil je het licht even aandoen?
-Will you turn on the light?

1241 hiervan
adv
['hirvan]

hereof
Weet iemand anders hiervan?
-Does anyone else know about this?

1242 opwinden
vb
['ɔpwɪndə(n)]

excite, wind up
Geen enkele vrouw kon me opwinden.
-I could never find a woman who could excite me.

1243 uitzoeken
vb
['œytsukə(n)]

sort, find out
Ik wil uitzoeken of mijn garantie al vervallen is.
-I want to find out if the warranty has expired yet.

1244 wensen
vb
['wɛnsə(n)]

wish
Ik wens je een prettige verjaardag.
-I wish you a happy birthday.

1245 wild
adj; het
[wɪlt]

wild; wildlife
In het bos leven wilde dieren.
-Wild animals live in the forest.

1246 vasthouden
vb
['vasthaudə(n)]

hold
Waarom kan ik al deze limoenen niet vasthouden?
-Why can't I hold all these limes?

1247 detail
het
[de'taj]

detail
Hij beschreef de omstandigheden in detail.
-He described the circumstances in detail.

1248 dossier

file

	het	Ik leende een dossier van de marechaussee.
	[dɔ'ʃe, dɔ'sir]	-Well, I sort of borrowed a file from the military police.
1249	**meemaken**	**experience**
	vb	Dat ik dit nog mag meemaken.
	['memakə(n)]	-I never thought I'd experience this.
1250	**badkamer**	**bathroom**
	de	Jane brengt uren in de badkamer door.
	['bɑtkamər]	-Jane spends hours in the bathroom.
1251	**dulden**	**tolerate, allow**
	vb	Dat mogen wij in geen geval dulden.
	['dʏldə(n)]	-We should not allow this under any circumstances.
1252	**eng**	**scary**
	adj	Mijn broer vindt enge films leuk.
	[ɛŋ]	-My brother likes watching scary movies.
1253	**afscheid**	**farewell**
	het	De tijd van het afscheid is gekomen.
	['ɑfsxɛit]	-It's time to say goodbye.
1254	**race**	**race**
	de	Het is leuk om de race te bekijken.
	[res]	-It's fun to watch the race.
1255	**ruim**	**spacious, amply**
	adj	De kamer is erg ruim.
	[rœym]	-The room is very spacious.
1256	**wedden**	**bet**
	vb	Ik wed dat je dat niet kan.
	['wɛdə(n)]	-I bet that you can not do that.
1257	**gerust**	**be at ease, safe**
	adj	Je kan gerust zwemmen of duiken.
	[xə'rʏst]	-There's no problem with swimming or diving.
1258	**gezond**	**healthy**
	adj	De gezonde man rookt niet.
	[xə'zɔnt]	-The healthy man does not smoke.
1259	**taart**	**cake**
	de	Snijd de taart in punten.
	[tart]	-Cut the pie into slices.
1260	**graf**	**grave**
	het	Mijn vroegere lerares Engels draait zich nu zeker weten om in haar graf.
	[xrɑf]	-My old English teacher is certainly rolling in her grave right now.
1261	**groen**	**green**
	adj	In de herfst worden deze groene bladeren rood.
	[xrun]	-These green leaves will turn red in the fall.
1262	**carrière**	**career**
	de	John heeft een voorbeeldige carrière als advocaat.
	[karijɛ:rə]	-John has an exemplary career as a lawyer.
1263	**nauwelijks**	**hardly**
	adv	We hebben nauwelijks genoeg tijd om te ontbijten.
	['nɑuwələks]	-We hardly have time to eat breakfast.
1264	**zojuist**	**just (now)**
	adv	Ik heb zojuist een goed idee gekregen.
	[zo'jœyst]	-I just had a good idea.
1265	**champagne**	**champagne**

de
[ʃɑmˈpɑɲe]

Sinaasappelsap of champagne?
-Orange juice or champagne?

1266 **natuur**
de
[naˈtyr]

nature
Ik hou van natuur.
-I love nature.

1267 **saai**
adj
[saj]

dull, boring
Wat zijn jullie saai.
-You guys are so boring.

1268 **vergissing**
de
[vərˈxɪsɪŋ]

mistake
Het is maar een vergissing.
-It is just a mistake.

1269 **priester**
de
[ˈpristər]

priest
Ben je een priester?
-Are you a priest?

1270 **graad**
de
[xrat]

degree
Uw graad in filosofie verbaast me.
-Your degree in philosophy surprises me.

1271 **verdieping**
de
[vərˈdipɪŋ]

floor
Mijn woning is op de vierde verdieping.
-My apartment is on the fourth floor.

1272 **signaal**
het
[sɪˈɲal]

signal
Hier komt het signaal beslist vandaan.
-This is definitely the origin of the signal.

1273 **oplossen**
vb
[ˈɔplɔsə(n)]

solve
Een neutraal land werd gevraagd om het geschil te helpen oplossen.
-A neutral country was asked to help solve the dispute.

1274 **manager**
de
[ˈmɛnədʒər]

manager
Dat is een van de voordelen wanneer je manager bent.
-That's one of the perks of being the manager.

1275 **schade**
de
[ˈsxadə]

damage
Wat is de schade?
-What is the damage?

1276 **flat**
de
[flɛt, flɑt]

flat
Heeft de flat drie slaapkamers?
-Has the flat got three bedrooms?

1277 **schattig**
adj
[ˈsxɑtəx]

sweet, cute
Je bent zo'n schattige jongen.
-You're such a cute boy.

1278 **hiervoor**
adv
[ˈhirvor]

theretofore
Ik voel me schuldig hiervoor.
-I feel guilty about it.

1279 **toegang**
de
[ˈtuxaŋ]

access
Studenten hebben toegang tot de bibliotheek.
-Students have access to the library.

1280 **waardoor**
con
[warˈdor]

whereby
Zwaartekracht is een natuurkracht, waardoor dingen elkaar aantrekken.
-Gravity is the natural force by which objects are attracted to each other.

1281 **ronde**
de
[ˈrɔndə]

round
Nog een ronde!
-Another round!

1282 **ondanks**

despite

prp
['ɔndaŋks]

Ondanks hun omvang en hun gewicht kunnen nijlpaarden snel zwemmen.
-Despite their bulk and weight, hippos can swim rapidly.

1283 **amen**
het
[aːmən]

amen
Ze zeggen amen, net als wij.
-They say amen, just like us.

1284 **achterlaten**
vb
['ɑxtərlatə(n)]

leave
Als we hem achterlaten zal hij doodbloeden.
-If we leave him, he'll bleed to death.

1285 **dertig**
de
['dɛrtəx]

thirty
Ze heeft dertig jaar lang muziekles gegeven.
-She taught music for thirty years.

1286 **politiek**
de
[poli'tik]

politics
Hij verloor de belangstelling voor politiek.
-He has lost interest in politics.

1287 **aannemen**
vb
['anemə(n)]

assume
Laten we aannemen dat het waar is.
-Let's assume it's true.

1288 **bewerken**
vb
[bə'wɛrkə(n)]

edit
Het resultaat zal ik persoonlijk bewerken.
-The product of which I shall personally edit.

1289 **genaamd**
adj
[xə'namt]

called
John werd verliefd op een meisje genaamd Jane.
-John fell in love with a girl called Jane.

1290 **schrikken**
vb
['sxrɪkə(n)]

start, jolt, scare
Dat lawaai zou iedereen het schrik op het lijf jagen.
-That noise would scare the daylights out of anyone.

1291 **genezen**
vb
[xə'nezə(n)]

cure
Veel mensen geloven dat acupunctuur ziektes kan genezen.
-Many people believe that acupuncture can cure diseases.

1292 **voorkomen**
vb; het
['vorkomə(n)]

prevent; appearance
De dokter raadde haar aan meer water te drinken om dehydratatie te voorkomen.
-The doctor suggested that she drink more water to keep from being dehydrated.

1293 **duits**
adj; het
[dœyts]

German; German
Je bent toch Duits? Of niet?
-You are German, right?

1294 **smaken**
vb
['smakə(n)]

taste
Die druiven smaken zuur.
-These grapes taste sour.

1295 **kast**
de
[kɑst]

closet
Ik heb vanmorgen de kast van Jane opgeruimd.
-This morning I cleaned out Jane's closet.

1296 **eenzaam**
adj
['enzam]

lonely, solitary
Ik vraag me af waarom ik me zo eenzaam voel wanneer het koud wordt.
-I wonder why I feel so lonely when it gets cold.

1297 **morgenochtend**
adv
[mɔrxə(n)'ɔxtənt]

tomorrow morning
Wacht tot morgenochtend.
-Wait until tomorrow morning.

1298 **cadeau**
het

gift
Oom John bezocht ons nooit zonder een of ander cadeau.

[ka'do]

-Uncle John never visited us without some present.

1299	**oceaan**	**ocean**
	de	Ik hou van de oceaan.
	[ose'jan]	-I love the ocean.

1300	**daarheen**	**there**
	adv	Jij beslist of we daarheen gaan of niet.
	[dar'hen]	-It is up to you to decide whether we will go there or not.

1301	**naakt**	**naked**
	adj	Ik slaap naakt.
	[nakt]	-I sleep in the nude.

1302	**omgeving**	**surroundings**
	de	Dit is het beste zeevruchtenrestaurant in de omgeving.
	[ɔm'xevɪŋ]	-This is by far the best seafood restaurant in this area.

1303	**binnenkomen**	**come in**
	vb	Mag ik binnenkomen?
	['bɪnə(n)komə(n)]	-Might I come in?

1304	**verband**	**connection, bandage**
	het	Ik zie het verband niet.
	[vər'bant]	-I don't see the connection.

1305	**engel**	**angel**
	de	Jane is een engel.
	['ɛŋəl]	-Jane is an angel.

1306	**bron**	**source**
	de	Inkomsten uit deze bron zijn niet belastbaar.
	[brɔn]	-Income from this source is nontaxable.

1307	**grijpen**	**grab**
	vb	Grijp hem. En knevel hem.
	['xrɛipə(n)]	-Grab him. And bind him.

1308	**heten**	**be named**
	vb	Ik wil vanaf nu John heten.
	['hetə(n)]	-From now on, I want to be called John.

1309	**aanraken**	**touch**
	vb	Raak het niet aan.
	['anrakə(n)]	-Don't touch it.

1310	**belang**	**importance**
	het	Het is onmogelijk het belang te overdrijven van vroeg opstaan.
	[bə'laŋ]	-One cannot overestimate the importance of getting up early.

1311	**steun**	**support**
	de	Niemand wilde mijn land steunen.
	[støn]	-Nobody wanted to support my country.

1312	**verslagen**	**defeated**
	adj	Hier ziet u een verslagen kampioen.
	[vər'slaxə(n)]	-Here, you see a defeated champion.

1313	**wei**	**whey**
	de	Ik hoop dat ze niet zonder zoete wei zitten.
	[wɛi]	-I hope they didn't run out of sweet whey.

1314	**waarheen**	**where to**
	adv	Maar ik ga waarheen ze mij sturen.
	[war'hen]	-But I'll go wherever they send me.

| 1315 | **verstoppen** | **hide** |
| | *vb* | John hoefde zich niet te verstoppen. |

[vər'stɔpə(n)]   -John didn't have to hide.

1316 doorheen — **through**
adv
Ze reisden met mij doorheen heel Europa.
[dor'hen] — -They traveled all throughout Europe with me!

1317 keizer — **emperor**
de
Julius Caesar was een Romeinse keizer.
['kɛizər] — -Julius Caesar was a Roman emperor.

1318 prettig — **gratifying**
adj
Ik wens je een prettige dag!
['prɛtəx] — -I wish you a nice day!

1319 genade — **mercy**
de
Verwacht geen genade.
[xə'nadə] — -Expect no mercy.

1320 vervelen — **bore**
vb
Het laatste weekeind was vervelend voor mij.
[vər'velə(n)] — -Last weekend was boring for me.

1321 vermist — **missing**
adj
Er is een kind vermist.
[vər'mɪst] — -A child is missing.

1322 lef — **courage**
het
John heeft veel lef.
[lɛf] — -John has a lot of courage.

1323 kwestie — **matter**
de
Ik werd gevraagd naar mijn persoonlijke mening over de kwestie.
['kwɛsti] — -I was asked for my personal opinion about the matter.

1324 schitteren — **shine**
vb
We moeten onze solist laten schitteren.
['sxɪtərə(n)] — -We have to allow our soloist to shine.

1325 hoogheid — **highness**
de
Bedankt hoogheid.
[ho:xhɛjt] — -Thank you, Your Highness.

1326 snelheid — **speed**
de
Het vliegtuig kan supersonische snelheden behalen.
['snɛlheit] — -The airplane is capable of supersonic speeds.

1327 groeten — **greet**
vb
Doe de groeten aan Judy.
['xrutə(n)] — -Please give my best regards to Judy.

1328 beveiliging — **safeguard, security**
de
Blijf daar niet zo staan, bel de beveiliging!
[bə'vɛiləxɪŋ] — -Don't just stand there, call security!

1329 regen — **rain**
de
Ik las gisteren een artikel over zure regen.
['rexə(n)] — -I read an article about acid rain yesterday.

1330 gereed — **ready**
adj
Is alles gereed voor dat liefdadigheidsbal?
[xə'ret] — -Are we all set for that charity ball?

1331 woestijn — **desert**
de
John stierf alleen in de woestijn.
[wus'tɛin] — -John died alone in the desert.

1332 opgeven — **quit, give up**
vb
John zal niet makkelijk opgeven.

['ɔpxevə(n)]   -John won't give up easily.

1333 eenheid — **unit, unity**
de
['enhɛit]
Berlijn is een symbool van de eenheid tussen Oost en West.
-Berlin is a symbol of the union between East and West.

1334 verantwoordelijkheid — **responsibility**
de
[vərant'wordələkhɛit]
Het is John die verantwoordelijk is voor de veiligheidszaken.
-In matters of security, it is John who is responsible.

1335 nogmaals — **once again**
adv
['nɔxmals]
Nee, nee en nogmaals nee!
-No, no, and once again, no!

1336 lelijk — **ugly**
adj
['le[lək]
Dat is lelijk. Net zoals je moeder.
-That's ugly. Just like your mom.

1337 vrees — **fear**
de
[vres]
Vrees mij, als je durft!
-Fear me, if you dare!

1338 aap — **monkey**
de
[ap]
Hij aapt een aap na.
-He is imitating a monkey.

1339 tellen — **count**
vb
['tɛlə(n)]
Hij kan niet tellen.
-He can't count.

1340 aankomen — **arrive**
verb
['ankomə(n)]
Ik zal contact met je opnemen zodra ik aankom.
-I will contact you as soon as I arrive.

1341 varken — **pig**
het
['vɑrkə(n)]
De koe loeit, de haan kraait, het varken knort, de eend kwaakt en de kat miauwt.
-The cow moos, the rooster crows, the pig oinks, the duck quacks, and the cat meows.

1342 min — **poor; minus**
adj; adv
[mɪn]
Hij begrijpt min of meer zijn problemen.
-He understands more or less his problems.

1343 scheiden — **separate**
vb
['sxɛidə(n)]
Men kan taal en cultuur niet van elkaar scheiden.
-You can't separate language from culture.

1344 pil — **pill**
de
[pɪl]
Slik je pillen.
-Take your pills.

1345 verbranden — **incinerate**
vb
[vər'brandə(n)]
Je kan niks verbranden zonder zuurstof.
-You cannot burn anything without oxygen.

1346 studeren — **study**
vb
[sty'derə(n)]
Bij deze hitte van vandaag heb ik geen zin om te studeren.
-As it is very hot today, I don't feel like studying.

1347 arts — **physician**
de
[arts]
Is zij geen arts?
-Isn't she a doctor?

1348 gedeelte — **part**
het
[xə'deltə]
Meer mensen wonen in het noordelijke gedeelte van de stad.
-More people live in the northern part of the city.

1349	**jury**		**jury**
	de		Hij is door een jury schuldig bevonden.
	[ˈʒyri]		-He was tried and convicted by a jury of his peers.
1350	**whisky**		**whiskey**
	de		De whisky is met water verdund.
	[ˈwɪski]		-The whiskey has been watered down.
1351	**strijken**		**iron**
	vb		Ik ben mijn zakdoeken aan het strijken.
	[ˈstrɛikə(n)]		-I'm ironing my handkerchiefs.
1352	**nachtmerrie**		**nightmare**
	de		Een vluchtelingenkamp is een nachtmerrie.
	[ˈnɑxtmɛri]		-A refugee camp is a nightmare.
1353	**netjes**		**neat**
	adj		Hou je kamer zo netjes als je kan.
	[ˈnɛcəs]		-Keep your room as neat as you can.
1354	**okee**		**okay**
	in		Okee Jane. Dikke doei-doei!
	[oʊˈkeɪ]		-Okay Jane. A big fat bye-bye!
1355	**verdedigen**		**defend**
	vb		Verdedig mij tegen mijzelf.
	[vərˈdedəxə(n)]		-Defend me from myself!
1356	**oosten**		**east**
	het		Er komt storm vanuit het oosten.
	[ˈostə(n)]		-It seems like there's a storm building to the east.
1357	**huur**		**rent**
	de		Ik kan de huur niet betalen.
	[hyr]		-I can't pay the rent.
1358	**schrijver**		**writer**
	de		John is een gepubliceerde schrijver.
	[ˈsxrɛivər]		-John is a published writer.
1359	**buik**		**belly**
	de		Ik heb kriebels in de buik.
	[bœyk]		-I have butterflies in my belly.
1360	**slaapkamer**		**bedroom**
	de		John heeft een bescheiden huis met twee slaapkamers in Boston.
	[ˈslapkamər]		-John has a modest two-bedroom house in Boston.
1361	**maagd**		**virgin**
	de		Ze was nog steeds maagd.
	[maxt]		-She was still a virgin.
1362	**borst**		**chest, breast**
	de		Waarom verberg je je borsten?
	[bɔrst]		-Why do you hide your breasts?
1363	**dief**		**thief**
	de		De dief rende weg.
	[dif]		-The thief ran away.
1364	**plicht**		**duty**
	de		Het is je plicht om te studeren.
	[plɪxt]		-It is your duty to study.
1365	**bezoeken**		**visit**
	vb		Ik moet mijn vriend in het ziekenhuis bezoeken.
	[bəˈzukə(n)]		-I must visit my friend in the hospital.

1366	**verzoek**	**request**
	het	Ze wees mijn verzoek af.
	[vər'zuk]	-She turned down my request.
1367	**dichter**	**poet**
	de	Dichters kunnen niet leven zonder liefde.
	[dixtər]	-Poets cannot live without love.
1368	**boerderij**	**farm**
	de	De boerderij kweekt aardappelen.
	[burdəˈrɛi]	-The farm grows potatoes.
1369	**horloge**	**watch**
	het	Dit horloge lijkt op datgene dat ik gisteren verloren heb.
	[hɔrˈloʒə]	-This watch is similar to mine I lost yesterday.
1370	**stijl**	**style, steep**
	de	John's stijl is veranderd.
	[stɛil]	-John's style has changed.
1371	**eeuw**	**century**
	de	In de loop van de twintigste eeuw is dit alles veranderd.
	[ew]	-In the course of the twentieth century all this changed.
1372	**wennen**	**get used to**
	vb	Je moet gewoon nog aan'm wennen.
	[ˈwɛnə(n)]	-You're not used to him yet.
1373	**pauze**	**pause, break**
	de	We hebben onderweg een kleine pauze genomen.
	[ˈpɑuzə]	-We took a short rest on the way.
1374	**piloot**	**pilot**
	de	John wil piloot worden.
	[piˈlot]	-John wants to be a pilot.
1375	**sigaret**	**cigarette**
	de	Ik heb een sigaret nodig.
	[sixaˈrɛt]	-I need a cigarette.
1376	**winnaar**	**winner**
	de	We hebben de winnaars gekozen!
	[ˈʋɪ.naːr]	-We've picked the winners!
1377	**behandelen**	**treat**
	vb	John behandelt Jane goed.
	[bəˈhɑndələ(n)]	-John treats Jane well.
1378	**aanvallen**	**attacks; attack**
	de; vb	Ik voel me aangevallen.
	[ˈɑnvɑlə(n)]	-I feel attacked.
1379	**medelijden**	**compassion, pity**
	het	Verwar medelijden nooit met liefde.
	[ˈmedəlɛidə(n)]	-Never confuse pity with love.
1380	**opsluiten**	**lock**
	vb	Sluit me alsjeblieft niet op.
	[ˈɔpslœytə(n)]	-Please don't lock me away.
1381	**verhuizen**	**move**
	vb	Laten we naar die tafel verhuizen.
	[vərˈhœyzə(n)]	-Let's move over to that table.
1382	**detective**	**detective**
	de	Zij huurde een privé-detective.
	[diˈtɛktɪf, detɛkˈtivə]	-She hired a private investigator.

1383	**smerig**	**filthy**
	adj	Dat is smerig.
	[ˈsmerəx]	-That's gross.
1384	**militair**	**military; soldier**
	adj; de	Militaire discipline is letterlijk rigide.
	[miliˈtɛːr]	-Military discipline is literally rigid.
1385	**groeien**	**grow**
	vb	Dat land zijn economie is aan het groeien.
	[ˈxrujə(n)]	-That country's economy is growing.
1386	**minister**	**minister**
	de	De eerste minister bracht een formeel bezoek aan het Witte Huis.
	[miˈnɪstər]	-The premier paid a formal visit to the White House.
1387	**stof**	**substance, dust**
	het	Hij gaat je in het stof laten bijten.
	[stɔf]	-He will make you bite the dust.
1388	**bord**	**plate, dish**
	het	Ik zal de borden nog eens afwassen.
	[bɔrt]	-I'll wash the dishes once again.
1389	**voorstel**	**proposal**
	het	Ik kan het voorstel helemaal niet steunen.
	[ˈvorstɛl]	-I absolutely cannot approve the proposal.
1390	**oefenen**	**practice**
	vb	We kunnen John niet zo laat in de nacht op de piano laten oefenen.
	[ˈufənə(n)]	-We can't let John practice piano so late at night.
1391	**buur**	**neighbor**
	de	Een goede buur is beter dan een slecht familielid.
	[byr]	-A good neighbor is better than a bad relative.
1392	**hierin**	**herein**
	adv	Ik dacht dat je hierin wel geïnteresseerd zou zijn.
	[ˈhirɪn]	-I thought you might be interested in this.
1393	**medisch**	**medical**
	adj	De medische benodigdheden raken op.
	[ˈmedis]	-Medical supplies are running out.
1394	**frans**	**French**
	adj	Belgen beweren dat frietjes niet Frans maar Belgisch zijn.
	[frɑns]	-Belgians claim that French fries are not French but Belgian.
1395	**ademen**	**breathe**
	vb	John hield zijn adem in.
	[ˈadəmə(n)]	-John held his breath.
1396	**waarde**	**value**
	de	Je bent goud waard.
	[ˈwardə]	-You're worth gold.
1397	**gouverneur**	**governor**
	de	Rockefeller was gouverneur van New York.
	[xuvərˈnør]	-Rockefeller was governor of New York.
1398	**gas**	**gas**
	het	Er ontsnapte gas uit een barst in de leiding.
	[xɑs]	-Gas was escaping from a crack in the pipe.
1399	**wassen**	**wash; wax**
	vb; adj	Ik stond op het punt mijn haar te wassen.
	[ˈwɑsə(n)]	-I was going to wash my hair.

1400	**touw**	**rope**
	het	Ik hield me stevig aan het touw vast om niet te vallen.
	[tɑu]	-I held on to the rope firmly as not to fall.
1401	**aanwezig**	**present**
	adj	Hij was niet aanwezig op de bijeenkomst.
	[anˈwezəx]	-He was not present at the meeting.
1402	**wegens**	**due to, because of**
	prp	Ik wil dat John gearresteerd wordt wegens moord.
	[ˈwexə(n)s]	-I want John arrested for murder.
1403	**voorbeeld**	**example**
	het	Probeer het goede voorbeeld te geven.
	[ˈvorbelt]	-Try to set a good example.
1404	**kaartje**	**card, ticket**
	het	Ik heb een kaartje nodig.
	[ˈkarcə]	-I need a ticket.
1405	**jeugd**	**youth**
	de	John heeft het graag over zijn jeugd.
	[jøxt]	-John likes talking about his youth.
1406	**reden**	**reason**
	de	Weet jij de reden waarom twee derde van de studenten niet bij de studentenvergadering was?
	[ˈredə(n)]	-Do you know the reason why two-thirds of the students did not attend the student meeting?
1407	**niveau**	**level**
	het	Verlaag je niet naar Johns niveau.
	[niˈvo]	-Don't stoop to John's level.
1408	**nederlands**	**Dutch; Dutch**
	adj; het	Ik begrijp geen Nederlands, omdat het moeilijk is.
	[ˈnedərlan(t)s]	-I don't understand Dutch, because it's difficult.
1409	**ontslag**	**dismissal**
	het	Wegens diefstal werd hij ontslagen.
	[ɔntˈslɑx]	-He was fired for stealing.
1410	**burger**	**citizen**
	de	Een democraat is een vrije burger die de wil van de meerderheid aanvaardt.
	[ˈbʏrxər]	-A democrat is a free citizen who yields to the will of the majority.
1411	**toeval**	**chance**
	het	Hij liet alles aan het toeval over.
	[ˈtuvɑl]	-He left everything to chance.
1412	**stinken**	**stink**
	vb	Deze vieze sokken stinken.
	[ˈstɪŋkə(n)]	-These dirty socks stink.
1413	**bril**	**glasses**
	de	Ik heb mijn bril kapotgemaakt.
	[brɪl]	-I've broken my glasses.
1414	**aanbieden**	**offer**
	vb	Je moet je excuses aanbieden aan John.
	[ˈambidə(n)]	-You must offer your apologies to John.
1415	**klap**	**blow, whack**
	de	John kreeg een klap.
	[klɑp]	-John was smacked.
1416	**keel**	**throat**

	de	Ik kreeg een droge keel.
	[kel]	-My throat went dry.
1417	**magie**	**magic**
	de	Vriendschap is magie.
	[ma'xi]	-Friendship is magic.
1418	**scène**	**scene**
	de	Ze lieten de scène vertraagd zien.
	['sɛ:nə]	-They showed the scene in slow motion.
1419	**koers**	**rate, course, track**
	de	John volgt de goede koers.
	[kurs]	-John follows the right track.
1420	**stroom**	**current, stream, electricity**
	de	De stroom is uitgevallen.
	[strom]	-The power's out.
1421	**graven**	**dig**
	vb	De hond was een put aan het graven.
	['xravə(n)]	-The dog was digging a hole.
1422	**diner**	**dinner**
	het	John zal dineren.
	[di'ne]	-John will have dinner.
1423	**hersens**	**brain**
	de	Mijn hersens doen pijn.
	['hɛrsəns]	-My brain hurts.
1424	**dekking**	**cover**
	de	Ik geef dekking terwijl jij nieuwe munitie haalt.
	['dɛkɪŋ]	-I'll cover you while you get more ammunition for the guns.
1425	**chauffeur**	**driver**
	de	Hou het wisselgeld maar, hoor, chauffeur.
	[ʃo'før]	-Keep the change, driver.
1426	**kist**	**chest**
	de	De nieuwe telescoop werd verstuurd in een enorme houten kist.
	[kɪst]	-The new telescope was shipped in a huge wooden box.
1427	**gezondheid**	**health**
	de	Je bent helemaal gezond.
	[xə'zɔnthɛit]	-You're completely healthy.
1428	**wellicht**	**perhaps**
	adv	John zal wellicht op u wachten.
	['wɛlɪxt, wɛ'lɪxt]	-John will perhaps wait for you.
1429	**omlaag**	**down**
	adv	Doe het deksel omlaag.
	[ɔm'lax]	-Put the lid down.
1430	**terrein**	**terrain**
	het	Dit terrein is goed verlicht.
	[tə'rɛin]	-This terrain is properly lit.
1431	**herkennen**	**recognize**
	vb	John schijnt Jane niet te herkennen.
	[hɛr'kɛnə(n)]	-John doesn't seem to recognize Jane.
1432	**beroep**	**profession**
	het	Wat doet u van beroep?
	[bə'rup]	-What do you do for a living?
1433	**kerstfeest**	**Christmas (party)**

	het [kɛrstfe:st]	Vrolijk kerstfeest! -Merry Christmas!
1434	**ernaar** *adv* [ɛr'nar]	**it, at it, after it** Streef ernaar om alles te vereenvoudigen. -Strive to simplify everything.
1435	**eindigen** *vb* ['ɛindəxə(n)]	**end** Aardige jongens eindigen als laatste. -Nice guys finish last.
1436	**wandelen** *vb* ['wɑndələ(n)]	**walk** Die oude man is, bij wijze van spreken, een wandelend woordenboek. -That old man is, so to speak, a walking dictionary.
1437	**hal** *de* [hɑl]	**hall** Mijn jas hangt in de hal. -My coat is hanging in the hall.
1438	**ongerust** *adj* [ɔnxəˈrʏst]	**anxious, worried** Na een poosje werd ik ongerust. -After a while, I got worried.
1439	**dubbel** *adj* ['dʏbəl]	**double** Jouw boek is dubbel zo groot als dat van mij. -Your book is double the size of mine.
1440	**jongeman** *de* [jɔŋəˈmɑn]	**young man** Deze jongeman heeft blauw haar. -This young man has blue hair.
1441	**toegeven** *vb* ['tuxevə(n)]	**admit** John wilde zijn fout niet toegeven. -John wouldn't admit his mistake.
1442	**momenteel** *adv* [momɛnˈtel]	**currently, at the moment** Ik woon momenteel in Tampa. -I live in Tampa at the moment.
1443	**noch** *con* [nɔx]	**nor** Hij schreef noch telefoneerde. -He neither wrote nor telephoned.
1444	**centrum** *het* ['sɛntrʏm]	**center** Welke trein gaat naar het centrum? -What train goes to the center of town?
1445	**wolf** *de* [wɔlf]	**wolf** De vrees maakt de wolf groter dan wat hij is. -The fear makes the wolf bigger than what it is.
1446	**duitser** *de* ['dœytsər]	**German** Duitsers zijn gewaarschuwd om geen komkommers te eten. -Germans have been warned not to eat cucumbers.
1447	**binden** *vb* ['bɪndə(n)]	**bind** We binden hem niet zo goed vast. -We do not tie him up well.
1448	**zwembad** *het* ['zwɛmbɑt]	**swimming pool** John is in het zwembad van zijn buur vedronken. -John drowned in his neighbor's pool.
1449	**poort** *de* [port]	**port** Haar vriend wachtte op haar bij de poort. -Her friend waited for her by the gate.
1450	**onthouden**	**remember**

	vb		Hij heeft moeite om namen te onthouden.
	[ɔntˈhɑudə(n)]		-He has trouble remembering names.
1451	**geur**		**smell**
	de		De geur van gemaaid gras roept beelden op van hete zomermiddagen.
	[xør]		-The smell of cut grass summons up images of hot summer afternoons.
1452	**theorie**		**theory**
	de		Het is niet mogelijk hem de nieuwe theorie te laten begrijpen.
	[tejoˈri]		-It is impossible to get him to understand the new theory.
1453	**geheugen**		**memory**
	het		Je hebt een goed geheugen.
	[xəˈhøxə(n)]		-You have a good memory.
1454	**benzine**		**petrol, gasoline**
	de		Mijn auto verbruikt veel benzine.
	[bɛnˈzinə]		-My car burns a lot of gas.
1455	**vals**		**FALSE**
	adj		Hij heeft een vals paspoort.
	[ˈvɑls]		-He has a false passport.
1456	**leugen**		**lie**
	de		Zij kan zonder blikken of blozen de meest schandalige leugen vertellen.
	[ˈløxə(n)]		-She can tell the most outrageous lie without batting an eye.
1457	**genie**		**genius**
	het		Edison was een genie.
	[ʒəˈni]		-Edison was a genius.
1458	**vanmiddag**		**this afternoon**
	adv		Laat ons vanmiddag gaan tennissen.
	[vaˈmɪdɑx]		-Let's play tennis this afternoon.
1459	**spiegel**		**mirror**
	de		John heeft voor de spiegel geoefend.
	[ˈspixəl]		-John practiced in front of the mirror.
1460	**opzoeken**		**visit**
	vb		Hij kwam me de morgen van de 15de mei opzoeken.
	[ˈɔpsukə(n)]		-He came to see me on the morning of May 15.
1461	**vijftien**		**fifteen**
	nu		Dit kostte minder dan vijftien dollar.
	[ˈvɛiftin]		-It was less than fifteen dollars.
1462	**herhalen**		**repeat**
	vb		Kunt u dat herhalen?
	[hɛrˈhalə(n)]		-Could you repeat that again?
1463	**waardeloos**		**worthless**
	adj		Deze website is waardeloos.
	[ˈwardəlos]		-This website is useless.
1464	**smeken**		**beg**
	vb		Ik smeek het je, geef me een fles.
	[ˈsmekə(n)]		-I beg you, give me a bottle!
1465	**markt**		**market**
	de		Mijn moeder gaat elke dag naar de markt om dingen te kopen.
	[mɑrkt]		-My mother goes to the market every day to buy things.
1466	**verloven**		**commit, betroth**
	vb		Ik kan me nu niet verloven.
	[fərloufə]		-I can't get engaged right now.
1467	**mogelijkheid**		**possibility**

	de	De enige mogelijkheid is via het afvalkanaal.
	['mɔxələkhɛit]	-The only possibility is through the waste disposal system.
1468	**veroorzaken**	**cause**
	vb	Koolstofmonoxidevergiftiging kan hallucinaties veroorzaken.
	[vər'orzakə(n)]	-Carbon monoxide poisoning can cause hallucinations.
1469	**blijken**	**prove**
	vb	Een alliantie tegen onze gezamenlijke vijand kan heel nuttig blijken.
	['blɛikə(n)]	-An alliance against our common enemy would prove extremely useful.
1470	**proosten**	**toast**
	vb	Proost! Ouwe dronkelap!
	['prostə(n)]	-Cheers! You old drunkard!
1471	**overwinning**	**victory**
	de	Overwinning is onwaarschijnlijk, maar mogelijk.
	[ovər'wɪnɪŋ]	-Victory is unlikely but not impossible.
1472	**vervangen**	**substitute, replace**
	vb	Ik probeer haar niet te vervangen.
	[vər'vaŋə(n)]	-Well, I'm not trying to replace her.
1473	**handel**	**trade, act**
	de	Nu dat je beslist hebt, moet je ook handelen.
	['handəl]	-Now that you have made your decision, you must act.
1474	**welnee**	**surely not**
	prt	Welnee, ik trakteer je op een drankje.
	[velne:j]	-Not at all. I am buying you a drink.
1475	**herinnering**	**reminder**
	de	Stuur me een herinnering
	[hɛr'ɪnərɪŋ]	-Send me a reminder.
1476	**verdediging**	**defense**
	de	Aanval is de beste verdediging.
	[vər'dedəxɪŋ]	-The attack is the best form of defense.
1477	**bevelen**	**order, command**
	vb	Jouw wens is mijn bevel.
	[bə'velə(n)]	-Your wishes are my commands.
1478	**verandering**	**change**
	de	Verander de vlag, alsjeblieft.
	[vər'andərɪŋ]	-Change the flag, please.
1479	**pizza**	**pizza**
	de	Houden jullie van pizza?
	['pitsa]	-Do you like pizza?
1480	**braaf**	**good**
	adj	Dat is een brave hond.
	[braf]	-That's a good dog.
1481	**dienen**	**serve**
	vb	Dien alstublieft zijn maaltijd eerst op.
	['dinə(n)]	-Please serve him his meal first.
1482	**beroemd**	**famous**
	adj	Ik denk dat John nooit beroemd zal worden.
	[bə'rumt]	-I think John will never become famous.
1483	**wc**	**toilet**
	de	Ik moet nodig plassen en kan geen wc vinden.
	[we'se]	-I'm bursting for a wee and I can't find a bathroom.
1484	**gave**	**gift**

	de	Lionel Messi heeft een gave.
	['xavə]	-Lionel Messi has a gift.
1485	**daardoor**	**thereby, therefore**
	adv	De traditionele zure roomkazen zijn daardoor in het nadeel.
	[dar'dor]	-Obviously the traditional sour milk cheeses are therefore at a disadvantage.
1486	**ramp**	**disaster**
	de	Zijn speech was een regelrechte ramp.
	[rɑmp]	-His speech was an unmitigated disaster.
1487	**pensioen**	**pension**
	het	De oude man leeft van zijn pensioen.
	[pɛn'ʃun]	-The old man lives on his pension.
1488	**russisch**	**Russian; Russian**
	adj; het	Ik spreek Engels en Russisch.
	['rʏsis]	-I speak English and Russian.
1489	**geheel**	**whole; whole; entirely**
	adj; het; adv	Hij werkt de gehele nacht en slaapt de gehele dag.
	[xə'hel]	-He works all night and he sleeps all day.
1490	**bescherming**	**protection**
	de	John kan mij bescherming geven.
	[bə'sxɛrmɪŋ]	-John can give me protection.
1491	**jacht**	**hunt, yacht**
	de, het	De baai heeft meer jachten dan zeilboten.
	[jɑxt]	-The bay has more yachts than sailboats.
1492	**wetenschap**	**science**
	de	Ik hou niet van wetenschap.
	['wetənsxɑp]	-I do not like science.
1493	**nationaal**	**national**
	adj	De nationale vlag van de VS heeft sterren.
	[na(t)ʃo'nal]	-The national flag of the USA contains stars.
1494	**daarin**	**therein**
	adv	Alle gegevens daarin zijn waarschijnlijk verloren.
	[dar'ɪn]	-All data in there is likely lost.
1495	**duwen**	**push**
	vb	Laten we vooruit duwen.
	['dywə(n)]	-Let's push on.
1496	**geregeld**	**regular**
	adj	Ik kom hier geregeld.
	[xə'rexəlt]	-I come here regularly.
1497	**interesse**	**interest**
	de	John toont interesse in Jane.
	[ɪntə'rɛsə]	-John shows interest in Jane.
1498	**vuren**	**fire**
	vb	Van dichtbij vuurde hij nog tweemaal.
	['vyrə(n)]	-He fired twice more from close up.
1499	**verbinden**	**link**
	vb	De nieuwe tunnel zal Groot-Brittannië verbinden met Frankrijk.
	[vər'bɪndə(n)]	-The new tunnel will link Great Britain and France.
1500	**bovendien**	**besides, moreover**
	adv	Bekeken van de zijkant, steken de tanden bovendien naar voren.
	[bovən'din]	-Moreover, when viewed from the side, the front teeth are protruding.
1501	**gegeven**	**given; given**

	adj; het	Op een gegeven moment ging ik naar huis.
	[xəˈxevə(n)]	-I went home at a given moment.
1502	**aanbod**	**offer**
	het	Dit is mijn laatste aanbod. Graag of niet.
	[ˈambɔt]	-This is my final offer. Take it or leave it.
1503	**verslag**	**report**
	het	Het doel van dit verslag is alle voor- en nadelen van dat voorstel te onderzoeken.
	[vərˈslɑx]	-The goal of this report is to research all the pros and cons of the proposal.
1504	**winter**	**winter**
	de	Heb je afgelopen winter geskied?
	[ˈwɪntər]	-Did you ski last winter?
1505	**tegelijk**	**at the same time**
	adv	Men kan niet op twee plaatsen tegelijk zijn.
	[təxəˈlɛik]	-You can't be at two places at once.
1506	**walgelijk**	**disgusting**
	adj	Johns keuken is walgelijk.
	[ˈwɑlxələk]	-John's kitchen is disgusting.
1507	**garage**	**garage**
	de	Johns garage zit vol met dingen die hij nooit gebruikt.
	[xaˈraʒə]	-John's garage is full of things he never uses.
1508	**omstandigheid**	**circumstance**
	de	Hij beschreef de omstandigheden in detail.
	[ɔmˈstandəxhɛit]	-He described the circumstances in detail.
1509	**zielig**	**pathetic**
	adj	Dit is gek en verschrikkelijk zielig.
	[ˈzilax]	-This is crazy and disgustingly pathetic
1510	**uniform**	**uniform**
	het	We moeten een uniform dragen op school.
	[ˈynifɔrm]	-We have to wear school uniforms at school.
1511	**waarschuwen**	**warn**
	vb	Ik waarschuw je.
	[ˈwarsxywə(n)]	-I warn you.
1512	**optreden**	**perform, appear**
	vb	Er kunnen overlappingen optreden.
	[ˈɔptredə(n)]	-Overlap can occur.
1513	**onderwerp**	**subject, topic**
	het	Het is de moeite waard dit onderwerp te bespreken.
	[ˈɔndərwɛrp]	-The topic is worth discussing.
1514	**meedoen**	**participate**
	vb	Kom maar meedoen.
	[ˈmedun]	-Join us.
1515	**ellende**	**misery**
	de	Dit is meer ellende dan ik kan verdragen.
	[ɛˈlɛndə]	-This misery is more than I can bear.
1516	**accepteren**	**accept**
	vb	Ik zal zijn verzoek accepteren.
	[aksɛpˈterə(n)]	-I will accept his request.
1517	**pop**	**doll**
	de	Het meisje maakte een pop van een stukje stof.
	[pɔp]	-The girl made a doll out of a piece of cloth.

1518	**fabriek**		**factory**
	de		Deze fabriek is volledig geautomatiseerd.
	[fa'brik]		-This factory is fully-automated.
1519	**lied**		**song**
	het		Je kunt een lied zingen.
	[lit]		-You can sing a song.
1520	**ophangen**		**hang**
	vb		Zeg haar, dat ik de was ophang.
	['ɔphaŋə(n)]		-Tell her that I am pegging up the washing.
1521	**verenigen**		**unite**
	vb		Ze hebben ook geholpen het land te verenigen.
	[vər'enəxə(n)]		-They also helped unite the country.
1522	**melden**		**report**
	vb		Ik meld me af, ik ga een douche nemen.
	['mɛldə(n)]		-Signing off, gonna take a shower.
1523	**rechtbank**		**court**
	de		Deze rechtbank had vandaag een opmerkelijke ervaring.
	['rɛx(t)baŋk]		-This court has had a remarkable experience today.
1524	**lijf**		**body**
	het		Heb je gezien hoeveel deze telefoon kost? Dat is een rib uit mijn lijf!
	[lɛif]		-Did you see how much this phone costs? It costs an arm and a leg!
1525	**aangezien**		**since**
	con		Aangezien je geen kind meer bent zou je verantwoordelijk moeten zijn voor wat je doet.
	[anxə'zin]		-Since you are no longer a child, you should be responsible for what you do.
1526	**geliefd**		**beloved**
	adj		De oude man was geliefd bij iedereen.
	[xə'lift]		-The old man was loved by everyone.
1527	**training**		**workout, training**
	de		John heeft training nodig.
	['trenɪŋ]		-John needs training.
1528	**plegen**		**commit**
	vb		Hij probeerde zelfmoord te plegen.
	['plexə(n)]		-He tried to commit suicide himself.
1529	**rat**		**rat**
	de		Katten doden ratten.
	[rɑt]		-Cats kill rats.
1530	**zacht**		**soft; gently**
	adj; adv		Zachte heelmeesters maken stinkende wonden.
	[zɑxt]		-Soft healers make stinking wounds.
1531	**artikel**		**article**
	het		Het artikel is authentiek.
	[ar'tikəl]		-The article is genuine.
1532	**ontvoeren**		**kidnap**
	vb		We moeten hem bestelen en ontvoeren.
	[ɔnt'furə(n)]		-We should rob and kidnap him.
1533	**partij**		**party**
	de		Voor de partij doe ik dat graag.
	[par'tɛi]		-It is a pleasure to do it for the party.
1534	**verderop**		**further ahead**
	adv		Ietsje verderop is een parkeerplaats.

[vɛrdər'ɔp]
  -There's a parking space a little further ahead.

1535 plannen
vb
['plɛnə(n)]
plan
We plannen een trip naar New York.
  -We are planning a trip to New York.

1536 mensheid
de
['mɛnshɛit]
humanity
De ontdekking van een nieuw soort maaltijd brengt de mensheid meer dan de ontdekking van een nieuwe ster.
  -The discovery of a new type of meal contributes more to humankind than the discovery of a new star.

1537 kaas
de
[kas]
cheese
Hij heeft boter en kaas.
  -He has butter and cheese.

1538 bruid
de
[brœyt]
bride
Zij is een bruid.
  -She's a bride.

1539 vies
adj; adv
[vis]
dirty; nastily
Dit vlees ruikt vies.
  -This meat smells bad.

1540 kasteel
het
[kas'tel]
castle
Het kasteel is aan de andere kant van de rivier.
  -The castle is across the river.

1541 vijftig
nu
['fɛiftəx]
fifty
Op de Amerikaanse vlag staan vijftig sterren.
  -There are fifty stars in the American flag.

1542 schaduw
de
['sxadyw]
shadow
Laat ons even in de schaduw uitrusten.
  -Let's take a rest in the shade.

1543 marine
de
[ma'rinə]
navy
De marine wilde m'n verhaal horen.
  -The Navy wanted to hear my story.

1544 belofte
de
[bə'lɔftə]
promise
John heeft zijn belofte niet gehouden.
  -John didn't keep his promise.

1545 lip
de
[lɪp]
lip
Je hebt iets op je lip.
  -You've got something on your lip.

1546 vanochtend
adv
[van'ɔxtənt]
this morning
Mijn oor bloedde vanochtend.
  -My ear was bleeding this morning.

1547 redelijk
adj; adv
['redələk]
reasonable; reasonably
Er waren redelijk wat leerlingen niet in de les vandaag.
  -A reasonable amount of students were absent from class today.

1548 uiteraard
adv
[œytər'art]
naturally
Het is uiteraard niet de bedoeling dat je in je schoolboek schrijft.
  -Of course, you are not supposed to write in your textbook.

1549 douche
de
[duʃ]
shower
Ik douche liever 's morgens.
  -I prefer to take a shower in the morning.

1550 logisch
adj
['loxis]
logical
Zijn antwoord was logisch.
  -His reply was logical.

1551	**komst**	**arrival**
	de	De orkaan Sandy is op komst.
	[kɔmst]	-Hurricane Sandy is coming.
1552	**heks**	**witch**
	de	Ik ben geen heks.
	[hɛks]	-I am not a witch.
1553	**voorlopig**	**temporary; for the time being**
	adj; adv	Dat is voorlopig genoeg.
	[vor'lopəx]	-This will do for now.
1554	**materiaal**	**material**
	het	Ik wil een pak gemaakt van dit materiaal.
	[matəri'jal]	-I want a suit made of this material.
1555	**cheque**	**check**
	de	Ik wil met een cheque betalen.
	[ʃɛk]	-I'd like to pay by check.
1556	**ontzettend**	**tremendous; enormously**
	adj; adv	Ik heb ontzettende hoofdpijn!
	[ɔnt'sɛtənt]	-I have a terrible headache!
1557	**voort**	**on**
	adv	Zet je werk voort.
	[vort]	-Carry on with your work.
1558	**meerdere**	**superior; multiple**
	de; adv	Het woord heeft meerdere betekenissen.
	['merdərə]	-The word has several meanings.
1559	**maag**	**stomach**
	de	Mijn maag doet pijn.
	[max]	-My stomach hurts.
1560	**bewaren**	**keep**
	vb	Kunnen jullie een geheim bewaren?
	[bəwarə(n)]	-Can you keep a secret?
1561	**toestand**	**state**
	de	De toestand van John wordt gecompliceerder.
	['tustɑnt]	-John's situation is getting more complicated.
1562	**jood**	**Jew**
	de	Zo joods ben ik ook weer niet, ook al ben ik een jood.
	[jout]	-I'm not that Jewish, even though I am a Jew.
1563	**dwars**	**contrary, across**
	adj	De boom ligt dwars over straat.
	[dwɑrs]	-The three lies across the road
1564	**nicht**	**niece**
	de	Ik ben je nicht.
	[nɪxt]	-I am your cousin.
1565	**klok**	**clock**
	de	Zet de klok goed. Hij loopt tien minuten voor.
	[klɔk]	-Set the clock right. It's ten minutes fast.
1566	**onszelf**	**ourselves**
	prn	Me moeten ermee ophouden onszelf te bedriegen.
	[ɔn'sɛlf]	-We can't keep on fooling ourselves.
1567	**slang**	**hose, snake**
	de	Ik hou niet van spinnen en slangen.
	[slɑŋ]	-I don't like spiders and snakes.

1568	**branden**	**burn**
	vb	De bossen branden gemakkelijk.
	[ˈbrɑndə(n)]	-Woods burn easily.
1569	**kleden**	**dress**
	vb	Hij baadde en kleedde zich aan.
	[ˈkledə(n)]	-He bathed and dressed.
1570	**minstens**	**at least**
	adv	Je moet minstens twee keer per dag je tanden poetsen.
	[ˈmɪnstəns]	-You should brush your teeth at least twice a day.
1571	**reputatie**	**reputation**
	de	John heeft een slechte reputatie.
	[repyˈta(t)si]	-John has a bad reputation.
1572	**junior**	**junior; minor**
	de; adj	Dan eindig je zoals junior daar.
	[ˈjynijɔr]	-Then you end up like Junior over there.
1573	**overtuigen**	**convince**
	vb	Dat is een overtuigende uitleg.
	[ovərˈtœyxə(n)]	-That's a convincing explanation.
1574	**diegene**	**he, she, those who**
	prn	Ik ben diegene die John vermoord heeft.
	[ˈdixenə]	-I'm the one who killed John.
1575	**cijfer**	**figure, grade, numeral**
	het	Mijn cijfers zijn hoger dan gemiddeld.
	[ˈsɛifər]	-My grades are above average.
1576	**voorbereiden**	**prepare**
	vb	Is voor morgen alles voorbereid?
	[ˈvorbərɛidə(n)]	-Is everything arranged for tomorrow?
1577	**masker**	**mask**
	het	Niemand herkent haar met dit masker.
	[ˈmɑskər]	-No one will recognize her in this mask.
1578	**ambulance**	**ambulance**
	de	John was dood tegen de tijd dat de ambulance aankwam.
	[ɑmbyˈlãsə]	-John was dead by the time the ambulance got there.
1579	**dek**	**deck**
	het	Op het deck in de zon.
	[dɛk]	-In the sun on the deck.
1580	**sneeuw**	**snow**
	de	Eet sneeuw. Maar niet de gele sneeuw.
	[snew]	-Eat snow. But don't eat the yellow snow.
1581	**waarschuwing**	**warning**
	de	John negeerde Jane's waarschuwing.
	[ˈwarsxywɪŋ]	-John ignored Jane's warning.
1582	**rus**	**Russian**
	de	Kijk naar die rus.
	[rʏs]	-Look at that Russian.
1583	**hekel**	**dislike**
	de	Hij heeft een hekel aan hardlopen.
	[ˈhekəl]	-He hates running.
1584	**reactie**	**reaction**
	de	Wat was Johns reactie op het nieuws?
	[reˈjɑksi]	-What was John's reaction to the news?

1585	**verdriet**	**grief**
	het	John wist dat ik verdrietig was.
	[vər'drit]	-John knew that I was sad.
1586	**bijbel**	**Bible**
	de	De Bijbel is duidelijk een complex geschrift, dat onmogelijk door één auteur geschreven kan zijn.
	['bɛibəl]	-The Bible is clearly a complex piece of writing that could not possibly have been written by a single author.
1587	**mijl**	**mile**
	de	John rijdt zestig mijlen per uur op de snelweg om brandstof te besparen.
	[mɛil]	-John drives at sixty miles an hour on the highway in order to save fuel.
1588	**tunnel**	**tunnel**
	de	De trein ging door een tunnel.
	['tʏnəl]	-The train went through a tunnel.
1589	**gelden**	**be valid**
	vb	Dat geldt niet meer
	['xɛldə(n)]	-That is not valid anymore.
1590	**kou(de)**	**cold**
	de	Deze morgen was het bitter koud.
	[kʌu(də)]	-This morning it was very cold.
1591	**lossen**	**unload**
	vb	Laden en lossen.
	['lɔsə(n)]	-Loading and unloading.
1592	**pen**	**pen**
	de	Deze pen schrijft niet goed.
	[pɛn]	-This pen doesn't write well.
1593	**graaf**	**count**
	de	Hij wordt graaf en krijgt landgoederen.
	[xraf]	-He will be made count and given estates.
1594	**kleding**	**clothing**
	de	Hij gaf ons niet alleen kleding, maar ook wat geld.
	['kledɪŋ]	-He gave us not only clothes but some money.
1595	**hieruit**	**from this**
	adv	Hieruit kan geconcludeerd worden dat het feminisme nog steeds nodig is.
	['hirœyt]	-From this you can conclude that feminism is still necessary.
1596	**vriendschap**	**friendship**
	de	Niets is belangrijker dan vriendschap.
	['vrintsxap]	-There is nothing more important than friendship.
1597	**chinees**	**Chinese; Chinese**
	adj; de	Ik hou echt van Chinees eten.
	[ʃi'nes]	-I really like Chinese food.
1598	**plotseling**	**suddenly; sudden**
	adv; adj	Plotseling ging het brandalarm af.
	['plɔtsəlɪŋ]	-All of a sudden, the fire alarm went off.
1599	**middag**	**noon**
	de	Wat doe je 's middags?
	['mɪdɑx]	-What do you do in the afternoon?
1600	**filmen**	**film**
	vb	Jullie filmen alles wat ik doe.
	['fɪlmə(n)]	-You film everything I do.
1601	**opeten**	**eat**

	vb [ˈɔpetə(n)]	Ik heb zoveel honger dat ik een koe kon opeten. -I am so hungry that I could eat a cow.
1602	**stand** de [stɑnt]	**position** De stand van de zon. -The position of the sun.
1603	**daarover** adv [darˈovər]	**about it** Ik herinner me dat ik daarover iets gelezen heb. -I remember reading about it.
1604	**amper** adv [ˈɑmpər]	**barely** Uw ideeën zijn amper praktisch. -Your ideas are hardly practical.
1605	**virus** het [ˈvirʏs]	**virus** Een virus heeft Johns computer besmet. -A virus infected John's computer.
1606	**invloed** de [ˈɪnvlut]	**influence** De fantasie heeft invloed op alle facetten van ons leven. -Imagination affects every aspect of our lives.
1607	**daarbuiten** adv [daːrbajtə]	**outside** Ze leken op je vriendjes daarbuiten. -They looked a lot like your friends outside.
1608	**schande** de [ˈsxɑndə]	**shame** Arm zijn is geen schande. -There is no shame in being poor.
1609	**daarbij** adv [darˈbɛi]	**thereby** Laten we het daarbij laten voor nu. -Let's leave it at that for now.
1610	**winst** de [wɪnst]	**profit** Een kleine winst is beter dan een groot verlies. -A small profit is better than a great loss.
1611	**gemeenschap** de [xəˈmensxɑp]	**community** John is in de LGBT gemeenschap. -John is in the LGBT community.
1612	**kruis** het [krœys]	**cross** Zij deed veel vrijwilligerswerk voor het Rode Kruis. -She did a lot of voluntary work for the Red Cross.
1613	**oppakken** vb [ˈɔpakə(n)]	**take up** Eén vinger kan geen kiezelsteen oppakken. -One finger can't pick up a pebble.
1614	**teruggaan** vb [təˈrʏxan]	**return** Ik wou dat ik kon teruggaan en de dingen anders doen. -I often wish I could go back and do things differently.
1615	**tank** de [tɛŋk]	**tank** Mijn tank vullen. -To fill up my tank.
1616	**hek** het [hɛk]	**fence** John heeft het hek gerepareerd. -John fixed the fence.
1617	**acteur** de [aktø:r]	**actor** De acteur had een geschil met zijn directeur. -The actor had a dispute with his director.
1618	**dwaas**	**silly; fool; foolishly**

adj; de; adv
[dwas]

Ik ben zo'n dwaas.
-I'm such a fool.

1619 **trainen**
vb; het
['trenə(n)]

train; training
Je moet blijven trainen.
-You must continue to train.

1620 **golf**
de
[gɔlf, xɔlf]

golf, wave
Men zegt dat golf erg populair is in Japan.
-They say that golf is very popular in Japan.

1621 **snijden**
vb; het
['snɛidə(n)]

cut; slicing
Ik heb mezelf gesneden.
-I cut myself.

1622 **teleurstellen**
vb
[təˈlørstɛlə(n)]

disappoint
Zijn nieuwe film is teleurstellend.
-His new movie is disappointing.

1623 **bleek**
adj; adv
[blek]

pale; wanly
Toen hij het nieuws hoorde, werd hij bleek.
-Hearing the news, he turned pale.

1624 **voordeel**
het
['vordel]

advantage
Het was een voordeel dat ik Chinees geleerd had toen ik op school zat.
-It was an advantage, having learned Chinese while I was in school.

1625 **bewaker**
de
[bəˈwakər]

guard
Een bewaker zat met zijn benen gekruist.
-A watchman sat with his legs crossed.

1626 **gezellig**
adj; adv
[xəˈzɛləx]

cozy; cozily
Het is niet zo gezellig als thuis.
-It's not as cozy as our house.

1627 **koninkrijk**
het
['konıŋkrɛik]

kingdom
Bahrein werd een koninkrijk in 2002.
-Bahrain became a kingdom in 2002.

1628 **helikopter**
de
[heliˈkɔptər]

helicopter
Hij weet hoe een helikopter te besturen.
-He knows how to fly a helicopter.

1629 **hout**
het
[hɑut]

wood
Al het speelgoed is van hout.
-All of the toys are wooden.

1630 **commissaris**
de
[kɔmıˈsarıs]

commissioner
Ik was het niet, commissaris!
-It wasn't me, commissioner!

1631 **duisternis**
de
['dœystərnıs]

darkness
Dan staat u de duisternis te wachten.
-You will be waiting in the darkness.

1632 **grootvader**
de
['xrotfadər]

grandfather
We noemden hem John, naar zijn grootvader.
-We named him John, after his grandfather.

1633 **meegaan**
vb
['mexan]

come
John moest met ons meegaan, maar hij kwam niet opdagen.
-John was supposed to come with us, but he didn't show up.

1634 **achterin**
adv
[ɑxtərˈın]

in the back
Jullie kunnen de bedden achterin gebruiken.
-There are some cots in the back you could use.

1635 **richten**

direct, aim

vb	Laten we ons richten op onze overeenkomsten.
[ˈrɪxtə(n)]	-Let's focus on what we have in common.
1636 legende	**legend**
de	Volgens de legende ontving hij persoonlijk zijn zwaard van de goden.
[ləˈxɛndə]	-The legend says he received his sword from the hands of the gods themselves.
1637 afsluiten	**close**
verb	Ik wou afsluiten met Winter Mist.
[ˈɑfslœytə(n)]	-I'd like to close with this piece, "Winter Mist".
1638 brits	**british**
adj	De Britse regering was kwaad.
[brɪts]	-The British government was angry.
1639 televisie	**television**
de	Kranten, televisie en radio heten massamedia.
[teləˈvizi]	-Newspapers, television, and radio are called mass media.
1640 beloning	**reward**
de	Elke inspanning verdient een beloning.
[bəˈlonɪŋ]	-Every effort deserves a reward.
1641 poging	**attempt**
de	Is dit een vroege poging om een cake te maken?
[ˈpoxɪŋ]	-Is this an early attempt at cake making?
1642 hut	**cabin**
de	Ja, de hut wordt bewaakt.
[hʏt]	-Yes, the cabin is being guarded.
1643 live	**on air**
adj	Ik ga zo live, Sherry.
[lɑjf]	-I'm about to go on air, Sherry.
1644 model	**model**
het	Lieveling, kijk eens naar dat model.
[moˈdɛl]	-Darling, you should look at this model.
1645 zegen	**blessing**
de;	Zo niet, betekent mijn zegen niks.
[ˈzexə(n)]	-If you're wrong, my blessing won't mean anything.
1646 suiker	**sugar**
de	John mengt bloem met suiker.
[ˈsœykər]	-John is mixing flour with sugar.
1647 vet	**fat**
het	Spek zit vol met vet.
[vɛt]	-Bacon is full of fat.
1648 voldoende	**satisfactory; sufficient**
adj; de	Eén taal is nooit voldoende.
[vɔlˈdundə]	-One language is never enough.
1649 daarbinnen	**in there**
adv	Die zwarte vrouw daarbinnen is heel belangrijk.
[da:rbinə]	-That's a very important black lady in there.
1650 wijzen	**point**
vb	Ik ben verdwaald. Kan je me de weg wijzen naar het station?
[ˈwɛizə(n)]	-I'm lost. Could you direct me to the station?
1651 woede	**rage**
de	Vol met woede doodde John zijn eigen broer.
[ˈwudə]	-Filled with anger, John killed his own brother.

1652	**sport**	**sport**
	de	Sommige mensen houden van sport, andere niet.
	[spɔrt]	-Some people like sports, and others don't.
1653	**ontspannen**	**relax**
	vb	Hoe kan ik me ontspannen voelen, als jij zo naar mij kijkt.
	[ɔntˈspanə(n)]	-How can I feel relaxed, with you watching me like that?
1654	**middernacht**	**midnight**
	de	Deze overeenkomst treedt om middernacht in kracht.
	[mɪdərˈnɑxt]	-This agreement becomes valid at midnight.
1655	**hartstikke**	**terribly**
	adv	John, ik ben hartstikke bang.
	[ˈhɑrtstɪkə]	-John, I'm terribly scared.
1656	**diamant**	**diamond**
	de	Deze diamant kost een fortuin.
	[dijaˈmɑnt]	-This diamond costs a fortune.
1657	**fan**	**fan**
	de	De fans juichten.
	[fɛn]	-The fans cheered.
1658	**dringen**	**push**
	vb	Het is niet goed om onze denkbeelden aan anderen op te dringen.
	[ˈdrɪŋə(n)]	-It's not good to force our ideas on others.
1659	**verschuldigd**	**indebted**
	adj	Nick is mij tien dollar verschuldigd.
	[vərˈsxʏldəxt]	-Nick owes me ten dollars.
1660	**verrassen**	**surprise**
	vb	Jongens, ik zal jullie verrassen.
	[vərˈɑsə(n)]	-Guys, I will surprise you.
1661	**verzet**	**resistance**
	het	Het hele verzet moest leren liplezen.
	[vərˈzɛt]	-Everyone in the resistance had to learn to lip-read.
1662	**klasse**	**class**
	de	De werkende klasse is groot.
	[ˈklɑsə]	-The working class is big.
1663	**daarboven**	**up there**
	adv	Hoe ben je daarboven gekomen?
	[darˈbovə(n)]	-How did you get up there?
1664	**uitzien**	**look**
	vb	Ik wil er rijk uitzien.
	[ˈœytsin]	-I want to look rich.
1665	**april**	**April**
	de	Het is één april.
	[aˈprɪl]	-It's April first.
1666	**theater**	**theater**
	het	Ik ben uit het theater verbannen.
	[teˈjatər]	-I'm banned from the theater.
1667	**nul**	**zero**
	het	Het standaardbedrag is nul.
	[nʏl]	-The default value is zero.
1668	**mamma**	**mum**
	de	Ik moet mamma even alleen spreken.
	[ˈmama]	-I need to talk to mommy alone for a second.

1669	**kanker**		**cancer**
	de		De man stierf aan kanker.
	[ˈkaŋkər]		-The man died of cancer.
1670	**fort**		**fortress**
	het		We zijn een fort.
	[fɔrt]		-We are a fortress.
1671	**ogenblik**		**moment**
	het		Voor het ogenblik ben ik op dieet.
	[ˈoxə(n)blɪk]		-I'm on a diet at the moment.
1672	**eventjes**		**momentarily**
	adv		Wacht eventjes.
	[ˈevə(n)cəs]		-Wait a minute.
1673	**hierover**		**hereof**
	adv		Spreek hierover met niemand.
	[ˈhirovər]		-Don't tell anyone this.
1674	**ruilen**		**exchange**
	vb		Ik zou graag dit hemd, dat ik gisteren gekocht heb, ruilen.
	[rœylə(n)]		-I would like to exchange this shirt that I bought yesterday.
1675	**scherp**		**sharp**
	adj		Ik heb een scherpe pijn in mijn borstkas.
	[sxɛrp]		-I have a sharp pain in my chest.
1676	**baseren**		**base**
	vb		Waar is dat precies op gebaseerd?
	[baze:jrə(n)]		-That is based on what exactly?
1677	**personeel**		**staff**
	het		Uitsluitend personeel.
	[pɛrsoˈnel]		-Staff members only.
1678	**zijde**		**side**
	de		Hoeveel kost een meter van deze rode zijde?
	[ˈzɛidə]		-How much is a meter of this red silk?
1679	**overval**		**raid, robbery**
	de		Die jongens gingen een overval plegen.
	[ˈovərval]		-Well, these guys were going to commit a robbery.
1680	**gras**		**grass**
	het		Het gras aan de andere kant is altijd groener.
	[xrɑs]		-The grass is always greener on the other side.
1681	**assistent**		**assistant**
	de		John zegt me dat je zijn assistent bent.
	[asisˈtɛnt]		-John tells me you're his assistant.
1682	**lunchen**		**lunch**
	vb		Waar ga je vandaag lunchen?
	[ˈlʏnʃə(n)]		-Where will you have lunch today?
1683	**lafaard**		**coward**
	de		Je bent een lafaard.
	[ˈlɑfart]		-You're a coward.
1684	**briljant**		**brilliant**
	adj		Wie heeft dat briljante artikel geschreven?
	[brɪlˈjant]		-Who wrote that brilliant article?
1685	**allerlei**		**all kinds of**
	prn		Ik heb met allerlei muzikanten gezongen.
	[ˈɑlərlɛi]		-I've sung with all kinds of musicians.

1686	**groots**	**grand, great**
	adj	Dit boek is van groot nut voor ons.
	[xrots]	-This book is of great use to us.
1687	**roze**	**pink**
	adj	John nam een paar roze rozen.
	['rɔːzə]	-John took some pink roses.
1688	**namelijk**	**namely**
	adv	Daarvoor bestaat een oplossing, namelijk onafhankelijke controle.
	['naməlak]	-There is a solution to this, namely independent supervision.
1689	**zand**	**sand**
	het	Wie vandaag zijn kop in het zand steekt, knarst morgen met zijn tanden.
	[zɑnt]	-He who buries his head in the sand today will grind his teeth tomorrow.
1690	**voorzitter**	**chairman**
	de	John, voorzitter van de club, zal spoedig komen.
	['vorzɪtər]	-John, chairman of the club, will soon come.
1691	**maal**	**time; meal**
	de; het	Hij begon de universiteit nadat hij twee maal gezakt was in de examens.
	[mal]	-He entered the university after failing the examination twice.
1692	**geschenk**	**gift**
	het	Ik neem geschenken aan.
	[xəˈsxɛŋk]	-I accept gifts.
1693	**rommel**	**clutter**
	de	Ik kan tegen een rommelig huis, maar ik houd er niet van als het vies is.
	['rɔməl]	-I can put up with a house being untidy, but I don't like it to be dirty.
1694	**daarop**	**thereon**
	adv	Ik ga advertentie ruimte daarop verkopen.
	[darˈɔp]	-I'm going to sell advertising space on that.
1695	**vlakbij**	**nearby**
	adv	Ze wonen vlakbij.
	['vlɑgˈbɛi]	-They live nearby.
1696	**doorlopen**	**go through**
	vb	We moeten de hele procedure opnieuw doorlopen.
	[dorˈlopə(n)]	-We shall have to go through the whole procedure again.
1697	**mankeren**	**lack, ail**
	vb	Hoe weten we wat we mankeren?
	[mɑŋˈkerə(n)]	-How do we know what is wrong with us?
1698	**verstandig**	**wise**
	adj	Ik vind dat een zeer verstandig besluit.
	[vərˈstɑndəx]	-I think that this was an extremely wise decision.
1699	**puur**	**pure**
	adj	Het was puur toeval dat ik haar leerde kennen.
	[pyr]	-It was by pure accident that I came to know her.
1700	**houding**	**attitude**
	de	Dit is niet de goeie houding.
	['haudɪŋ]	-That is not the right attitude.
1701	**bovenop**	**on top**
	adv	Mijn haar wordt erg dun bovenop.
	[bovə(n)ˈɔp]	-My hair is getting very thin on top.
1702	**jarig**	**have a birthday**
	adj	Maar ik ben morgen pas echt jarig.
	['jarəx]	-But it's not officially my birthday until tomorrow.

1703	**besef**		**realization**
	het		Dat besef ging mijn leven veranderen.
	[bəˈsɛf]		-And that realization was about to change my life.
1704	**merken**		**notice**
	vb		Niet dat hij ooit zou merken.
	[ˈmɛrkə(n)]		-Not that he'd ever notice.
1705	**vloek**		**curse**
	de		De vloek werd verbroken.
	[vluk]		-The curse was broken.
1706	**seizoen**		**season**
	het		Dit is het beste seizoen om te wandelen.
	[sɛiˈzun]		-This is the best season for hiking.
1707	**route**		**route**
	de		Op deze route kan er niks gebeuren.
	[ˈrutə]		-Just stay on this route and nothing will happen.
1708	**Vietnam**		**Vietnam**
	het		De hoofdstad van Vietnam is Hanoi.
	[vjɛtnam]		-The capital of Vietnam is Hanoi.
1709	**realiteit**		**reality**
	de		Realiteit en fantasie zijn moeilijk te onderscheiden.
	[rejaliˈtɛit]		-Reality and fantasy are hard to distinguish.
1710	**as**		**ash**
	de		Alles is in de as gelegd.
	[ɑs]		-Everything was burnt to ashes.
1711	**droog**		**dry**
	adj		Zijn mijn sokken al droog?
	[drox]		-Are my socks dry already?
1712	**doodgaan**		**die**
	vb		Hij mag niet ontsnappen of doodgaan.
	[ˈdotxan]		-He mustn't escape or die.
1713	**podium**		**stage**
	het		Wie is het meisje dat op het podium zingt?
	[ˈpodijʏm]		-Who is the girl singing on the stage?
1714	**romantisch**		**romantic**
	adj		Hoe romantisch!
	[roˈmɑntis]		-How romantic!
1715	**fiets**		**bike**
	de		Ik heb een nieuwe fiets nodig.
	[fits]		-I need a new bicycle.
1716	**toren**		**tower**
	de		Hoe hoog is die toren?
	[ˈtorə(n)]		-How high is that tower?
1717	**heleboel**		**a lot**
	nu		Ik denk dat je een heleboel vragen hebt.
	[ˈheləbul]		-I guess you've got a lot of questions.
1718	**pappa**		**daddy**
	de		Je mamma en pappa zijn zeer belangrijke mensen.
	[ˈpɑpa]		-Your mom and dad are very important people.
1719	**mannetje**		**small/little man**
	het		Dan verschijnt er een ouder mannetje.
	[ˈmɑnəcə]		-Then, an older male appears.

1720	**gedurende**	**during**
	prp	Gedurende de week lees ik het nieuws in het Frans.
	[xəˈdyrəndə]	-During the week I read the news in French.
1721	**geschikt**	**suited, eligible**
	adj	Deze film is geschikt voor kinderen.
	[xəˈsxɪkt]	-This movie is suitable for children.
1722	**staart**	**tail**
	de	Misschien kunnen we de staart vinden.
	[start]	-Maybe we can find the tail.
1723	**traan**	**tear**
	de	Haar ogen vulden zich met tranen.
	[tran]	-Her eyes filled with tears.
1724	**attentie**	**attention**
	de	We lanceren al dagenlang vuursignalen voor attentie.
	[aˈtɛn(t)si]	-We launched flares for days to get their attention.
1725	**museum**	**museum**
	het	Waar is de bushalte voor het museum?
	[myˈzejʏm]	-Where is the bus stop for the museum?
1726	**constant**	**constant**
	adj	Ik controleer haar Facebookpagina constant.
	[kɔnˈstɑnt]	-I check her Facebook page constantly.
1727	**omgaan**	**handle**
	vb	De leraar kan goed met zijn leerlingen omgaan.
	[ˈɔmxan]	-The teacher handles his pupils well.
1728	**klagen**	**complain**
	vb	Stop met klagen.
	[ˈklaxə(n)]	-Quit complaining.
1729	**pest**	**plague**
	de	Muizen brengen de pest over.
	[pɛst]	-Mice carry the plague.
1730	**knop**	**button**
	de	Druk op de rode knop in uw hut.
	[knɔp]	-Press the red button in your cabin.
1731	**volkomen**	**utterly**
	adv	John was volkomen zat.
	[vɔlˈkomə(n)]	-John was utterly wasted.
1732	**tekst**	**text**
	de	Ik was het niet die die tekst vertaald heeft.
	[tɛkst]	-It wasn't me who translated this text.
1733	**jungle**	**jungle**
	de	Wat is een jungle?
	[ˈdʒʏŋɡəl]	-What's a jungle?
1734	**dapper**	**brave**
	adj	Zijn dappere daad leverde hem respect op.
	[ˈdapər]	-His brave deed earned him respect.
1735	**vleugel**	**wing**
	de	Er stroomt brandstof uit de vleugel.
	[ˈvløxəl]	-There's gas coming out of the wing.
1736	**koe**	**cow**
	de	Zij molk de koe.
	[ku]	-She milked the cow.

1737	**huiswerk**	**homework**
	het	Heb jij je huiswerk al af?
	[ˈhœyswɛrk]	-Have you finished doing your homework yet?

1738	**uitzicht**	**view**
	het	Het uitzicht vanaf de top van de berg was adembenemend.
	[ˈœytsɪxt]	-The view from the top of the mountain was breathtaking.

1739	**verrader**	**traitor**
	de	Jij verrader! Hier zal je voor boeten!
	[vərraːdːr]	-You traitor! You'll pay for this!

1740	**pakje**	**packet**
	het	Hij legde een pakje sigaretten op de tafel.
	[ˈpakjə]	-He put a pack of cigarettes on the table.

1741	**schoppen**	**kick**
	vb	Schop alsjeblieft tegen de bal.
	[ˈsxɔpə(n)]	-Please kick the ball.

1742	**overheid**	**government**
	de	De overheid probeert ons te sluiten.
	[ˈovərhɛit]	-The government is trying to shut us down.

1743	**helder**	**clear**
	adj	Bij helder weer is de kust van Estland zichtbaar vanaf Helsinki.
	[ˈhɛldər]	-During clear weather, the coast of Estonia is visible from Helsinki.

1744	**rand**	**edge**
	de	De kerk staat aan de rand van de stad.
	[rɑnt]	-The church sits on the outskirts of town.

1745	**indiaan**	**Indian**
	de	Generaal Custer heeft geen enkele Indiaan gedood. Het waren zijn kogels die het deden.
	[ɪndiˈjan]	-General Custer didn't kill any Native American. It was his bullets that did it.

1746	**spannend**	**exciting**
	adj	Dat was een spannend spel.
	[ˈspɑnənt]	-That was an exciting game.

1747	**blazen**	**blow**
	vb	Blaas de kaarsjes uit.
	[ˈblazə(n)]	-Blow out the candles.

1748	**ontmoeting**	**encounter**
	de	Dat was onze eerste ontmoeting.
	[ɔntˈmutɪŋ]	-That was our first encounter.

1749	**overkant**	**other side**
	de	Zijn huis is aan de overkant van de straat.
	[ˈovərkɑnt]	-His house is across the street.

1750	**schudden**	**shake**
	vb	Als je het bed opmaakt, vergeet dan niet de kussens op te schudden.
	[ˈsxʏdə(n)]	-When you make the bed, don't forget to fluff up the pillows.

1751	**handtekening**	**signature**
	de	Bekende honkbalspelers worden vaak om handtekeningen gevraagd.
	[ˈhɑntekənɪŋ]	-Famous baseball players are often asked for autographs.

1752	**voorgoed**	**permanently**
	adv	Plotseling was ik genoodzaakt een gedrag aan te nemen dat mijn leven voorgoed zou veranderen.
	[vorˈxut]	-All at once, I was forced to take an attitude that would change my life forever.

| 1753 | **gunst** | **favor** |

	de	Hij vroeg me of ik hem een gunst kon bewijzen.
	[xʏnst]	-He asked me if I could do him a favor.
1754	**doof**	**deaf**
	adj	Mijn twee zusters zijn zowat doof.
	[dof]	-My two sisters are almost deaf.
1755	**soep**	**soup**
	de	Deze soep is te zout om te eten.
	[sup]	-This soup is too salty to eat.
1756	**eis**	**demand**
	de	Mijn regering heeft uw eis afgewezen.
	[ɛis]	-My government has rejected your demand.
1757	**alcohol**	**alcohol**
	de	De dokter zei hem dat hij alcohol moest mijden.
	[ˈɑlkohɔl]	-He was told to abstain from alcohol by the doctor.
1758	**schamen**	**be ashamed**
	vb	Ik schaam me er niet voor dat ik arm ben.
	[sxaːmə(n)]	-I'm not ashamed that I am poor.
1759	**wijf**	**hag**
	het	Dat ouwe wijf liever dan wij.
	[wɛif]	-Better the old hag than us.
1760	**heuvel**	**hill**
	de	Ik liep de heuvel op.
	[ˈhøvəl]	-I walked up the hill.
1761	**bevrijden**	**liberate**
	vb	John bevrijdde de vogel.
	[bəˈvrɛidə(n)]	-John freed the bird.
1762	**verbinding**	**connection**
	de	Ik krijg alleen geen goede verbinding.
	[vərˈbɪndɪŋ]	-I can't seem to get a good connection.
1763	**gevoelig**	**sensitive**
	adj	John is verrassend gevoelig voor de kou.
	[xəˈvuləx]	-John is surprisingly sensitive to cold.
1764	**hof**	**court**
	het	God behoede Amerika en dit achtenswaardige hof.
	[hɔf]	-God save the United States and this honorable court.
1765	**organisatie**	**organization**
	de	De Verenigde Naties is een internationale organisatie.
	[ɔrxaniˈza(t)si]	-The United Nations is an international organization.
1766	**dader**	**perpetrator**
	de	Alles wijst op een mannelijke dader.
	[ˈdadər]	-Everything about this screams male perpetrator.
1767	**nieuwsgierig**	**curious**
	adj	Ze is nieuwsgierig naar wie de bloemen stuurde.
	[niwsˈxirəx]	-She's curious to find out who sent the flowers.
1768	**geboorte**	**birth**
	de	Hij woont daar vanaf zijn geboorte.
	[xəˈbortə]	-He's lived there all his life.
1769	**behandeling**	**treatment**
	de	Mensen lijken me anders te behandelen vandaag.
	[bəˈhandəlɪŋ]	-People seem to be treating me differently today.
1770	**gewicht**	**weight**

het
[xəˈwɪxt]
We hebben gewicht verloren.
-We lost weight.

1771 **zusje**
het
[zysjə]
little sister
Mijn zusje is beroemd.
-My younger sister is famous.

1772 **dromen**
vb
[ˈdromə(n)]
dream
Het was bijna als een droom.
-It was almost like a dream.

1773 **opruimen**
vb
[ˈɔprœymə(n)]
tidy up
Wel, ga je je kamer nu opruimen of niet?
-Well, are you going to clean up your room or not?

1774 **speelgoed**
het
[ˈspelxut]
toy
Ze kocht een stuk speelgoed voor de jongen.
-She bought a toy for the boy.

1775 **grot**
de
[xrɔt]
cave
Deze ondergrondse grot is zo ontstaan.
-This underground cavern was created in that way.

1776 **meekomen**
vb
[ˈmekomə(n)]
come along with
Je moet met mij meekomen.
-You have to come with me.

1777 **daaraan**
adv
[darˈan]
on that
Hij zei dat hij honger had en voegde daaraan toe dat hij ook dorst had.
-He said he was hungry, and then he added that he was also thirsty.

1778 **plas**
de
[plɑs]
puddle
Vreemd zoals je in die plas terechtkwam.
-Sure was weird the way you hit that puddle.

1779 **verzamelen**
vb
[vərˈzamələ(n)]
collect, gather
De eekhoorn was bezig met noten verzamelen.
-The squirrel was busy gathering nuts.

1780 **plat**
adj
[plɑt]
flat
Mijn vader had een zeldzaam plat gezicht.
-My father, he had an exceptionally flat face.

1781 **pech**
de
[pɛx]
bad luck
Hij schrijft zijn mislukkingen vaak toe aan pech.
-He often attributes his failures to bad luck.

1782 **allang**
adv
[aˈlɑŋ]
a long time ago
Zonder jou zou ik allang weggeweest zijn.
-Without you, I would have left a long time ago.

1783 **illegaal**
adj
[ɪləˈxal]
illegal
De overheid heeft een strenge wet tegen illegale immigratie aangenomen.
-The government has passed a strict law against illegal immigration.

1784 **collega**
de
[kɔˈlexa]
colleague
Heb je je collega's graag?
-Do you like your coworkers?

1785 **avontuur**
het
[avɔnˈtyr]
adventure
Ik beloof u een grandioos avontuur.
-I promise you a grand adventure.

1786 **nep**
adj
[nɛp]
fake
Die is duidelijk nep.
-It's clearly a fake.

1787 **bemanning**
crew

de
[bəˈmɑnɪŋ]

Het schip zonk met bemanning en al.
-The ship sank with all her crew on board.

1788 **studio**
de
[ˈstydijo]

studio
Gewapende militairen zijn de studio binnengedrongen.
-Several soldiers have just broken into the studio.

1789 **interview**
het
[ˈɪntərvjuː]

interview
Bedankt voor het interview.
-Thank you for agreeing to this interview.

1790 **student**
de
[styˈdɛnt]

student
Er zijn veel studenten in de bibliotheek.
-There are a lot of students in the library.

1791 **explosie**
de
[ɛksˈplozi]

explosion
Het was zo'n krachtige explosie dat het dak eraf geblazen werd.
-It was such a powerful explosion that the roof was blown off.

1792 **bibliotheek**
de
[biblijoˈtek]

library
De bibliotheek is naar rechts.
-The library is to the right.

1793 **bezwaar**
het
[bəˈzwar]

objection
Hebt u er bezwaar tegen dat ik ga?
-Do you mind if I go?

1794 **afschuwelijk**
adj; adv
[afˈsxywələk]

horrible; awfully
Ik heb een afschuwelijke fout begaan.
-I made a horrible mistake.

1795 **overeenkomst**
de
[ovərˈenkɔmst]

agreement
Bovendien moet de overeenkomst representatief zijn.
-In addition, we must insist on the agreement being representative.

1796 **opname**
de
[ˈɔpnamə]

recording
De opname is op een digitaal signaal gecomprimeerd.
-The recording is compressed on a digital signal.

1797 **expert**
de
[ɛksˈpɛːr, ɛksˈpɛrt]

expert
We hebben experts nodig.
-We need experts.

1798 **magisch**
adj
[ˈmaxis]

magic
Wat is het magische woord?
-What's the magic word?

1799 **leveren**
vb
[ˈlevərə(n)]

deliver
Wij leveren verse sinaasappelen aan je deur.
-We deliver fresh orange juice straight to your door.

1800 **speler**
de
[ˈspelər]

player
Werkt deze cd-speler?
-Does this CD player work?

1801 **kopje**
het
[kopjə]

cup
Ik ga koffie maken. Hebt u ook zin in een kopje?
-I'm going to make some coffee. Would you like a cup?

1802 **humor**
de
[ˈhymɔr]

humor
Ze kijkt op me neer omdat ik geen gevoel voor humor heb.
-She looks down on me for not having a sense of humor.

1803 **koekje**
het
[ˈkukjə]

cookie
Een lekker koekje kan zelfs een sombere dag opvrolijken.
-A nice cookie can brighten up even the darkest day.

1804 **veroordelen**
condemn

	vb	Sommige religieuze personen kunnen zeer veroordelend zijn.
	[vər'ordelə(n)]	-Some religious people can be very judgemental.
1805	**titel**	**title**
	de	Die titel kreeg ik als beeldhouwer.
	['titəl]	-That title was bestowed on me when I became a sculptor.
1806	**truc**	**trick**
	de	Oude honden kunnen nieuwe trucs leren.
	[tryk]	-Old dogs can learn new tricks.
1807	**haven**	**port**
	de	Vroeger reden ze naar de Haven van Nagoya voor het weekend.
	['havə(n)]	-They used to go for a drive to Nagoya Port on weekends.
1808	**terugtrekken**	**withdraw**
	vb	Jullie kunnen je nog altijd terugtrekken.
	[tə'ryxtrɛkə(n)]	-You can always withdraw.
1809	**bijten**	**bite**
	vb	Bijt nooit de hand die je voedt.
	['bɛitə(n)]	-Never bite the hand that feeds you.
1810	**gij**	**thou**
	prn	Gezegend zijt gij boven alle vrouwen.
	[xɛi]	-Blessed are thou amongst women.
1811	**verwijderen**	**remove**
	vb	Verwijder zijn naam van de lijst met kandidaten.
	[vər'wɛidərə(n)]	-Delete his name from the list of the applicants.
1812	**ofwel**	**or**
	con	Hij is leeg, ofwel gloednieuw.
	[ɔf'wɛl]	-It's empty, or brand new.
1813	**rollen**	**roll**
	vb	Mooie woorden rollen zo van je tong.
	['rɔlə(n)]	-Terrific words just roll right out of your mouth.
1814	**proef**	**test**
	de	Deze leerlingen hebben beiden de proef gefaald.
	[pruf]	-Those students didn't both pass the test.
1815	**zenuwachtig**	**nervous**
	adj	Lang wachten op een vriend maakt me zenuwachtig.
	['zenywɑxtəx]	-Waiting a long time for a friend makes me nervous.
1816	**fantasie**	**fantasy**
	de	Kan je fantasie en realiteit niet van elkaar scheiden?
	[fɑntaˈzi]	-Can't you separate fantasy from reality?
1817	**dominee**	**pastor**
	de	We spreken morgen de dominee en regelen alles.
	['domine]	-We'll talk to the pastor and arrange everything tomorrow.
1818	**verstaan**	**understand, hear**
	vb	Ik kan amper verstaan wat hij zegt.
	[vər'stan]	-I can hardly make out what he says.
1819	**meebrengen**	**bring**
	vb	Je mag meebrengen wie je maar wil.
	['mebrɛŋə(n)]	-You may bring whomever you like.
1820	**opleiding**	**training**
	de	Ik weet nog niet welke opleiding ik wil gaan volgen na de middelbare school.
	['ɔplɛidɪŋ]	-I still don't know what I want to study after my A-levels.
1821	**vers**	**fresh**

adj
Misschien was de appel niet vers.
[vɛrs]
-Maybe the apple wasn't fresh.

1822 **verplaatsen**
move
vb
We zouden onze kantoren hierheen moeten verplaatsen.
[vər'platsə(n)]
-We should move our offices here.

1823 **tenslotte**
finally
adv
En tenslotte, natuurlijk het hart.
[tɛn'slɔtə]
-And finally, of course, the heart.

1824 **bewust**
aware, conscious
adj
Hij moet zich bewust zijn van het gevaar.
[bə'wʏst]
-He must be aware of the danger.

1825 **beantwoorden**
answer
vb
Ik heb deze vraag al beantwoord.
[bə'ɑntwordə(n)]
-I've already answered this question.

1826 **zone**
zone
de
We moeten naar de neutrale zone.
['zɔːnə]
-We have to get into the neutral zone.

1827 **tape**
tape
de
Ik moet een tape bekijken.
[tep]
-I have to watch a tape.

1828 **vat**
container, keg
het
Het vat vertoont inderdaad sporen van ionisatie.
[vɑt]
-The container does show evidence of residual ionization.

1829 **bodem**
bottom
de
Je bent tot aan de bodem geraakt.
['bodəm]
-You have arrived at the bottom.

1830 **indien**
if
con
Indien mogelijk, zou ik nu naar huis willen gaan.
[ɪn'din]
-If possible, I'd like to go home now.

1831 **penis**
penis
de
Na Tsjernobyl valt m'n penis eraf.
['penɪs]
-After Chernobyl, my penis is falling off.

1832 **ex**
ex
de
John is een ex-gedetineerde.
[ɛks]
-John is an ex-con.

1833 **samenwerken**
co-operate; teamwork
vb; het
We kunnen misschien samenwerken.
['samə(n)wɛrkə(n)]
-Maybe we could collaborate.

1834 **lawaai**
noise
het
De deur viel plots dicht met veel lawaai.
[la'waj]
-Suddenly, the door closed with a loud noise.

1835 **echter**
however
adv
Mijn vader hing echter vaak rond met vrouwen.
['ɛxtər]
-However, my father used to fool around with women a lot.

1836 **bagage**
luggage
de
Mijn bagage ontbreekt.
[ba'xaʒə]
-My baggage is missing.

1837 **strak**
tight; tightly
adj; adv
Deze rok is een beetje te strak.
[strɑk]
-This skirt is a little too tight.

1838 **verkrachten**
rape

	vb		Verkrachting is iets verschrikkelijks.
	[vərˈkrɑxtə(n)]		-Rape is a horrible thing.
1839	**mekaar**	**each other**	
	prn		Gelukkig kunnen we onze gedachten afschermen van mekaar.
	[məˈkar]		-Luckily, we can shield our thoughts from each other.
1840	**indrukwekkend**	**impressive**	
	adj		Dat is waarlijk indrukwekkend.
	[ɪndrʏkˈwɛkənt]		-That's really impressive.
1841	**ondertussen**	**meanwhile**	
	adv		Ondertussen is er niet veel tijd meer.
	[ɔndərˈtʏsə(n)]		-Meanwhile, time is running out.
1842	**moeilijkheid**	**difficulty**	
	de		De vraag was te moeilijk voor mij om op te lossen.
	[ˈmujləkhɛit]		-The problem was too difficult for me to solve.
1843	**onbekend**	**unknown**	
	adj		De hond blafte naar de onbekende.
	[ɔmbəˈkɛnt]		-The dog barked at the stranger.
1844	**vijfde**	**fifth**	
	adj		John is nu in het vijfde jaar.
	[ˈvɛivdə]		-John is now in the fifth year.
1845	**uitdaging**	**challenge**	
	de		Ik wil je theorie niet uitdagen.
	[ˈœydaxɪŋ]		-I don't mean to challenge your theory.
1846	**lieveling**	**favorite**	
	de		Wie is jullie lievelings-dj?
	[li:fəliŋ]		-Who's your favorite DJ?
1847	**psychiater**	**psychiatrist**	
	de		John is een jonge psychiater.
	[psixiˈjatər]		-John is a young psychiatrist.
1848	**vak**	**section, compartment, profession**	
	het		In het bovenste vak rechts.
	[vɑk]		-In the top right compartment.
1849	**bemoeien**	**interfere**	
	vb		Bemoei je niet met mijn zaken.
	[bəmu:jə(n)]		-Don't interfere in my affairs.
1850	**handelen**	**act**	
	vb		Eerst denken, dan handelen!
	[ˈhɑndələ(n)]		-Think before you act!
1851	**flauw**	**faint**	
	adj		Zij viel flauw vanwege de slechte lucht.
	[flɑu]		-She's fainted because of the bad air.
1852	**schilderij**	**painting**	
	het		Jouw schilderijen zijn mooi.
	[sxɪldəˈrɛi]		-Your paintings are beautiful.
1853	**vlag**	**flag**	
	de		De nationale vlag van de VS heet de "Stars and Stripes".
	[vlɑx]		-The national flag of the USA is called the "Stars and Stripes".
1854	**concentreren**	**concentrate**	
	vb		Concentreer je, John.
	[kɔnsɛnˈtrerə(n)]		-Concentrate, John.
1855	**applaus**	**applause**	

het
[aˈplaus]

Laten we John applaus geven.
-Let's give John a round of applause.

1856 **opgroeien**
vb
[ˈɔpxrujə(n)]

grow up
Je moest zoveel sneller opgroeien dan ik.
-You had to grow up so much faster than I did.

1857 **gewoonlijk**
adv
[xəˈwonlək]

usually
Hier noemen we het gewoonlijk jeukpoeder.
-Here we usually call it itching powder.

1858 **schouder**
de
[ˈsxaudər]

shoulder
Jane masseerde mijn schouders.
-Jane massaged my shoulders.

1859 **namens**
prp
[ˈnaməns]

on behalf of
Gegroet namens de volkeren van onze planeet.
-I send greetings on behalf of the people of our planet.

1860 **centrale**
de
[sentra:lə]

headquarters, station, power plant
Het reddingsteam verlaat zojuist de centrale.
-The nuclear emergency team has just emerged from the plant.

1861 **rit**
de
[rɪt]

ride
We hadden een erg comfortabele rit.
-We had a very smooth ride.

1862 **spoedig**
adv; adj
[ˈspudəx]

soon; early
John, voorzitter van de club, zal spoedig komen.
-John, president of the club, will soon come.

1863 **duiken**
het; vb
[ˈdœykə(n)]

diving; dive
Ik mag binnen 24 uur niet duiken en vliegen.
-I can't dive and fly in the same 24 hours.

1864 **verklaren**
vb
[vərˈklarə(n)]

explain
Ik zou graag een verklaring willen hebben.
-I'd love an explanation.

1865 **aanklacht**
de
[ˈanklaxt]

charge
De aanklacht luidt mishandeling met een uiterst ongevaarlijk wapen.
-The charge, Your Honour, is assault with a very undeadly weapon.

1866 **paleis**
het
[paˈlɛis]

palace
Het paleis heeft een hoge toren.
-The palace has a tall tower.

1867 **reageren**
vb
[rejaˈxerə(n)]

react
Mensen hebben de neiging om emotioneel op gebeurtenissen te reageren.
-People tend to react emotionally to events.

1868 **werkelijkheid**
de
[ˈwɛrkələkhɛit]

reality
Mijn droom is werkelijkheid geworden.
-My dream has come true.

1869 **gemak**
het
[xəˈmak]

convenience
Je onderschat het gemak van een zak.
-I think you underestimate the convenience of a pocket.

1870 **morgenavond**
adv
[mɔrxə(n)ˈavɔnt]

tomorrow
Heb je zin om naar een film te gaan morgenavond?
-Would you like to go to a movie tomorrow night?

1871 **effect**
het
[ɛˈfɛkt]

effect
Het effect van het geneesmiddel was bewonderenswaardig.
-The effect of the medicine was amazing.

1872 **konijn**

rabbit

	het [koˈnɛin]	Konijnen hebben lange oren. -Rabbits have long ears.
1873	**crimineel** *adj* [krimiˈnel]	**criminal** De crimineel is gewapend en zeer gevaarlijk. -The criminal is armed and highly dangerous.
1874	**ingang** *de* [ˈɪnxɑŋ]	**entrance** Sommige mensen hingen wat rond aan de ingang. -Some people were hanging around at the entrance.
1875	**waarbij** *con; adv* [warˈbɛi]	**whereby; whereat** Een ongeluk waarbij alle vijf cadetten omkwamen. -An accident in which all five cadets lost their lives.
1876	**vullen** *vb* [ˈvʏlə(n)]	**fill** John is een fles met water aan het vullen. -John is filling a bottle with water.
1877	**resultaat** *het* [rezʏlˈtat]	**result** Ze waren tevreden met het resultaat. -They were satisfied with the result.
1878	**bot** *het; adj* [bɔt]	**bone; blunt** Hij gaf een bot aan de hond. -He gave the dog a bone.
1879	**uitnodiging** *de* [ˈœytnodəxɪŋ]	**invitation** Ik kan de uitnodiging niet aannemen want ik heb een andere verplichting. -I can't accept the invitation because I have another engagement.
1880	**lokaal** *adj; het* [loˈkal]	**local; place** Waar is het lokale internetcafé? -Where is the local Internet café?
1881	**negeren** *vb* [nəˈxerə(n)]	**ignore** Had ik dit gewoon moeten negeren? -Was I supposed to just ignore it?
1882	**aanwezigheid** *de* [anˈwezəxhɛit]	**presence** Ze stelde zich aan de aanwezigen voor. -She introduced herself to the people who were there.
1883	**openbaar** *adj; adv* [opə(n)ˈbar]	**public; openly** Jane denkt dat spreken in openbaar zwaar is. -Jane thinks there's something stressful about speaking in public.
1884	**Juli** *de* [ˈjyli]	**July** Ik ga van 20 juli tot 8 augustus op vakantie. -I'm taking a vacation from July 20 through August 8.
1885	**vrachtwagen** *de* [ˈvrɑxtwaxə(n)]	**truck** Kom uit de vrachtwagen. -Get out of the truck.
1886	**gerechtigheid** *de* [xəˈrɛxtəxhɛit]	**righteousness** Ik wil gerechtigheid voor ze allemaal. -I want justice for all of them.
1887	**draak** *de* [drak]	**dragon** Draken zijn gevaarlijke wezens. -Dragons are dangerous creatures.
1888	**bekennen** *vb* [bəˈkɛnə(n)]	**confess** John begon alles te bekennen. -John began to confess everything.
1889	**veroorloven**	**afford, permit**

vb	Ik kan mij niet veroorloven een dure auto te kopen.
[fro:rloufə(n)]	-I can't afford to buy an expensive car.
1890 overgeven	**hand over, vomit**
vb	Liefde, boven alles, gaat om jezelf overgeven.
['ovərxevə(n)]	-Love, before everything, is about surrendering oneself.
1891 lust	**lust**
de	Een zuiver instinctief wezen vol gevoelens van lust, genot en woede.
[lʏst]	-A purely instinctual creature, all desire and joy and rage.
1892 scheiding	**divorce**
de	Ik heb gehoord dat Jane een scheiding wil.
['sxɛidɪŋ]	-I heard that Jane wants a divorce.
1893 weglopen	**walk away**
vb	Ik wilde weglopen met John.
['wɛxlopə(n)]	-I wanted to walk away with John.
1894 reeds	**already**
adv	Dergelijke onderhandelingen zijn trouwens reeds bezig.
[rets]	-In fact, negotiations in this respect are already under way.
1895 steunen	**support**
vb	Ik zal je vandaag en altijd steunen.
['stønə(n)]	-I'll support you today and always.
1896 sindsdien	**since then**
adv	John brak vorig jaar zijn been en hinkt sindsdien.
[sɪn(t)s'din]	-John broke his leg last year and has limped ever since.
1897 vrijen	**have sex**
vb	Daarom wil je niet met me vrijen.
['vrɛijə(n)]	-That is why you don't want to sleep with me.
1898 Juni	**June**
de	Juni is perfect voor allerlei evenementen.
['jyni]	-June is perfect for all kinds of events.
1899 uitgaan	**go out**
vb	Ik wil met haar uitgaan.
['œytxan]	-I want to go out with her.
1900 tovenaar	**wizard**
de	Ben je een tovenaar?
[toufəna:r]	-Are you a wizard?
1901 college	**college**
het	Ik moet dit college bijwonen.
[kɔ'leʒə]	-I have to attend this class.
1902 maaltijd	**meal**
de	De jeuk kwam op enkele uren na de maaltijd.
['maltɛit]	-The itching appeared several hours after the meal.
1903 goedendag	**goodbye**
int	Goedendag! Hoe gaat het met U?
[xudə(n)'dɑx]	-Goodbye! How are you?
1904 munitie	**ammunition**
de	Onze munitie is opgeraakt.
[my'ni(t)si]	-Our ammunition has run out.
1905 herstellen	**restore**
vb	We moeten de orde gaan herstellen.
[hɛr'stɛlə(n)]	-We should restore the order.
1906 dwingen	**force**

	vb	We willen je natuurlijk niet dwingen.
	[ˈdwɪŋə(n)]	-Of course, we do not want to force you.
1907	**raket**	**rocket**
	de	De raket lijkt intact.
	[raˈkɛt]	-The rocket looks intact.
1908	**vanzelf**	**self, by itself**
	adv	Het licht ging vanzelf uit.
	[vanˈzɛlf]	-The light went out by itself.
1909	**paspoort**	**passport**
	het	Mijn paspoort is verlopen.
	[ˈpɑsport]	-My passport has expired.
1910	**lading**	**cargo**
	de	Opschieten met de lading, jongens.
	[ˈladɪŋ]	-Hurry with the cargo, boys.
1911	**geel**	**yellow**
	adj	De bloem is geel.
	[xel]	-The flower is yellow.
1912	**duw**	**push**
	de	Gelukkig heeft onze baby de duw overleefd.
	[dyw]	-Luckily, our baby survived the push.
1913	**mijzelf**	**myself**
	prn	Ik sloot mijzelf buiten.
	[mɛiˈzɛlf]	-I locked myself out.
1914	**terugkeren**	**return**
	vb	Ooit zal hij terugkeren naar Japan.
	[təˈrʏxkerə(n)]	-One day he will return to Japan.
1915	**nood**	**need**
	de	In tijden van nood.
	[not]	-In times of need.
1916	**bezetten**	**occupy**
	vb	Onze troepen hebben de stad bezet.
	[bəˈzɛtə(n)]	-Our forces occupied the city.
1917	**gerucht**	**rumor**
	het	Er gaat een gerucht de ronde.
	[xəˈrʏxt]	-There's a rumor going around.
1918	**set**	**set**
	de	We wachten op je op de set.
	[sɛt]	-We are waiting for you on the set.
1919	**telkens**	**constantly, again and again**
	adv	telkens vergeten de dop op de tube te doen.
	[ˈtɛlkəns]	-to constantly forget to put the lid back on the tube.
1920	**chaos**	**chaos**
	de	Er is geweld en chaos in de straten.
	[ˈxaɔs]	-There is violence and chaos in the streets.
1921	**overvallen**	**ambush, rob**
	vb	Het tankstation is overvallen door twee jongens op een motorfiets.
	[ovərˈvalə(n)]	-The gas station was held up by two youngsters on a motorbike.
1922	**ongelukkig**	**unhappy; unfortunately**
	adj	We zijn niet zo gelukkig of ongelukkig als we onszelf inbeelden.
	[ɔnxəˈlʏkəx]	-We are not as happy or unhappy as we imagine ourselves to be.
1923	**terrorist**	**terrorist**

	de	De terroristen zwoeren wraak op dat land.
	[tɛrɔ'rɪst]	-The terrorists swore vengeance on that country.
1924	**hartaanval**	**heart attack**
	de	John had vorig jaar een hartaanval.
	['hɑrtanvɑl]	-John had a heart attack last year.
1925	**erdoor**	**through it**
	adv	Laat die stretcher erdoor.
	[ɛr'dor]	-Let the stretcher through.
1926	**schuur**	**barn, shed**
	de	Ik schuur de schuur vandaag.
	[sxyr]	-I'm sanding the shed today.
1927	**zekerheid**	**certainty**
	de	Zij krijgt geld, zekerheid en maatschappelijke status.
	['zekərhɛit]	-She gets money, certainty and social standing.
1928	**verrotten**	**rot**
	vb	We moeten ze verbranden vooraleer ze verrotten.
	[və'rɔtə(n)]	-We've got to burn them before they rot.
1929	**stemming**	**vote; mood**
	de	Ik ben niet in de stemming.
	['stɛmɪŋ]	-I'm not in the mood.
1930	**technologie**	**technology**
	de	Technologie op zichzelf is zinloos tenzij het nuttig is voor de mensheid.
	[tɛxnolo'gi]	-Technology is in itself meaningless unless it serves mankind.
1931	**wanhopig**	**desperate**
	adj	Onthoudt dat John wanhopig is.
	[wɑn'hopəx]	-Remember that John is a desperate man.
1932	**hol**	**empty; hole**
	adv; het	Een holle ruimte onder de weg.
	[hɔl]	-A hole under the road.
1933	**gedragen**	**behave**
	vbr	Hebben ze zich gedragen?
	[xədra:xə(n)]	-Did they behave themselves?
1934	**aantrekkelijk**	**attractive**
	adj	Ze zijn beiden erg aantrekkelijk.
	[an'trɛkələk]	-Both of them are very attractive.
1935	**karakter**	**personality**
	het	Hij heeft een lastig karakter.
	[ka'rɑktər]	-He has a difficult personality.
1936	**doorbrengen**	**pass, spend**
	vb	Ik begrijp dat je jouw vakantie in Nieuw-Zeeland gaat doorbrengen?
	['dorbrɛŋə(n)]	-I understand you are going to spend your vacation in New Zealand?
1937	**kleintje**	**little one**
	het	Je kan niet ontsnappen, kleintje.
	[klɛjncjə]	-There's no escape for you, little one.
1938	**periode**	**period**
	de	Ze was bijgelovig, zoals de mensen uit die periode meestal waren.
	[peri'jodə]	-She was superstitious, as the people of that period usually were.
1939	**verspreiden**	**spread**
	vb	De brand verspreidde zich snel.
	[vər'sprɛidə(n)]	-The fire spread rapidly.
1940	**Spanje**	**Spain**

	het	Frankrijk grenst aan Spanje.
	[spanjə]	-France is adjacent to Spain.

1941 ketting — chain
de
[ˈkɛtɪŋ]
Deze ketting is gemaakt van jade.
-This necklace is made of jade.

1942 apparaat — device
het
[apaˈrat]
Wie heeft dat apparaat uitgevonden?
-Who invented this device?

1943 loon — wage
het
[lon]
Als je die vaas laat vallen, zal ik het op je loon inhouden.
-If you drop that vase, I'll take it out of your wage.

1944 hoofdkwartier — headquarters
het
[ˈhoftkwartir]
Ons nieuw hoofdkwartier is in Tokio.
-Our new head office is in Tokyo.

1945 bereik — range
het
[bəˈrɛik]
De rebellenbasis is in zeven minuten binnen bereik.
-The rebel base will be in range in seven minutes.

1946 slaaf — slave
de
[slaf]
Een man maakt keuzes; een slaaf gehoorzaamt.
-A man chooses; a slave obeys.

1947 verbazen — surprise
vb
[vərˈbazə(n)]
Hij zou je nog kunnen verbazen.
-He could surprise you.

1948 verontschuldigen — apologize
vb
[fərontsxyldixə(n)]
We verontschuldigen ons.
-We apologize.

1949 repareren — repair
vb
[repaˈrerə(n)]
Ik heb de deur laten repareren.
-I had the door repaired.

1950 naaien — sew; dressmaking
vb; het
[ˈnajə(n)]
Kan je naaien?
-Do you know how to sew?

1951 overheen — across, over
adv
[ovərˈhen]
Er ligt een kleed overheen.
-There is a cover over it.

1952 sociaal — social
adj
[soˈʃal]
Je bent net zo warm en sociaal als altijd.
-You're just as warm and sociable as ever.

1953 dagboek — diary
het
[ˈdaxbuk]
John schreef daarover in zijn dagboek.
-John wrote about that in his journal.

1954 achterkant — back
de
[ˈaxtərkant]
De voor en achterkant zijn hetzelfde.
-The front and back are the same.

1955 betekenis — meaning
de
[bəˈtekənɪs]
De leraar verklaarde ons de betekenis van dat woord.
-The teacher explained the meaning of the word to us.

1956 verdrietig — sad; sadly
adj; adv
[vərˈdritəx]
Waarom kijkt ze zo verdrietig?
-Why does she look so sad?

1957 verraad — betrayal

	het	De admiraal ziet het niet als verraad.
	[vər'at]	-The Admiral doesn't see it as betrayal.
1958	**schreeuw**	**scream**
	de	Die oude dame hoort geen schreeuw.
	[sxrew]	-The old lady doesn't hear a scream.
1959	**verpesten**	**spoil**
	vb	Je hebt alles verpest.
	[vər'pɛstə(n)]	-You ruined everything.
1960	**krankzinnig**	**insane; frantically**
	adj; adv;	Wat een krankzinnige wereld waar we in leven.
	[kraŋk'sınəx]	-What an insane world we live in.
1961	**vee**	**cattle**
	het	We eten het vee op.
	[ve]	-We are eating the cattle.
1962	**kosten**	**price; cost**
	de; vb	De zonnebril kost twintig euro.
	['kɔstə(n)]	-The sunglasses cost twenty euros.
1963	**buitenlands**	**foreign**
	adj	Het is een stukje buitenlands gebied.
	['bœytə(n)lɑn(t)s]	-It's a little piece of a foreign country.
1964	**triest**	**sad**
	adj	Wat soort zaken maken je triest?
	[trist]	-What sort of things make you feel sad?
1965	**verkeer**	**traffic**
	het	Je moet oppassen voor het verkeer als je de straat oversteekt.
	[vər'ker]	-You must be careful of the traffic when you cross the street.
1966	**universum**	**universe**
	het	Er zijn miljoenen sterren in het universum.
	[yni'vɛrsʏm]	-There are millions of stars in the universe.
1967	**omdraaien**	**turn around**
	verb	Het spijt me. Kunt u zich even omdraaien?
	['ɔmdrajə(n)]	-I'm sorry. Would you mind turning around?
1968	**schoonmaken**	**clean**
	vb	Als ik begin met schoonmaken, kan ik mezelf niet meer tegenhouden.
	['sxonmakə(n)]	-Once I start cleaning, I can't stop myself.
1969	**chocolade**	**chocolate**
	de	Een stukje chocolade per dag houdt de dokter weg.
	[ʃoko'ladə]	-A piece of chocolate a day keeps the doctor away.
1970	**ondergoed**	**underwear**
	het	Ik slaap in mijn ondergoed.
	['ɔndərxut]	-I sleep in my underwear.
1971	**boer**	**farmer**
	de	John is een heel goede boer.
	[buːr]	-John is a really good farmer.
1972	**behoefte**	**need**
	de	Er is dringend behoefte aan water.
	[bə'huftə]	-Water is urgently needed.
1973	**fase**	**phase**
	de	De ziekte is nog altijd in de eerste fase.
	['fazə]	-The disease is still in the primary phase.
1974	**revolutie**	**revolution**

de
[revoˈly(t)si]

De industriële revolutie begon in Engeland.
-The Industrial Revolution began in England.

1975 ten minste
adv
[tɛnˈmɪnstə]

at least
Ik ga naar de bibliotheek ten minste een keer per week.
-I go to the library at least once a week.

1976 lente
de
[ˈlɛntə]

spring
Boeren zaaien in de lente.
-Farmers sow seeds in the spring.

1977 zowel
adv
[zoˈwɛl]

both
Zowel John als Jane zijn Pools.
-Both John and Jane are Polish.

1978 spion
de
[spiˈjɔn]

spy
De man werd gearresteerd als spion.
-The man was arrested as a spy.

1979 promotie
de
[proˈmo(t)si]

promotion
John kreeg promotie.
-John was promoted.

1980 onderhandelen
vb
[ɔndərˈhandələ(n)]

negotiate
Ze zullen onderhandelen.
-They will negotiate.

1981 plant
de
[plant]

plant
De plant heeft groene bladeren.
-The plant has green leaves.

1982 rots
de
[rɔts]

rock
Als kind kwam ik vaak naar deze rots.
-I used to come to this rock all the time when I was a kid.

1983 boeten
vb
[ˈbutə(n)]

to atone for
Hij moet voor beide misdaden boeten.
-He should pay for both crimes.

1984 stok
de
[stɔk]

stick
We koken met een stok.
-We cook with a stick.

1985 kwart
het
[kwart]

quarter
Het laatste kwart van de wedstrijd.
-The final quarter of the game.

1986 eikel
de
[ˈɛikəl]

acorn, jerk
Wat ben je toch een eikel.
-You're such a jerk.

1987 leeuw
de
[lew]

lion
Wat zou je doen als je hier een leeuw zou tegenkomen?
-What would you do if you met a lion here?

1988 veertig
nu
[ˈvertəx]

forty
Veertig dollar voor zeven dagen.
-Forty dollars for seven days.

1989 aanpakken
vb
[ˈanpakə(n)]

tackle
Wij moeten de zaak Europees aanpakken.
-We need to tackle the issue at European level.

1990 proeven
vb
[ˈpruvə(n)]

taste
Wil je niet wat van mijn wijn proeven?
-Do you not want to taste some of my wine?

1991 grazen

graze

	vb	Koeien grazen in de wei.
	[ˈxrazə(n)]	-Cows are eating grass in the meadow.
1992	**goedkoop**	**cheap**
	adj	Dit artikel is goedkoop.
	[xutˈkop]	-This article is cheap.
1993	**huidig**	**current**
	adj	De huidige regering heeft veel problemen.
	[ˈhœydəx]	-The present government has many problems.
1994	**zout**	**salt; salt**
	adj; het	Zout en peper zijn belangrijke ingredienten.
	[zɑut]	-Salt and pepper are important ingredients.
1995	**beleefd**	**polite; politely**
	adj; adv	John was te beleefd om nee te zeggen.
	[bəˈleft]	-John was too polite to say no.
1996	**bestellen**	**order**
	vb	Laten we Chinees bestellen.
	[bəˈstɛlə(n)]	-Let's order Chinese takeout.
1997	**daad**	**act**
	de	Een goede daad verdwijnt niet spoorloos.
	[dat]	-A good deed will never vanish without leaving a trace.
1998	**miljard**	**billion**
	nu	Een miljard volwassenen zijn analfabeten.
	[mɪlˈjɑrt]	-A billion adults are illiterate.
1999	**passie**	**passion**
	de	Skiën is mijn passie.
	[ˈpɑsi]	-Skiing is my passion.
2000	**piano**	**piano**
	de	John oefent drie uur per dag op de piano.
	[piˈjano]	-John practices the piano for three hours a day.
2001	**uitkomen**	**come**
	vb	Ik hoop dat al je dromen uitkomen, op één na, zodat je steeds iets hebt om na
	[ˈœytkomə(n)]	te streven.
		-I hope all but one of your dreams come true, so you always have something
		to strive for.
2002	**ingewikkeld**	**complicated**
	adj	Mensen zijn ingewikkeld.
	[ɪnxəˈwɪkəlt]	-People are complicated.
2003	**uitgang**	**exit**
	de(m)	Waar is de uitgang?
	[ˈœytxɑŋ]	-Where is the way out?
2004	**betrappen**	**catch**
	vb	Als ze ons betrappen ben ik m'n beurs kwijt.
	[bəˈtrapə(n)]	-If we get caught, I will lose my scholarship.
2005	**gespannen**	**tense**
	adj	Waarom is iedreen zo gespannen?
	[xeˈspanə(n)]	-Why is everyone so tense?
2006	**rijbewijs**	**driving license**
	het	Mijn rijbewijs verloopt eind deze maand.
	[ˈrɛibəwɛis]	-My driver's license expires at the end of this month.
2007	**tempel**	**temple**
	de	Kyoto staat bekend om zijn tempels.

['tɛmpəl]   -Kyoto is famous for its temples.

2008   **instructie**   **instruction**
de   Je was niet bij de instructie.
[ɪnˈstrʏksi]   -You weren't at the briefing.

2009   **admiraal**   **admiral**
de   De admiraal is een redelijk man.
[admira:l]   -The Admiral's a decent man.

2010   **correct**   **correct, proper**
adj   Wat hij zegt is absoluut correct.
[kɔˈrɛkt]   -What he says is absolutely correct.

2011   **dadelijk**   **immediate, soon**
adv   Ik zal uw afrekening dadelijk brengen.
[ˈdadələk]   -I'll bring your check right away.

2012   **opdagen**   **turn up**
vb   Ik vroeg me af of je vandaag zou komen opdagen.
[ˈɔpdaxə(n)]   -I was wondering if you were going to show up today.

2013   **jonger**   **younger**
adj   John is jonger dan Jane, nietwaar?
[joŋər]   -John is younger than Jane, isn't he?

2014   **eigendom**   **property**
het   We erkennen je recht op dit eigendom.
[ˈɛixə(n)dɔm]   -We concede your right to this property.

2015   **borrel**   **drink**
de   Ik heb echt een borrel nodig.
[ˈbɔrəl]   -I really need an alcoholic drink.

2016   **onlangs**   **recently**
adv   De prijzen zijn onlangs gedaald.
[ˈɔnlaŋs]   -Prices have dropped recently.

2017   **excuseren**   **excuse**
vb   Excuseer mij. Ik moet er even langs.
[ɛkskyˈzerə(n)]   -Excuse me. I just need to pass you real quick.

2018   **pissen**   **piss**
vb   Hij stond daar en beweerde dat hij tegen het gerechtsgebouw ging pissen.
[ˈpɪsə(n)]   -He stood there and said he would urinate on the courthouse.

2019   **spanning**   **tension, voltage, pressure**
de   De spanning kan elk moment op geweld uitdraaien.
[ˈspanɪŋ]   -The tension can lead to violence at any moment.

2020   **brein**   **brain**
het   Computers worden vaak vergeleken met het menselijk brein.
[brɛin]   -The computer is often compared to the human brain.

2021   **aandeel**   **share**
het   Ik neem m'n aandeel en verdwijn.
[ˈandel]   -I'll take my share and disappear.

2022   **experiment**   **experiment**
het   Laat het ons eerst hebben over de experimenten die uitgevoerd worden in laboratoria.
[ɛksperiˈmɛnt]   -First, let us talk about the experiments conducted in laboratories.

2023   **staren**   **stare**
vb   Ik kon niet ophouden ernaar te staren.
[ˈstarə(n)]   -I couldn't stop staring at it.

2024   **stevig**   **firmly; firm**

	adv; adj	Ze hield mijn arm stevig vast.
	['stevəx]	-She held my arm firmly.
2025	**beschikbaar**	**available**
	adj	Hij is niet beschikbaar.
	[bə'sxɪgbar]	-He is not available.
2026	**glimlach**	**smile**
	de	Hij begroette me met een glimlach.
	['xlɪmlɑx]	-He greeted me with a smile.
2027	**gelegenheid**	**opportunity, occasion**
	de	Dit was de ideale gelegenheid.
	[xə'lexənhɛit]	-This was the perfect occasion.
2028	**bewijzen**	**prove**
	vb	John moest dat bewijzen.
	[bə'wɛizə(n)]	-John had to prove that.
2029	**koninklijk**	**royal; regally**
	adj; adv	Het koninklijk paleis.
	['konɪŋklək]	-The Royal Palace.
2030	**ezel**	**donkey**
	de	Een ezel is een dier.
	[e:jzəl]	-A donkey is an animal.
2031	**voetbal**	**football (ball), football (sport)**
	de/het	We hebben voetbal gespeeld gisteren.
	['vudbɑl]	-We played football yesterday.
2032	**lade**	**drawer**
	de	Deze lade klemt.
	['ladə]	-This drawer is stuck.
2033	**voortaan**	**henceforth**
	adv	Voortaan overleg je eerst met mij.
	[vor'tan]	-From now on you talk to me first.
2034	**middel**	**waist, method**
	het	Een betaalmiddel.
	['mɪdəl]	-A payment method.
2035	**traditie**	**tradition**
	de	Deze traditie slaat nergens op.
	[tra'di(t)si]	-This tradition is bogus.
2036	**commissie**	**committee, commission**
	de	Gelukkig werken we niet op commissie.
	[kɔ'mɪsi]	-I'm glad we're not working on commission.
2037	**hoofdpijn**	**headache**
	de	Hij had hoofdpijn.
	['hoftpɛin]	-He had a headache.
2038	**lever**	**liver**
	de	Het eten van de lever van een ijsbeer kan dodelijk zijn.
	['levər]	-Eating a polar bear's liver can kill you.
2039	**vrouwelijk**	**feminine, female**
	adj	Een hinde is een vrouwelijk hert.
	['vrɑuwelək]	-A doe is a female deer.
2040	**oefening**	**exercise**
	de	Ik wil met je oefenen.
	['ufənɪŋ]	-I want to practice with you.
2041	**gevolg**	**result**

	het	Jouw hoest is het gevolg van roken.
	[xəˈvɔlx]	-Your cough is the consequence of smoking.
2042	**kopie**	**copy**
	de	Je zoon is bijna een kopie van je vader.
	[koˈpi]	-Your son is almost a copy of your father.
2043	**kok**	**cook**
	de	Wat zijn jullie aan het koken?
	[kɔk]	-What are you cooking?
2044	**veronderstellen**	**assume**
	vb	We moeten niet het ergste veronderstellen.
	[vərɔndərˈstɛlə(n)]	-We don't have to assume the worst.
2045	**brandstof**	**fuel**
	de	Bier is mijn brandstof.
	[ˈbrɑntstɔf]	-Beer is my fuel.
2046	**studie**	**study**
	de	John startte pas op zijn dertigste met een studie Frans.
	[ˈstydi]	-John didn't start to study French until he was thirty.
2047	**uitweg**	**solution, way out**
	de	Het is noodzakelijk een andere uitweg te vinden uit deze situatie.
	[ˈœytwɛx]	-It is imperative that we find another way out of this situation.
2048	**actrice**	**actress**
	de	Mijn vriendin is een actrice.
	[aktrisə]	-My girlfriend is an actress.
2049	**ras**	**race, breed**
	het	Sommige hondenrassen zijn populair bij tokkies.
	[rɑs]	-Some dog breeds are populair with white trash people.
2050	**japans**	**Japanese**
	adj	Ik vroeg niet of je japans spreekt.
	[jaˈpɑns]	-I didn't ask if you speak Japanese.
2051	**das**	**tie**
	de	Ik denk dat ik deze das ga kopen.
	[dɑs]	-I think I will buy this tie.
2052	**voeden**	**feed**
	vb	Ze voeden zich met honing en brood.
	[ˈvudə(n)]	-They feed on honey and bread.
2053	**tja**	**well**
	interj	En tja, dan zijn er de kinderen.
	[ca]	-And, well, then there are the kids.
2054	**medium**	**medium; medium**
	adj; het	Ik heb mijn biefstuk graag medium gebakken.
	[ˈmedijʏm]	-I like my steak medium.
2055	**pijnlijk**	**painful; painfully**
	adj; adv	Dat zou minder pijnlijk zijn.
	[ˈpɛinlək]	-That would be less painful.
2056	**datum**	**date**
	de	Leg een datum vast voor de bijeenkomst.
	[ˈdatʏm]	-Fix a date for the meeting.
2057	**zeep**	**soap**
	de	Ik zal je mond met zeep spoelen!
	[zep]	-I'll wash your mouth out with soap!
2058	**waanzin**	**madness**

de ['wanzɪn]	Waanzin is dezelfde fouten herhalen maar verschillende resultaten verwachten. -Madness is repeating the same mistakes and expecting different results.
2059 bevestigen vb [bəˈvɛstəxə(n)]	**confirm** Uitzonderingen bevestigen de regel. -Exceptions prove the rule.
2060 verzekering de [vərˈzekərɪŋ]	**insurance** Het kan ook via de verzekering. -It can be done through insurance.
2061 kom de [kɔm]	**bowl** Een grote kom met soep. -A big bowl of soup.
2062 fris adj; adv [frɪs]	**fresh; freshly** Laat wat frisse lucht binnen. -Let some fresh air in.
2063 circus het ['sɪrkʏs]	**circus** De olifanten zijn de hoofdattractie in het circus. -The elephants are the chief attraction at the circus.
2064 passagier de [pɑsaˈʒir]	**passenger** Gelukkig raakte geen van de passagiers gewond. -Fortunately none of the passengers were injured.
2065 paradijs het [paraˈdɛis]	**paradise** Het eiland is een paradijs voor kinderen. -The island is a paradise for children.
2066 onderdeel het ['ɔndərdel]	**part, component** Nieuwsgierigheid is een onderdeel van intelligentie. -Curiosity is a component of intelligence.
2067 seksueel adj [sɛksyˈwel]	**sexual** Ik moest seksueel getint commentaar aanhoren. -I was subjected to remarks of a sexual nature.
2068 klimmen vb ['klɪmə(n)]	**climb** Apen klimmen in bomen. -Monkeys climb trees.
2069 bedreiging de [bəˈdrɛixɪŋ]	**threat** Terrorisme is vormt een bedreiging, -Terrorism is a threat.
2070 winden vb ['wɪndə(n)]	**wrap** Hij windt verband om zijn vinger. -He wraps a bandage around his finger.
2071 bijeenkomst de [bɛiˈenkɔmst]	**meeting** Kom niet naar de bijeenkomst. -Don't come to the meeting!
2072 plaat de [plat]	**panel, illustration, record** Ik heb veel platen. -I have many records.
2073 uzelf prn [yˈzɛlf]	**yourself** U kan er een voor uzelf maken. -You can make your own.
2074 zaal de [zal]	**room** Ik weet niet precies wanneer ik terug zal zijn. -I don't know exactly when I'll be back.
2075 laars	**boot**

de
[lars]
Ik heb nieuwe laarzen.
-I have new boots.

2076 hierbij
adv
['hirbɛi]
hereby
Maar ik wil je niet hierbij betrekken.
-But I don't want to involve you in this.

2077 versie
de
['vɛrzi]
version
Geef me jouw versie van de feiten.
-Tell me your version of the events.

2078 modern
adj; adv
[mo'dɛrn]
modern; contemporary
Wat vind je van moderne kunst?
-What do you think about contemporary art?

2079 zenuw
de
['zenyw]
nerve
Zijn manier van praten werkt op mijn zenuwen.
-His way of speaking gets on my nerves.

2080 dodelijk
adj; adv
['dodələk]
deadly; deadly
Het is een dodelijk vergif.
-It's a deadly poison.

2081 technisch
adj
['tɛxnis]
technical
Het proces was echter allesbehalve technisch.
-The process, however, was anything but a technical one.

2082 spaans
adj
[spans]
Spanish
Spaans is haar moedertaal.
-Spanish is her native language.

2083 verlangen
het; vb
[vər'laŋə(n)]
desire; desire
We verlangen allemaal naar succes.
-We all desire success.

2084 aard
de
[art]
nature
Het ligt in zijn aard.
-It lies in his nature.

2085 versterking
de
[vər'stɛrkɪŋ]
reinforcement
Breng versterking.
-Bring backup.

2086 metro
de
['metro]
metro
De zombies zijn in de metro!
-The zombies are in the metro!

2087 nut
het
[nʏt]
utility
De info die je me gaf is van weinig nut.
-The information you gave me is of little use.

2088 maatschappij
de
[matsxɑ'pɛi]
society
Zelfs de primitiefste maatschappij.
-Even the most primitive society.

2089 verzinnen
vb
[vər'zɪnə(n)]
invent, come up with
Ik denk niet dat het al te moeilijk is een beter systeem te verzinnen.
-I think it wouldn't be too hard to come up with a better system.

2090 fortuin
het
[fɔr'tœyn]
fortune
Hij liet zijn zoon een fortuin na.
-He left his son a fortune.

2091 huren
vb
['hyrə(n)]
rent
Ik kan me niet veroorloven om zo'n huis in Tokio te huren.
-I can't afford to rent a house like this in Tokyo.

2092 kameraad
comrade

	de	Zwaar om een kameraad te begraven.
	[kamə'rat]	-Tough to bury a comrade.
2093	**letterlijk**	**literal; to the letter**
	adj; adv	Iets letterlijk uit het Engels vertalen.
	['lɛtərlək]	-Translate something from English literally.
2094	**gok**	**gamble**
	de	Mijn gok is op Barcelona.
	[xɔk]	-My gamble is on Barcelona.
2095	**laden**	**load**
	vb	Daarom moeten we ons eigen munitie laden.
	['ladə(n)]	-That is why we have to load our own ammo.
2096	**afhandelen**	**settle, handle**
	vb	Alsjeblieft, laat mij dit afhandelen.
	['afhandələ(n)]	-Please, let me handle this.
2097	**varen**	**sail; fern, sailing**
	vb; het	Varen is mijn favoriete ding.
	['varə(n)]	-Sailing is my favorite thing.
2098	**tip**	**tip**
	de	Geef me een tip.
	[tɪp]	-Give me a tip.
2099	**ridder**	**knight; cavalier**
	de; adj	John is een ridder.
	['rɪdər]	-John is a knight.
2100	**internationaal**	**international**
	adj	Esperanto is een internationale plantaal.
	[ɪntərnɑ(t)ʃoˈnal]	-Esperanto is an international planned language.
2101	**waarderen**	**appreciate**
	vb	Ik waardeer jouw.
	[warˈderə(n)]	-I appreciate you.
2102	**knie**	**knee**
	de	Wil je niet op mijn knie zitten?
	[kni]	-Won't you sit on my knee?
2103	**concert**	**concert**
	het	Laten we samen naar een concert gaan.
	[kɔnˈsɛrt]	-Let's go to a concert together.
2104	**identiteit**	**identity**
	de	Maar hou je identiteit wel geheim.
	[idɛntiˈtɛit]	-But keep your identity secret.
2105	**verspillen**	**waste**
	vb	Ik had mijn tijd niet moeten verspillen.
	[vərˈspɪlə(n)]	-I shouldn't have wasted my time.
2106	**populair**	**popular**
	adj	Toen ze jong was, was ze zeer populair.
	[popyˈlɛ:r]	-When she was young, she was very popular.
2107	**mail**	**mail**
	de	Ik wilde gewoon mijn e-mail checken.
	[mel]	-I just wanted to check my email.
2108	**ministerie**	**ministry**
	het	We werken voor het ministerie van Volksgezondheid.
	[minɪsˈteri]	-Those are my orders from the ministry of health.
2109	**finale**	**final**

	de		Ik wil de finale tegen jou spelen.
	[fiˈnalə]		-I want to play against you in the final.
2110	**therapie**		**therapy**
	de		Misschien moet je in therapie.
	[teraˈpi]		-Maybe you should go into therapy.
2111	**vooruitgang**		**progress**
	de		De wetenschap heeft een opmerkelijke vooruitgang geboekt.
	[vorˈœytxɑŋ]		-Science has made remarkable progress.
2112	**wreed**		**cruel**
	adj		Het doden van olifanten, tijgers en andere bedreigde diersoorten is niet alleen wreed, het is ook illegaal.
	[vret]		-Murdering elephants, tigers and other endangered species, is not just cruel, it's also illegal.
2113	**vervolgens**		**then**
	adv		Eerst zagen ze de rommel, vervolgens keken ze elkaar aan.
	[vərˈvɔlxə(n)s]		-They looked at the rubbish, then they looked at each other.
2114	**vermogen**		**power, ability**
	het		De mens heeft het vermogen om te spreken.
	[vərˈmoxə(n)]		-Man has the ability to speak.
2115	**Justitie**		**justice**
	de		Minister van Justitie.
	[jʏsˈti(t)si]		-Justice Minister.
2116	**toestaan**		**allow**
	vb		John zal geen Amerikaanse aanwezigheid toestaan.
	[ˈtustan]		-John will not allow an American presence.
2117	**betwijfelen**		**doubt**
	vb		Dat betwijfel ik zeer.
	[bəˈtwɛifələ(n)]		-I very much doubt it.
2118	**bedrag**		**amount**
	het		Indien nodig heb ik geen bezwaar tegen het betalen van een bepaald bedrag.
	[bəˈdrɑx]		-If necessary, I have no objection to paying a certain amount.
2119	**zuurstof**		**oxygen**
	de		John overleed ten gevolge van een gebrek aan zuurstof.
	[ˈzyrstɔf]		-John died from lack of oxygen.
2120	**winkelen**		**shop**
	vb		Waar is de winkel?
	[ˈwɪŋkələ(n)]		-Where is the store?
2121	**schema**		**scheme, schedule**
	het		We lopen achter op het schema.
	[ˈsxema]		-We are behind schedule.
2122	**zooi**		**mess**
	de		John is verantwoordelijk voor deze zooi.
	[zoj]		-John is responsible for this mess.
2123	**gebeurtenis**		**event**
	de		Mijn geboorte was kennelijk geen gezegende gebeurtenis.
	[xəˈbørtənɪs]		-Apparently my birth was not considered a blessed event.
2124	**commentaar**		**comment**
	het		Verwijder het commentaar alstublieft.
	[kɔmɛnˈtar]		-Delete the comment, please.
2125	**kanaal**		**channel**
	het		John heeft een YouTube kanaal.

[kaˈnal]   -John has a Youtube channel.

2126 trekker   **tractor**
de   Een trekker en een houtduif.
[ˈtrɛkər]   -A tractor and a wood pigeon.

2127 ton   **tonne**
de   Deze walrus weegt wel een ton.
[tɔn]   -This walrus weighs as much as a tonne.

2128 daarnet   **earlier**
adv   Trouwens, ik wilde daarnet geen problemen veroorzaken.
[darˈnɛt]   -By the way, I did not mean to cause a problem earlier.

2129 journalist   **journalist**
de   Hij is een onafhankelijk journalist.
[ʒurnaˈlɪst]   -He is an independent journalist.

2130 jasje   **jacket**
het   Ik hou niet van dat jasje.
[ˈjɑʃə]   -I don't like that jacket.

2131 tuig   **rig, harness, scum**
het   Het tuig van een trekdier.
[tœyx]   -The harness of a draught animal.

2132 tof   **great, amazing**
adj   Is dat niet tof?
[tɔf]   -Isn't it awesome?

2133 snoep   **candy**
de   Geef John geen snoep meer.
[snup]   -Don't give John any more candy.

2134 overnemen   **take over**
vb   De bewoners gaan het district overnemen.
[ˈovərnemə(n)]   -The residents will take over the district.

2135 discussie   **discussion**
de   Wat we nu nodig hebben is actie, niet discussie.
[dɪsˈkʏsi]   -What we need now is action, not discussion.

2136 gewoonte   **habit**
de   Hij heeft de gewoonte om de krant tijdens de maaltijden te lezen.
[xəˈwontə]   -He has the habit of reading the newspaper during meals.

2137 positief   **positive; positive**
adj; het   Bespaar op energie, wees positief!
[posiˈtif]   -Save energy, be positive!

2138 kwetsen   **hurt**
vb   Ik wilde John nooit kwetsen.
[ˈkwɛtsə(n)]   -I never wanted to hurt John.

2139 timen   **time**
vb   Je moet 't proces goed timen.
[ˈtɑjmə(n)]   -One has to time the process right.

2140 tijger   **tiger**
de   Wat eten tijgers?
[ˈtɛixər]   -What do tigers eat?

2141 regenen   **rain**
vb   We vertrekken zodra het stopt met regenen.
[ˈrexənə(n)]   -We'll leave as soon as it stops raining.

2142 hoofdstuk   **chapter**
het   Jane leest elke dag een hoofdstuk van de Koran.

['hoftstɣk]   -Jane reads a chapter of the Quran every day.

2143	**weigeren**	**refuse**
	vb	Ik weiger om nog langer genegeerd te worden.
	['wɛixərə(n)]	-I refuse to be ignored any longer.

2144	**crisis**	**crisis**
	de	Weet iemand hoe je geld kunt verdienen in tijden van crisis?
	['krizɪs]	-Does someone know how to earn money in time of crisis?

2145	**kennelijk**	**evident**
	adj	John is kennelijk bezorgd.
	['kɛnələk]	-John is obviously worried.

2146	**revolver**	**revolver**
	de	En doe alsjeblieft die revolver weg.
	[rəˈvɔlvər]	-And please, put the revolver down.

2147	**beurs**	**exchange, scholarship**
	de	Ik raakte mijn beurs kwijt.
	[børs]	-I lost my scholarship.

2148	**leerling**	**pupil, student**
	de	Ik ben niet een slechte leerling.
	['lerlɪŋ]	-I'm not a bad student.

2149	**reclame**	**advertisement**
	de	Hier zou uw reclame kunnen staan.
	[rəˈklamə]	-Your ad could be here.

2150	**beu**	**sick**
	adj	Ik ben het beu om naar zijn gezeur te luisteren.
	[bø]	-I'm sick of listening to his complaints.

2151	**zoenen**	**kiss**
	vb	Jij bent mij een zoen verschuldigd.
	['zunə(n)]	-You owe me a kiss.

2152	**long**	**lung**
	de	Men kan de long eruit halen.
	[lɔŋ]	-You can take the lung out.

2153	**noord**	**north**
	adj	De Noordpool ligt ten noorden van de Zuidpool.
	[no:rt]	-The North Pole lies north of the South Pole.

2154	**verplichten**	**oblige**
	vb	Je bent het verplicht.
	[vərˈplɪxtə(n)]	-You are obliged.

2155	**scherm**	**screen**
	het	Dat is een groot scherm!
	[sxɛrm]	-That is a big screen!

2156	**politieagent**	**policeman**
	de	De politieagent bestuurt de auto.
	[poˈli(t)siaxɛnt]	-The policeman is driving the car.

2157	**uitmaken**	**extinguish**
	vb	Maak het vuur uit!
	['œytmakə(n)]	-Extinguish the fire!

2158	**uitstappen**	**get off**
	vb	Kunt u mij alstublieft vertellen wanneer ik moet uitstappen?
	['œytstapə(n)]	-Would you please tell me when to get off?

2159	**greep**	**hold, grasp**
	de	Ze is verlost van Satans greep.

[xrep]   -She's been released from Satan's grip.

2160 rechtstreeks   **directly; direct**
adv; adj   John negeerde een rechtstreekse order van zijn meerdere.
[rɛx(t)ˈstreks]   -John disobeyed a direct order from a superior officer.

2161 ranch   **ranch**
de   Ik wilde eigenlijk op de ranch werken.
[rɛntʃ]   -Actually I wanted to work on the ranch.

2162 weghalen   **take away**
vb   Ik moest hem daar gewoon weghalen.
[ˈwɛxhalə(n)]   -I just had to get him out of there.

2163 document   **document**
het   Dit document is alleen voor jou bestemd.
[dokyˈmɛnt]   -This document is for your eyes only.

2164 pan   **pan**
de   De pan kookt over.
[pɑn]   -The pot is boiling over.

2165 beseffen   **realize, be aware**
vb   Besef je wat je hebt gedaan?
[bəˈsɛfə(n)]   -Are you aware of what you have done?

2166 inclusief   **including; inclusively**
adj; adv   Is die prijs inclusief btw?
[ɪnklyˈsif]   -Does that price include tax?

2167 commando   **command**
de   Ik kan niet op commando vrolijk zijn.
[kɔˈmɑndo]   -I can not be happy on command.

2168 pijp   **pipe**
de   Hij zat daar met een pijp in zijn mond.
[pɛip]   -He was sitting there with a pipe in his mouth.

2169 tijdelijk   **temporarily; temporary**
adv; adj   Het effect is tijdelijk.
[ˈtɛidələk]   -The effect is temporary.

2170 vreugde   **joy**
de   Ze barstte uit in tranen van vreugde toen ze het nieuws hoorde.
[ˈvrøxdə]   -She burst out crying with joy when she heard the news.

2171 ticket   **ticket**
het   Ik heb geen ticket.
[ˈtɪkət]   -I don't have a ticket.

2172 negatief   **negative; negative**
adj; het   Wees niet zo negatief.
[nexaˈtif]   -Don't be so negative.

2173 allemachtig   **mighty**
adv   Maar allemachtig, wat zijn we saai.
[ɑ.ləˈmɑx.təx]   -But almighty, what are we boring.

2174 afwijzen   **reject**
vb   Het register kon aanvragen niet om andere redenen afwijzen.
[ˈɑfwɛizə(n)]   -The Registry could not reject an application for any other reason.

2175 pet   **cap**
de   Hoeveel kost deze pet?
[pɛt]   -What is the price of this cap?

2176 kooi   **cage**
de   Je zou deze dieren uit hun kooien moeten bevrijden.

[koj] -You should free those animals from the cage.

2177 bevinden   **be, find oneself**
vbr   De herenshirts bevinden zich op de eerste verdieping.
[bəˈvɪndə(n)]   -Men's shirts are on the second floor.

2178 centimeter   **centimeter**
de   Een centimeter is een lengtemaat.
[ˈsɛntimetər]   -A centimeter is a unit of length.

2179 overdag   **in the daytime**
adv   Overdag of in de nacht?
[ovərˈdɑx]   -In the daytime or at night?

2180 tweeling   **twin**
de   Ook al zijn John en Jane een tweeling, ze lijken niet erg veel op elkaar.
[ˈtwelɪŋ]   -Even though John and Jane are twins, they don't look very much alike.

2181 doodsbang   **mortified**
adj   John was doodsbang.
[ˈdotsbɑŋ]   -John was terrified.

2182 uitputten   **exhaust**
vb   Nee, ik wil je niet uitputten.
[ˈœytpʏtə(n)]   -No, I wouldn't want to exhaust you.

2183 verpleegster   **nurse**
de   De verpleegster is in het wit gekleed.
[vərˈplexstər]   -The nurse is dressed in white.

2184 oordeel   **judgment**
het   Het oordeel van de rechter is definitief.
[ˈordel]   -The judge's decision is final.

2185 opgeblazen   **bloated**
adj   Ik voel me opgeblazen.
[ˈɔpxəblazə(n)]   -I feel bloated.

2186 aanklager   **prosecutor**
de   John is de aanklager.
[ˈanklaxər]   -John is the prosecutor.

2187 zowat   **almost**
adv   Hij heeft de knuppel zowat tussen z'n tanden.
[zoˈwat]   -He says he's practically got the stick between his teeth now.

2188 beroven   **rob**
vb   Hij heeft de winkel beroofd.
[bəˈrovə(n)]   -He robbed the store.

2189 juweel   **jewel**
het   Herken je een van deze juwelen?
[jyˈwel]   -Do you recognize any of these jewels?

2190 opvoeden   **bring up**
vb   Ik wil m'n puppy's kunnen opvoeden.
[ˈɔpfudə(n)]   -I want the opportunity to raise my puppies.

2191 ambassade   **embassy**
de   Je bent van de ambassade, toch?
[ɑmbaˈsadə]   -You're from the embassy, aren't you?

2192 bewusteloos   **unconscious**
adj   John werd bewusteloos.
[bəˈwʏstəlos]   -John passed out.

2193 loslaten   **release**
vb   Misschien moet ik haar ook loslaten.

['lɔslatə(n)]   -Maybe I need to let go of her, too.

2194 **schakel**   **link**
de   De keten is niet sterker dan de zwakste schakel.
['sxakəl]   -A chain is no stronger than its weakest link.

2195 **verknallen**   **mess up**
vb   Wil je je eerste opdracht verknallen?
[vər'knalə(n)]   -Do you want to mess up your first assignment?

2196 **heelal**   **universe**
het   Maar het heelal is oneindig.
[he'lal]   -But the universe is infinite.

2197 **overeind**   **upright**
adv   Help hem overeind.
[ovər'ɛint]   -Help him stand up.

2198 **uitvoer**   **export**
de   De uitvoer is groter dan de invoer.
[œytvur]   -The exports exceed the imports.

2199 **achtergrond**   **background**
de   Ze is verlegen en blijft altijd op de achtergrond.
['axtərxrɔnt]   -She is shy and always remains in the background.

2200 **lamp**   **lamp**
de   Aladdin vond een magische lamp.
[lamp]   -Aladdin found a magic lamp.

2201 **contant**   **cash**
adj   Ik heb geen contant geld bij me.
[kɔn'tant]   -I don't have any cash on me.

2202 **doodschieten**   **shoot**
vb   En uiteindelijk zullen we je doodschieten.
['dotsxitə(n)]   -And in the end we shall shoot you.

2203 **baard**   **beard**
de   Er zit een kruimel in zijn baard.
[bart]   -There is a crumb in his beard.

2204 **wegkomen**   **escape**
vb   Ik kon nog net wegkomen.
['wɛxkomə(n)]   -I could barely escape.

2205 **mysterie**   **mystery**
het   John is een mysterie.
[mɪs'teri]   -John is a mystery.

2206 **begaan**   **commit**
vb   Welke misdaden hebben jullie begaan?
[bə'xan]   -What crimes have you committed?

2207 **stout**   **naughty**
adj   Het stoute jongetje verdwaalde en keek om zich heen.
[staut]   -The naughty boy got lost and looked around.

2208 **vandaar**   **hence**
adv   We werden bespioneerd, vandaar die gordijnen.
[van'dar]   -We were spied on, hence the curtains.

2209 **serie**   **series**
de   Het hoofdpersonage van deze serie is een pratende eekhoorn.
['seri]   -This series main character is a talking squirrel.

2210 **versieren**   **decorate**
vb   Laat ons de kerstboom versieren.

[vər'sirə(n)]   -Let's decorate the Christmas tree.

2211	**service**	**service**
	de	Ik wil een klacht indienen over de service.
	['sʏːrvɪs]	-I want to complain about the service.
2212	**helm**	**helmet**
	de	Ik heb een helm nodig.
	[hɛlm]	-I need a helmet.
2213	**knal**	**bang**
	de	De bom explodeerde met een knal.
	[knɑl]	-The bomb exploded with a bang.
2214	**afval**	**garbage**
	het	Stop het in de afvalbak.
	['ɑfɑl]	-Put in in the garbage bin.
2215	**overstuur**	**upset**
	adj	De buren zijn nogal overstuur.
	[ovər'styr]	-The neighbors are pretty upset.
2216	**koorts**	**fever**
	de	Je hebt koorts.
	[korts]	-You've got a fever.
2217	**achterlijk**	**backward**
	adj	Deze mensen zijn achterlijk.
	['ɑxtərlək]	-These people are backward.
2218	**toestel**	**device**
	het	Het weer lijkt gergeld te worden met dit toestel.
	['tustɛl]	-The weather seems to be regulated by this device.
2219	**spijtig**	**regrettable, unfortunate**
	adj	Het is spijtig dat je dat niet weet.
	['spɛitəx]	-It's a pity that you don't know that.
2220	**waaraan**	**whereat**
	adv	Waarom wil je weten waaraan wij denken?
	[war'an]	-Why do you want to know what we are thinking about?
2221	**vergelijken**	**compare**
	vb	Vergelijk me niet met een filmster.
	[vɛrxə'lɛikə(n)]	-Don't compare me to a movie star.
2222	**verwoesten**	**destroy**
	vb	De storm heeft de hele stad verwoest.
	[vər'wustə(n)]	-The storm destroyed the whole town.
2223	**gokken**	**gamble**
	vb	Het moet ook helpen tegen gokken.
	['xɔkə(n)]	-It's supposed to help against gambling too.
2224	**apart**	**separate; separately**
	adj; adv	Een aparte kassa voor rookwaren.
	[a'pɑrt]	-A separate cash register for smoking goods.
2225	**opzetten**	**put on**
	vb	Ik zet mijn hoed op.
	['ɔpsɛtə(n)]	-I put my hat on.
2226	**inzet**	**effort, bet**
	de	Je werk met veel inzet doen.
	['ɪnzɛt]	-To put a lot of effort into your work.
2227	**gebrek**	**lack; vice**
	het; adj	Hij heeft gebrek aan ervaring.

[xə'brɛk]   -He is lacking in experience.

2228	**koelkast**	**refrigerator**

de   Er bleef niets in de koelkast over.
['kulkɑst]   -Nothing remained in the refrigerator.

2229 **riem**   **belt**
de   Anders moet ik mijn riem uitdoen.
[rim]   -Otherwise I'd have to undo my belt.

2230 **voorzien**   **provide; anticipate**
vb; adj   Ik moet in mijn levensonderhoud voorzien.
[vor'zin]   -I have to earn a living.

2231 **'s ochtends**   **in the morning**
adv   Heb je 's ochtends tijd om de krant te lezen?
['sɔx.tən(t)s]   -Do you have time to read the newspaper in the morning?

2232 **zegenen**   **bless**
vb   Ik wilde ons huwelijk zegenen volgens de oude leer.
['zexənə(n)]   -I was trying to bless our marriage, like in the ancient teachings.

2233 **oproep**   **call**
de   Laatste oproep, dames en heren.
['ɔprup]   -Last call, please, ladies and gentlemen.

2234 **menigte**   **crowd**
de   Een menigte verzamelde zich in deze straat.
['menəxtə]   -A crowd gathered on this street.

2235 **ambassadeur**   **ambassador**
de   Ik heb gepraat met de Poolse ambassadeur.
[ɑmbɑsaˈdør]   -I spoke with the Polish ambassador.

2236 **toekomstig**   **future**
adj   Maak je klaar voor de toekomst.
[tuˈkɔmstəx]   -Prepare yourself for the future.

2237 **intelligent**   **intelligent**
adj   John lijkt intelligent.
[ɪntɛliˈxɛnt]   -John seems intelligent.

2238 **ervaren**   **experienced; experience**
adj; vb   Dit verhaal is gebaseerd op zijn eigen ervaring.
[ɛrˈvarə(n)]   -The story is based on his own experience.

2239 **bruin**   **brown**
adj   Die kat is bruin.
[brœyn]   -That cat is brown.

2240 **achteraan**   **in the back**
adv   Helemaal achteraan.
[ɑxtərˈan]   -All the way in the back

2241 **aangeven**   **indicate, pass**
vb   Kan je mij de schroevendraaier aangeven?
['anxevə(n)]   -Would you hand me the screwdriver?

2242 **portemonnee**   **wallet**
de   Gisteren heb ik mijn portemonnee verloren.
[pɔrtəmɔˈne]   -Yesterday, I lost my wallet.

2243 **douchen**   **shower**
vb   Ik ga douchen.
['duʃə(n)]   -I'll take a shower.

2244 **opblazen**   **blow**
vb   Blaas deze pop op.

['ɔblazə(n)]   -Blow up this doll.

2245 staf   **stave**
de   De staf van sinterklaas is van goud
[stɑf]   -Sinterklaas' stave is made out of gold.

2246 erbuiten   **out (it)**
adv   Je houdt een bepaalde partij erbuiten.
[ɛrbœy.tə(n)]   -You leave a certain party out of it.

2247 moeras   **swamp**
het   Er zijn krokodillen in het moeras.
[muˈrɑs]   -There are crocodiles in the swamp.

2248 wapenen   **arm**
vb   Je moet je wapenen.
[ˈwapənə(n)]   -You have to arm yourself.

2249 klaarmaken   **prepare**
vb   Mijn vader zal morgen lekker eten voor mij klaarmaken.
[ˈklarmakə(n)]   -My father will prepare a tasty meal for me tomorrow.

2250 grootmoeder   **grandmother**
de   Mijn grootmoeder sms't sneller dan jij.
[ˈxrotmudər]   -My grandmother texts faster than you.

2251 vrijlaten   **release; release**
het; vb   John komt over vijf jaar in aanmerking voor vervroegde vrijlating.
[ˈvrɛilatə(n)]   -John will be eligible for parole in five years.

2252 schutter   **shooter**
de   Ze stond hier met de schutter.
[ˈsxʏtər]   -She was standing right here with the gunman.

2253 cirkel   **circle**
de   Jane plaatste de stoelen in een halve cirkel.
[ˈsɪrkəl]   -Jane placed the chairs in a semicircle.

2254 behoren   **belong; should**
vb; av   Dat ding behoort mij toe.
[bəhorə(n)]   -That thing belongs to me.

2255 mazzel   **luck**
de   Je hebt mazzel, ze zijn beroemd.
[ˈmazəl]   -You're lucky, they are famous.

2256 incident   **incident**
het   Ik herinner me niks van het incident.
[ɪnsiˈdɛnt]   -I don't remember anything about the incident.

2257 kliniek   **clinic**
de   Ik ging naar de kliniek.
[kliˈnik]   -I went to the clinic.

2258 knopen   **knot**
vb   Twee twoutjes aan elkaar knopen.
[ˈknopə(n)]   -Tie two strings together.

2259 combinatie   **combination**
de   Originaliteit is slechts een nieuwe combinatie van clichés.
[kɔmbiˈna(t)si]   -Originality is merely a new combination of clichés.

2260 bestemming   **destination**
de   Wij kennen de bestemming nooit.
[bəˈstɛmɪŋ]   -We never know the destination.

2261 beslag   **batter**
het   Ze maakte een speciaal beslag, een familierecept.

[bəˈslɑx] -She made this special batter, a family recipe.

2262 gitaar **guitar**
de John probeerde de gitaar te bespelen.
[xiˈtar] -John tried to play the guitar.

2263 generatie **generation**
de De jongere generatie ziet de zaken anders.
[xenəˈra(t)si] -The younger generation looks at things differently.

2264 pagina **page**
de Sla alstublieft de pagina om.
[ˈpaxina] -Please turn the page.

2265 machtig **powerful; powerfully**
adj; adv Hij is machtig.
[ˈmɑxtəx] -He is powerful.

2266 optie **option**
de Niets doen is gewoon geen optie.
[ˈɔpsi] -Doing nothing is simply not an option.

2267 congres **congress**
het Ik ga naar het congres.
[kɔŋˈxrɛs] -I am going to the congress.

2268 haak **hook**
de Ik wil vissen maar ik ben mijn haak kwijt.
[hak] -I want to go fishing but I lost my hook.

2269 vervloeken **curse**
vb Mij vervloeken zal je niet helpen.
[vərˈvlukə(n)] -It will do you no good to curse me.

2270 ham **ham**
de Hamburgers zijn niet gemaakt van ham.
[hɑm] -Hamburgers aren't made of ham.

2271 regisseur **director**
de De Amerikaanse regisseur creëerde een eerbetoon aan de spaghetti western
[rexiˈsør] films.
  -The American director made an homage to spaghetti western films.

2272 kwartier **fifteen minutes**
het Kastanjes moeten minimaal een kwartier gekookt worden.
[kwarˈtir] -Chestnuts have to be boiled for at least fifteen minutes.

2273 inzetten **insert, make an effort**
vb2 Ik wil me voor je inzetten.
[ˈɪnzɛtə(n)] -I want to make an effort for you.

2274 hitte **heat**
de De hitte van de zon verhardt klei.
[ˈhɪtə] -The heat of the sun hardens clay.

2275 begrip **understanding**
het Het muggenziften is net zo vaak een teken van onwetendheid als een teken van
[bəˈxrɪp] begrip.
  -Nitpicking is just as often a sign of ignorance as it is a sign of understanding.

2276 natie **nation**
de Hij gaf zijn leven voor de natie.
[ˈna(t)si] -He gave his life for the nation.

2277 gereedschap **tool**
het John had niet het juiste gereedschap voor de taak.
[xəˈretsxap] -John didn't have the right tools for the job.

2278 gids — guide
de
[xɪts]
Als je naar Rio komt, vergeet dan niet mij te bellen en te vragen om jouw gids te zijn.
-If you come to Rio, don't forget to call me to be your guide!

2279 poot — leg
de
[pot]
Insecten hebben zes poten.
-Insects have six legs.

2280 straffen — punish
vb
['strɑfə(n)]
Wij zullen ze straffen volgens onze wetten.
-We will punish them according to our own rules.

2281 korporaal — corporal
de
[ˌkɔr.poˈraːl]
Ze is getrouwd met korporaal John.
-She's married to Corporal John.

2282 doorgeven — pass down
vb
['dorxevə(n)]
Gezien ik hem morgen zal zien kan ik hem een boodschap doorgeven, als je dat wilt.
-Since I will see him tomorrow, I can give him a message if you want.

2283 aanwijzing — instruction
de
['ɑnwɛizɪŋ]
Lees de aanwijzingen aandachtig.
-Read the instructions carefully.

2284 glorie — glory
de
['xlori]
Het gevecht om liefde en glorie.
-The fight for love and glory.

2285 volhouden — hold on
vb
['vɔlhɑudə(n)]
Nog even volhouden, het gaat prima.
-You're doing fine, just hold on.

2286 bedrogen — deceived
adj
[bədro:xə]
Ik kwam tot de vaststelling dat ik bedrogen geweest was.
-I came to the conclusion that I had been deceived.

2287 ontwerpen — design
vb
[ɔntˈwɛrpə(n)]
Ontwerpen vind ik leuk.
-I like to design.

2288 zender — transmitter
de
['zɛndər]
Een microfoon bevat een zender.
-A microphone contains a transmitter.

2289 verbazingwekkend — astounding
adj
[vərbazɪŋ'wɛkənt]
Dat is best wel verbazingwekkend.
-That's pretty astounding.

2290 behouden — maintain
vb
[bə'hɑudən]
U moet het dieet kunnen behouden.
-You'll have to be able to maintain the diet.

2291 techniek — technique
de
[tɛx'nik]
Je techniek is uitzonderlijk.
-Your technique is extraordinary.

2292 uiterlijk — appearance
het
['œytərlək]
Jane is geobsedeerd door haar uiterlijk.
-Jane is obsessed with her appearance.

2293 zweet — sweat
het
[zwet]
Er rolde een druppel zweet over zijn wang.
-A drop of sweat ran down his cheek.

2294 verblijf — stay

het	Hoe was uw verblijf?
[vər'blɛif]	-How was your stay?
2295 bewaking	**surveillance**
de	Beleid, personeel en bewaking zijn verbeterd.
[bə'wakɪŋ]	-Policy, staff and surveillance have been improved.
2296 star	**rigid**
adj	Een starre manager.
[stɑr]	-A rigid manager.
2297 fruit	**fruit**
het	Jullie houden van fruit.
[frœyt]	-You like fruit.
2298 bestuur	**management**
het	Het dagelijks bestuur.
[bə'styr]	-Everyday management.
2299 bevroren	**frozen**
adj	De kinderen pakten hun schaatsen en gingen richting de bevroren vijver.
[bəfro:rə]	-The children took their ice skates and made for the frozen pond.
2300 wetenschapper	**scientist**
de	Hij is fier dat zijn vader een vooraanstaande wetenschapper was.
['wetənsxapər]	-He is proud that his father was a great scientist.
2301 geniaal	**ingenious**
adj	John is geniaal.
[xeni'jal]	-John is ingenious.
2302 gedicht	**poem**
het	De studenten leerden dit gedicht uit hun hoofd.
[xə'dɪxt]	-The students learned this poem by heart.
2303 temperatuur	**temperature**
de	Laat me je temperatuur opnemen.
[tɛmpəra'tyr]	-Let me take your temperature.
2304 vanwaar	**from where**
adv	Vanwaar ken je dat?
[van'war]	-Where do you know it from?
2305 plastic	**plastic**
het	Ik heb bier gedronken uit een plastic beker
['plɛstɪk]	-I drank beer from a plastic cup.
2306 figuur	**figure**
het	Ze heeft een slank figuur.
[fi'xyr]	-She has a slender figure.
2307 uitvinden	**figure out**
vb	Ik wou dat ik kon uitvinden hoe ik een dvd moet branden.
['œytfɪndə(n)]	-I wish I could figure out how to burn a DVD.
2308 kruipen	**crawl; crawling**
vb; het	Ik kruip over de ground.
['krœypə(n)]	-I am crawling on the ground.
2309 symbool	**symbol**
het	De legenda van een kaart toont wat elk symbool betekent.
[sɪm'bol]	-The map's legend shows what each symbol stands for.
2310 bevolking	**population**
de	De stedelijke bevolking van Amerika neemt toe.
[bə'vɔlkɪŋ]	-The urban population of America is increasing.
2311 olifant	**elephant**

	de	Van een afstand gezien, lijkt de heuvel op een olifant.
	['olifɑnt]	-Seen from a distance, the hill looks like an elephant.
2312	**testament**	**will**
	het	Je moet een testament maken.
	[tɛstaˈmɛnt]	-You have to make a will.
2313	**schrik**	**scare**
	de	Ik zal geen schrik hebben.
	[sxrɪk]	-I will not be afraid.
2314	**emotie**	**emotion**
	de	Kolinahr: waardoor alle emotie eindelijk verdwijnt.
	[eˈmo(t)si]	-Kolinahr: through which all emotion is finally shed.
2315	**mobiel**	**mobile**
	adj	Kan ik alsjeblieft je mobiel lenen?
	[moˈbil]	-Can I borrow your cellphone, please?
2316	**bloeden**	**bleed**
	vb	Mijn vinger bloedt.
	[ˈbludə(n)]	-My finger is bleeding.
2317	**aanslag**	**assault**
	de	De aanslag is uitgevoerd en gelukt.
	[ˈɑnslɑx]	-The attack was carried out and succeeded.
2318	**plots**	**suddenly; sudden**
	adv; adj	Haar uitdrukking veranderde plots.
	[plɔts]	-Her expression underwent a sudden change.
2319	**december**	**December**
	de	Maciek heeft in december het leven verloren.
	[deˈsɛmbər]	-Maciek lost his life in December.
2320	**modder**	**mud, dirt**
	de	De kinderen zaten in de modder te spelen.
	[ˈmɔdər]	-The children were playing in the mud.
2321	**tandarts**	**dentist**
	de	Is je tandarts bijziend?
	[ˈtɑndɑrts]	-Is your dentist nearsighted?
2322	**campagne**	**campaign**
	de	Elke campagne krijgt met een crisis te maken.
	[kɑmˈpɑɲə]	-Every campaign has a crisis point.
2323	**kostuum**	**costume**
	het	Ik had me een kostuum laten maken.
	[kɔsˈtym]	-I had the tailor make a costume for me.
2324	**verzekeren**	**ensure**
	vb	En ik moet zijn voortbestaan verzekeren.
	[vərˈzekərə(n)]	-And I must do all that I can to ensure his survival.
2325	**bukken**	**bend**
	vb	Oke, nu omdraaien en bukken.
	[ˈbʏkə(n)]	-Alright, now turn around and bend over.
2326	**status**	**status**
	de	Een symbool van status en rangorde.
	[ˈstatʏs]	-A symbol of status and rank.
2327	**stoer**	**tough, seasoned**
	adj	Oh, dus jij denkt dat je stoer bent, hè?
	[stur]	-Oh, so you think you're a tough, huh?
2328	**herrie**	**noise**

	de	Hij klaagde over de herrie.
	['hɛri]	-He complained about the noise.
2329	**ruimen**	**clear**
	vb	We hoeven zelfs niet op te ruimen.
	['rœymə(n)]	-We don't even have to clean up.
2330	**bijeen**	**together**
	adv	We komen eenmaal per jaar bijeen.
	[bɛi'en]	-We get together once a year.
2331	**november**	**November**
	de	Mijn verjaardag is op tien november.
	[no'vɛmbər]	-My birthday is on November 10th.
2332	**kwijtraken**	**lose**
	vb	John, je moet je telefoon niet kwijtraken.
	['kwɛitrakə(n)]	-John, you must not lose your phone.
2333	**telefoonnummer**	**telephone number**
	het	Mijn telefoonnummer is…
	[telə'fonʏmər]	-My telephone number is…
2334	**secretaresse**	**secretary**
	de	Mijn zus werkt als secretaresse bij een bank.
	[sɪkrətaˈrɛssə]	-My sister works as a secretary at a bank.
2335	**oorzaak**	**cause**
	de	De politie onderzoekt de oorzaak van het ongeval.
	['orzak]	-The police are investigating the cause of the accident.
2336	**deken**	**blanket**
	de	Ik heb een deken nodig.
	['dekə(n)]	-I need a blanket.
2337	**link**	**link; dangerous**
	de; adj	De link met een terroristische organisatie.
	[lɪŋk]	-The link with a terrorist organization.
2338	**vreemdeling**	**stranger**
	de	Ik was een vreemdeling in Boston.
	['vremdəlɪŋ]	-I was a stranger in Boston.
2339	**pols**	**wrist**
	de	Een gebroken pols.
	[pɔls]	-A broken wrist.
2340	**beledigen**	**offend**
	vb	Niemand wil mijn land beledigen.
	[bə'ledəxə(n)]	-Nobody wants to insult my country.
2341	**voorwaarts**	**forward; forward**
	adj; adv	We moeten voorwaarts kijken naar onze toekomst.
	['vorwarts]	-We should look forward to our future.
2342	**maffia**	**mafia**
	de	De maffia is een criminele organisatie.
	['mɑfija]	-The mafia is a criminal organization.
2343	**wolk**	**cloud**
	de	Die donkere wolken voorspellen regen.
	[wɔlk]	-Those dark clouds foretell rain.
2344	**teen**	**toe**
	de	Ik kan mijn vingers en tenen niet voelen.
	[ten]	-I can't feel my fingers or my toes.
2345	**troon**	**throne**

de	De koning zit op de troon.
[tron]	-The king is sitting on the throne.

2346 voorstelling — **performance**
de
['vorstɛlɪŋ]
De voorstelling start bijna.
-The performance is about to start.

2347 tegenstander — **opponent**
de
['texə(n)standər]
Hij haalt altijd voordeel uit de gemaakte fouten van zijn tegenstanders.
-He always takes advantage of the mistakes made by his opponents.

2348 verwarren — **confuse**
vb
[vər'warə(n)]
Jij verwart mij!
-You confuse me!

2349 zonsopgang — **sunrise**
de
[zɔns'ɔpxaŋ]
De vissers stonden op voor zonsopgang.
-The fishermen got up before dawn.

2350 hakken — **heels; chop**
de; vb
['hɑkə(n)]
Misschien dat je morgen hout voor ons kunt hakken.
-Maybe you can chop wood for us tomorrow.

2351 ontploffen — **explode**
vb
[ɔnt'plɔfə(n)]
De bom ontplofte met een knal.
-The bomb exploded with a bang.

2352 zeuren — **whine**
vb
['zørə(n)]
Zijn vrouw zit voortdurend aan zijn kop te zeuren.
-His wife nags him constantly.

2353 aantrekken — **attract**
vb
['antrɛkə(n)]
Voedsel trekt dieren aan.
-Food attracts animals.

2354 communicatie — **communication**
de
[kɔmyni'ka(t)si]
Wat bedoelt je met communicatie?
-What do you mean by communication?

2355 salaris — **salary**
het
[sa'larɪs]
Zijn salaris is twee keer zo hoog als zeven jaar geleden.
-His salary is double what it was seven years ago.

2356 topper — **top class**
de
['tɔpər]
Deze film is een topper.
-This film is top class.

2357 baron — **baron**
de
[baron]
De Rode Baron was een goede Nazi-piloot.
-The Red Baron was a good Nazi-pilot.

2358 misselijk — **nauseous**
adj
['mɪsələk]
Ik denk dat ik misselijk word.
-I'm going to be nauseous.

2359 treffen — **meet; encounter**
vb; het
['trɛfə(n)]
Ik ga John daar treffen.
-I'm going to meet John there.

2360 klappen — **clap**
vb
['klɑpə(n)]
Klap in je handen.
-Clap your hands.

2361 muis — **mouse**
de
[mœys]
Een hond achtervolgt een kat, en de kat achtervolgt een muis.
-A dog runs after a cat, and the cat after a mouse.

2362 terugbrengen — **bring back**

	vb	Ik moet dit boek naar de bibliotheek terugbrengen.
	[təˈrʏxbrɛŋə(n)]	-I have to return this book to the library.
2363	**brigadier**	**constable, brigadier**
	de	Die kerel daar is brigadier bij de Londense politie.
	[briɣaːˈdiːr]	-That bloke is a constable with the London police force.
2364	**kroon**	**crown**
	de	Dit boek gaat over een koning die zijn kroon verliest.
	[kron]	-This book is about a king who loses his crown.
2365	**netwerk**	**network**
	het	Het netwerk is niet verbonden.
	[ˈnɛtwɛrk]	-The network is not connected.
2366	**roos**	**rose**
	de	Deze roos is heel mooi.
	[ros]	-This rose is very beautiful.
2367	**smeren**	**lubricate**
	vb	Smeer het in met olie.
	[ˈsmerə(n)]	-Lubricate it with oil.
2368	**realiseren**	**realize**
	vb	Daarna vertrek ik, maar dan realiseer ik me dat ik m'n rugzak bij hen thuis heb
	[rejaliˈzerə(n)]	laten liggen.
		-After that, I left, but then I realized that I forgot my backpack at their house.
2369	**innemen**	**take**
	vb	Het is niet gemakkelijk om iemand te vinden, die zijn plaats kan innemen.
	[ˈɪnemə(n)]	-It won't be easy to find someone capable of taking his place.
2370	**uitvoeren**	**execute**
	vb	Hij is wat taken gaan uitvoeren.
	[ˈœytfurə(n)]	-He went to run errands.
2371	**porno**	**porn**
	de	Kijk jij naar porno?
	[ˈpɔrno]	-Do you watch porn?
2372	**algemeen**	**general**
	adj	In het algemeen houden jongeren niet van formaliteit.
	[ˈɑlxəmen]	-In general, young people dislike formality.
2373	**charmant**	**charming; charmingly**
	adj; adv	Je hebt iets heel charmants.
	[ʃarˈmɑnt]	-There is something very charming about you.
2374	**handschoen**	**glove**
	de	Ik heb de handschoenen gevonden die onder de stoel lagen.
	[ˈhɑntsxun]	-I found the gloves that were under the chair.
2375	**sparen**	**save**
	vb	We moeten onze uitgaven beperken om geld te sparen.
	[ˈsparə(n)]	-We must cut our expenses to save money.
2376	**handig**	**convenient**
	adj; adv	De bandrecorder is een handig hulpmiddel in het onderwijs.
	[ˈhandəx]	-The tape recorder is a useful aid to teaching.
2377	**pastoor**	**priest**
	de	Iedereen wil graag de nieuwe pastoor ontmoeten.
	[pasˈtor]	-Everybody is anxious to meet their new pastor.
2378	**rechtszaak**	**trial**
	de	De rechtszaak is morgen om middernacht.
	[ˈrɛx(t)sak]	-The trial is tomorrow at the stroke of midnight.

2379	**schilderen**	**paint**
	vb	We lieten John de muren schilderen.
	[ˈsxɪldərə(n)]	-We had John paint the wall.
2380	**stam**	**tribe**
	de	Een primitieve stam.
	[stɑm]	-A primitive tribe.
2381	**heden**	**given moment; now**
	adv; het	We kunnen het verleden en het heden registreren.
	[ˈhedə(n)]	-We can record the past and present.
2382	**onbeleefd**	**rude; discourteously**
	adj; adv	Wees niet onbeleefd.
	[ɔmbəˈleft]	-Don't be rude.
2383	**krachtig**	**powerful; vigorously**
	adj; adv	Draken zijn krachtige wezens.
	[ˈkrɑxtəx]	-Dragons are powerful creatures.
2384	**emotioneel**	**emotional**
	adj	John is emotioneel.
	[emo(t)ʃoˈnel]	-John is emotional.
2385	**misverstand**	**misunderstanding**
	het	Er was een misverstand tussen ons.
	[ˈmɪsfərstɑnt]	-We've had a misunderstanding.
2386	**procedure**	**procedure**
	de	Hou je maar gewoon aan de procedure.
	[prosəˈdyrə]	-Just follow the procedure and you will be fine.
2387	**beschuldigen**	**accuse**
	vb	En mij durft ze te beschuldigen.
	[bəˈsxʏldəxə(n)]	-And she has the nerve to accuse me.
2388	**beheersen**	**control**
	vb	Bob kon zijn woede niet beheersen.
	[bəˈhersə(n)]	-Bob could not control his anger.
2389	**uniek**	**unique**
	adj	Ieder molecuul in ons lichaam heeft een unieke vorm.
	[yˈnik]	-Each molecule in our body has a unique shape.
2390	**verdragen**	**bear**
	vb	Ik kon de kou niet verdragen.
	[vərˈdraxə(n)]	-I couldn't stand the cold.
2391	**grof**	**coarse; grossly**
	adj; adv	Hij werd aangeklaagd wegens grof taalgebruik.
	[xrɔf]	-He was charged with the crime of coarse language.
2392	**boon**	**bean**
	de	Ik haat bonen.
	[bon]	-I hate beans.
2393	**joods**	**jewish**
	adj	De meeste dokters hier zijn joods.
	[jots]	-Most of the doctors here are Jewish.
2394	**puinhoop**	**mess**
	de	Het is een puinhoop.
	[ˈpœynhop]	-It's a mess.
2395	**wijsheid**	**wisdom**
	de	Wijsheid en kracht.
	[ˈwɛishɛit]	-Wisdom and power.

2396	**kandidaat**	**candidate**
	de	Deze kandidaat is duidelijk beter dan zijn voorganger.
	[kandiˈdat]	-This candidate is significantly better compared to his predecessor.
2397	**hopeloos**	**hopeless; past hope**
	adj; adv	Ze is hopeloos verliefd.
	[ˈhopəlos]	-She's hopelessly in love.
2398	**diefstal**	**theft**
	de	Hij beschuldigde de man van diefstal.
	[ˈdifstal]	-He accused the man of stealing.
2399	**accent**	**accent**
	het	Hij spreekt zonder accent.
	[akˈsɛnt]	-He speaks without an accent.
2400	**economie**	**economy**
	de	Ze vreesden dat het geschil de economie zou schaden.
	[ekonoˈmi]	-They feared that the dispute would hurt the economy.
2401	**rente**	**interest**
	de	De rente is te hoog, meneer Goldschmidt.
	[ˈrɛntə]	-The interest is too high, Mr. Goldschmidt.
2402	**drijven**	**float**
	vb	Olie zal op water drijven.
	[ˈdrɛivə(n)]	-Oil will float on water.
2403	**sectie**	**section**
	de	Verlaat alstublieft sectie A.
	[ˈsɛksi]	-Please leave section A.
2404	**verf**	**paint**
	de	Raak de natte verf niet aan.
	[vɛrf]	-Don't touch the wet paint.
2405	**verhouding**	**ratio**
	de	In dezelfde verhouding als voorheen.
	[vərˈhaudɪŋ]	-In the exact same ratio as before.
2406	**uitschakelen**	**switch off**
	vb	Schakel jij de lichten uit?
	[ˈœytsxakələ(n)]	-Will you switch off the lights?
2407	**angel**	**sting**
	de	Deze bijen hebben een buitengewoon giftige angel.
	[ˈaŋəl]	-These bees have an exceptionally venomous sting.
2408	**cultuur**	**culture**
	de	Elk land heeft een specifieke cultuur.
	[kʏlˈtyr]	-Every country has a specific culture.
2409	**zogenaamd**	**supposed; allegedly**
	adv; adj	Twee minuten nadat je zogenaamd z'n leven had gered.
	[zoxəˈnamt]	-Two minutes after you supposedly saved his life.
2410	**overdrijven**	**exaggerate**
	vb	Probeer overdrijving te vermijden.
	[ovərˈdrɛivə(n)]	-Try to avoid exaggerating
2411	**buurman**	**neighbor**
	de	We hebben een nieuwe buurman.
	[ˈbyrman]	-We have a new neighbor.
2412	**zinloos**	**pointless**
	adj	Dat lijkt me wat zinloos.
	[ˈzɪnlos]	-That seems a bit pointless to me.

2413	**kap**		**hood**
	de		Allereerst moet de kap naar beneden.
	[kɑp]		-First of all, you should put the hood down.
2414	**legaal**		**legal**
	adj		Is dit wel legaal?
	[lə'xal]		-Is this even legal?
2415	**beweren**		**claim**
	vb		John en Jane beweren dat ze nooit tegen elkaar liegen.
	[bə'werə(n)]		-John and Jane claim that they never lie to each other.
2416	**toneel**		**stage**
	het		Wat heeft John op het toneel gezongen?
	[to'nel]		-What did John sing on the stage?
2417	**handdoek**		**towel**
	de		Er zijn geen handdoeken in kamer vijftien.
	['hɑnduk]		-There are no towels in room fifteen.
2418	**roman**		**novel**
	de		Deze film is gebaseerd op een roman.
	[ro'mɑn]		-This film is based on a novel.
2419	**staal**		**steel**
	het		Staal is erg sterk.
	[stal]		-Steel is very strong.
2420	**falen**		**fail**
	vb		Je hebt je falen aan Jane te danken.
	['falə(n)]		-You have Jane to thank for your failure.
2421	**wang**		**cheek**
	de		Mijn driejarige nicht kuste me op de wang.
	[wɑŋ]		-My three-year-old niece kissed me on the cheek.
2422	**put**		**well**
	de		Het geld ligt in de put.
	['pʏt]		-The money is in the well.
2423	**huisje**		**cottage**
	het		Naar een huisje buiten de stad.
	[hɑjʃjə]		-To a cottage outside the city.
2424	**tempo**		**pace**
	het		Ja, het tempo is moordend.
	['tɛmpo]		-Yes, it's a pace of torture.
2425	**typisch**		**typical**
	adj		Hij is een typische Japanse man.
	['tipis]		-He's a typical Japanese man.
2426	**bouw**		**construction**
	de		Mijn oom zou alles bouwen.
	[bɑu]		-My uncle would build everything.
2427	**draad**		**wire**
	de		Ze naait met naald en draad.
	[drat]		-She sews with a needle and thread.
2428	**toespraak**		**speech**
	de		Wat vond je van Johns toespraak?
	['tusprak]		-What did you think of John's speech?
2429	**opening**		**opening**
	de		Alle andere schepen naar de opening.
	['opənɪŋ]		-All other ships to that opening.

2430	**artiest**	**artist**	
	de	Veel beroemde artiesten wonen in New York.	
	[ɑrˈtist]	-Many famous artists live in New York.	
2431	**privacy**	**privacy**	
	de	Willen jullie soms wat meer privacy?	
	[ˈprɑjvəsi]	-Would you like some more privacy?	
2432	**blok**	**block**	
	het	Kinderen spelen met blokken.	
	[blɔk]	-Children play with blocks.	
2433	**onzichtbaar**	**invisible**	
	adj	Lucht is onzichtbaar.	
	[ɔnˈzɪx(t)bar]	-Air is invisible.	
2434	**handje**	**hand**	
	het	Hij zei dat hij hen een handje zou helpen.	
	[hant]	-He said he would give a helping hand to them.	
2435	**drama**	**drama**	
	het	Hoe eindigt dit drama?	
	[ˈdrama]	-How does this drama end?	
2436	**voertuig**	**vehicle**	
	het	Open nooit de deur van een voertuig in beweging.	
	[ˈvurtœyx]	-Never open the door of a car that is in motion.	

2437 **verschijnen** — **appear**
vb
[vərˈsxɛinə(n)]
Een geactualiseerde versie van de encyclopedie zal de volgende maand verschijnen.
-An up-to-date edition of the encyclopedia will come out next month.

2438	**goor**	**revolting**	
	adj	Het zal luid en goor zijn.	
	[xor]	-It'll be loud and nasty.	
2439	**zelden**	**rarely**	
	adv	Hij is zelden goed gehumeurd.	
	[ˈzɛldə(n)]	-He is rarely in a good mood.	
2440	**nest**	**nest**	
	het	De twee vogels bouwden een nest zonder bouwvergunning.	
	[nɛst]	-The two birds built a nest without a building permit.	
2441	**krijt**	**chalk**	
	het	Het jonge kind gebruikt krijt om een tekening te maken.	
	[krɛit]	-The young child uses chalk to draw a picture.	
2442	**afhankelijk**	**dependent**	
	adj	Ze wil niet afhankelijk zijn van haar ouders.	
	[afˈhaŋkələk]	-She does not want to be dependent on her parents.	
2443	**compagnie**	**company**	
	de	De gehele compagnie - behalve mij natuurlijk.	
	[kɔmpaˈɲi]	-The entire company - except me, of course.	
2444	**rijzen**	**rise**	
	vb	Grote risico's rijzen ook als mensen van baan veranderen.	
	[ˈrɛizə(n)]	-Major risks also arise when people change jobs.	
2445	**boksen**	**box**	
	vb	Het boksen is niet altijd een ruige sport.	
	[ˈbɔksə(n)]	-Boxing is not always a rough sport.	
2446	**nuttig**	**useful**	
	adj	Esperanto is een nuttige taal.	

['nʏtəx]   -Esperanto is a useful language.

2447 vereren — **honor**
vb
Ze vereren hem door er weg te blijven.
[vər'erə(n)]   -They honor him by staying away.

2448 warmte — **heat**
de
Door de warmte kon ik niet slapen.
['wɑrmtə]   -I couldn't sleep because of the heat.

2449 afzetten — **drop off**
vb
Wilt u me bij het station afzetten?
['ɑfsɛtə(n)]   -Please drop me off at the station.

2450 record — **record**
het
Zijn record is een nieuw wereldrecord op de honderd meter sprint.
[rə'kɔ:r]   -His record is a new world record in the 100-meter dash.

2451 pater — **father (priest)**
de
Echt, pater, het is gewoon een ongeluk.
['patər]   -Honestly, father, the whole thing is just an accident.

2452 dagelijks — **daily; daily**
adj; adv
Het bijhouden van een dagboek geeft ons ook de kans om op ons dagelijks
['daxələks]   leven te reflecteren.
-Keeping a diary also gives us a chance to reflect on our daily life.

2453 weduwe — **widow**
de
Er zit een enorme zwarte weduwe in mijn kamer!
['wedywə]   -There's a huge black widow spider in my room!

2454 tekort — **deficit**
het
Ik kom op het moment wat geld tekort.
[tə'kɔrt]   -I'm a bit short of money now.

2455 front — **front**
het
Zij probeerden het vijandelijk front te doorbreken.
[frɔnt]   -They attempted to break through the enemy front.

2456 praktisch — **practical**
adj
De noodzaak van een theoretische en praktische voorbereiding ligt voor de
['prɑktis]   hand.
-The need for theoretical and practical preparation is obvious.

2457 bliksem — **lightning**
de
De bliksem sloeg in op de toren.
['blɪksəm]   -Lightning struck the tower.

2458 aanvaarden — **accept**
vb
Goed. Ik aanvaard je aanbod.
[an'vardə(n)]   -All right. I'll accept your offer.

2459 oost — **east**
adj
Jemen is een land in het Midden-Oosten.
[oust]   -Yemen is a country in the Middle East.

2460 kwaliteit — **quality**
de
De kwaliteit van de rijst vermindert.
[kwali'tɛit]   -The quality of rice is going down.

2461 opletten — **pay attention**
vb
Jullie moeten beter opletten wat jullie zeggen.
['ɔplɛtə(n)]   -You should pay more attention to what you say.

2462 jager — **hunter**
de
Daarom heb ik een interessantere jager uitgenodigd.
['jaxər]   -So I've invited a more interesting hunter.

2463	**tred**	**pace**
	de	Ik verkies zijn tred boven die van het grotere paard.
	[trɛt]	-I prefer his pace to that of the larger horse.
2464	**federaal**	**federal**
	adj	Hij zal rest van zijn leven onder federaal toezicht zijn.
	[fedə'ral]	-He'll be under federal supervision for the rest of his life.
2465	**district**	**district**
	het	De bewoners gaan het district overnemen.
	[dɪs'trɪkt]	-The residents will take over the district.
2466	**sector**	**sector**
	de	De concurrentiemogelijkheden binnen de sector worden hierdoor beknot.
	['sɛktɔr]	-The opportunities for competition within this area are in this way reduced.
2467	**schild**	**shield**
	het	Het leger gebruikt burgers als menselijk schild.
	[sxɪlt]	-The army uses civilians as a human shield.
2468	**kerkhof**	**cemetery**
	het	Ik probeer te vermijden na zonsondergang langs het kerkhof te lopen.
	['kɛrkhɔf]	-I try to avoid walking by the cemetery after dark.
2469	**overlijden**	**death; decease**
	het; vb	Hierdoor overlijden elke dag wel 5000 kinderen.
	[ovər'lɛidə(n)]	-This results in the death of as many as 5000 children a day.
2470	**bewustzijn**	**consciousness**
	het	Hij is nog niet bij bewustzijn gekomen.
	[bə'wʏstsɛin]	-He has not yet recovered consciousness.
2471	**bevriend**	**friendly**
	adj	Japan en de VSA werden bevriende landen.
	[bə'vrint]	-Japan and the United States became friendly nations.
2472	**recept**	**recipe**
	het	Kunt u mij het recept voor uw salade geven?
	[rə'sɛpt]	-Could you give me the recipe for your salad?
2473	**tegelijkertijd**	**at the same time**
	adv	Ze begonnen tegelijkertijd.
	[təxəlɛikər'tɛit]	-They started at the same time.
2474	**gijzelaar**	**hostage**
	de	De gijzelaars worden morgen vrijgelaten.
	['xɛizəlar]	-The hostages will be released tomorrow.
2475	**wond**	**wound**
	de	Hij bloedde uit zijn wonden.
	[wɔnt]	-He was bleeding from his wounds.
2476	**schuilplaats**	**shelter**
	de	Maar u moet een schuilplaats hebben.
	['sxœylplats]	-I think you must have shelter.
2477	**naderen**	**approach**
	vb	Ik nader mijn bestemming.
	['nadərə(n)]	-I approach my destination.
2478	**cake**	**cake**
	de	Jij was het niet die de cake hebt gegeten die ik heb gemaakt, het was je zus.
	[kek]	-It was not you who ate the cake I made, it was your sister.
2479	**ontkennen**	**deny**
	vb	U kunt het gebeurde niet ontkennen.
	[ɔnt'kɛnə(n)]	-You can't deny what happened.

2480	**rondlopen**	**walkabout**
	vb	ik zou hier niet alleen rondlopen.
	[ˈrɔntlopə(n)]	-I would not walk around alone.
2481	**offer**	**sacrifice**
	het	Het leven is rijk aan offers en arm aan vergeldingen.
	[ˈɔfər]	-Life is rich in sacrifices and poor in retributions.
2482	**ontwikkelen**	**develop**
	vb	Creativiteit is een belangrijk aspect voor de ontwikkeling van de mens.
	[ɔntˈwɪkələ(n)]	-Creativity is an important aspect of the development of humans.
2483	**wiskunde**	**mathematics**
	de	Zij studeert wiskunde.
	[ˈwɪskʏndə]	-She studies mathematics.
2484	**examen**	**examination**
	het	Jij zult hard moeten werken, als jij voor het examen wilt slagen.
	[ɛkˈsamə(n)]	-You'll have to work hard if you want to pass the exam.
2485	**vloot**	**fleet**
	de	Een vloot met boten.
	[vlot]	-A fleet of ships.
2486	**avondeten**	**supper**
	het	Ik moet mijn ouders opbellen en ze vertellen dat ik laat zal zijn voor het avondeten.
	[ˈavɔntetə(n)]	-I need to call my parents and tell them I'll be late for dinner.
2487	**uitkijken**	**be careful**
	vb	Je moet uitkijken dat je niet weer dezelfde fout maakt.
	[ˈœytkɛikə(n)]	-You should be careful not to make the same mistake again.
2488	**tering**	**typhus**
	de	Tering is een ziekte.
	[ˈterɪŋ]	-Typhus is a disease.
2489	**zonsondergang**	**sunset**
	de	De berg Fuji ziet er mooi uit bij zonsondergang.
	[zɔnsˈɔndərxaŋ]	-Mt. Fuji is a beautiful sight at sunset.
2490	**teruggeven**	**give back**
	vb	Ik zal alles gauw teruggeven.
	[təˈrʏxevə(n)]	-I will give everything back quickly.
2491	**alvast**	**in advance**
	adv	Alvast bedankt voor je samenwerking.
	[alˈvast]	-Thank you in advance for your cooperation.
2492	**honkbal**	**baseball**
	het	Ik houd ervan honkbal te spelen.
	[ˈhɔŋkbal]	-I like playing baseball.
2493	**mode**	**fashion**
	de	Ze weet veel over de laatste mode.
	[ˈmodə]	-She knows a lot about the latest fashions.
2494	**autoriteit**	**authority**
	de	Respecteer mijn autoriteit.
	[autoriˈtɛit]	-Respect my authority.
2495	**oppassen**	**babysit; beware**
	het; vb	Kun je me vannacht een pleziertje doen en op mijn kinderen oppassen?
	[ˈɔpasə(n)]	-Could you do me a favor and babysit my kids tonight?
2496	**belasting**	**tax**
	de	John betaalde zijn belastingen niet.

[bə'lɑstɪŋ]   -John didn't pay taxes.

2497 **scoren**   **score**
      vb   Hij scoort een doelpunt.
      ['skorə(n)]   -He scores a goal.

2498 **verbeteren**   **improve**
      vb   Denk je dat de situatie zich kan verbeteren?
      [vər'betərə(n)]   -Do you think the situation can improve?

2499 **ontbreken**   **lack**
      vb   Waar is de ontbrekende dollar?
      [ɔnd'brekə(n)]   -Where is the missing dollar?

2500 **zesde**   **sixth**
      nu   Ze heeft het zesde en zevende uur vrij.
      ['zɛzdə]   -She is free the sixth and seventh period.

2501 **spier**   **muscle**
      de   Hun spieren zijn stijf.
      [spir]   -Their muscles are stiff.

2502 **knoop**   **button**
      de   Een knoop aan je jas naaien.
      [knop]   -To sew a button on your coat.

2503 **streng**   **strand; strict; strictly**
      de; adj; adv   John is streng maar eerlijk.
      [strɛŋ]   -John is strict but fair.

2504 **rondje**   **round**
      het   Niet als jij het eerste rondje trakteert.
      ['rɔncə]   -Not if you treat us to the first round.

2505 **voortduren**   **continue**
      vb   Zijn vrouw zit voortdurend aan zijn kop te zeuren.
      ['vordyrə(n)]   -His wife nags him constantly.

2506 **vermaak**   **entertainment**
      het   Er wordt voor vermaak gezorgd.
      [vər'mak]   -Entertainment will be provided.

2507 **levenslang**   **lifelong**
      adj   John zit levenslang in de gevangenis.
      [levə(n)s'laŋ]   -John is serving a life sentence in prison.

2508 **opstand**   **rebellion**
      de   De ergste opstand had in Chicago plaats.
      ['ɔpstɑnt]   -The worst riot was in Chicago.

2509 **dertien**   **thirteen**
      nu   Kinderen onder de dertien jaar mogen dit zwembad niet in.
      ['dɛrtin]   -Children under thirteen years of age are not admitted to this swimming pool.

2510 **schedel**   **skull**
      de   De schedel van een 16-jarig meisje.
      ['sxedəl]   -It's the skull of a 16-year-old girl.

2511 **zestien**   **sixteen**
      nu   Tien, elf, twaalf, dertien, veertien, vijftien, zestien, zeventien, achttien,
      ['zɛstin]   negentien, twintig.
                                  -Ten, eleven, twelve, thirteen, fourteen, fifteen, sixteen, seventeen, eighteen,
                                  nineteen, twenty.

2512 **uitzending**   **broadcast; transmission**
      adj; de   We beginnen onze rechtstreekse uitzending over twee minuten.
      ['œytsɛndɪŋ]   -We will begin our live television transmission in two minutes.

2513	**hetgeen** *prn* [hɛt'xen]	**which** John gaf Jane met tegenzin hetgeen waar ze om vroeg. -John reluctantly gave Jane what she asked for.
2514	**wisselen** *vb* ['wɪsələ(n)]	**exchange** Wissel van plaats met me. -Switch places with me.
2515	**opvallen** *vb* ['ɔpfɑlə(n)]	**notice** Fantastisch hoe jou twee dingen kunnen opvallen. -It's amazing the way you notice two things.
2516	**hemd** *het* [hɛmt]	**shirt** John draagt zelden zijn zwarte hemd. -John seldom wears his black shirt.
2517	**beschaving** *de* [bə'sxavɪŋ]	**civilization** Europeanen probeerden de stam beschaving bij te brengen. -Europeans tried to civilize the tribe.
2518	**marinier** *de* [mari'nir]	**marine** Je wordt nu meteen een marinier. -You're going to become a Marine, right now.
2519	**schijn** *de* [sxɛin]	**appearance** We moeten de schijn van fatsoenlijkheid ophouden. -We have to keep up the appearance of respectability.
2520	**inwoner** *de* ['ɪnwonər]	**resident, inhabitant** China heeft meer dan een miljard inwoners. -China has more than a billion inhabitants.
2521	**leed** *het* [let]	**anguish, grief** Iemand leed aandoen. -To cause someone grief.
2522	**sowieso** *adv* [sowi'zo]	**definitely** Ze weten het sowieso. -They definitely know.
2523	**vermijden** *vb* [vər'mɛidə(n)]	**avoid** Kan u niet vermijden dat uw hond in mijn tuin komt? -Can't you avoid your dog from coming into my garden?
2524	**wodka** *de* [vodka]	**vodka** Waar is de wodka? -Where is the vodka?
2525	**politieman** *de* [po'li(t)simɑn]	**policeman** De dief liep weg toen hij een politieman zag. -The thief ran away when he saw a policeman.

Adjectives

Rank	Dutch-PoS	English Equivalent
15	op-*prp; adv; adj*	on, up, at; on, up; spent
29	aan-*prp; adj*	to, on; on
32	naar-*prp; adv; adj*	to, for; along; awful
38	geen-*art; adj; adv; prn; nu*	not one, no; no; no; none
42	wel-*adv; adj; con*	well; alright; as many as
44	goed-*adj; adv; het*	good, correct; well; estate
47	waar-*adv; con; adj; de*	where; where; true; merchandise
52	uit-*prp; adv; adj*	from; out; off
65	meer-*adj; adv; het*	more; more; lake
74	eens-*adv; adj*	once; agree
75	echt-*adv; adj*	really; real
80	alleen-*adv; con; adj*	only, merely; only; alone
87	even-*adv; adj*	momentarily; even
99	gewoon-*adv; adj*	just, plainly; ordinary
101	nodig-*adj*	necessary, required
109	net-*adv; het; adj*	just; net; elegant
110	heel-*adj; adv*	very, whole
113	dood-*de; adj*	death; dead
115	af-*adv; adj*	off; ready
120	zeker-*adj; adv*	confident; sure
131	zoals-*adv; con; adj; prp*	as; as; such as; like
135	erg-*adv; adj*	very; terrible
140	ander-*adj; prn*	other; other
144	beter-*adv; adj*	better; superior
155	genoeg-*adj; adv*	enough; enough
156	klaar-*adj; adv*	ready, finished; clear
157	leuk-*adj*	nice, fun
158	mooi-*adj*	beautiful, pretty
170	gek-*adj; de; adv*	crazy; fool; fool
172	groot-*adj*	large, big
173	lang-*adj; adv*	long, tall; long
184	beetje-*het; adj*	bit; little
186	snel-*adv; adj*	fast; quick
191	bang-*adj; adv*	afraid, scared; anxious
200	geweldig-*adj*	great, awesome
204	nieuw-*adj*	new, novel
207	laatst-*adj; adv*	last, latest; lately
212	best-*adj; adv*	best; sufficiently
217	rustig-*adj; adv*	calm; quietly
218	enig-*adv; adj; prn*	any; solely; single
221	klein-*adj*	small, little
223	eerst-*adj; adv*	first, primary; first
226	eigen-*adj*	own
230	open-*adj; adv*	open, overt; overtly
232	elk-*prn; adj; adv*	each, any; every
233	geleden-*adv; adj*	ago; past
238	gelijk-*adj; het*	equal, similar; right
241	eigenlijk-*adv; adj*	really; actually
247	precies-*adv; adj*	exactly, precise; exact
248	heet-*adj;*	hot, warm
250	verder-*adj; adv*	further; moreover
259	oud-*adj*	old
273	slecht-*adj; adv*	bad, evil; badly
279	blij-*adj; adv*	happy, joyous; glad
289	lekker-*adj; adv*	tasty, nice; deliciously
290	later-*adv; adj*	later, hereafter; after
295	juist-*adj; adv*	just, correct; just
297	prima-*adj;adv*	great, fine
301	week-*de; adj*	week; soft
319	vrij-*adj; adv*	free, clear; free
325	los-*adj; adv*	loose; loose
326	mis-*adj; adv; de*	wrong, erroneous; wrong; mass
331	wakker-*adj*	awake
333	voorbij-*adj; adv; prp*	gone; past; beyond
334	leren-*vb; adj*	learn; teach
337	vol-*adj; adv*	full, crowded; full
342	druk-*de; adj; adv*	pressure; busy; busily
343	dicht-*adj; adv*	close, closed; densely
346	zoiets-*adj*	such a thing
347	gelukkig-*adj*	happy
351	moeilijk-*adj*	difficult, tough
357	hetzelfde-*prn; adj; adv*	same; ditto; ditto
359	bezig-*adj*	busy
360	ver-*adj; adv*	far, remote; far
361	eerder-*adj*	earlier, rather
368	waarschijnlijk-*adv; adj*	probably, presumably; likely
378	rond-*adv; adj*	around; round
380	zeer-*adj; adv; het*	very, highly; very; sore
381	welkom-*int, adj*	welcome, appreciated
384	veilig-*adj; adv*	safe, sure; safely
385	stuk-*het; adj*	piece, part; broken
386	aardig-*adj; adv*	nice, pretty; nicely
388	fijn-*adj; adv*	fine, nice; delicately
390	mogelijk-*adj; adv*	possible, eventual; possibly
394	eerlijk-*adj; adv*	honest, straight; honestly
396	stil-*adj; adv*	quiet, still; quietly
402	ouder-*adj; de*	older, senior; parent

403	recht-*adj; adv; het*	right; right; right
408	belangrijk-*adj*	important
409	fout-*de; adj*	error, mistake; wrong
411	hard-*adj; adv*	hard, loud; hard
413	duidelijk-*adj; adv*	clear, obvious; clearly
418	prachtig-*adj; adv*	wonderful, magnificent
432	voorzichtig-*adj; adv*	careful, cautious; carefully
434	licht-*adj; het; adv*	light, mild; light; slightly
435	enkel-*adj; adv; de*	only, single; only; ankle
437	lief-*adj; adv*	lovable, nice; sweet
447	kwaad-*adj; het*	evil, angry; evil
452	grappig-*adj*	funny
455	idioot-*de; adj*	idiot; idiotic
459	kwijt-*adj*	lost
473	ziek-*adj*	sick
480	fantastisch-*adj*	fantastic
489	normaal-*adj*	normal
491	vreemd-*adj; adv*	strange; strangely
495	nogal-*adv; adj*	rather; pretty
496	minder-*adj; adv*	less; less, fewer
502	verkeerd-*adj; adv*	wrong; wrong
506	allebei-*adj*	both
509	perfect-*adj*	perfect
510	waard-*adj*	worth
515	vroeger-*adv; adj*	earlier; former
517	trots-*de; adj*	pride; proud
521	hierheen-*adv; adj*	here; hither
526	serieus-*adj*	serious
529	verlaten-*vb; adj*	leave; abandoned
533	stom-*adj*	stupid
534	slim-*adj*	smart
543	zwart-*adj*	black
544	sommige-*adj; prn*	some; some
550	verliefd-*adj*	in love
551	ieder-*prn; adj*	each; every
555	makkelijk-*adj; adv*	easy; easy
556	boos-*adj; adv*	angry; angrily
568	koud-*adj*	cold
570	weinig-*adj*	little, few
574	vreselijk-*adj; adv*	terrible; terribly
584	sterk-*adj*	strong
587	geheim-*adj; het*	secret; secret
588	rot-*het; adj*	rot; rotten
590	absoluut-*adv; adj*	absolutely; absolute
596	afgelopen-*adj; adv*	over, last; out
597	moe-*adj*	tired
598	geboren-*adj*	born
600	jong-*adj; het*	young; cub
601	naast-*adj; prp*	near; next to
621	gevaarlijk-*adj; adv*	dangerous; hazardous
623	hel-*de; adj; adv*	hell; bright; glaringly
628	jammer-*adj; adv*	unfortunate; unfortunately
631	raar-*adj; adv*	strange; strangely
635	bekend-*adj*	known
636	arm-*de; adj*	arm; poor
644	dom-*adj;*	stupid
657	rijk-*adj; het*	rich; empire
660	schuldig-*adj*	guilty
661	zwaar-*adj*	heavy
667	vorig-*adj*	last
673	dronken-*adj*	drunk
676	kapot-*adj; adv*	broken; to pieces
683	onmogelijk-*adj; adv*	impossible; impossibly
686	links-*adj*	left
689	wit-*adj*	white
690	warm-*adj*	warm
704	diep-*adj; adv*	deep; deep
706	direct-*adv; adj*	directly; direct
708	kalm-*adj; adv*	calm; calmly
718	gisteravond-*adj*	last night
724	midden-*het; adj; prp*	middle; mid; amidst
725	rood-*adj*	red
726	beide-*adj; prn*	both; either
730	heerlijk-*adj; adv*	delicious; deliciously
731	rechts-*adj*	right
732	hoog-*adj; adv*	high; high
737	donker-*adj; het*	dark; dark
742	vuil-*het; adj; adv*	dirt; dirty; filthily
743	kwalijk-*adj; adv*	bad, wrong; amiss
749	zulk-*adj*	such
761	werkelijk-*adv; adj*	really; real
765	uiteindelijk-*adj; adv*	finally; sooner or later
778	teveel-*het; adj*	excess; excess, too much
780	extra-*adj; adv*	extra; extra
788	knap-*adj; adv*	handsome; cleverly
791	gewond-*adj*	injured
797	lastig-*adj*	difficult
798	speciaal-*adj; adv*	special; especially
801	ongelooflijk-*adj*	incredible, unbelievable
805	interessant-*adj*	interesting
807	rechter-*adj; de*	right; judge
808	heilig-*adj*	holy, sacred
809	leeg-*adj; adv*	empty; vacantly

812	belachelijk-*adj*	ridiculous		1137	uitstekend-*adj*	excellent
813	persoonlijk-*adj*	personal		1153	blind-*adj*	blind
827	volledig-*adj; adv*	full; completely		1155	gouden-*adj*	golden
838	aangenaam-*adj*	pleasant		1160	compleet-*adj*	complete
839	kort-*adj*	short, brief		1166	tegenwoordig-*adv; adj*	current; currently
845	bar-*de; adj*	bar; severe				
849	vlug-*adv; adj*	quickly; quick		1172	zwak-*adj*	weak
854	engels-*adj; het*	English; English		1176	duur-*de; adj*	duration; expensive
857	zwanger-*adj*	pregnant		1179	laag-*adj; de*	low; layer
886	simpel-*adj*	simple, basic		1180	zonde-*de; adj*	sin; too bad
887	langzaam-*adj*	slow		1191	menselijk-*adj*	human
891	totaal-*adj; het; adv*	total; total; totally		1200	vrolijk-*adj*	cheerful, happy
				1206	wijs-*adj; de*	wise; tune
901	blauw-*adj*	blue		1218	nat-*adj*	wet
907	onmiddellijk-*adj*	immediate		1221	dankbaar-*adj*	grateful
923	schoon-*adj*	clean		1227	straf-*de; adj*	punishment; strong
927	bezorgd-*adj*	concerned, troubled		1228	super-*adj*	super, great
934	gratis-*adj*	free		1231	verborgen-*adj*	hidden
945	trouw-*de; adj*	faith; loyal		1233	ernstig-*adj*	serious
958	publiek-*het; adj*	audience; public		1235	flink-*adj; adv*	robust, firm; substantial
963	verschrikkelijk-*adj; adv*	horrible; terrible		1239	eenvoudig-*adj*	plain, simple
				1245	wild-*adj; het*	wild; wildlife
970	bereid-*adj*	prepared		1252	eng-*adj*	scary
990	vlak-*adj; het; adv*	flat; surface; just		1255	ruim-*adj*	spacious, amply
994	enorm-*adj; adv*	enormous; vast		1257	gerust-*adj*	be at ease, safe
998	gemakkelijk-*adj*	easy		1258	gezond-*adj*	healthy
1000	blank-*adj*	white, blank		1261	groen-*adj*	green
1008	sexy-*adj*	sexy		1267	saai-*adj*	dull, boring
1012	papieren-*adj; de*	paper; papers		1277	schattig-*adj*	sweet, cute
1014	eeuwig-*adj*	eternal; forever		1289	genaamd-*adj*	called
1020	dik-*adj*	thick, fat		1293	duits-*adj; het*	German; German
1022	volwassen-*adj*	adult		1296	eenzaam-*adj*	lonely, solitary
1029	gemeen-*adj*	mean		1301	naakt-*adj*	naked
1033	behoorlijk-*adj*	quite		1312	verslagen-*adj*	defeated
1035	verantwoordelijk-*adj*	responsible		1318	prettig-*adj*	gratifying
				1321	vermist-*adj*	missing
1036	toevallig-*adj*	accidental		1330	gereed-*adj*	ready
1037	dol-*adj*	crazy		1336	lelijk-*adj*	ugly
1039	nerveus-*adj*	nervous		1342	min-*adj; adv*	poor; minus
1044	verboden-*adj*	forbidden		1353	netjes-*adj*	neat
1048	onschuldig-*adj*	innocent		1383	smerig-*adj*	filthy
1053	jaloers-*adj*	jealous, envious		1384	militair-*adj; de*	military; soldier
1054	tevreden-*adj*	satisfied		1393	medisch-*adj*	medical
1063	bijzonder-*adj; adv*	extraordinary; thoroughly		1394	frans-*adj*	French
				1399	wassen-*vb; adj*	wash; wax
1068	gaaf-*adj*	whole, great		1401	aanwezig-*adj*	present
1077	terecht-*adj;adv*	justified; back, found		1408	nederlands-*adj; het*	Dutch; Dutch
1083	overleden-*adj*	deceased				
1112	hartelijk-*adj*	cordial, warm		1438	ongerust-*adj*	anxious, worried
1125	vriendelijk-*adj*	friendly, kind		1439	dubbel-*adj*	double
1133	heus-*adj*	real		1455	vals-*adj*	FALSE

1463	waardeloos-*adj*	worthless
1480	braaf-*adj*	good
1482	beroemd-*adj*	famous
1488	russisch-*adj; het*	Russian; Russian
1489	geheel-*adj; het; adv*	whole; whole; entirely
1493	nationaal-*adj*	national
1496	geregeld-*adj*	regular
1501	gegeven-*adj; het*	given; given
1506	walgelijk-*adj*	disgusting
1509	zielig-*adj*	pathetic
1526	geliefd-*adj*	beloved
1530	zacht-*adj; adv*	soft; gently
1539	vies-*adj; adv*	dirty; nastily
1547	redelijk-*adj; adv*	reasonable; reasonably
1550	logisch-*adj*	logical
1553	voorlopig-*adj; adv*	temporary; for the time being
1556	ontzettend-*adj; adv*	tremendous; enormously
1563	dwars-*adj*	contrary, across
1572	junior-*de; adj*	junior; minor
1597	chinees-*adj; de*	Chinese; Chinese
1598	plotseling-*adv; adj*	suddenly; sudden
1618	dwaas-*adj; de; adv*	silly; fool; foolishly
1623	bleek-*adj; adv*	pale; wanly
1626	gezellig-*adj; adv*	cozy; cozily
1638	brits-*adj*	british
1643	live-*adj*	on air
1648	voldoende-*adj; de*	satisfactory; sufficient
1659	verschuldigd-*adj*	indebted
1675	scherp-*adj*	sharp
1684	briljant-*adj*	brilliant
1686	groots-*adj*	grand, great
1687	roze-*adj*	pink
1698	verstandig-*adj*	wise
1699	puur-*adj*	pure
1702	jarig-*adj*	have a birthday
1711	droog-*adj*	dry
1714	romantisch-*adj*	romantic
1721	geschikt-*adj*	suited, eligible
1726	constant-*adj*	constant
1734	dapper-*adj*	brave
1743	helder-*adj*	clear
1746	spannend-*adj*	exciting
1754	doof-*adj*	deaf
1763	gevoelig-*adj*	sensitive
1767	nieuwsgierig-*adj*	curious
1780	plat-*adj*	flat
1783	illegaal-*adj*	illegal
1786	nep-*adj*	fake
1794	afschuwelijk-*adj; adv*	horrible; awfully
1798	magisch-*adj*	magic
1815	zenuwachtig-*adj*	nervous
1821	vers-*adj*	fresh
1824	bewust-*adj*	aware, conscious
1837	strak-*adj; adv*	tight; tightly
1840	indrukwekkend-*adj*	impressive
1843	onbekend-*adj*	unknown
1844	vijfde-*adj*	fifth
1851	flauw-*adj*	faint
1862	spoedig-*adv; adj*	soon; early
1873	crimineel-*adj*	criminal
1878	bot-*het; adj*	bone; blunt
1880	lokaal-*adj; het*	local; place
1883	openbaar-*adj; adv*	public; openly
1911	geel-*adj*	yellow
1922	ongelukkig-*adj*	unhappy; unfortunately
1931	wanhopig-*adj*	desperate
1934	aantrekkelijk-*adj*	attractive
1952	sociaal-*adj*	social
1956	verdrietig-*adj; adv*	sad; sadly
1960	krankzinnig-*adj; adv;*	insane; frantically
1963	buitenlands-*adj*	foreign
1964	triest-*adj*	sad
1992	goedkoop-*adj*	cheap
1993	huidig-*adj*	current
1994	zout-*adj; het*	salt; salt
1995	beleefd-*adj; adv*	polite; politely
2002	ingewikkeld-*adj*	complicated
2005	gespannen-*adj*	tense
2010	correct-*adj*	correct, proper
2013	jonger-*adj*	younger
2024	stevig-*adv; adj*	firmly; firm
2025	beschikbaar-*adj*	available
2029	koninklijk-*adj; adv*	royal; regally
2039	vrouwelijk-*adj*	feminine, female
2050	japans-*adj*	Japanese
2054	medium-*adj; het*	medium; medium
2055	pijnlijk-*adj; adv*	painful; painfully
2062	fris-*adj; adv*	fresh; freshly
2067	seksueel-*adj*	sexual
2078	modern-*adj; adv*	modern; contemporary

2080	dodelijk-*adj; adv*	deadly; deadly
2081	technisch-*adj*	technical
2082	spaans-*adj*	Spanish
2093	letterlijk-*adj; adv*	literal; to the letter
2099	ridder-*de; adj*	knight; cavalier
2100	internationaal-*adj*	international
2106	populair-*adj*	popular
2112	wreed-*adj*	cruel
2132	tof-*adj*	great, amazing
2137	positief-*adj; het*	positive; positive
2145	kennelijk-*adj*	evident
2150	beu-*adj*	sick
2153	noord-*adj*	north
2160	rechtstreeks-*adv; adj*	directly; direct
2166	inclusief-*adj; adv*	including; inclusively
2169	tijdelijk-*adv; adj*	temporarily; temporary
2172	negatief-*adj; het*	negative; negative
2181	doodsbang-*adj*	mortified
2185	opgeblazen-*adj*	bloated
2192	bewusteloos-*adj*	unconscious
2201	contant-*adj*	cash
2207	stout-*adj*	naughty
2215	overstuur-*adj*	upset
2217	achterlijk-*adj*	backward
2219	spijtig-*adj*	regrettable, unfortunate
2224	apart-*adj; adv*	separate; separately
2227	gebrek-*het; adj*	lack; vice
2230	voorzien-*vb; adj*	provide; anticipate
2236	toekomstig-*adj*	future
2237	intelligent-*adj*	intelligent
2238	ervaren-*adj; vb*	experienced; experience
2239	bruin-*adj*	brown
2265	machtig-*adj; adv*	powerful; powerfully
2286	bedrogen-*adj*	deceived
2289	verbazingwekkend-*adj*	astounding
2296	star-*adj*	rigid
2299	bevroren-*adj*	frozen
2301	geniaal-*adj*	ingenious
2315	mobiel-*adj*	mobile
2318	plots-*adv; adj*	suddenly; sudden
2327	stoer-*adj*	tough, seasoned
2337	link-*de; adj*	link; dangerous
2341	voorwaarts-*adj; adv*	forward; forward
2358	misselijk-*adj*	nauseous
2372	algemeen-*adj*	general
2373	charmant-*adj; adv*	charming; charmingly
2376	handig-*adj; adv*	convenient

2382	onbeleefd-*adj; adv*	rude; discourteously
2383	krachtig-*adj; adv*	powerful; vigorously
2384	emotioneel-*adj*	emotional
2389	uniek-*adj*	unique
2391	grof-*adj; adv*	coarse; grossly
2393	joods-*adj*	jewish
2397	hopeloos-*adj; adv*	hopeless; past hope
2409	zogenaamd-*adv; adj*	supposed; allegedly
2412	zinloos-*adj*	pointless
2414	legaal-*adj*	legal
2425	typisch-*adj*	typical
2433	onzichtbaar-*adj*	invisible
2438	goor-*adj*	revolting
2442	afhankelijk-*adj*	dependent
2446	nuttig-*adj*	useful
2452	dagelijks-*adj; adv*	daily; daily
2456	praktisch-*adj*	practical
2459	oost-*adj*	east
2464	federaal-*adj*	federal
2471	bevriend-*adj*	friendly
2503	streng-*de; adj; adv*	strand; strict; strictly
2507	levenslang-*adj*	lifelong
2512	uitzending-*adj; de*	broadcast; transmission

Adverbs

Rank	Dutch-*PoS*	English Equivalent
8	niet-*adv*	not
10	wat-*con; prn; adv*	what; what; few
15	op-*prp; adv; adj*	on, up, at; on, up; spent
16	te-*adv; prp*	too, to; in
18	er-*adv*	there
19	maar-*adv; con*	however, just; but
23	voor-*prp; adv; con*	for; before; ere
24	met-*prp; adv*	with; along with
25	als-*adv; con; prp*	as; as; like
30	hier-*adv*	here
31	om-*prp; adv*	to, for; about
32	naar-*prp; adv; adj*	to, for; along; awful
33	dan-*con; adv*	than; then
38	geen-*art; adj; adv; prn; nu*	not one, no; no; no; none
39	zo-*adv; con;*	so, that; if
40	nog-*adv*	yet, still
42	wel-*adv; adj; con*	well; alright; as many as
44	goed-*adj; adv; het*	good, correct; well; estate
47	waar-*adv; con; adj; de*	where; where; true; merchandise
48	nu-*adv; con*	now; now
49	hoe-*adv; prn*	how; how
52	uit-*prp; adv; adj*	from; out; off
55	ook-*adv*	also, as well
57	over-*prp; adv*	about; over
59	daar-*adv; con*	there; as
61	al-*adv; het; con*	already; all; though
63	bij-*prp; de; adv*	at; bee; up to date
65	meer-*adj; adv; het*	more; more; lake
66	waarom-*adv; con*	why; why
67	iets-*prn; adv*	something; some
74	eens-*adv; adj*	once; agree
75	echt-*adv; adj*	really; real
77	weg-*de; adv*	road; away, gone
78	toch-*adv; con*	yet, so, right; nevertheless
80	alleen-*adv; con; adj*	only, merely; only; alone
81	nou-*adv*	now
82	dus-*adv; con*	so, consequently; therefore
83	nooit-*adv*	never, no way
84	terug-*adv*	back, again
85	mee-*adv*	also, with
87	even-*adv; adj*	momentarily; even
88	niets-*het; prn; adv*	nothing; nothing; none
90	misschien-*adv*	maybe
94	veel-*adv*	much, a lot
99	gewoon-*adv; adj*	just, plainly; ordinary
100	weer-*het; adv*	weather; again
106	tegen-*prp; adv*	against
107	toen-*con; adv*	when; then
109	net-*adv; het; adj*	just; net; elegant
110	heel-*adj; adv*	very, whole
114	altijd-*adv*	always
115	af-*adv; adj*	off; ready
120	zeker-*adj; adv*	confident; sure
131	zoals-*adv; con; adj; prp*	as; as; such as; like
135	erg-*adv; adj*	very; terrible
136	anders-*adv; con*	different, else; otherwise
141	niks-*prn; adv*	nothing; none
142	binnen-*adv; prp*	within; inside
144	beter-*adv; adj*	better; superior
155	genoeg-*adj; adv*	enough; enough
156	klaar-*adj; adv*	ready, finished; clear
161	na-*prp; adv*	after; post
163	toe-*prp; adv*	to; towards
165	elkaar-*adv; prn*	each other; each other
170	gek-*adj; de; adv*	crazy; fool; fool
173	lang-*adj; adv*	long, tall; long
175	graag-*adv*	gladly, willingly
177	eerste-*de; adv*	first; initial
183	steeds-*adv*	always, still
185	achter-*adv; prp*	behind; behind
186	snel-*adv; adj*	fast; quick
188	ooit-*adv*	ever
189	wanneer-*adv; con*	when; when
190	onder-*adv; prp*	under, underneath; under
191	bang-*adj; adv*	afraid, scared; anxious
207	laatst-*adj; adv*	last, latest; lately
209	vandaag-*adv*	today
212	best-*adj; adv*	best; sufficiently
213	heen-*adv*	there, away
216	zelfs-*adv*	even
217	rustig-*adj; adv*	calm; quietly
218	enig-*adv; adj; prn*	any; solely; single
219	thuis-*adv*	home
220	buiten-*adv; prp*	outside, out; outside
223	eerst-*adj; adv*	first, primary; first
224	samen-*adv*	together
230	open-*adj; adv*	open, overt; overtly
232	elk-*prn; adj; adv*	each, any; every

233	geleden-*adv; adj*	ago; past		396	stil-*adj; adv*	quiet, still; quietly
235	bijna-*adv*	almost		403	recht-*adj; adv; het*	right; right; right
240	soms-*adv*	sometimes		405	ermee-*adv*	with it
241	eigenlijk-*adv; adj*	really; actually		407	overal-*adv*	everywhere
243	vanavond-*adv*	tonight		411	hard-*adj; adv*	hard, loud; hard
244	alsof-*con; adv*	like; as if		413	duidelijk-*adj; adv*	clear, obvious; clearly
247	precies-*adv; adj*	exactly, precise; exact		416	straks-*adv*	soon, later
250	verder-*adj; adv*	further; moreover		418	prachtig-*adj; adv*	wonderful, magnificent
251	pas-*adv; de*	just now; pass		421	vaak-*adv*	often, regularly
256	eruit-*adv*	out		423	erop-*adv*	on
268	daarom-*con; adv*	therefore; hence		432	voorzichtig-*adj; adv*	careful, cautious; carefully
273	slecht-*adj; adv*	bad, evil; badly		434	licht-*adj; het; adv*	light, mild; light; slightly
279	blij-*adj; adv*	happy, joyous; glad		435	enkel-*adj; adv; de*	only, single; only; ankle
286	vooruit-*adv*	forward, ahead		437	lief-*adj; adv*	lovable, nice; sweet
289	lekker-*adj; adv*	tasty, nice; deliciously		439	erin-*adv*	in it
290	later-*adv; adj*	later, hereafter; after		446	inderdaad-*adv*	indeed, actually
291	volgens-*adv*	according to		449	nergens-*adv*	nowhere
292	boven-*adv; prp*	above, over; above		461	daarna-*adv; con*	then, after; whereupon
293	ergens-*adv; prn*	somewhere; someplace		464	naartoe-*adv*	there
295	juist-*adj; adv*	just, correct; just		469	omhoog-*adv*	up
297	prima-*adj;adv*	great, fine		471	ervoor-*adv*	for it
300	zoveel-*adv*	so many, so much		485	gisteren-*adv*	yesterday
319	vrij-*adj; adv*	free, clear; free		488	eindelijk-*adv*	finally
325	los-*adj; adv*	loose; loose		491	vreemd-*adj; adv*	strange; strangely
326	mis-*adj; adv; de*	wrong, erroneous; wrong; mass		492	daarmee-*adv*	therewith, with that
328	beneden-*adv; prp*	down, below; below		495	nogal-*adv; adj*	rather; pretty
333	voorbij-*adj; adv; prp*	gone; past; beyond		496	minder-*adj; adv*	less; less, fewer
336	neer-*adv*	down		502	verkeerd-*adj; adv*	wrong; wrong
337	vol-*adj; adv*	full, crowded; full		505	hoezo-*adv; con*	why; why
342	druk-*de; adj; adv*	pressure; busy; busily		511	erbij-*adv*	at, with, there
343	dicht-*adj; adv*	close, closed; densely		512	zomaar-*adv*	just
350	meteen-*adv*	immediately		514	half-*het; adv*	half; semi
353	sinds-*adv; con*	since; since		515	vroeger-*adv; adj*	earlier; former
357	hetzelfde-*prn; adj; adv*	same; ditto; ditto		521	hierheen-*adv; adj*	here; hither
360	ver-*adj; adv*	far, remote; far		524	opnieuw-*adv*	again
362	eraan-*adv*	with it		536	ongeveer-*adv*	about, approximately
368	waarschijnlijk-*adv; adj*	probably, presumably; likely		553	tenminste-*adv*	at least
				554	slechts-*adv*	only
378	rond-*adv; adj*	around; round		555	makkelijk-*adj; adv*	easy; easy
380	zeer-*adj; adv; het*	very, highly; very; sore		556	boos-*adj; adv*	angry; angrily
384	veilig-*adj; adv*	safe, sure; safely		562	trouwens-*adv*	by the way
386	aardig-*adj; adv*	nice, pretty; nicely		574	vreselijk-*adj; adv*	terrible; terribly
388	fijn-*adj; adv*	fine, nice; delicately		590	absoluut-*adv; adj*	absolutely; absolute
390	mogelijk-*adj; adv*	possible, eventual; possibly		596	afgelopen-*adj; adv*	over, last; out
394	eerlijk-*adj; adv*	honest, straight; honestly		604	erover-*adv*	about
395	langs-*adv; prp*	along; along		621	gevaarlijk-*adj; adv*	dangerous; hazardous

623	hel-*de; adj; adv*	hell; bright; glaringly	963	verschrikkelijk-*adj; adv*	horrible; terrible
628	jammer-*adj; adv*	unfortunate; unfortunately	975	waarover-*adv*	about which/what
631	raar-*adj; adv*	strange; strangely	984	binnenkort-*adv*	shortly
655	zover-*adv*	as far as	985	waarin-*adv*	wherein
666	vooral-*adv*	especially, above all	990	vlak-*adj; het; adv*	flat; surface; just
676	kapot-*adj; adv*	broken; to pieces	994	enorm-*adj; adv*	enormous; vast
678	haast-*de; adv*	hurry; almost	1006	ineens-*adv*	suddenly
683	onmogelijk-*adj; adv*	impossible; impossibly	1061	opeens-*adv*	suddenly
694	daarvoor-*adv*	therefor, for that	1063	bijzonder-*adj; adv*	extraordinary; thoroughly
704	diep-*adj; adv*	deep; deep	1077	terecht-*adj;adv*	justified; back, found
706	direct-*adv; adj*	directly; direct	1100	erachter-*adv*	behind
707	vannacht-*adv*	tonight	1104	dichterbij-*adv*	closer
708	kalm-*adj; adv*	calm; calmly	1164	bijvoorbeeld-*adv*	for instance
711	waarvoor-*adv*	for what	1166	tegenwoordig-*adv; adj*	current; currently
721	onderweg-*adv*	en route, on the way			
730	heerlijk-*adj; adv*	delicious; deliciously	1177	vandoor-*adv*	away
732	hoog-*adj; adv*	high; high	1235	flink-*adj; adv*	robust, firm; substantial
742	vuil-*het; adj; adv*	dirt; dirty; filthily	1236	erom-*adv*	around it, about it
743	kwalijk-*adj; adv*	bad, wrong; amiss	1241	hiervan-*adv*	hereof
755	eraf-*adv*	off	1263	nauwelijks-*adv*	hardly
756	achteruit-*adv; de*	backwards; reverse	1264	zojuist-*adv*	just (now)
761	werkelijk-*adv; adj*	really; real	1278	hiervoor-*adv*	theretofore
765	uiteindelijk-*adj; adv*	finally; sooner or later	1297	morgenochtend-*adv*	tomorrow morning
773	daarvan-*adv*	of it	1300	daarheen-*adv*	there
780	extra-*adj; adv*	extra; extra	1314	waarheen-*adv*	where to
788	knap-*adj; adv*	handsome; cleverly	1316	doorheen-*adv*	through
798	speciaal-*adj; adv*	special; especially	1335	nogmaals-*adv*	once again
799	alweer-*adv*	again	1342	min-*adj; adv*	poor; minus
809	leeg-*adj; adv*	empty; vacantly	1392	hierin-*adv*	herein
817	blijkbaar-*adv*	apparently	1428	wellicht-*adv*	perhaps
819	waarop-*con; adv*	when; whereupon	1429	omlaag-*adv*	down
827	volledig-*adj; adv*	full; completely	1434	ernaar-*adv*	it, at it, after it
835	helaas-*adv*	unfortunately, alas	1442	momenteel-*adv*	currently, at the moment
849	vlug-*adv; adj*	quickly; quick			
852	meestal-*adv*	usually	1458	vanmiddag-*adv*	this afternoon
875	dichtbij-*adv*	near, nearby	1485	daardoor-*adv*	thereby, therefore
883	gauw-*adv*	soon, quickly	1489	geheel-*adj; het; adv*	whole; whole; entirely
890	eenmaal-*adv*	once			
891	totaal-*adj; het; adv*	total; total; totally	1494	daarin-*adv*	therein
			1500	bovendien-*adv*	besides, moreover
896	hopelijk-*adv*	hopefully	1505	tegelijk-*adv*	at the same time
905	vanmorgen-*adv*	this morning	1530	zacht-*adj; adv*	soft; gently
908	waarvan-*adv*	of which, whose, where from	1534	verderop-*adv*	further ahead
			1539	vies-*adj; adv*	dirty; nastily
916	hiermee-*adv*	herewith	1546	vanochtend-*adv*	this morning
918	hoelang-*adv*	how long	1547	redelijk-*adj; adv*	reasonable; reasonably
939	waarmee-*adv*	with which	1548	uiteraard-*adv*	naturally

1553	voorlopig-*adj; adv*	temporary; for the time being	1932	hol-*adv; het*	empty; hole
1556	ontzettend-*adj; adv*	tremendous; enormously	1951	overheen-*adv*	across, over
1557	voort-*adv*	on	1956	verdrietig-*adj; adv*	sad; sadly
1558	meerdere-*de; adv*	superior; multiple	1960	krankzinnig-*adj; adv;*	insane; frantically
1570	minstens-*adv*	at least	1975	ten minste-*adv*	at least
1595	hieruit-*adv*	from this	1977	zowel-*adv*	both
1598	plotseling-*adv; adj*	suddenly; sudden	1995	beleefd-*adj; adv*	polite; politely
1603	daarover-*adv*	about it	2011	dadelijk-*adv*	immediate, soon
1604	amper-*adv*	barely	2016	onlangs-*adv*	recently
1607	daarbuiten-*adv*	outside	2024	stevig-*adv; adj*	firmly; firm
1609	daarbij-*adv*	thereby	2029	koninklijk-*adj; adv*	royal; regally
1618	dwaas-*adj; de; adv*	silly; fool; foolishly	2033	voortaan-*adv*	henceforth
1623	bleek-*adj; adv*	pale; wanly	2055	pijnlijk-*adj; adv*	painful; painfully
1626	gezellig-*adj; adv*	cozy; cozily	2062	fris-*adj; adv*	fresh; freshly
1634	achterin-*adv*	in the back	2076	hierbij-*adv*	hereby
1649	daarbinnen-*adv*	in there	2078	modern-*adj; adv*	modern; contemporary
1655	hartstikke-*adv*	terribly	2080	dodelijk-*adj; adv*	deadly; deadly
1663	daarboven-*adv*	up there	2093	letterlijk-*adj; adv*	literal; to the letter
1672	eventjes-*adv*	momentarily	2113	vervolgens-*adv*	then
1673	hierover-*adv*	hereof	2128	daarnet-*adv*	earlier
1688	namelijk-*adv*	namely	2160	rechtstreeks-*adv; adj*	directly; direct
1694	daarop-*adv*	thereon	2166	inclusief-*adj; adv*	including; inclusively
1695	vlakbij-*adv*	nearby	2169	tijdelijk-*adv; adj*	temporarily; temporary
1701	bovenop-*adv*	on top	2173	allemachtig-*adv*	mighty
1731	volkomen-*adv*	utterly	2179	overdag-*adv*	in the daytime
1752	voorgoed-*adv*	permanently	2187	zowat-*adv*	almost
1777	daaraan-*adv*	on that	2197	overeind-*adv*	upright
1782	allang-*adv*	a long time ago	2208	vandaar-*adv*	hence
1794	afschuwelijk-*adj; adv*	horrible; awfully	2220	waaraan-*adv*	whereat
			2224	apart-*adj; adv*	separate; separately
1823	tenslotte-*adv*	finally	2231	's ochtends-*adv*	in the morning
1835	echter-*adv*	however	2240	achteraan-*adv*	in the back
1837	strak-*adj; adv*	tight; tightly	2246	erbuiten-*adv*	out (it)
1841	ondertussen-*adv*	meanwhile	2265	machtig-*adj; adv*	powerful; powerfully
1857	gewoonlijk-*adv*	usually	2304	vanwaar-*adv*	from where
1862	spoedig-*adv; adj*	soon; early	2318	plots-*adv; adj*	suddenly; sudden
1870	morgenavond-*adv*	tomorrow	2330	bijeen-*adv*	together
1875	waarbij-*con; adv*	whereby; whereat	2341	voorwaarts-*adj; adv*	forward; forward
1883	openbaar-*adj; adv*	public; openly	2373	charmant-*adj; adv*	charming; charmingly
1894	reeds-*adv*	already	2376	handig-*adj; adv*	convenient
1896	sindsdien-*adv*	since then	2381	heden-*adv; het*	given moment; now
1908	vanzelf-*adv*	self, by itself	2382	onbeleefd-*adj; adv*	rude; discourteously
1919	telkens-*adv*	constantly, again and again	2383	krachtig-*adj; adv*	powerful; vigorously
1925	erdoor-*adv*	through it	2391	grof-*adj; adv*	coarse; grossly

2397	hopeloos-*adj; adv*	hopeless; past hope
2409	zogenaamd-*adv; adj*	supposed; allegedly
2439	zelden-*adv*	rarely
2452	dagelijks-*adj; adv*	daily; daily
2473	tegelijkertijd-*adv*	at the same time
2491	alvast-*adv*	in advance
2503	streng-*de; adj; adv*	strand; strict; strictly
2522	sowieso-*adv*	definitely

Conjunctions

Rank	Dutch-PoS	English Equivalent
6	dat-*con; prn*	that; that
9	en-*con*	and
10	wat-*con; prn; adv*	what; what; few
19	maar-*adv; con*	however, just; but
21	die-*prn; con*	that; which
23	voor-*prp; adv; con*	for; before; ere
25	als-*adv; con; prp*	as; as; like
33	dan-*con; adv*	than; then
39	zo-*adv; con;*	so, that; if
42	wel-*adv; adj; con*	well; alright; as many as
47	waar-*adv; con; adj; de*	where; where; true; merchandise
48	nu-*adv; con*	now; now
58	of-*con*	or, whether
59	daar-*adv; con*	there; as
61	al-*adv; het; con*	already; all; though
66	waarom-*adv; con*	why; why
70	wie-*con; prn*	who; who
78	toch-*adv; con*	yet, so, right; nevertheless
80	alleen-*adv; con; adj*	only, merely; only; alone
82	dus-*adv; con*	so, consequently; therefore
93	tot-*prp; con*	to; until
107	toen-*con; adv*	when; then
118	omdat-*con*	because
131	zoals-*adv; con; adj; prp*	as; as; such as; like
136	anders-*adv; con*	different, else; otherwise
189	wanneer-*adv; con*	when; when
210	want-*con; de*	because; mitten
244	alsof-*con; adv*	like; as if
268	daarom-*con; adv*	therefore; hence
278	welk-*con; prn*	which; which
332	voordat-*prp; con*	prior to; ere
338	zodat-*con*	so that
353	sinds-*adv; con*	since; since
383	terwijl-*con*	while, whereas
461	daarna-*adv; con*	then, after; whereupon
505	hoezo-*adv; con*	why; why
591	zolang-*con*	as long as
641	totdat-*con*	until
651	nadat-*con*	after
663	zodra-*con*	once, as soon as
681	eer-*de; con*	honor; ere
722	tenzij-*con*	unless
819	waarop-*con; adv*	when; whereupon
1158	hoewel-*con*	although
1280	waardoor-*con*	whereby
1443	noch-*con*	nor
1525	aangezien-*con*	since
1812	ofwel-*con*	or
1830	indien-*con*	if
1875	waarbij-*con; adv*	whereby; whereat

Prepositions

Rank	Dutch-*PoS*	English Equivalent
11	van-*prp*	of, from
13	in-*prp*	in
15	op-*prp; adv; adj*	on, up, at; on, up; spent
16	te-*adv; prp*	too, to; in
23	voor-*prp; adv; con*	for; before; ere
24	met-*prp; adv*	with; along with
25	als-*adv; con; prp*	as; as; like
29	aan-*prp; adj*	to, on; on
31	om-*prp; adv*	to, for; about
32	naar-*prp; adv; adj*	to, for; along; awful
52	uit-*prp; adv; adj*	from; out; off
57	over-*prp; adv*	about; over
63	bij-*prp; de; adv*	at; bee; up to date
93	tot-*prp; con*	to; until
106	tegen-*prp; adv*	against
131	zoals-*adv; con; adj; prp*	as; as; such as; like
142	binnen-*adv; prp*	within; inside
161	na-*prp; adv*	after; post
163	toe-*prp; adv*	to; towards
179	zonder-*prp*	without
185	achter-*adv; prp*	behind; behind
190	onder-*adv; prp*	under, underneath; under
220	buiten-*adv; prp*	outside, out; outside
292	boven-*adv; prp*	above, over; above
299	tussen-*prp*	between
328	beneden-*adv; prp*	down, below; below
332	voordat-*prp; con*	prior to; ere
333	voorbij-*adj; adv; prp*	gone; past; beyond
358	per-*prp*	by
395	langs-*adv; prp*	along; along
404	vandaan-*prp*	from
427	vanaf-*prp*	from
458	tijdens-*prp*	during
566	ter-*prp*	to
577	behalve-*prp*	except
601	naast-*adj; prp*	near; next to
648	via-*prp*	via
665	vanuit-*prp*	from
691	vanwege-*prp*	because of
724	midden-*het; adj; prp*	middle; mid; amidst
1049	dankzij-*prp*	due to
1211	tegenover-*prp*	opposite
1282	ondanks-*prp*	despite
1402	wegens-*prp*	due to, because of
1720	gedurende-*prp*	during
1859	namens-*prp*	on behalf of

Pronouns

Rank	Dutch-*PoS*	English Equivalent
1	je-*prn*	you
2	het-*art; prn*	the; it
4	ik-*prn*	I
5	zijn-*prn; vb*	his, its; be
6	dat-*con; prn*	that; that
7	een-*art; nu; prn*	a; one; any
10	wat-*con; prn; adv*	what; what; few
12	we-*prn*	we
14	ze-*prn*	she, they
17	hij-*prn*	he
20	me-*prn*	me
21	die-*prn; con*	that; which
26	mijn-*prn*	my, mine
27	u-*prn*	you
28	dit-*prn*	this
34	jij-*prn*	you
38	geen-*art; adj; adv; prn; nu*	not one, no; no; no; none
45	hem-*prn*	him
49	hoe-*adv; prn*	how; how
53	haar-*prn; het*	her; hair
56	mij-*prn*	me
62	jullie-*prn*	you
64	ons-*prn; het/de*	us; ounce
67	iets-*prn; adv*	something; some
69	deze-*prn*	this
70	wie-*con; prn*	who; who
71	jou-*prn*	you
72	alles-*prn*	all, everything
88	niets-*het; prn; adv*	nothing; nothing; none
91	iemand-*prn*	someone; person
97	onze-*prn*	our
102	wij-*prn*	we
105	uw-*prn*	your
121	allemaal-*prn*	everything, everybody
125	zij-*prn; de*	she, they; side
128	jouw-*prn*	your
132	hun-*prn*	their
138	iedereen-*prn*	everyone
139	niemand-*prn*	nobody
140	ander-*adj; prn*	other; other
141	niks-*prn; adv*	nothing; none
150	zich-*prn*	himself
165	elkaar-*adv; prn*	each other; each other
169	alle-*prn*	every, all
211	zelf-*prn*	self
218	enig-*adv; adj; prn*	any; solely; single
227	hen-*prn; de*	them; hen
232	elk-*prn; adj; adv*	each, any; every
267	jezelf-*prn*	yourself
278	welk-*con; prn*	which; which
293	ergens-*adv; prn*	somewhere; someplace
324	ervan-*prn*	from it
357	hetzelfde-*prn; adj; adv*	same; ditto; ditto
412	mezelf-*prn*	myself
436	dezelfde-*prn*	same
478	zichzelf-*prn*	himself
487	men-*prn*	people, one
539	eentje-*prn*	alone, by yourself
544	sommige-*adj; prn*	some; some
546	degene-*prn*	the one, those
551	ieder-*prn; adj*	each; every
726	beide-*adj; prn*	both; either
1566	onszelf-*prn*	ourselves
1574	diegene-*prn*	he, she, those who
1685	allerlei-*prn*	all kinds of
1810	gij-*prn*	thou
1839	mekaar-*prn*	each other
1913	mijzelf-*prn*	myself
2073	uzelf-*prn*	yourself
2513	hetgeen-*prn*	which

Nouns

Rank	Dutch-*PoS*	English Equivalent
44	goed-*adj; adv; het*	good, correct; well; estate
47	waar-*adv; con; adj; de*	where; where; true; merchandise
53	haar-*prn; het*	her; hair
54	doen-*vb; het*	do, perform; doing
61	al-*adv; het; con*	already; all; though
63	bij-*prp; de; adv*	at; bee; up to date
64	ons-*prn; het/de*	us; ounce
65	meer-*adj; adv; het*	more; more; lake
76	man-*de*	man
77	weg-*de; adv*	road; away, gone
88	niets-*het; prn; adv*	nothing; nothing; none
96	mens-*het*	human
98	leven-*het; vb*	life; live
100	weer-*het; adv*	weather; again
104	tijd-*de*	time
109	net-*adv; het; adj*	just; net; elegant
113	dood-*de; adj*	death; dead
119	dag-*de; int*	day; bye
123	huis-*het*	house
125	zij-*prn; de*	she, they; side
126	jaar-*het*	year
127	vader-*de*	father
129	geld-*het*	money, cash
130	vrouw-*de*	woman, wife
133	god-*de*	god
134	keer-*de*	time
143	spijt-*de*	regret
149	werk-*het*	work
151	moeder-*de*	mother
154	meneer-*de*	mister
160	uur-*het*	hour
170	gek-*adj; de; adv*	crazy; fool; fool
176	ding-*het*	thing, object
177	eerste-*de; adv*	first; initial
180	vriend-*de*	friend
181	naam-*de*	name
182	jongen-*de*	boy
184	beetje-*het; adj*	bit; little
187	kind-*het*	child
192	hand-*de*	hand
194	eten-*vb; het*	eat; food
196	auto-*de*	car
197	idee-*het*	idea, notion
198	paar-*het*	couple
201	wereld-*de*	world
202	vraag-*de*	question
205	morgen-*de*	tomorrow, morning
208	lijken-*vb; de*	seem, resemble; cadavers
210	want-*con; de*	because; mitten
214	meisje-*het*	girl
222	geloof-*het*	faith, belief
227	hen-*prn; de*	them; hen
229	zoon-*de*	son
231	probleem-*het*	problem
234	orde-*de*	order, discipline
236	kant-*de*	side, lace
238	gelijk-*adj; het*	equal, similar; right
239	politie-*de*	police
242	hoofd-*het*	head, principal
251	pas-*adv; de*	just now; pass
253	familie-*de*	family
261	stad-*de*	city
263	oog-*het*	eye
264	plaats-*de*	place, location
265	manier-*de*	way, how
269	minuut-*de*	minute
270	school-*de*	school
274	moment-*het*	moment
275	pijn-*de*	pain
276	dollar-*de*	dollar
277	kamer-*de*	room, chamber
281	schat-*de*	treasure, honey
282	water-*het*	water
283	kans-*de*	chance
284	deur-*de*	door
285	land-*het*	land, earth, country
288	broer-*de*	brother
298	papa-*de*	dad
301	week-*de; adj*	week; soft
302	soort-*de*	kind
303	hulp-*de*	help, assistance
306	plan-*het*	plan, scheme
307	dokter-*de*	doctor
311	kop-*de*	head, cup
313	mevrouw-*de*	lady
314	nacht-*de*	night
315	bed-*het*	bed
317	mama-*de*	mom
320	zorg-*de*	care, worry
321	zaak-*de*	case, matter
323	liefde-*de*	love
326	mis-*adj; adv; de*	wrong, erroneous; wrong; mass
329	hart-*het*	heart
330	verhaal-*het*	story, redress

335	nummer-*het*	number, digit
341	Jezus-*de*	Jesus
342	druk-*de; adj; adv*	pressure; busy; busily
344	dochter-*de*	daughter
348	gezicht-*het*	face, sight
352	stel-*het*	set, bunch, couple
354	plek-*de*	place, spot
355	begin-*het*	beginning, start
363	baas-*de*	boss
364	baby-*de*	baby, nursling
365	agent-*de*	agent, policeman
366	film-*de*	film
367	mond-*de*	mouth
369	vent-*de*	fellow, geezer, guy
371	oorlog-*de*	war
374	hond-*de*	dog
375	waarheid-*de*	truth
376	geluk-*het*	happiness, luck
377	heer-*de*	lord, gentleman
379	avond-*de*	evening, night
380	zeer-*adj; adv; het*	very, highly; very; sore
382	nieuws-*het*	news, novelty
385	stuk-*het; adj*	piece, part; broken
387	maand-*de*	month
389	bloed-*het*	blood
391	mam-*de*	mom
393	rest-*de*	rest, remainder
397	vriendin-*de*	girlfriend
398	schuld-*de*	debt, blame
400	buurt-*de*	neighborhood, district
401	kerel-*de*	guy, fellow
402	ouder-*adj; de*	older, senior; parent
403	recht-*adj; adv; het*	right; right; right
406	rede-*de*	reason, speech
409	fout-*de; adj*	error, mistake; wrong
410	telefoon-*de*	phone
414	baan-*de*	job, track
415	boek-*het*	book
417	klinken-*vb; het*	sound, ring; clink
419	woord-*het*	word
420	kapitein-*de*	captain
424	pa-*de*	dad
425	zin-*de*	sentence
426	deel-*het*	part, segment
429	team-*het*	team
431	lieverd-*de*	darling, honey
433	geval-*het*	case
434	licht-*adj; het; adv*	light, mild; light; slightly
435	enkel-*adj; adv; de*	only, single; only; ankle
440	president-*de*	president
445	lichaam-*het*	body
447	kwaad-*adj; het*	evil, angry; evil
448	verliezen-*het; vb*	loss; lose
450	antwoord-*het*	answer
453	wapen-*het*	weapon
454	verdommen-*het*	refuse
455	idioot-*de; adj*	idiot; idiotic
456	stap-*de*	step, move
457	einde-*het*	end
460	vertrouwen-*het; vb*	confidence, faith; trust
462	plezier-*het*	fun
463	pap-*de*	dad
466	koning-*de*	king
467	spel-*het*	game
468	koffie-*de*	coffee
470	gevoel-*het*	feeling
474	gang-*de*	corridor, hallway
475	trek-*de*	pull
476	lucht-*de*	air, sky
477	meid-*de*	girl
483	zus-*de*	sister
484	onzin-*de*	nonsense, rubbish
486	muziek-*de*	music
490	oom-*de*	uncle
494	pardon-*het*	pardon, excuse me
498	grond-*de*	ground
503	kantoor-*het*	office
504	droom-*de*	dream
507	hemel-*de*	sky, heaven
508	foto-*de*	photo
513	gebruik-*het*	use
514	half-*het; adv*	half; semi
517	trots-*de; adj*	pride; proud
518	aarde-*de*	earth
519	vuur-*het*	fire
520	gevangenis-*de(f)*	prison
522	leger-*het*	army
523	persoon-*de*	person
525	kracht-*de*	force
527	ziekenhuis-*het*	hospital
528	moord-*de*	murder
535	vertrek-*het*	departure, room
537	punt-*het*	point
540	pistool-*het*	pistol
541	straat-*de*	street
542	toekomst-*de*	future
545	bank-*de*	bank; couch

547	spul-*het*	stuff	
549	vliegtuig-*het*	airplane	
552	informatie-*de*	information	
558	generaal-*de*	general	
559	boot-*de*	boat	
560	succes-*het*	success	
561	feest-*het*	party	
564	geest-*de*	spirit, ghost	
565	ongeluk-*het*	accident	
567	kleren-*de*	clothes	
569	liefje-*het*	sweetheart	
572	onderzoek-*het*	research, study	
573	honger-*de*	hunger	
575	hotel-*het*	hotel	
576	bal-*het*	ball	
578	controle-*de*	control	
579	zak-*de*	bag	
581	contact-*het*	contact	
582	meter-*de*	meter	
583	schip-*het*	ship	
586	show-*de*	show	
587	geheim-*adj; het*	secret; secret	
588	rot-*het; adj*	rot; rotten	
592	dienst-*de*	service	
594	rug-*de*	back	
595	advocaat-*de*	lawyer	
599	meester-*de*	master, teacher	
600	jong-*adj; het*	young; cub	
603	bestaan-*het; vb*	existence; exist	
605	bewijs-*het*	proof	
607	reis-*de*	travel	
608	afspraak-*de*	appointment	
609	rij-*de*	row	
612	kont-*de*	buttocks, bum	
615	seks-*de*	sex	
616	dame-*de*	lady	
617	prijs-*de*	price, prize	
618	trekken-*vb; het*	pull; draft	
622	maat-*de*	size, buddy	
623	hel-*de; adj; adv*	hell; bright; glaringly	
625	seconde-*de*	second	
626	regel-*de*	rule	
627	sla-*de*	lettuce	
630	doel-*het*	purpose, goal	
632	stem-*de*	vote, voice	
634	gevaar-*het*	danger	
636	arm-*de; adj*	arm; poor	
638	kolonel-*de*	colonel	
639	paard-*het*	horse	
640	tafel-*de*	table	
642	groep-*de*	group	

643	wedstrijd-*de*	match, game	
645	wagen-*de; vb*	car; risk	
646	grap-*de*	joke	
647	gat-*het*	hole	
650	band-*de*	tire, band	
652	moordenaar-*de*	killer, murderer	
653	ma-*de*	mom	
654	kaart-*de*	map	
656	kerk-*de*	church	
657	rijk-*adj; het*	rich; empire	
658	macht-*de*	power	
662	ruimte-*de*	space	
668	brief-*de*	letter	
669	gedachte-*de*	thought	
670	zuster-*de*	sister	
672	wet-*de*	law	
674	ziel-*de*	soul	
675	drug-*de*	drug	
677	sleutel-*de*	key	
678	haast-*de; adv*	hurry; almost	
679	eind-*het*	end	
681	eer-*de; con*	honor; ere	
682	zee-*de*	sea	
684	lijn-*de*	line	
685	teken-*het*	sign	
687	gast-*de*	guest, man	
688	situatie-*de*	situation	
692	zon-*de*	sun	
693	trein-*de*	train	
695	gebouw-*het*	building	
697	huwelijk-*het*	wedding	
698	draai-*de*	turn	
699	oma-*de*	grandmother	
700	schoen-*de*	shoe	
701	bus-*de*	bus	
702	bedrijf-*het*	business, company	
705	respect-*het*	respect	
709	muur-*de*	wall	
712	angst-*de*	fear	
713	been-*het*	leg	
714	keuze-*de*	choice	
715	broek-*de*	pants, trousers	
717	sergeant-*de*	sergeant	
719	gezin-*het*	family	
724	midden-*het; adj; prp*	middle; mid; amidst	
727	les-*de*	lesson	
729	brand-*de*	fire	
733	neus-*de*	nose	
734	verleden-*het*	past	
735	bericht-*het*	message	

736	goud-*het*	gold		818	ring-*de*	ring
737	donker-*adj; het*	dark; dark		820	klas-*de*	class
738	club-*de*	club		821	dier-*het*	animal
739	helft-*de*	half		822	geschiedenis-*de*	history
740	winkel-*de*	shop		823	wind-*de*	wind
742	vuil-*het; adj; adv*	dirt; dirty; filthily		824	missie-*de*	mission
745	sheriff-*de*	sheriff		828	adem-*de*	breath
746	vlees-*het*	meat		830	verjaardag-*de*	birthday
748	relatie-*de*	relation(ship)		831	weekend-*het*	weekend
750	raam-*het*	window		832	aantal-*het*	number
751	partner-*de*	partner		833	eiland-*het*	island
752	moeite-*de*	trouble, effort		834	nek-*de*	neck
753	professor-*de*	professor		836	rekening-*de*	account, check
754	camera-*de*	camera		840	regering-*de*	government
756	achteruit-*adv; de*	backwards; reverse		841	boodschap-*de*	message
				842	boord-*het*	board, collar
757	lift-*de*	lift, elevator, ride		843	dak-*het*	roof
758	lijst-*de*	list		844	verschil-*het*	difference
759	vrede-*de*	peace		845	bar-*de; adj*	bar; severe
762	geweer-*het*	rifle		846	zelfmoord-*de*	suicide
764	tante-*de*	aunt		847	kennis-*de*	knowledge
769	vijand-*de*	enemy		850	bom-*de*	bomb
770	volk-*het*	people, folk		851	vakantie-*de*	holiday, vacation
771	gebied-*het*	area		853	knul-*de*	young fellow
772	dorp-*het*	village		854	engels-*adj; het*	English; English
774	bureau-*het*	desk		855	kat-*de*	cat
775	gevecht-*het*	fight, battle		856	soldaat-*de*	soldier
776	held-*de*	hero		858	glas-*het*	glass
777	voet-*de*	foot		859	systeem-*het*	system
778	teveel-*het; adj*	excess; excess, too much		860	aanval-*de*	attack
779	bevel-*het*	order		861	opa-*de*	grandpa
781	slag-*de*	battle, stroke		862	mes-*het*	knife
782	la-*de*	drawer		863	hoek-*de*	corner
783	positie-*de*	position		865	stoel-*de*	chair
786	gesprek-*het*	conversation		866	taxi-*de*	taxi
787	wens-*de*	wish		867	mijnheer-*de*	sir, mister
789	beurt-*de*	turn		868	kus-*de*	kiss
790	radio-*de*	radio		869	krant-*de*	newspaper
792	lot-*het*	fate		870	keus-*de*	choice
793	luitenant-*de*	lieutenant		872	park-*het*	park
795	boom-*de*	tree		874	adres-*het*	address
802	vis-*de*	fish		876	richting-*de*	direction
803	koningin-*de*	queen		879	bier-*het*	beer
804	bezoek-*het*	visit		881	beest-*het*	beast
806	tas-*de*	bag		882	geluid-*het*	sound, noise
807	rechter-*adj; de*	right; judge		885	vrijheid-*de*	freedom
810	wijn-*de*	wine		888	prinses-*de*	princess
811	verrassing-*de*	surprise		889	lol-*de*	fun
814	aandacht-*de*	attention		891	totaal-*adj; het; adv*	total; total; totally
815	ijs-*het*	ice				
816	rivier-*de*	river		892	bek-*de*	beak, mouth

893	computer-*de*	computer
894	leer-*het; de*	leather; teaching
897	monster-*het*	sample, monster
898	juffrouw-*de*	female teacher, unmarried woman
902	maan-*de*	moon
903	jurk-*de*	gown, dress
904	keuken-*de*	kitchen
909	trap-*de*	stairs
910	beweging-*de*	movement
911	kilometer-*de*	kilometer
913	actie-*de*	action
914	rol-*de*	role
915	last-*de*	burden, bother
919	jas-*de*	coat
920	planeet-*de*	planet
922	neef-*de*	cousin
924	indruk-*de*	impression
926	broeder-*de*	brother
928	toestemming-*de*	permission
929	ster-*de*	star
931	bos-*het*	forest
935	mist-*de*	fog
936	brug-*de*	bridge
937	kussen-*het; vb*	pillow; kiss
938	excuus-*het*	excuse
941	rook-*de*	smoke
942	procent-*het*	percent
945	trouw-*de; adj*	faith; loyal
946	leider-*de*	leader
948	leeftijd-*de*	age
949	code-*de*	code
950	feit-*het*	fact
951	hoogte-*de*	height
953	homo-*de*	gay
955	commandant-*de*	commander
956	ervaring-*de*	experience
958	publiek-*het; adj*	audience; public
961	slot-*het*	lock
962	strijd-*de*	fight, competition
965	test-*de*	test
967	opdracht-*de*	assignment
969	prins-*de*	prince
973	tand-*de*	tooth
974	zomer-*de*	summer
976	duivel-*de*	devil
977	motor-*de*	engine
979	bloem-*de*	flower
980	operatie-*de*	operation
981	restaurant-*het*	restaurant
982	spoor-*het*	track
983	inspecteur-*de*	inspector
986	wonder-*het*	wonder, miracle
987	basis-*de*	basis, base
988	vertaling-*de*	translation
990	vlak-*adj; het; adv*	flat; surface; just
991	beeld-*het*	image, sculpture
993	boel-*de*	a lot
995	veiligheid-*de*	safety
996	top-*de*	top, peak
997	coach-*de*	coach
1001	pad-*het*	path
1004	ontbijt-*het*	breakfast
1005	beslissing-*de*	decision
1007	energie-*de*	energy
1010	wezen-*het; vb*	being; be
1011	cel-*de*	cell
1012	papieren-*adj; de*	paper; papers
1013	ochtend-*de*	morning
1015	amerikaan-*de*	American
1016	wraak-*de*	revenge
1018	vorm-*de*	form
1019	verklaring-*de*	statement
1021	directeur-*de*	director
1023	leiding-*de*	leadership
1024	zwaard-*het*	sword
1025	afstand-*de*	distance
1026	oor-*het*	ear
1027	lunch-*de*	lunch
1028	toilet-*het*	toilet
1031	programma-*het*	program
1032	fles-*de*	bottle
1034	opzij-*het*	aside
1038	gevoelens-*de*	feelings
1041	appartement-*het*	apartment
1042	universiteit-*de*	university
1043	moed-*de*	courage
1045	taak-*de*	task
1046	kamp-*het*	camp
1047	kip-*de*	chicken
1051	truck-*de*	truck
1052	misdaad-*de*	crime
1055	veld-*het*	field
1057	slachtoffer-*het*	victim
1058	troep-*de*	flock, pack, mess
1059	drankje-*het*	drink
1060	majesteit-*de*	majesty
1062	melk-*de*	milk
1064	post-*de*	post
1065	strand-*het*	beach

1067	getuige-*de*	witness	1151	tuin-*de*	garden
1069	donder-*de*	thunder	1152	doos-*de*	box
1071	steen-*de*	stone	1154	voedsel-*het*	food
1072	kogel-*de*	bullet, ball	1156	bende-*de*	mess, gang
1073	hoed-*de*	hat	1161	talent-*het*	talent, gift
1074	chef-*de*	chef	1162	kunst-*de*	art
1076	gedoe-*het*	hassle	1167	elf-*de; nu*	elf; eleven
1080	bedoeling-*de*	intention	1168	noorden-*het*	north
1082	pond-*het*	pound	1169	project-*het*	project
1086	pak-*het*	suit, pack	1170	advies-*het*	advice
1087	cent-*de*	cent	1171	koffer-*de*	suitcase
1088	risico-*het*	risk	1173	westen-*het*	west
1090	kleur-*de*	color	1174	vloer-*de*	floor
1092	berg-*de*	mountain	1175	zondag-*de*	Sunday
1093	genoegen-*het*	pleasure	1176	duur-*de; adj*	duration; expensive
1095	type-*het*	type	1178	vogel-*de*	bird
1096	stilte-*de*	silence	1179	laag-*adj; de*	low; layer
1097	medicijn-*het*	medicine	1180	zonde-*de; adj*	sin; too bad
1098	mening-*de*	opinion	1181	papier-*het*	paper
1099	schoonheid-*de*	beauty	1182	brood-*het*	bread
1102	twijfel-*de*	doubt	1185	alarm-*het*	alarm
1106	tent-*de*	tent	1186	station-*het*	station
1107	hoop-*de*	hope	1187	storm-*de*	storm
1108	geweld-*het*	violence	1188	oplossing-*de*	solution
1110	officier-*de*	officer	1190	schot-*het*	shot
1114	taal-*de*	language	1193	bruiloft-*de*	wedding
1117	klant-*de*	customer	1195	vergadering-*de*	meeting
1118	stappen-*het; vb*	step, go, stride; night out	1196	zuiden-*het*	south
1119	akkoord-*het*	agreement	1198	eigenaar-*de*	owner
1121	gedrag-*het*	behavior	1199	contract-*het*	contract
1123	Vrijdag-*de*	Friday	1201	beer-*de*	bear
1124	verstand-*het*	intellect, sense	1202	proces-*het*	process, trial
1126	hersenen-*de*	brain	1203	tong-*de*	tongue
1127	raad-*de*	advice	1204	leraar-*de*	teacher
1128	vinger-*de*	finger	1206	wijs-*adj; de*	wise; tune
1129	vaarwel-*het*	goodbye	1210	kust-*de*	coast
1131	toon-*de*	tone	1213	stront-*de*	shit
1132	favoriet-*de*	favorite	1214	ei-*het*	egg
1134	huid-*de*	skin	1215	pers-*de*	press, media
1136	machine-*de*	machine	1216	kampioen-*de*	champion
1138	echtgenoot-*de*	husband	1219	pot-*de*	crock, pot
1139	afdeling-*de*	department	1220	rechercheur-*de*	detective
1140	grens-*de*	border, limit	1222	ziekte-*de*	disease
1141	drank-*de*	beverage, booze	1223	kilo-*de*	kilo
1142	blik-*de*	look, tin	1224	lid-*het*	member
1144	burgemeester-*de*	mayor	1225	kelder-*de*	basement
			1226	klus-*de*	job
1145	rapport-*het*	report	1227	straf-*de; adj*	punishment; strong
1146	paniek-*de*	panic	1229	senator-*de*	senator
1147	begrafenis-*de*	funeral	1232	shirt-*het*	shirt
1148	gezelschap-*het*	company	1234	vliegveld-*het*	airport

1237	lach-*de*	smile	1337	vrees-*de*	fear
1238	west-*de*	west	1338	aap-*de*	monkey
1245	wild-*adj; het*	wild; wildlife	1341	varken-*het*	pig
1247	detail-*het*	detail	1344	pil-*de*	pill
1248	dossier-*het*	file	1347	arts-*de*	physician
1250	badkamer-*de*	bathroom	1348	gedeelte-*het*	part
1253	afscheid-*het*	farewell	1349	jury-*de*	jury
1254	race-*de*	race	1350	whisky-*de*	whiskey
1259	taart-*de*	cake	1352	nachtmerrie-*de*	nightmare
1260	graf-*het*	grave	1356	oosten-*het*	east
1262	carrière-*de*	career	1357	huur-*de*	rent
1265	champagne-*de*	champagne	1358	schrijver-*de*	writer
1266	natuur-*de*	nature	1359	buik-*de*	belly
1268	vergissing-*de*	mistake	1360	slaapkamer-*de*	bedroom
1269	priester-*de*	priest	1361	maagd-*de*	virgin
1270	graad-*de*	degree	1362	borst-*de*	chest, breast
1271	verdieping-*de*	floor	1363	dief-*de*	thief
1272	signaal-*het*	signal	1364	plicht-*de*	duty
1274	manager-*de*	manager	1366	verzoek-*het*	request
1275	schade-*de*	damage	1367	dichter-*de*	poet
1276	flat-*de*	flat	1368	boerderij-*de*	farm
1279	toegang-*de*	access	1369	horloge-*het*	watch
1281	ronde-*de*	round	1370	stijl-*de*	style, steep
1283	amen-*het*	amen	1371	eeuw-*de*	century
1285	dertig-*de*	thirty	1373	pauze-*de*	pause, break
1286	politiek-*de*	politics	1374	piloot-*de*	pilot
1292	voorkomen-*vb; het*	prevent; appearance	1375	sigaret-*de*	cigarette
			1376	winnaar-*de*	winner
1293	duits-*adj; het*	German; German	1378	aanvallen-*de; vb*	attacks; attack
1295	kast-*de*	closet	1379	medelijden-*het*	compassion, pity
1298	cadeau-*het*	gift	1382	detective-*de*	detective
1299	oceaan-*de*	ocean	1384	militair-*adj; de*	military; soldier
1302	omgeving-*de*	surroundings	1386	minister-*de*	minister
1304	verband-*het*	connection, bandage	1387	stof-*het*	substance, dust
1305	engel-*de*	angel	1388	bord-*het*	plate, dish
1306	bron-*de*	source	1389	voorstel-*het*	proposal
1310	belang-*het*	importance	1391	buur-*de*	neighbor
1311	steun-*de*	support	1396	waarde-*de*	value
1313	wei-*de*	whey	1397	gouverneur-*de*	governor
1317	keizer-*de*	emperor	1398	gas-*het*	gas
1319	genade-*de*	mercy	1400	touw-*het*	rope
1322	lef-*het*	courage	1403	voorbeeld-*het*	example
1323	kwestie-*de*	matter	1404	kaartje-*het*	card, ticket
1325	hoogheid-*de*	highness	1405	jeugd-*de*	youth
1326	snelheid-*de*	speed	1406	reden-*de*	reason
1328	beveiliging-*de*	safeguard, security	1407	niveau-*het*	level
1329	regen-*de*	rain	1408	nederlands-*adj; het*	Dutch; Dutch
1331	woestijn-*de*	desert			
1333	eenheid-*de*	unit, unity	1409	ontslag-*het*	dismissal
1334	verantwoordelijkheid-*de*	responsibility	1410	burger-*de*	citizen
			1411	toeval-*het*	chance

1413	bril-*de*	glasses	1502	aanbod-*het*	offer
1415	klap-*de*	blow, whack	1503	verslag-*het*	report
1416	keel-*de*	throat	1504	winter-*de*	winter
1417	magie-*de*	magic	1507	garage-*de*	garage
1418	scène-*de*	scene	1508	omstandigheid-*de*	circumstance
1419	koers-*de*	rate, course, track	1510	uniform-*het*	uniform
1420	stroom-*de*	current, stream, electricity	1513	onderwerp-*het*	subject, topic
1422	diner-*het*	dinner	1515	ellende-*de*	misery
1423	hersens-*de*	brain	1517	pop-*de*	doll
1424	dekking-*de*	cover	1518	fabriek-*de*	factory
1425	chauffeur-*de*	driver	1519	lied-*het*	song
1426	kist-*de*	chest	1523	rechtbank-*de*	court
1427	gezondheid-*de*	health	1524	lijf-*het*	body
1430	terrein-*het*	terrain	1527	training-*de*	workout, training
1432	beroep-*het*	profession	1529	rat-*de*	rat
1433	kerstfeest-*het*	Christmas (party)	1531	artikel-*het*	article
1437	hal-*de*	hall	1533	partij-*de*	party
1440	jongeman-*de*	young man	1536	mensheid-*de*	humanity
1444	centrum-*het*	center	1537	kaas-*de*	cheese
1445	wolf-*de*	wolf	1538	bruid-*de*	bride
1446	duitser-*de*	German	1540	kasteel-*het*	castle
1448	zwembad-*het*	swimming pool	1542	schaduw-*de*	shadow
1449	poort-*de*	port	1543	marine-*de*	navy
1451	geur-*de*	smell	1544	belofte-*de*	promise
1452	theorie-*de*	theory	1545	lip-*de*	lip
1453	geheugen-*het*	memory	1549	douche-*de*	shower
1454	benzine-*de*	petrol, gasoline	1551	komst-*de*	arrival
1456	leugen-*de*	lie	1552	heks-*de*	witch
1457	genie-*het*	genius	1554	materiaal-*het*	material
1459	spiegel-*de*	mirror	1555	cheque-*de*	check
1465	markt-*de*	market	1558	meerdere-*de; adv*	superior; multiple
1467	mogelijkheid-*de*	possibility			
1471	overwinning-*de*	victory	1559	maag-*de*	stomach
1473	handel-*de*	trade, act	1561	toestand-*de*	state
1475	herinnering-*de*	reminder	1562	jood-*de*	Jew
1476	verdediging-*de*	defense	1564	nicht-*de*	niece
1478	verandering-*de*	change	1565	klok-*de*	clock
1479	pizza-*de*	pizza	1567	slang-*de*	hose, snake
1483	wc-*de*	toilet	1571	reputatie-*de*	reputation
1484	gave-*de*	gift	1572	junior-*de; adj*	junior; minor
1486	ramp-*de*	disaster	1575	cijfer-*het*	figure, grade, numeral
1487	pensioen-*het*	pension	1577	masker-*het*	mask
1488	russisch-*adj; het*	Russian; Russian	1578	ambulance-*de*	ambulance
1489	geheel-*adj; het; adv*	whole; whole; entirely	1579	dek-*het*	deck
			1580	sneeuw-*de*	snow
1490	bescherming-*de*	protection	1581	waarschuwing-*de*	warning
1491	jacht-*de, het*	hunt, yacht			
1492	wetenschap-*de*	science	1582	rus-*de*	Russian
1497	interesse-*de*	interest	1583	hekel-*de*	dislike
1501	gegeven-*adj; het*	given; given	1584	reactie-*de*	reaction

1585	verdriet-*het*	grief
1586	bijbel-*de*	Bible
1587	mijl-*de*	mile
1588	tunnel-*de*	tunnel
1590	kou(de)-*de*	cold
1592	pen-*de*	pen
1593	graaf-*de*	count
1594	kleding-*de*	clothing
1596	vriendschap-*de*	friendship
1597	chinees-*adj; de*	Chinese; Chinese
1599	middag-*de*	noon
1602	stand-*de*	position
1605	virus-*het*	virus
1606	invloed-*de*	influence
1608	schande-*de*	shame
1610	winst-*de*	profit
1611	gemeenschap-*de*	community
1612	kruis-*het*	cross
1615	tank-*de*	tank
1616	hek-*het*	fence
1617	acteur-*de*	actor
1618	dwaas-*adj; de; adv*	silly; fool; foolishly
1619	trainen-*vb; het*	train; training
1620	golf-*de*	golf, wave
1621	snijden-*vb; het*	cut; slicing
1624	voordeel-*het*	advantage
1625	bewaker-*de*	guard
1627	koninkrijk-*het*	kingdom
1628	helikopter-*de*	helicopter
1629	hout-*het*	wood
1630	commissaris-*de*	commissioner
1631	duisternis-*de*	darkness
1632	grootvader-*de*	grandfather
1636	legende-*de*	legend
1639	televisie-*de*	television
1640	beloning-*de*	reward
1641	poging-*de*	attempt
1642	hut-*de*	cabin
1644	model-*het*	model
1645	zegen-*de;*	blessing
1646	suiker-*de*	sugar
1647	vet-*het*	fat
1648	voldoende-*adj; de*	satisfactory; sufficient
1651	woede-*de*	rage
1652	sport-*de*	sport
1654	middernacht-*de*	midnight
1656	diamant-*de*	diamond
1657	fan-*de*	fan
1661	verzet-*het*	resistance
1662	klasse-*de*	class
1665	april-*de*	April
1666	theater-*het*	theater
1667	nul-*het*	zero
1668	mamma-*de*	mum
1669	kanker-*de*	cancer
1670	fort-*het*	fortress
1671	ogenblik-*het*	moment
1677	personeel-*het*	staff
1678	zijde-*de*	side
1679	overval-*de*	raid, robbery
1680	gras-*het*	grass
1681	assistent-*de*	assistant
1683	lafaard-*de*	coward
1689	zand-*het*	sand
1690	voorzitter-*de*	chairman
1691	maal-*de; het*	time; meal
1692	geschenk-*het*	gift
1693	rommel-*de*	clutter
1700	houding-*de*	attitude
1703	besef-*het*	realization
1705	vloek-*de*	curse
1706	seizoen-*het*	season
1707	route-*de*	route
1708	Vietnam-*het*	Vietnam
1709	realiteit-*de*	reality
1710	as-*de*	ash
1713	podium-*het*	stage
1715	fiets-*de*	bike
1716	toren-*de*	tower
1718	pappa-*de*	daddy
1719	mannetje-*het*	small/little man
1722	staart-*de*	tail
1723	traan-*de*	tear
1724	attentie-*de*	attention
1725	museum-*het*	museum
1729	pest-*de*	plague
1730	knop-*de*	button
1732	tekst-*de*	text
1733	jungle-*de*	jungle
1735	vleugel-*de*	wing
1736	koe-*de*	cow
1737	huiswerk-*het*	homework
1738	uitzicht-*het*	view
1739	verrader-*de*	traitor
1740	pakje-*het*	packet
1742	overheid-*de*	government
1744	rand-*de*	edge
1745	indiaan-*de*	Indian
1748	ontmoeting-*de*	encounter

1749	overkant-*de*	other side	
1751	handtekening-*de*	signature	
1753	gunst-*de*	favor	
1755	soep-*de*	soup	
1756	eis-*de*	demand	
1757	alcohol-*de*	alcohol	
1759	wijf-*het*	hag	
1760	heuvel-*de*	hill	
1762	verbinding-*de*	connection	
1764	hof-*het*	court	
1765	organisatie-*de*	organization	
1766	dader-*de*	perpetrator	
1768	geboorte-*de*	birth	
1769	behandeling-*de*	treatment	
1770	gewicht-*het*	weight	
1771	zusje-*het*	little sister	
1774	speelgoed-*het*	toy	
1775	grot-*de*	cave	
1778	plas-*de*	puddle	
1781	pech-*de*	bad luck	
1784	collega-*de*	colleague	
1785	avontuur-*het*	adventure	
1787	bemanning-*de*	crew	
1788	studio-*de*	studio	
1789	interview-*het*	interview	
1790	student-*de*	student	
1791	explosie-*de*	explosion	
1792	bibliotheek-*de*	library	
1793	bezwaar-*het*	objection	
1795	overeenkomst-*de*	agreement	
1796	opname-*de*	recording	
1797	expert-*de*	expert	
1800	speler-*de*	player	
1801	kopje-*het*	cup	
1802	humor-*de*	humor	
1803	koekje-*het*	cookie	
1805	titel-*de*	title	
1806	truc-*de*	trick	
1807	haven-*de*	port	
1814	proef-*de*	test	
1816	fantasie-*de*	fantasy	
1817	dominee-*de*	pastor	
1820	opleiding-*de*	training	
1826	zone-*de*	zone	
1827	tape-*de*	tape	
1828	vat-*het*	container, keg	
1829	bodem-*de*	bottom	
1831	penis-*de*	penis	
1832	ex-*de*	ex	

1833	samenwerken-*vb; het*	co-operate; teamwork
1834	lawaai-*het*	noise
1836	bagage-*de*	luggage
1842	moeilijkheid-*de*	difficulty
1845	uitdaging-*de*	challenge
1846	lieveling-*de*	favorite
1847	psychiater-*de*	psychiatrist
1848	vak-*het*	section, compartment, profession
1852	schilderij-*het*	painting
1853	vlag-*de*	flag
1855	applaus-*het*	applause
1858	schouder-*de*	shoulder
1860	centrale-*de*	headquarters, station, power plant
1861	rit-*de*	ride
1863	duiken-*het; vb*	diving; dive
1865	aanklacht-*de*	charge
1866	paleis-*het*	palace
1868	werkelijkheid-*de*	reality
1869	gemak-*het*	convenience
1871	effect-*het*	effect
1872	konijn-*het*	rabbit
1874	ingang-*de*	entrance
1877	resultaat-*het*	result
1878	bot-*het; adj*	bone; blunt
1879	uitnodiging-*de*	invitation
1880	lokaal-*adj; het*	local; place
1882	aanwezigheid-*de*	presence
1884	Juli-*de*	July
1885	vrachtwagen-*de*	truck
1886	gerechtigheid-*de*	righteousness
1887	draak-*de*	dragon
1891	lust-*de*	lust
1892	scheiding-*de*	divorce
1898	Juni-*de*	June
1900	tovenaar-*de*	wizard
1901	college-*het*	college
1902	maaltijd-*de*	meal
1904	munitie-*de*	ammunition
1907	raket-*de*	rocket
1909	paspoort-*het*	passport
1910	lading-*de*	cargo
1912	duw-*de*	push
1915	nood-*de*	need
1917	gerucht-*het*	rumor
1918	set-*de*	set
1920	chaos-*de*	chaos
1923	terrorist-*de*	terrorist
1924	hartaanval-*de*	heart attack

1926	schuur-*de*	barn, shed
1927	zekerheid-*de*	certainty
1929	stemming-*de*	vote; mood
1930	technologie-*de*	technology
1932	hol-*adv; het*	empty; hole
1935	karakter-*het*	personality
1937	kleintje-*het*	little one
1938	periode-*de*	period
1940	Spanje-*het*	Spain
1941	ketting-*de*	chain
1942	apparaat-*het*	device
1943	loon-*het*	wage
1944	hoofdkwartier-*het*	headquarters
1945	bereik-*het*	range
1946	slaaf-*de*	slave
1950	naaien-*vb; het*	sew; dressmaking
1953	dagboek-*het*	diary
1954	achterkant-*de*	back
1955	betekenis-*de*	meaning
1957	verraad-*het*	betrayal
1958	schreeuw-*de*	scream
1961	vee-*het*	cattle
1962	kosten-*de; vb*	price; cost
1965	verkeer-*het*	traffic
1966	universum-*het*	universe
1969	chocolade-*de*	chocolate
1970	ondergoed-*het*	underwear
1971	boer-*de*	farmer
1972	behoefte-*de*	need
1973	fase-*de*	phase
1974	revolutie-*de*	revolution
1976	lente-*de*	spring
1978	spion-*de*	spy
1979	promotie-*de*	promotion
1981	plant-*de*	plant
1982	rots-*de*	rock
1984	stok-*de*	stick
1985	kwart-*het*	quarter
1986	eikel-*de*	acorn, jerk
1987	leeuw-*de*	lion
1994	zout-*adj; het*	salt; salt
1997	daad-*de*	act
1999	passie-*de*	passion
2000	piano-*de*	piano
2003	uitgang-*de(m)*	exit
2006	rijbewijs-*het*	driving license
2007	tempel-*de*	temple
2008	instructie-*de*	instruction
2009	admiraal-*de*	admiral
2014	eigendom-*het*	property
2015	borrel-*de*	drink
2019	spanning-*de*	tension, voltage, pressure
2020	brein-*het*	brain
2021	aandeel-*het*	share
2022	experiment-*het*	experiment
2026	glimlach-*de*	smile
2027	gelegenheid-*de*	opportunity, occasion
2030	ezel-*de*	donkey
2031	voetbal-*de/het*	football (ball), football (sport)
2032	lade-*de*	drawer
2034	middel-*het*	waist, method
2035	traditie-*de*	tradition
2036	commissie-*de*	committee, commission
2037	hoofdpijn-*de*	headache
2038	lever-*de*	liver
2040	oefening-*de*	exercise
2041	gevolg-*het*	result
2042	kopie-*de*	copy
2043	kok-*de*	cook
2045	brandstof-*de*	fuel
2046	studie-*de*	study
2047	uitweg-*de*	solution, way out
2048	actrice-*de*	actress
2049	ras-*het*	race, breed
2051	das-*de*	tie
2054	medium-*adj; het*	medium; medium
2056	datum-*de*	date
2057	zeep-*de*	soap
2058	waanzin-*de*	madness
2060	verzekering-*de*	insurance
2061	kom-*de*	bowl
2063	circus-*het*	circus
2064	passagier-*de*	passenger
2065	paradijs-*het*	paradise
2066	onderdeel-*het*	part, component
2069	bedreiging-*de*	threat
2071	bijeenkomst-*de*	meeting
2072	plaat-*de*	panel, illustration, record
2074	zaal-*de*	room
2075	laars-*de*	boot
2077	versie-*de*	version
2079	zenuw-*de*	nerve
2083	verlangen-*het; vb*	desire; desire
2084	aard-*de*	nature
2085	versterking-*de*	reinforcement
2086	metro-*de*	metro
2087	nut-*het*	utility
2088	maatschappij-*de*	society
2090	fortuin-*het*	fortune

2092	kameraad-*de*	comrade	2176	kooi-*de*	cage
2094	gok-*de*	gamble	2178	centimeter-*de*	centimeter
2097	varen-*vb; het*	sail; fern, sailing	2180	tweeling-*de*	twin
2098	tip-*de*	tip	2183	verpleegster-*de*	nurse
2099	ridder-*de; adj*	knight; cavalier	2184	oordeel-*het*	judgment
2102	knie-*de*	knee	2186	aanklager-*de*	prosecutor
2103	concert-*het*	concert	2189	juweel-*het*	jewel
2104	identiteit-*de*	identity	2191	ambassade-*de*	embassy
2107	mail-*de*	mail	2194	schakel-*de*	link
2108	ministerie-*het*	ministry	2196	heelal-*het*	universe
2109	finale-*de*	final	2198	uitvoer-*de*	export
2110	therapie-*de*	therapy	2199	achtergrond-*de*	background
2111	vooruitgang-*de*	progress	2200	lamp-*de*	lamp
2114	vermogen-*het*	power, ability	2203	baard-*de*	beard
2115	Justitie-*de*	justice	2205	mysterie-*het*	mystery
2118	bedrag-*het*	amount	2209	serie-*de*	series
2119	zuurstof-*de*	oxygen	2211	service-*de*	service
2121	schema-*het*	scheme, schedule	2212	helm-*de*	helmet
2122	zooi-*de*	mess	2213	knal-*de*	bang
2123	gebeurtenis-*de*	event	2214	afval-*het*	garbage
2124	commentaar-*het*	comment	2216	koorts-*de*	fever
2125	kanaal-*het*	channel	2218	toestel-*het*	device
2126	trekker-*de*	tractor	2226	inzet-*de*	effort, bet
2127	ton-*de*	tonne	2227	gebrek-*het; adj*	lack; vice
2129	journalist-*de*	journalist	2228	koelkast-*de*	refrigerator
2130	jasje-*het*	jacket	2229	riem-*de*	belt
2131	tuig-*het*	rig, harness, scum	2233	oproep-*de*	call
2133	snoep-*de*	candy	2234	menigte-*de*	crowd
2135	discussie-*de*	discussion	2235	ambassadeur-*de*	ambassador
2136	gewoonte-*de*	habit	2242	portemonnee-*de*	wallet
2137	positief-*adj; het*	positive; positive			
2140	tijger-*de*	tiger	2245	staf-*de*	stave
2142	hoofdstuk-*het*	chapter	2247	moeras-*het*	swamp
2144	crisis-*de*	crisis	2250	grootmoeder-*de*	grandmother
2146	revolver-*de*	revolver	2251	vrijlaten-*het; vb*	release; release
2147	beurs-*de*	exchange, scholarship	2252	schutter-*de*	shooter
2148	leerling-*de*	pupil, student	2253	cirkel-*de*	circle
2149	reclame-*de*	advertisement	2255	mazzel-*de*	luck
2152	long-*de*	lung	2256	incident-*het*	incident
2155	scherm-*het*	screen	2257	kliniek-*de*	clinic
2156	politieagent-*de*	policeman	2259	combinatie-*de*	combination
2159	greep-*de*	hold, grasp	2260	bestemming-*de*	destination
2161	ranch-*de*	ranch	2261	beslag-*het*	batter
2163	document-*het*	document	2262	gitaar-*de*	guitar
2164	pan-*de*	pan	2263	generatie-*de*	generation
2167	commando-*de*	command	2264	pagina-*de*	page
2168	pijp-*de*	pipe	2266	optie-*de*	option
2170	vreugde-*de*	joy	2267	congres-*het*	congress
2171	ticket-*het*	ticket	2268	haak-*de*	hook
2172	negatief-*adj; het*	negative; negative	2270	ham-*de*	ham
2175	pet-*de*	cap	2271	regisseur-*de*	director

2272	kwartier-*het*	fifteen minutes		2345	troon-*de*	throne
2274	hitte-*de*	heat		2346	voorstelling-*de*	performance
2275	begrip-*het*	understanding		2347	tegenstander-*de*	opponent
2276	natie-*de*	nation		2349	zonsopgang-*de*	sunrise
2277	gereedschap-*het*	tool		2350	hakken-*de; vb*	heels; chop
2278	gids-*de*	guide		2354	communicatie-*de*	communication
2279	poot-*de*	leg		2355	salaris-*het*	salary
2281	korporaal-*de*	corporal		2356	topper-*de*	top class
2283	aanwijzing-*de*	instruction		2357	baron-*de*	baron
2284	glorie-*de*	glory		2359	treffen-*vb; het*	meet; encounter
2288	zender-*de*	transmitter		2361	muis-*de*	mouse
2291	techniek-*de*	technique		2363	brigadier-*de*	constable, brigadier
2292	uiterlijk-*het*	appearance		2364	kroon-*de*	crown
2293	zweet-*het*	sweat		2365	netwerk-*het*	network
2294	verblijf-*het*	stay		2366	roos-*de*	rose
2295	bewaking-*de*	surveillance		2371	porno-*de*	porn
2297	fruit-*het*	fruit		2374	handschoen-*de*	glove
2298	bestuur-*het*	management		2377	pastoor-*de*	priest
2300	wetenschapper-*de*	scientist		2378	rechtszaak-*de*	trial
2302	gedicht-*het*	poem		2380	stam-*de*	tribe
2303	temperatuur-*de*	temperature		2381	heden-*adv; het*	given moment; now
2305	plastic-*het*	plastic		2385	misverstand-*het*	misunderstanding
2306	figuur-*het*	figure		2386	procedure-*de*	procedure
2308	kruipen-*vb; het*	crawl; crawling		2392	boon-*de*	bean
2309	symbool-*het*	symbol		2394	puinhoop-*de*	mess
2310	bevolking-*de*	population		2395	wijsheid-*de*	wisdom
2311	olifant-*de*	elephant		2396	kandidaat-*de*	candidate
2312	testament-*het*	will		2398	diefstal-*de*	theft
2313	schrik-*de*	scare		2399	accent-*het*	accent
2314	emotie-*de*	emotion		2400	economie-*de*	economy
2317	aanslag-*de*	assault		2401	rente-*de*	interest
2319	december-*de*	December		2403	sectie-*de*	section
2320	modder-*de*	mud, dirt		2404	verf-*de*	paint
2321	tandarts-*de*	dentist		2405	verhouding-*de*	ratio
2322	campagne-*de*	campaign		2407	angel-*de*	sting
2323	kostuum-*het*	costume		2408	cultuur-*de*	culture
2326	status-*de*	status		2411	buurman-*de*	neighbor
2328	herrie-*de*	noise		2413	kap-*de*	hood
2331	november-*de*	November		2416	toneel-*het*	stage
2333	telefoonnummer-*het*	telephone number		2417	handdoek-*de*	towel
2334	secretaresse-*de*	secretary		2418	roman-*de*	novel
2335	oorzaak-*de*	cause		2419	staal-*het*	steel
2336	deken-*de*	blanket		2421	wang-*de*	cheek
2337	link-*de; adj*	link; dangerous		2422	put-*de*	well
2338	vreemdeling-*de*	stranger		2423	huisje-*het*	cottage
2339	pols-*de*	wrist		2424	tempo-*het*	pace
2342	maffia-*de*	mafia		2426	bouw-*de*	construction
2343	wolk-*de*	cloud		2427	draad-*de*	wire
2344	teen-*de*	toe		2428	toespraak-*de*	speech
				2429	opening-*de*	opening

2430	artiest-*de*	artist
2431	privacy-*de*	privacy
2432	blok-*het*	block
2434	handje-*het*	hand
2435	drama-*het*	drama
2436	voertuig-*het*	vehicle
2440	nest-*het*	nest
2441	krijt-*het*	chalk
2443	compagnie-*de*	company
2448	warmte-*de*	heat
2450	record-*het*	record
2451	pater-*de*	father (priest)
2453	weduwe-*de*	widow
2454	tekort-*het*	deficit
2455	front-*het*	front
2457	bliksem-*de*	lightning
2460	kwaliteit-*de*	quality
2462	jager-*de*	hunter
2463	tred-*de*	pace
2465	district-*het*	district
2466	sector-*de*	sector
2467	schild-*het*	shield
2468	kerkhof-*het*	cemetery
2469	overlijden-*het; vb*	death; decease
2470	bewustzijn-*het*	consciousness
2472	recept-*het*	recipe
2474	gijzelaar-*de*	hostage
2475	wond-*de*	wound
2476	schuilplaats-*de*	shelter
2478	cake-*de*	cake
2481	offer-*het*	sacrifice
2483	wiskunde-*de*	mathematics
2484	examen-*het*	examination
2485	vloot-*de*	fleet
2486	avondeten-*het*	supper
2488	tering-*de*	typhus
2489	zonsondergang-*de*	sunset
2492	honkbal-*het*	baseball
2493	mode-*de*	fashion
2494	autoriteit-*de*	authority
2495	oppassen-*het; vb*	babysit; beware
2496	belasting-*de*	tax
2501	spier-*de*	muscle
2502	knoop-*de*	button
2503	streng-*de; adj; adv*	strand; strict; strictly
2504	rondje-*het*	round
2506	vermaak-*het*	entertainment
2508	opstand-*de*	rebellion
2510	schedel-*de*	skull
2512	uitzending-*adj; de*	broadcast; transmission
2516	hemd-*het*	shirt
2517	beschaving-*de*	civilization
2518	marinier-*de*	marine
2519	schijn-*de*	appearance
2520	inwoner-*de*	resident, inhabitant
2521	leed-*het*	anguish
2524	wodka-*de*	vodka
2525	politieman-*de*	policeman

Numerals

Rank	Dutch-*PoS*	English Equivalent
7	een-*art; nu; prn*	a; one; any
38	geen-*art; adj; adv; prn; nu*	not one, no; no; no; none
103	twee-*nu*	two
162	drie-*nu*	three
257	vijf-*nu*	five
262	hoeveel-*nu*	how much; what
280	vier-*nu*	four
327	tien-*nu*	ten
349	zes-*nu*	six
430	miljoen-*nu*	million
438	tweede-*nu*	second
482	zeven-*nu*	seven
637	derde-*nu*	third
664	negen-*nu*	nine
900	twintig-*nu*	twenty
912	honderd-*nu*	hundred
917	twaalf-*nu*	twelve
964	duizend-*nu*	thousand
1167	elf-*de; nu*	elf; eleven
1461	vijftien-*nu*	fifteen
1541	vijftig-*nu*	fifty
1717	heleboel-*nu*	a lot
1988	veertig-*nu*	forty
1998	miljard-*nu*	billion
2500	zesde-*nu*	sixth
2509	dertien-*nu*	thirteen
2511	zestien-*nu*	sixteen

Verbs

Rank	Dutch-PoS	English Equivalent
5	zijn-*prn; vb*	his, its; be
22	hebben-*av; vb*	have; have
35	weten-*vb*	know
37	kunnen-*vb*	can
41	willen-*vb*	want
43	moeten-*vb; av*	must, need; should
50	gaan-*vb; av*	go, work; shall
51	komen-*vb*	come, come to
54	doen-*vb; het*	do, perform; doing
60	zullen-*vb; av*	will; shall
68	laten-*vb*	let, leave
73	denken-*vb*	think, think of
79	zien-*vb*	see, look
86	houden-*vb*	keep, hold
89	zeggen-*vb*	say
92	kijken-*vb*	look
95	worden-*vb*	will be, become
98	leven-*het; vb*	life; live
108	zitten-*vb*	sit
111	maken-*vb*	make
112	mogen-*vb*	may, like
116	wachten-*vb*	wait
117	geven-*vb*	give
122	danken-*vb*	thank
137	bedanken-*vb*	thank
146	nemen-*vb*	take
147	vinden-*vb*	find
148	staan-*vb*	stand
152	praten-*vb*	talk
153	bedoelen-*vb*	mean
159	luisteren-*vb*	listen
167	blijven-*vb*	stay
171	helpen-*vb;*	help
174	wissen-*vb*	wipe
178	krijgen-*vb*	get
193	vertellen-*vb*	tell
194	eten-*vb; het*	eat; food
195	horen-*vb*	hear
199	zorgen-*vb*	care, worry
203	gebeuren-*vb*	happen
206	vragen-*vb*	ask
208	lijken-*vb; de*	seem, resemble; cadavers
215	kennen-*vb*	know
225	halen-*vb*	get, fetch
228	hopen-*vb*	hope
237	begrijpen-*vb*	understand, grasp
245	zetten-*vb*	put, place
246	voelen-*vb*	feel
249	proberen-*vb*	try, attempt
252	werken-*vb*	work
254	volgen-*vb*	follow, track
255	bellen-*vb*	dial
258	vermoorden-*vb*	murder, assassinate
260	schieten-*vb*	shoot, fire
266	zoeken-*vb*	search
271	geloven-*vb*	believe, think
272	spelen-*vb*	play, game
287	brengen-*vb*	bring
294	liggen-*vb*	lie
296	spreken-*vb*	speak
304	vergeten-*vb*	forget
305	pakken-*vb*	grab
308	betekenen-*vb*	mean
310	kloppen-*vb*	knock, beat
312	beginnen-*vb*	start, begin
316	lopen-*vb*	walk
318	stoppen-*vb*	stop, cease
322	gebruiken-*vb*	use
334	leren-*vb; adj*	learn; teach
339	hoeven-*av*	need, have to
340	slapen-*vb*	sleep
345	snappen-*vb*	understand, get
356	drinken-*vb*	drink
370	vallen-*vb*	fall, drop
372	rusten-*vb*	rest, lie
373	sterven-*vb*	die
392	redden-*vb*	save, rescue
399	betalen-*vb*	pay
417	klinken-*vb; het*	sound, ring; clink
422	haten-*vb*	hate
428	rijden-*vb*	ride, drive
441	ontmoeten-*vb*	meet
442	noemen-*vb*	call, mention
443	vechten-*vb*	fight, battle
444	trouwen-*vb*	marry
448	verliezen-*het; vb*	loss; lose
451	veranderen-*vb*	change
460	vertrouwen-*het; vb*	confidence, faith; trust
465	kopen-*vb*	buy
472	achten-*vb*	deem
479	leggen-*vb*	lay, put
481	winnen-*vb*	win
493	herinneren-*vb*	remember
497	verwachten-*vb*	expect
501	beloven-*vb*	promise
516	sturen-*vb*	send, steer
529	verlaten-*vb; adj*	leave; abandoned

530	lezen-*vb*	read	880	draaien-*vb*	turn
538	stellen-*vb*	suppose, put	884	overleven-*vb*	survive
548	schrijven-*vb*	write	895	zagen-*vb*	saw
557	slaan-*vb*	beat, hit	899	ontslaan-*vb*	dismiss, fire
563	vliegen-*vb*	fly	906	plaatsen-*vb*	place, plant, put
580	wonen-*vb*	live	921	bouwen-*vb*	build
585	verkopen-*vb*	sell	925	betrekken-*vb*	involve
589	doden-*vb*	kill	930	springen-*vb*	jump
593	wegwezen-*vb*	get out	932	passen-*vb*	suit, fit
602	beschermen-*vb*	protect	933	ontdekken-*vb*	discover
603	bestaan-*het; vb*	existence; exist	937	kussen-*het; vb*	pillow; kiss
606	lachen-*vb*	laugh	940	ontvangen-*vb*	receive
610	voorstellen-*vb*	propose	943	getuigen-*vb*	testify
611	raken-*vb*	hit, touch	944	durven-*vb*	dare
613	schelen-*vb*	differ, care	947	bidden-*vb*	pray
614	lukken-*vb*	succeed	952	starten-*vb*	start
618	trekken-*vb; het*	pull; draft	954	vieren-*vb*	celebrate
619	stelen-*vb*	steal	957	nadenken-*vb*	reflect, think
620	dragen-*vb;*	wear, carry	959	roepen-*vb*	call
624	rennen-*vb*	run	960	slagen-*vb*	succeed
629	missen-*vb*	miss	966	besluiten-*vb*	decide
645	wagen-*de; vb*	car; risk	968	roken-*vb*	smoke
649	raden-*vb*	guess	971	storen-*vb*	disturb
659	vluchten-*vb*	flee	972	vernietigen-*vb*	destroy
671	gooien-*vb*	throw	978	bezitten-*vb*	own
680	duren-*vb*	last, take	989	betreffen-*vb*	concern
696	delen-*vb*	share	992	wijten-*vb*	blame
703	bewegen-*vb*	move	999	genieten-*vb*	enjoy
710	breken-*vb*	break	1002	opstaan-*vb*	stand up, rise, get up
716	regelen-*vb*	arrange	1003	tonen-*vb*	show
720	zingen-*vb*	sing	1009	zwemmen-*vb*	swim
723	weggaan-*vb*	go away, leave	1010	wezen-*het; vb*	being; be
728	sluiten-*vb*	close	1017	tekenen-*vb*	draw, sign
741	verdienen-*vb*	earn	1030	ruiken-*vb*	smell
760	bereiken-*vb*	reach	1040	neerschieten-*vb*	shoot
763	hangen-*vb*	hang	1050	vertalen-*vb*	translate
766	uitleggen-*vb*	explain	1056	sukkelen-*vb*	struggle
767	leiden-*vb*	lead	1066	terugkomen-*vb*	return
784	opschieten-*vb*	hurry	1070	openen-*vb*	open
794	ophouden-*vb*	stop	1075	antwoorden-*vb*	answer
796	verdwijnen-*vb*	disappear	1078	ophalen-*vb*	collect
825	bekijken-*vb*	view, look at	1079	vangen-*vb*	catch
826	meenemen-*vb*	take, bring	1081	steken-*vb*	put, poke, stab
829	doorgaan-*vb*	go on, continue	1084	afmaken-*vb*	finish
837	kiezen-*vb*	choose	1085	verslaan-*vb*	defeat
848	huilen-*vb*	cry	1089	schijnen-*vb*	seem
864	begraven-*vb*	bury	1091	afspreken-*vb*	arrange
871	ontsnappen-*vb*	escape	1094	bespreken-*vb*	discuss
873	liegen-*vb*	lie	1101	omkeren-*vb*	turn
877	vergeven-*vb*	forgive	1103	bepalen-*vb*	determine
878	ruziën-*vb*	argue, fight	1105	controleren-*vb*	check

1109	vertrekken-*vb*	leave		1327	groeten-*vb*	greet
1111	arresteren-*vb*	arrest		1332	opgeven-*vb*	quit, give up
1113	bevallen-*vb*	please, give birth		1339	tellen-*vb*	count
1115	opnemen-*vb*	record, take		1343	scheiden-*vb*	separate
1116	onderzoeken-*vb*	examine		1345	verbranden-*vb*	incinerate
1118	stappen-*het; vb*	step, go, stride; night out		1346	studeren-*vb*	study
				1351	strijken-*vb*	iron
1120	verdenken-*vb*	suspect		1355	verdedigen-*vb*	defend
1122	bedenken-*vb*	think		1365	bezoeken-*vb*	visit
1130	rekenen-*vb*	calculate, count		1372	wennen-*vb*	get used to
1135	overkomen-*vb*	happen, visit		1377	behandelen-*vb*	treat
1149	tegenhouden-*vb*	retain, hold		1378	aanvallen-*de; vb*	attacks; attack
1150	bakken-*vb*	bake		1380	opsluiten-*vb*	lock
1157	voeren-*vb*	feed, pursue		1381	verhuizen-*vb*	move
1159	lijden-*vb*	suffer		1385	groeien-*vb*	grow
1163	uitnodigen-*vb*	invite		1390	oefenen-*vb*	practice
1184	interesseren-*vb*	interest		1395	ademen-*vb*	breathe
1189	loven-*vb*	praise		1399	wassen-*vb; adj*	wash; wax
1192	verraden-*vb*	betray		1412	stinken-*vb*	stink
1194	jagen-*vb*	hunt		1414	aanbieden-*vb*	offer
1197	reizen-*vb*	travel		1421	graven-*vb*	dig
1205	beslissen-*vb*	decide		1431	herkennen-*vb*	recognize
1207	koken-*vb*	cook		1435	eindigen-*vb*	end
1208	pikken-*vb*	steal, peck, put up with		1436	wandelen-*vb*	walk
1209	zwijgen-*vb*	keep silent		1441	toegeven-*vb*	admit
1212	verbergen-*vb*	hide		1447	binden-*vb*	bind
1217	bieden-*vb*	offer		1450	onthouden-*vb*	remember
1230	schreeuwen-*vb*	shout		1460	opzoeken-*vb*	visit
1240	aandoen-*vb*	put on		1462	herhalen-*vb*	repeat
1242	opwinden-*vb*	excite, wind up		1464	smeken-*vb*	beg
1243	uitzoeken-*vb*	sort, find out		1466	verloven-*vb*	commit, betroth
1244	wensen-*vb*	wish		1468	veroorzaken-*vb*	cause
1246	vasthouden-*vb*	hold		1469	blijken-*vb*	prove
1249	meemaken-*vb*	experience		1470	proosten-*vb*	toast
1251	dulden-*vb*	tolerate, allow		1472	vervangen-*vb*	substitute, replace
1256	wedden-*vb*	bet		1477	bevelen-*vb*	order, command
1273	oplossen-*vb*	solve		1481	dienen-*vb*	serve
1284	achterlaten-*vb*	leave		1495	duwen-*vb*	push
1287	aannemen-*vb*	assume		1498	vuren-*vb*	fire
1288	bewerken-*vb*	edit		1499	verbinden-*vb*	link
1290	schrikken-*vb*	start, jolt, scare		1511	waarschuwen-*vb*	warn
1291	genezen-*vb*	cure		1512	optreden-*vb*	perform, appear
1292	voorkomen-*vb; het*	prevent; appearance		1514	meedoen-*vb*	participate
1294	smaken-*vb*	taste		1516	accepteren-*vb*	accept
1303	binnenkomen-*vb*	come in		1520	ophangen-*vb*	hang
1307	grijpen-*vb*	grab		1521	verenigen-*vb*	unite
1308	heten-*vb*	be named		1522	melden-*vb*	report
1309	aanraken-*vb*	touch		1528	plegen-*vb*	commit
1315	verstoppen-*vb*	hide		1532	ontvoeren-*vb*	kidnap
1320	vervelen-*vb*	bore		1535	plannen-*vb*	plan
1324	schitteren-*vb*	shine		1560	bewaren-*vb*	keep

1568	branden-*vb*	burn
1569	kleden-*vb*	dress
1573	overtuigen-*vb*	convince
1576	voorbereiden-*vb*	prepare
1589	gelden-*vb*	be valid
1591	lossen-*vb*	unload
1600	filmen-*vb*	film
1601	opeten-*vb*	eat
1613	oppakken-*vb*	take up
1614	teruggaan-*vb*	return
1619	trainen-*vb; het*	train; training
1621	snijden-*vb; het*	cut; slicing
1622	teleurstellen-*vb*	disappoint
1633	meegaan-*vb*	come
1635	richten-*vb*	direct, aim
1650	wijzen-*vb*	point
1653	ontspannen-*vb*	relax
1658	dringen-*vb*	push
1660	verrassen-*vb*	surprise
1664	uitzien-*vb*	look
1674	ruilen-*vb*	exchange
1676	baseren-*vb*	base
1682	lunchen-*vb*	lunch
1696	doorlopen-*vb*	go through
1697	mankeren-*vb*	lack, ail
1704	merken-*vb*	notice
1712	doodgaan-*vb*	die
1727	omgaan-*vb*	handle
1728	klagen-*vb*	complain
1741	schoppen-*vb*	kick
1747	blazen-*vb*	blow
1750	schudden-*vb*	shake
1758	schamen-*vb*	be ashamed
1761	bevrijden-*vb*	liberate
1772	dromen-*vb*	dream
1773	opruimen-*vb*	tidy up
1776	meekomen-*vb*	come along with
1779	verzamelen-*vb*	collect, gather
1799	leveren-*vb*	deliver
1804	veroordelen-*vb*	condemn
1808	terugtrekken-*vb*	withdraw
1809	bijten-*vb*	bite
1811	verwijderen-*vb*	remove
1813	rollen-*vb*	roll
1818	verstaan-*vb*	understand, hear
1819	meebrengen-*vb*	bring
1822	verplaatsen-*vb*	move
1825	beantwoorden-*vb*	answer
1833	samenwerken-*vb; het*	co-operate; teamwork
1838	verkrachten-*vb*	rape
1849	bemoeien-*vb*	interfere
1850	handelen-*vb*	act
1854	concentreren-*vb*	concentrate
1856	opgroeien-*vb*	grow up
1863	duiken-*het; vb*	diving; dive
1864	verklaren-*vb*	explain
1867	reageren-*vb*	react
1876	vullen-*vb*	fill
1881	negeren-*vb*	ignore
1888	bekennen-*vb*	confess
1889	veroorloven-*vb*	afford, permit
1890	overgeven-*vb*	hand over, vomit
1893	weglopen-*vb*	walk away
1895	steunen-*vb*	support
1897	vrijen-*vb*	have sex
1899	uitgaan-*vb*	go out
1905	herstellen-*vb*	restore
1906	dwingen-*vb*	force
1914	terugkeren-*vb*	return
1916	bezetten-*vb*	occupy
1921	overvallen-*vb*	ambush, rob
1928	verrotten-*vb*	rot
1933	gedragen-*vbr*	behave
1936	doorbrengen-*vb*	pass, spend
1939	verspreiden-*vb*	spread
1947	verbazen-*vb*	surprise
1948	verontschuldigen-*vb*	apologize
1949	repareren-*vb*	repair
1950	naaien-*vb; het*	sew; dressmaking
1959	verpesten-*vb*	spoil
1962	kosten-*de; vb*	price; cost
1968	schoonmaken-*vb*	clean
1980	onderhandelen-*vb*	negotiate
1983	boeten-*vb*	to atone for
1989	aanpakken-*vb*	tackle
1990	proeven-*vb*	taste
1991	grazen-*vb*	graze
1996	bestellen-*vb*	order
2001	uitkomen-*vb*	come
2004	betrappen-*vb*	catch
2012	opdagen-*vb*	turn up
2017	excuseren-*vb*	excuse
2018	pissen-*vb*	piss
2023	staren-*vb*	stare
2028	bewijzen-*vb*	prove
2044	veronderstellen-*vb*	assume
2052	voeden-*vb*	feed
2059	bevestigen-*vb*	confirm
2068	klimmen-*vb*	climb
2070	winden-*vb*	wrap

2083	verlangen-*het; vb*	desire; desire		2280	straffen-*vb*	punish
2089	verzinnen-*vb*	invent, come up with		2282	doorgeven-*vb*	pass down
2091	huren-*vb*	rent		2285	volhouden-*vb*	hold on
2095	laden-*vb*	load		2287	ontwerpen-*vb*	design
2096	afhandelen-*vb*	settle, handle		2290	behouden-*vb*	maintain
2097	varen-*vb; het*	sail; fern, sailing		2307	uitvinden-*vb*	figure out
2101	waarderen-*vb*	appreciate		2308	kruipen-*vb; het*	crawl; crawling
2105	verspillen-*vb*	waste		2316	bloeden-*vb*	bleed
2116	toestaan-*vb*	allow		2324	verzekeren-*vb*	ensure
2117	betwijfelen-*vb*	doubt		2325	bukken-*vb*	bend
2120	winkelen-*vb*	shop		2329	ruimen-*vb*	clear
2134	overnemen-*vb*	take over		2332	kwijtraken-*vb*	lose
2138	kwetsen-*vb*	hurt		2340	beledigen-*vb*	offend
2139	timen-*vb*	time		2348	verwarren-*vb*	confuse
2141	regenen-*vb*	rain		2350	hakken-*de; vb*	heels; chop
2143	weigeren-*vb*	refuse		2351	ontploffen-*vb*	explode
2151	zoenen-*vb*	kiss		2352	zeuren-*vb*	whine
2154	verplichten-*vb*	oblige		2353	aantrekken-*vb*	attract
2157	uitmaken-*vb*	extinguish		2359	treffen-*vb; het*	meet; encounter
2158	uitstappen-*vb*	get off		2360	klappen-*vb*	clap
2162	weghalen-*vb*	take away		2362	terugbrengen-*vb*	bring back
2165	beseffen-*vb*	realize, be aware		2367	smeren-*vb*	lubricate
2174	afwijzen-*vb*	reject		2368	realiseren-*vb*	realize
2177	bevinden-*vbr*	be, find oneself		2369	innemen-*vb*	take
2182	uitputten-*vb*	exhaust		2370	uitvoeren-*vb*	execute
2188	beroven-*vb*	rob		2375	sparen-*vb*	save
2190	opvoeden-*vb*	bring up		2379	schilderen-*vb*	paint
2193	loslaten-*vb*	release		2387	beschuldigen-*vb*	accuse
2195	verknallen-*vb*	mess up		2388	beheersen-*vb*	control
2202	doodschieten-*vb*	shoot		2390	verdragen-*vb*	bear
2204	wegkomen-*vb*	escape		2402	drijven-*vb*	float
2206	begaan-*vb*	commit		2406	uitschakelen-*vb*	switch off
2210	versieren-*vb*	decorate		2410	overdrijven-*vb*	exaggerate
2221	vergelijken-*vb*	compare		2415	beweren-*vb*	claim
2222	verwoesten-*vb*	destroy		2420	falen-*vb*	fail
2223	gokken-*vb*	gamble		2437	verschijnen-*vb*	appear
2225	opzetten-*vb*	put on		2444	rijzen-*vb*	rise
2230	voorzien-*vb; adj*	provide; anticipate		2445	boksen-*vb*	box
2232	zegenen-*vb*	bless		2447	vereren-*vb*	honor
2238	ervaren-*adj; vb*	experienced; experience		2449	afzetten-*vb*	drop off
				2458	aanvaarden-*vb*	accept
2241	aangeven-*vb*	indicate, pass		2461	opletten-*vb*	pay attention
2243	douchen-*vb*	shower		2469	overlijden-*het; vb*	death; decease
2244	opblazen-*vb*	blow		2477	naderen-*vb*	approach
2248	wapenen-*vb*	arm		2479	ontkennen-*vb*	deny
2249	klaarmaken-*vb*	prepare		2480	rondlopen-*vb*	walkabout
2251	vrijlaten-*het; vb*	release; release		2482	ontwikkelen-*vb*	develop
2254	behoren-*vb; av*	belong; should		2487	uitkijken-*vb*	be careful
2258	knopen-*vb*	knot		2490	teruggeven-*vb*	give back
2269	vervloeken-*vb*	curse		2495	oppassen-*het; vb*	babysit; beware
2273	inzetten-*vb2*	insert, make an effort		2497	scoren-*vb*	score

2498	verbeteren-*vb*	improve
2499	ontbreken-*vb*	lack
2505	voortduren-*vb*	continue
2514	wisselen-*vb*	exchange
2515	opvallen-*vb*	notice
2523	vermijden-*vb*	avoid

Alphabetical Order

Rank	Dutch-*PoS*	English Equivalent
	A	
1414	aanbieden-*vb*	offer
1502	aanbod-*het*	offer
814	aandacht-*de*	attention
2021	aandeel-*het*	share
1240	aandoen-*vb*	put on
838	aangenaam-*adj*	pleasant
2241	aangeven-*vb*	indicate, pass
1525	aangezien-*con*	since
1865	aanklacht-*de*	charge
2186	aanklager-*de*	prosecutor
1340	aankomen-*verb*	arrive
1287	aannemen-*vb*	assume
1989	aanpakken-*vb*	tackle
29	aan-*prp; adj*	to, on; on
1309	aanraken-*vb*	touch
2317	aanslag-*de*	assault
832	aantal-*het*	number
1934	aantrekkelijk-*adj*	attractive
2353	aantrekken-*vb*	attract
2458	aanvaarden-*vb*	accept
860	aanval-*de*	attack
1378	aanvallen-*de; vb*	attacks; attack
1401	aanwezig-*adj*	present
1882	aanwezigheid-*de*	presence
2283	aanwijzing-*de*	instruction
1338	aap-*de*	monkey
2084	aard-*de*	nature
518	aarde-*de*	earth
386	aardig-*adj; adv*	nice, pretty; nicely
590	absoluut-*adv; adj*	absolutely; absolute
2399	accent-*het*	accent
1516	accepteren-*vb*	accept
768	ach-*int*	oh, ah
472	achten-*vb*	deem
2240	achteraan-*adv*	in the back
185	achter-*adv; prp*	behind; behind
2199	achtergrond-*de*	background
1634	achterin-*adv*	in the back
1954	achterkant-*de*	back
1284	achterlaten-*vb*	leave
2217	achterlijk-*adj*	backward
756	achteruit-*adv; de*	backwards; reverse
1617	acteur-*de*	actor
913	actie-*de*	action
2048	actrice-*de*	actress
828	adem-*de*	breath
1395	ademen-*vb*	breathe
2009	admiraal-*de*	admiral
874	adres-*het*	address
1170	advies-*het*	advice
595	advocaat-*de*	lawyer
115	af-*adv; adj*	off; ready
1139	afdeling-*de*	department
596	afgelopen-*adj; adv*	over, last; out
2096	afhandelen-*vb*	settle, handle
2442	afhankelijk-*adj*	dependent
1084	afmaken-*vb*	finish
1253	afscheid-*het*	farewell
1794	afschuwelijk-*adj; adv*	horrible; awfully
1637	afsluiten-*verb*	close
608	afspraak-*de*	appointment
1091	afspreken-*vb*	arrange
1025	afstand-*de*	distance
2214	afval-*het*	garbage
2174	afwijzen-*vb*	reject
2449	afzetten-*vb*	drop off
365	agent-*de*	agent, policeman
1119	akkoord-*het*	agreement
61	al-*adv; het; con*	already; all; though
1185	alarm-*het*	alarm
1757	alcohol-*de*	alcohol
2372	algemeen-*adj*	general
1782	allang-*adv*	a long time ago
506	allebei-*adj*	both
80	alleen-*adv; con; adj*	only, merely; only; alone
121	allemaal-*prn*	everything, everybody
2173	allemachtig-*adv*	mighty
169	alle-*prn*	every, all
1685	allerlei-*prn*	all kinds of
72	alles-*prn*	all, everything
25	als-*adv; con; prp*	as; as; like
164	alsjeblieft-*int*	please (coll)
244	alsof-*con; adv*	like; as if
114	altijd-*adv*	always
2491	alvast-*adv*	in advance
799	alweer-*adv*	again
2191	ambassade-*de*	embassy
2235	ambassadeur-*de*	ambassador
1578	ambulance-*de*	ambulance
1283	amen-*het*	amen
1015	amerikaan-*de*	American
1604	amper-*adv*	barely

140	ander-*adj; prn*	other; other
136	anders-*adv; con*	different, else; otherwise
2407	angel-*de*	sting
712	angst-*de*	fear
1075	antwoorden-*vb*	answer
450	antwoord-*het*	answer
2224	apart-*adj; adv*	separate; separately
1942	apparaat-*het*	device
1041	appartement-*het*	apartment
1855	applaus-*het*	applause
1665	april-*de*	April
636	arm-*de; adj*	arm; poor
1111	arresteren-*vb*	arrest
2430	artiest-*de*	artist
1531	artikel-*het*	article
1347	arts-*de*	physician
1710	as-*de*	ash
1681	assistent-*de*	assistant
1724	attentie-*de*	attention
196	auto-*de*	car
2494	autoriteit-*de*	authority
379	avond-*de*	evening, night
2486	avondeten-*het*	supper
1785	avontuur-*het*	adventure

B

414	baan-*de*	job, track
2203	baard-*de*	beard
363	baas-*de*	boss
364	baby-*de*	baby, nursling
1250	badkamer-*de*	bathroom
1836	bagage-*de*	luggage
1150	bakken-*vb*	bake
576	bal-*het*	ball
650	band-*de*	tire, band
191	bang-*adj; adv*	afraid, scared; anxious
545	bank-*de*	bank; couch
845	bar-*de; adj*	bar; severe
2357	baron-*de*	baron
1676	baseren-*vb*	base
987	basis-*de*	basis, base
1825	beantwoorden-*vb*	answer
137	bedanken-*vb*	thank
1122	bedenken-*vb*	think
315	bed-*het*	bed
153	bedoelen-*vb*	mean
1080	bedoeling-*de*	intention
2118	bedrag-*het*	amount
2069	bedreiging-*de*	threat

702	bedrijf-*het*	business, company
2286	bedrogen-*adj*	deceived
991	beeld-*het*	image, sculpture
713	been-*het*	leg
1201	beer-*de*	bear
881	beest-*het*	beast
184	beetje-*het; adj*	bit; little
2206	begaan-*vb*	commit
355	begin-*het*	beginning, start
312	beginnen-*vb*	start, begin
1147	begrafenis-*de*	funeral
864	begraven-*vb*	bury
237	begrijpen-*vb*	understand, grasp
2275	begrip-*het*	understanding
577	behalve-*prp*	except
1377	behandelen-*vb*	treat
1769	behandeling-*de*	treatment
2388	beheersen-*vb*	control
1972	behoefte-*de*	need
1033	behoorlijk-*adj*	quite
2254	behoren-*vb; av*	belong; should
2290	behouden-*vb*	maintain
726	beide-*adj; prn*	both; either
892	bek-*de*	beak, mouth
635	bekend-*adj*	known
1888	bekennen-*vb*	confess
825	bekijken-*vb*	view, look at
812	belachelijk-*adj*	ridiculous
1310	belang-*het*	importance
408	belangrijk-*adj*	important
2496	belasting-*de*	tax
2340	beledigen-*vb*	offend
1995	beleefd-*adj; adv*	polite; politely
255	bellen-*vb*	dial
1544	belofte-*de*	promise
1640	beloning-*de*	reward
501	beloven-*vb*	promise
1787	bemanning-*de*	crew
1849	bemoeien-*vb*	interfere
1156	bende-*de*	mess, gang
328	beneden-*adv; prp*	down, below; below
1454	benzine-*de*	petrol, gasoline
1103	bepalen-*vb*	determine
970	bereid-*adj*	prepared
760	bereiken-*vb*	reach
1945	bereik-*het*	range
1092	berg-*de*	mountain
735	bericht-*het*	message
1482	beroemd-*adj*	famous
1432	beroep-*het*	profession

2188	beroven-*vb*	rob		1916	bezetten-*vb*	occupy
2517	beschaving-*de*	civilization		359	bezig-*adj*	busy
602	beschermen-*vb*	protect		978	bezitten-*vb*	own
1490	bescherming-*de*	protection		1365	bezoeken-*vb*	visit
2025	beschikbaar-*adj*	available		804	bezoek-*het*	visit
2387	beschuldigen-*vb*	accuse		927	bezorgd-*adj*	concerned, troubled
2165	beseffen-*vb*	realize, be aware		1793	bezwaar-*het*	objection
1703	besef-*het*	realization		1792	bibliotheek-*de*	library
2261	beslag-*het*	batter		947	bidden-*vb*	pray
1205	beslissen-*vb*	decide		1217	bieden-*vb*	offer
1005	beslissing-*de*	decision		879	bier-*het*	beer
966	besluiten-*vb*	decide		1586	bijbel-*de*	Bible
1094	bespreken-*vb*	discuss		2330	bijeen-*adv*	together
603	bestaan-*het; vb*	existence; exist		2071	bijeenkomst-*de*	meeting
212	best-*adj; adv*	best; sufficiently		235	bijna-*adv*	almost
1996	bestellen-*vb*	order		63	bij-*prp; de; adv*	at; bee; up to date
2260	bestemming-*de*	destination		1809	bijten-*vb*	bite
2298	bestuur-*het*	management		1164	bijvoorbeeld-*adv*	for instance
399	betalen-*vb*	pay		1063	bijzonder-*adj;*	extraordinary;
308	betekenen-*vb*	mean			*adv*	thoroughly
1955	betekenis-*de*	meaning		1447	binden-*vb*	bind
144	beter-*adv; adj*	better; superior		142	binnen-*adv; prp*	within; inside
2004	betrappen-*vb*	catch		1303	binnenkomen-*vb*	come in
989	betreffen-*vb*	concern		984	binnenkort-*adv*	shortly
925	betrekken-*vb*	involve		1000	blank-*adj*	white, blank
2117	betwijfelen-*vb*	doubt		901	blauw-*adj*	blue
2150	beu-*adj*	sick		1747	blazen-*vb*	blow
2147	beurs-*de*	exchange, scholarship		1623	bleek-*adj; adv*	pale; wanly
789	beurt-*de*	turn		279	blij-*adj; adv*	happy, joyous; glad
1113	bevallen-*vb*	please, give birth		817	blijkbaar-*adv*	apparently
1328	beveiliging-*de*	safeguard, security		1469	blijken-*vb*	prove
1477	bevelen-*vb*	order, command		167	blijven-*vb*	stay
779	bevel-*het*	order		1142	blik-*de*	look, tin
2059	bevestigen-*vb*	confirm		2457	bliksem-*de*	lightning
2177	bevinden-*vbr*	be, find oneself		1153	blind-*adj*	blind
2310	bevolking-*de*	population		2316	bloeden-*vb*	bleed
2471	bevriend-*adj*	friendly		389	bloed-*het*	blood
1761	bevrijden-*vb*	liberate		979	bloem-*de*	flower
2299	bevroren-*adj*	frozen		2432	blok-*het*	block
1625	bewaker-*de*	guard		1829	bodem-*de*	bottom
2295	bewaking-*de*	surveillance		415	boek-*het*	book
1560	bewaren-*vb*	keep		993	boel-*de*	a lot
703	bewegen-*vb*	move		1971	boer-*de*	farmer
910	beweging-*de*	movement		1368	boerderij-*de*	farm
2415	beweren-*vb*	claim		1983	boeten-*vb*	to atone for
1288	bewerken-*vb*	edit		2445	boksen-*vb*	box
605	bewijs-*het*	proof		850	bom-*de*	bomb
2028	bewijzen-*vb*	prove		841	boodschap-*de*	message
1824	bewust-*adj*	aware, conscious		795	boom-*de*	tree
2192	bewusteloos-*adj*	unconscious		2392	boon-*de*	bean
2470	bewustzijn-*het*	consciousness		842	boord-*het*	board, collar

556	boos-*adj; adv*	angry; angrily
559	boot-*de*	boat
1388	bord-*het*	plate, dish
2015	borrel-*de*	drink
1362	borst-*de*	chest, breast
931	bos-*het*	forest
1878	bot-*het; adj*	bone; blunt
2426	bouw-*de*	construction
921	bouwen-*vb*	build
292	boven-*adv; prp*	above, over; above
1500	bovendien-*adv*	besides, moreover
1701	bovenop-*adv*	on top
1480	braaf-*adj*	good
729	brand-*de*	fire
1568	branden-*vb*	burn
2045	brandstof-*de*	fuel
2020	brein-*het*	brain
710	breken-*vb*	break
287	brengen-*vb*	bring
668	brief-*de*	letter
2363	brigadier-*de*	constable, brigadier
1413	bril-*de*	glasses
1684	briljant-*adj*	brilliant
1638	brits-*adj*	british
926	broeder-*de*	brother
715	broek-*de*	pants, trousers
288	broer-*de*	brother
1306	bron-*de*	source
1182	brood-*het*	bread
936	brug-*de*	bridge
1538	bruid-*de*	bride
1193	bruiloft-*de*	wedding
2239	bruin-*adj*	brown
1359	buik-*de*	belly
220	buiten-*adv; prp*	outside, out; outside
1963	buitenlands-*adj*	foreign
2325	bukken-*vb*	bend
774	bureau-*het*	desk
1144	burgemeester-*de*	mayor
1410	burger-*de*	citizen
701	bus-*de*	bus
1391	buur-*de*	neighbor
2411	buurman-*de*	neighbor
400	buurt-*de*	neighborhood, district

C

1298	cadeau-*het*	gift
2478	cake-*de*	cake
754	camera-*de*	camera
2322	campagne-*de*	campaign

1262	carrière-*de*	career
1011	cel-*de*	cell
1087	cent-*de*	cent
2178	centimeter-*de*	centimeter
1860	centrale-*de*	headquarters, station, power plant
1444	centrum-*het*	center
1265	champagne-*de*	champagne
1920	chaos-*de*	chaos
2373	charmant-*adj; adv*	charming; charmingly
1425	chauffeur-*de*	driver
1074	chef-*de*	chef
1555	cheque-*de*	check
1597	chinees-*adj; de*	Chinese; Chinese
1969	chocolade-*de*	chocolate
785	christus-*pn*	Christ
1575	cijfer-*het*	figure, grade, numeral
2063	circus-*het*	circus
2253	cirkel-*de*	circle
738	club-*de*	club
997	coach-*de*	coach
949	code-*de*	code
1784	collega-*de*	colleague
1901	college-*het*	college
2259	combinatie-*de*	combination
955	commandant-*de*	commander
2167	commando-*de*	command
2124	commentaar-*het*	comment
1630	commissaris-*de*	commissioner
2036	commissie-*de*	committee, commission
2354	communicatie-*de*	communication
2443	compagnie-*de*	company
1160	compleet-*adj*	complete
893	computer-*de*	computer
1854	concentreren-*vb*	concentrate
2103	concert-*het*	concert
2267	congres-*het*	congress
1726	constant-*adj*	constant
581	contact-*het*	contact
2201	contant-*adj*	cash
1199	contract-*het*	contract
578	controle-*de*	control
1105	controleren-*vb*	check
2010	correct-*adj*	correct, proper
1873	crimineel-*adj*	criminal
2144	crisis-*de*	crisis
2408	cultuur-*de*	culture

D

1997	daad-*de*	act	1656	diamant-*de*	diamond
1777	daaraan-*adv*	on that	343	dicht-*adj; adv*	close, closed; densely
59	daar-*adv; con*	there; as	875	dichtbij-*adv*	near, nearby
1609	daarbij-*adv*	thereby	1104	dichterbij-*adv*	closer
1649	daarbinnen-*adv*	in there	1367	dichter-*de*	poet
1663	daarboven-*adv*	up there	1363	dief-*de*	thief
1607	daarbuiten-*adv*	outside	2398	diefstal-*de*	theft
1485	daardoor-*adv*	thereby, therefore	1574	diegene-*prn*	he, she, those who
1300	daarheen-*adv*	there	1481	dienen-*vb*	serve
1494	daarin-*adv*	therein	592	dienst-*de*	service
492	daarmee-*adv*	therewith, with that	704	diep-*adj; adv*	deep; deep
461	daarna-*adv; con*	then, after; whereupon	21	die-*prn; con*	that; which
2128	daarnet-*adv*	earlier	821	dier-*het*	animal
268	daarom-*con; adv*	therefore; hence	1020	dik-*adj*	thick, fat
1694	daarop-*adv*	thereon	1422	diner-*het*	dinner
1603	daarover-*adv*	about it	176	ding-*het*	thing, object
773	daarvan-*adv*	of it	706	direct-*adv; adj*	directly; direct
694	daarvoor-*adv*	therefor, for that	1021	directeur-*de*	director
2011	dadelijk-*adv*	immediate, soon	2135	discussie-*de*	discussion
1766	dader-*de*	perpetrator	2465	district-*het*	district
1953	dagboek-*het*	diary	28	dit-*prn*	this
119	dag-*de; int*	day; bye	344	dochter-*de*	daughter
2452	dagelijks-*adj; adv*	daily; daily	2163	document-*het*	document
843	dak-*het*	roof	2080	dodelijk-*adj; adv*	deadly; deadly
616	dame-*de*	lady	589	doden-*vb*	kill
33	dan-*con; adv*	than; then	630	doel-*het*	purpose, goal
1221	dankbaar-*adj*	grateful	54	doen-*vb; het*	do, perform; doing
122	danken-*vb*	thank	307	dokter-*de*	doctor
1049	dankzij-*prp*	due to	1037	dol-*adj*	crazy
531	dansen-*verb*	dance	276	dollar-*de*	dollar
1734	dapper-*adj*	brave	644	dom-*adj;*	stupid
2051	das-*de*	tie	1817	dominee-*de*	pastor
6	dat-*con; prn*	that; that	1069	donder-*de*	thunder
2056	datum-*de*	date	737	donker-*adj; het*	dark; dark
3	de-*art*	the	113	dood-*de; adj*	death; dead
2319	december-*de*	December	1712	doodgaan-*vb*	die
426	deel-*het*	part, segment	2181	doodsbang-*adj*	mortified
546	degene-*prn*	the one, those	2202	doodschieten-*vb*	shoot
2336	deken-*de*	blanket	1754	doof-*adj*	deaf
1579	dek-*het*	deck	1936	doorbrengen-*vb*	pass, spend
1424	dekking-*de*	cover	829	doorgaan-*vb*	go on, continue
696	delen-*vb*	share	2282	doorgeven-*vb*	pass down
73	denken-*vb*	think, think of	1316	doorheen-*adv*	through
637	derde-*nu*	third	1696	doorlopen-*vb*	go through
2509	dertien-*nu*	thirteen	1152	doos-*de*	box
1285	dertig-*de*	thirty	772	dorp-*het*	village
1247	detail-*het*	detail	1248	dossier-*het*	file
1382	detective-*de*	detective	1549	douche-*de*	shower
284	deur-*de*	door	2243	douchen-*vb*	shower
436	dezelfde-*prn*	same	2427	draad-*de*	wire
69	deze-*prn*	this	698	draai-*de*	turn

880	draaien-*vb*	turn
1887	draak-*de*	dragon
620	dragen-*vb;*	wear, carry
2435	drama-*het*	drama
1141	drank-*de*	beverage, booze
1059	drankje-*het*	drink
162	drie-*nu*	three
2402	drijven-*vb*	float
1658	dringen-*vb*	push
356	drinken-*vb*	drink
1772	dromen-*vb*	dream
673	dronken-*adj*	drunk
1711	droog-*adj*	dry
504	droom-*de*	dream
675	drug-*de*	drug
342	druk-*de; adj; adv*	pressure; busy; busily
1439	dubbel-*adj*	double
413	duidelijk-*adj; adv*	clear, obvious; clearly
1863	duiken-*het; vb*	diving; dive
1631	duisternis-*de*	darkness
1293	duits-*adj; het*	German; German
1446	duitser-*de*	German
976	duivel-*de*	devil
964	duizend-*nu*	thousand
1251	dulden-*vb*	tolerate, allow
680	duren-*vb*	last, take
944	durven-*vb*	dare
82	dus-*adv; con*	so, consequently; therefore
1176	duur-*de; adj*	duration; expensive
1912	duw-*de*	push
1495	duwen-*vb*	push
1618	dwaas-*adj; de; adv*	silly; fool; foolishly
1563	dwars-*adj*	contrary, across
1906	dwingen-*vb*	force

E

75	echt-*adv; adj*	really; real
1835	echter-*adv*	however
1138	echtgenoot-*de*	husband
2400	economie-*de*	economy
7	een-*art; nu; prn*	a; one; any
1333	eenheid-*de*	unit, unity
890	eenmaal-*adv*	once
74	eens-*adv; adj*	once; agree
539	eentje-*prn*	alone, by yourself
1239	eenvoudig-*adj*	plain, simple
1296	eenzaam-*adj*	lonely, solitary
681	eer-*de; con*	honor; ere

361	eerder-*adj*	earlier, rather
394	eerlijk-*adj; adv*	honest, straight; honestly
223	eerst-*adj; adv*	first, primary; first
177	eerste-*de; adv*	first; initial
1371	eeuw-*de*	century
1014	eeuwig-*adj*	eternal; forever
1871	effect-*het*	effect
1198	eigenaar-*de*	owner
226	eigen-*adj*	own
2014	eigendom-*het*	property
241	eigenlijk-*adv; adj*	really; actually
1214	ei-*het*	egg
1986	eikel-*de*	acorn, jerk
833	eiland-*het*	island
457	einde-*het*	end
488	eindelijk-*adv*	finally
679	eind-*het*	end
1435	eindigen-*vb*	end
1756	eis-*de*	demand
1167	elf-*de; nu*	elf; eleven
165	elkaar-*adv; prn*	each other; each other
232	elk-*prn; adj; adv*	each, any; every
1515	ellende-*de*	misery
2314	emotie-*de*	emotion
2384	emotioneel-*adj*	emotional
9	en-*con*	and
1007	energie-*de*	energy
1252	eng-*adj*	scary
1305	engel-*de*	angel
854	engels-*adj; het*	English; English
218	enig-*adv; adj; prn*	any; solely; single
435	enkel-*adj; adv; de*	only, single; only; ankle
994	enorm-*adj; adv*	enormous; vast
362	eraan-*adv*	with it
1100	erachter-*adv*	behind
18	er-*adv*	there
755	eraf-*adv*	off
511	erbij-*adv*	at, with, there
2246	erbuiten-*adv*	out (it)
1925	erdoor-*adv*	through it
135	erg-*adv; adj*	very; terrible
293	ergens-*adv; prn*	somewhere; someplace
439	erin-*adv*	in it
405	ermee-*adv*	with it
1434	ernaar-*adv*	it, at it, after it
1233	ernstig-*adj*	serious
1236	erom-*adv*	around it, about it
423	erop-*adv*	on
604	erover-*adv*	about

256	eruit-*adv*	out
324	ervan-*prn*	from it
2238	ervaren-*adj; vb*	experienced; experience
956	ervaring-*de*	experience
471	ervoor-*adv*	for it
194	eten-*vb; het*	eat; food
87	even-*adv; adj*	momentarily; even
1672	eventjes-*adv*	momentarily
2484	examen-*het*	examination
2017	excuseren-*vb*	excuse
938	excuus-*het*	excuse
1832	ex-*de*	ex
2022	experiment-*het*	experiment
1797	expert-*de*	expert
1791	explosie-*de*	explosion
780	extra-*adj; adv*	extra; extra
2030	ezel-*de*	donkey

F

1518	fabriek-*de*	factory
2420	falen-*vb*	fail
253	familie-*de*	family
1657	fan-*de*	fan
1816	fantasie-*de*	fantasy
480	fantastisch-*adj*	fantastic
1973	fase-*de*	phase
1132	favoriet-*de*	favorite
2464	federaal-*adj*	federal
561	feest-*het*	party
950	feit-*het*	fact
1715	fiets-*de*	bike
2306	figuur-*het*	figure
388	fijn-*adj; adv*	fine, nice; delicately
366	film-*de*	film
1600	filmen-*vb*	film
2109	finale-*de*	final
1276	flat-*de*	flat
1851	flauw-*adj*	faint
1032	fles-*de*	bottle
1235	flink-*adj; adv*	robust, firm; substantial
1670	fort-*het*	fortress
2090	fortuin-*het*	fortune
508	foto-*de*	photo
409	fout-*de; adj*	error, mistake; wrong
1394	frans-*adj*	French
2062	fris-*adj; adv*	fresh; freshly
2455	front-*het*	front
2297	fruit-*het*	fruit

G

1068	gaaf-*adj*	whole, great
50	gaan-*vb; av*	go, work; shall
474	gang-*de*	corridor, hallway
1507	garage-*de*	garage
1398	gas-*het*	gas
687	gast-*de*	guest, man
647	gat-*het*	hole
883	gauw-*adv*	soon, quickly
1484	gave-*de*	gift
203	gebeuren-*vb*	happen
2123	gebeurtenis-*de*	event
771	gebied-*het*	area
1768	geboorte-*de*	birth
598	geboren-*adj*	born
695	gebouw-*het*	building
2227	gebrek-*het; adj*	lack; vice
322	gebruiken-*vb*	use
513	gebruik-*het*	use
669	gedachte-*de*	thought
1348	gedeelte-*het*	part
2302	gedicht-*het*	poem
1076	gedoe-*het*	hassle
1933	gedragen-*vbr*	behave
1121	gedrag-*het*	behavior
1720	gedurende-*prp*	during
1911	geel-*adj*	yellow
38	geen-*art; adj; adv; prn; nu*	not one, no; no; no; none
564	geest-*de*	spirit, ghost
1501	gegeven-*adj; het*	given; given
1489	geheel-*adj; het; adv*	whole; whole; entirely
587	geheim-*adj; het*	secret; secret
1453	geheugen-*het*	memory
170	gek-*adj; de; adv*	crazy; fool; fool
1589	gelden-*vb*	be valid
129	geld-*het*	money, cash
233	geleden-*adv; adj*	ago; past
2027	gelegenheid-*de*	opportunity, occasion
1526	geliefd-*adj*	beloved
238	gelijk-*adj; het*	equal, similar; right
222	geloof-*het*	faith, belief
271	geloven-*vb*	believe, think
882	geluid-*het*	sound, noise
376	geluk-*het*	happiness, luck
347	gelukkig-*adj*	happy
1869	gemak-*het*	convenience
998	gemakkelijk-*adj*	easy
1029	gemeen-*adj*	mean
1611	gemeenschap-*de*	community

1289	genaamd-*adj*	called
1319	genade-*de*	mercy
558	generaal-*de*	general
2263	generatie-*de*	generation
1291	genezen-*vb*	cure
2301	geniaal-*adj*	ingenious
1457	genie-*het*	genius
999	genieten-*vb*	enjoy
155	genoeg-*adj; adv*	enough; enough
1093	genoegen-*het*	pleasure
1886	gerechtigheid-*de*	righteousness
1330	gereed-*adj*	ready
2277	gereedschap-*het*	tool
1496	geregeld-*adj*	regular
1917	gerucht-*het*	rumor
1257	gerust-*adj*	be at ease, safe
1692	geschenk-*het*	gift
822	geschiedenis-*de*	history
1721	geschikt-*adj*	suited, eligible
2005	gespannen-*adj*	tense
786	gesprek-*het*	conversation
1067	getuige-*de*	witness
943	getuigen-*vb*	testify
1451	geur-*de*	smell
634	gevaar-*het*	danger
621	gevaarlijk-*adj; adv*	dangerous; hazardous
433	geval-*het*	case
520	gevangenis-*de(f)*	prison
775	gevecht-*het*	fight, battle
117	geven-*vb*	give
1038	gevoelens-*de*	feelings
470	gevoel-*het*	feeling
1763	gevoelig-*adj*	sensitive
2041	gevolg-*het*	result
762	geweer-*het*	rifle
1108	geweld-*het*	violence
200	geweldig-*adj*	great, awesome
1770	gewicht-*het*	weight
791	gewond-*adj*	injured
99	gewoon-*adv; adj*	just, plainly; ordinary
1857	gewoonlijk-*adv*	usually
2136	gewoonte-*de*	habit
1626	gezellig-*adj; adv*	cozy; cozily
1148	gezelschap-*het*	company
348	gezicht-*het*	face, sight
719	gezin-*het*	family
1258	gezond-*adj*	healthy
1427	gezondheid-*de*	health
2278	gids-*de*	guide
1810	gij-*prn*	thou

2474	gijzelaar-*de*	hostage
718	gisteravond-*adj*	last night
485	gisteren-*adv*	yesterday
2262	gitaar-*de*	guitar
858	glas-*het*	glass
2026	glimlach-*de*	smile
2284	glorie-*de*	glory
133	god-*de*	god
744	godsnaam-*int*	for god's sake
44	goed-*adj; adv; het*	good, correct; well; estate
1903	goedendag-*int*	goodbye
1992	goedkoop-*adj*	cheap
2094	gok-*de*	gamble
2223	gokken-*vb*	gamble
1620	golf-*de*	golf, wave
671	gooien-*vb*	throw
2438	goor-*adj*	revolting
1155	gouden-*adj*	golden
736	goud-*het*	gold
1397	gouverneur-*de*	governor
1270	graad-*de*	degree
1593	graaf-*de*	count
175	graag-*adv*	gladly, willingly
1260	graf-*het*	grave
646	grap-*de*	joke
452	grappig-*adj*	funny
1680	gras-*het*	grass
934	gratis-*adj*	free
1421	graven-*vb*	dig
1991	grazen-*vb*	graze
2159	greep-*de*	hold, grasp
1140	grens-*de*	border, limit
1307	grijpen-*vb*	grab
1385	groeien-*vb*	grow
1261	groen-*adj*	green
642	groep-*de*	group
1327	groeten-*vb*	greet
2391	grof-*adj; adv*	coarse; grossly
498	grond-*de*	ground
172	groot-*adj*	large, big
2250	grootmoeder-*de*	grandmother
1686	groots-*adj*	grand, great
1632	grootvader-*de*	grandfather
1775	grot-*de*	cave
1753	gunst-*de*	favor

H

2268	haak-*de*	hook
53	haar-*prn; het*	her; hair

678	haast-*de; adv*	hurry; almost		1475	herinnering-*de*	reminder
2350	hakken-*de; vb*	heels; chop		1431	herkennen-*vb*	recognize
1437	hal-*de*	hall		2328	herrie-*de*	noise
225	halen-*vb*	get, fetch		1126	hersenen-*de*	brain
514	half-*het; adv*	half; semi		1423	hersens-*de*	brain
145	hallo-*int*	hello		1905	herstellen-*vb*	restore
2270	ham-*de*	ham		2	het-*art; prn*	the; it
192	hand-*de*	hand		1308	heten-*vb*	be named
2417	handdoek-*de*	towel		2513	hetgeen-*prn*	which
1473	handel-*de*	trade, act		357	hetzelfde-*prn; adj; adv*	same; ditto; ditto
1850	handelen-*vb*	act				
2376	handig-*adj; adv*	convenient		1133	heus-*adj*	real
2434	handje-*het*	hand		1760	heuvel-*de*	hill
2374	handschoen-*de*	glove		30	hier-*adv*	here
1751	handtekening-*de*	signature		2076	hierbij-*adv*	hereby
763	hangen-*vb*	hang		521	hierheen-*adv; adj*	here; hither
411	hard-*adj; adv*	hard, loud; hard				
1924	hartaanval-*de*	heart attack		1392	hierin-*adv*	herein
1112	hartelijk-*adj*	cordial, warm		916	hiermee-*adv*	herewith
329	hart-*het*	heart		1673	hierover-*adv*	hereof
1655	hartstikke-*adv*	terribly		1595	hieruit-*adv*	from this
422	haten-*vb*	hate		1241	hiervan-*adv*	hereof
1807	haven-*de*	port		1278	hiervoor-*adv*	theretofore
22	hebben-*av; vb*	have; have		17	hij-*prn*	he
2381	heden-*adv; het*	given moment; now		2274	hitte-*de*	heat
110	heel-*adj; adv*	very, whole		49	hoe-*adv; prn*	how; how
2196	heelal-*het*	universe		1073	hoed-*de*	hat
213	heen-*adv*	there, away		863	hoek-*de*	corner
377	heer-*de*	lord, gentleman		918	hoelang-*adv*	how long
730	heerlijk-*adj; adv*	delicious; deliciously		262	hoeveel-*nu*	how much; what
248	heet-*adj;*	hot, warm		339	hoeven-*av*	need, have to
808	heilig-*adj*	holy, sacred		1158	hoewel-*con*	although
1583	hekel-*de*	dislike		505	hoezo-*adv; con*	why; why
1616	hek-*het*	fence		1764	hof-*het*	court
1552	heks-*de*	witch		309	hoi-*int*	hi
835	helaas-*adv*	unfortunately, alas		1143	ho-*interj*	stop
776	held-*de*	hero		1932	hol-*adv; het*	empty; hole
623	hel-*de; adj; adv*	hell; bright; glaringly		953	homo-*de*	gay
1743	helder-*adj*	clear		374	hond-*de*	dog
1717	heleboel-*nu*	a lot		912	honderd-*nu*	hundred
739	helft-*de*	half		573	honger-*de*	hunger
1628	helikopter-*de*	helicopter		2492	honkbal-*het*	baseball
2212	helm-*de*	helmet		242	hoofd-*het*	head, principal
171	helpen-*vb;*	help		1944	hoofdkwartier-*het*	headquarters
2516	hemd-*het*	shirt				
507	hemel-*de*	sky, heaven		2037	hoofdpijn-*de*	headache
1183	hemelsnaam-*in*	heaven's name		2142	hoofdstuk-*het*	chapter
45	hem-*prn*	him		732	hoog-*adj; adv*	high; high
227	hen-*prn; de*	them; hen		1325	hoogheid-*de*	highness
1462	herhalen-*vb*	repeat		951	hoogte-*de*	height
493	herinneren-*vb*	remember		1107	hoop-*de*	hope

896	hopelijk-*adv*	hopefully
2397	hopeloos-*adj; adv*	hopeless; past hope
228	hopen-*vb*	hope
195	horen-*vb*	hear
1369	horloge-*het*	watch
575	hotel-*het*	hotel
86	houden-*vb*	keep, hold
1700	houding-*de*	attitude
1629	hout-*het*	wood
1134	huid-*de*	skin
1993	huidig-*adj*	current
848	huilen-*vb*	cry
123	huis-*het*	house
2423	huisje-*het*	cottage
1737	huiswerk-*het*	homework
303	hulp-*de*	help, assistance
1802	humor-*de*	humor
132	hun-*prn*	their
2091	huren-*vb*	rent
1642	hut-*de*	cabin
1357	huur-*de*	rent
697	huwelijk-*het*	wedding

I

197	idee-*het*	idea, notion
2104	identiteit-*de*	identity
455	idioot-*de; adj*	idiot; idiotic
138	iedereen-*prn*	everyone
551	ieder-*prn; adj*	each; every
91	iemand-*prn*	someone; person
67	iets-*prn; adv*	something; some
815	ijs-*het*	ice
4	ik-*prn*	I
1783	illegaal-*adj*	illegal
2256	incident-*het*	incident
2166	inclusief-*adj; adv*	including; inclusively
446	inderdaad-*adv*	indeed, actually
1745	indiaan-*de*	Indian
1830	indien-*con*	if
924	indruk-*de*	impression
1840	indrukwekkend-*adj*	impressive
1006	ineens-*adv*	suddenly
552	informatie-*de*	information
1874	ingang-*de*	entrance
2002	ingewikkeld-*adj*	complicated
2369	innemen-*vb*	take
13	in-*prp*	in
983	inspecteur-*de*	inspector

2008	instructie-*de*	instruction
2237	intelligent-*adj*	intelligent
805	interessant-*adj*	interesting
1497	interesse-*de*	interest
1184	interesseren-*vb*	interest
2100	internationaal-*adj*	international
1789	interview-*het*	interview
1606	invloed-*de*	influence
2520	inwoner-*de*	resident, inhabitant
2226	inzet-*de*	effort, bet
2273	inzetten-*vb2*	insert, make an effort

J

126	jaar-*het*	year
1491	jacht-*de, het*	hunt, yacht
1194	jagen-*vb*	hunt
2462	jager-*de*	hunter
1053	jaloers-*adj*	jealous, envious
628	jammer-*adj; adv*	unfortunate; unfortunately
2050	japans-*adj*	Japanese
36	ja-*prt*	yes
1702	jarig-*adj*	have a birthday
919	jas-*de*	coat
2130	jasje-*het*	jacket
571	jawel-*int*	yes, sure enough
1165	jazeker-*int*	surely so
1	je-*prn*	you
1405	jeugd-*de*	youth
267	jezelf-*prn*	yourself
341	Jezus-*de*	Jesus
34	jij-*prn*	you
600	jong-*adj; het*	young; cub
1440	jongeman-*de*	young man
182	jongen-*de*	boy
2013	jonger-*adj*	younger
1562	jood-*de*	Jew
2393	joods-*adj*	jewish
71	jou-*prn*	you
2129	journalist-*de*	journalist
128	jouw-*prn*	your
898	juffrouw-*de*	female teacher, unmarried woman
295	juist-*adj; adv*	just, correct; just
1884	Juli-*de*	July
62	jullie-*prn*	you
1733	jungle-*de*	jungle
1898	Juni-*de*	June
1572	junior-*de; adj*	junior; minor

903	jurk-*de*	gown, dress
1349	jury-*de*	jury
2115	Justitie-*de*	justice
2189	juweel-*het*	jewel

K

654	kaart-*de*	map
1404	kaartje-*het*	card, ticket
1537	kaas-*de*	cheese
708	kalm-*adj; adv*	calm; calmly
2092	kameraad-*de*	comrade
277	kamer-*de*	room, chamber
1046	kamp-*het*	camp
1216	kampioen-*de*	champion
2125	kanaal-*het*	channel
2396	kandidaat-*de*	candidate
1669	kanker-*de*	cancer
283	kans-*de*	chance
236	kant-*de*	side, lace
503	kantoor-*het*	office
2413	kap-*de*	hood
420	kapitein-*de*	captain
676	kapot-*adj; adv*	broken; to pieces
1935	karakter-*het*	personality
1295	kast-*de*	closet
1540	kasteel-*het*	castle
855	kat-*de*	cat
1416	keel-*de*	throat
134	keer-*de*	time
1317	keizer-*de*	emperor
1225	kelder-*de*	basement
2145	kennelijk-*adj*	evident
215	kennen-*vb*	know
847	kennis-*de*	knowledge
401	kerel-*de*	guy, fellow
656	kerk-*de*	church
2468	kerkhof-*het*	cemetery
1433	kerstfeest-*het*	Christmas (party)
1941	ketting-*de*	chain
904	keuken-*de*	kitchen
870	keus-*de*	choice
714	keuze-*de*	choice
837	kiezen-*vb*	choose
92	kijken-*vb*	look
1223	kilo-*de*	kilo
911	kilometer-*de*	kilometer
187	kind-*het*	child
1047	kip-*de*	chicken
1426	kist-*de*	chest
156	klaar-*adj; adv*	ready, finished; clear

2249	klaarmaken-*vb*	prepare
1728	klagen-*vb*	complain
1117	klant-*de*	customer
1415	klap-*de*	blow, whack
2360	klappen-*vb*	clap
820	klas-*de*	class
1662	klasse-*de*	class
1569	kleden-*vb*	dress
1594	kleding-*de*	clothing
221	klein-*adj*	small, little
1937	kleintje-*het*	little one
567	kleren-*de*	clothes
1090	kleur-*de*	color
2068	klimmen-*vb*	climb
2257	kliniek-*de*	clinic
417	klinken-*vb; het*	sound, ring; clink
1565	klok-*de*	clock
310	kloppen-*vb*	knock, beat
1226	klus-*de*	job
2213	knal-*de*	bang
788	knap-*adj; adv*	handsome; cleverly
2102	knie-*de*	knee
2502	knoop-*de*	button
1730	knop-*de*	button
2258	knopen-*vb*	knot
853	knul-*de*	young fellow
1736	koe-*de*	cow
1803	koekje-*het*	cookie
2228	koelkast-*de*	refrigerator
1419	koers-*de*	rate, course, track
1171	koffer-*de*	suitcase
468	koffie-*de*	coffee
1072	kogel-*de*	bullet, ball
2043	kok-*de*	cook
1207	koken-*vb*	cook
638	kolonel-*de*	colonel
2061	kom-*de*	bowl
51	komen-*vb*	come, come to
1551	komst-*de*	arrival
1872	konijn-*het*	rabbit
466	koning-*de*	king
803	koningin-*de*	queen
2029	koninklijk-*adj; adv*	royal; regally
1627	koninkrijk-*het*	kingdom
612	kont-*de*	buttocks, bum
2176	kooi-*de*	cage
2216	koorts-*de*	fever
311	kop-*de*	head, cup
465	kopen-*vb*	buy
2042	kopie-*de*	copy

1801	kopje-*het*	cup
2281	korporaal-*de*	corporal
839	kort-*adj*	short, brief
1962	kosten-*de; vb*	price; cost
2323	kostuum-*het*	costume
1590	kou(de)-*de*	cold
568	koud-*adj*	cold
525	kracht-*de*	force
2383	krachtig-*adj; adv*	powerful; vigorously
1960	krankzinnig-*adj; adv;*	insane; frantically
869	krant-*de*	newspaper
178	krijgen-*vb*	get
2441	krijt-*het*	chalk
2364	kroon-*de*	crown
2308	kruipen-*vb; het*	crawl; crawling
1612	kruis-*het*	cross
37	kunnen-*vb*	can
1162	kunst-*de*	art
868	kus-*de*	kiss
937	kussen-*het; vb*	pillow; kiss
1210	kust-*de*	coast
447	kwaad-*adj; het*	evil, angry; evil
743	kwalijk-*adj; adv*	bad, wrong; amiss
2460	kwaliteit-*de*	quality
1985	kwart-*het*	quarter
2272	kwartier-*het*	fifteen minutes
1323	kwestie-*de*	matter
2138	kwetsen-*vb*	hurt
459	kwijt-*adj*	lost
2332	kwijtraken-*vb*	lose

L

1179	laag-*adj; de*	low; layer
2075	laars-*de*	boot
207	laatst-*adj; adv*	last, latest; lately
1237	lach-*de*	smile
606	lachen-*vb*	laugh
782	la-*de*	drawer
2032	lade-*de*	drawer
2095	laden-*vb*	load
1910	lading-*de*	cargo
1683	lafaard-*de*	coward
2200	lamp-*de*	lamp
285	land-*het*	land, earth, country
173	lang-*adj; adv*	long, tall; long
395	langs-*adv; prp*	along; along
887	langzaam-*adj*	slow
915	last-*de*	burden, bother
797	lastig-*adj*	difficult

68	laten-*vb*	let, leave
290	later-*adv; adj*	later, hereafter; after
1834	lawaai-*het*	noise
2521	leed-*het*	anguish
948	leeftijd-*de*	age
809	leeg-*adj; adv*	empty; vacantly
894	leer-*het; de*	leather; teaching
2148	leerling-*de*	pupil, student
1987	leeuw-*de*	lion
1322	lef-*het*	courage
2414	legaal-*adj*	legal
1636	legende-*de*	legend
522	leger-*het*	army
479	leggen-*vb*	lay, put
767	leiden-*vb*	lead
946	leider-*de*	leader
1023	leiding-*de*	leadership
289	lekker-*adj; adv*	tasty, nice; deliciously
1336	lelijk-*adj*	ugly
1976	lente-*de*	spring
1204	leraar-*de*	teacher
334	leren-*vb; adj*	learn; teach
727	les-*de*	lesson
2093	letterlijk-*adj; adv*	literal; to the letter
1456	leugen-*de*	lie
157	leuk-*adj*	nice, fun
98	leven-*het; vb*	life; live
2507	levenslang-*adj*	lifelong
2038	lever-*de*	liver
1799	leveren-*vb*	deliver
530	lezen-*vb*	read
445	lichaam-*het*	body
434	licht-*adj; het; adv*	light, mild; light; slightly
1224	lid-*het*	member
1519	lied-*het*	song
437	lief-*adj; adv*	lovable, nice; sweet
323	liefde-*de*	love
569	liefje-*het*	sweetheart
873	liegen-*vb*	lie
1846	lieveling-*de*	favorite
431	lieverd-*de*	darling, honey
757	lift-*de*	lift, elevator, ride
294	liggen-*vb*	lie
1159	lijden-*vb*	suffer
1524	lijf-*het*	body
208	lijken-*vb; de*	seem, resemble; cadavers
684	lijn-*de*	line
758	lijst-*de*	list
2337	link-*de; adj*	link; dangerous
686	links-*adj*	left

1545	lip-*de*	lip
1643	live-*adj*	on air
1550	logisch-*adj*	logical
1880	lokaal-*adj; het*	local; place
889	lol-*de*	fun
2152	long-*de*	lung
1943	loon-*het*	wage
316	lopen-*vb*	walk
325	los-*adj; adv*	loose; loose
2193	loslaten-*vb*	release
1591	lossen-*vb*	unload
792	lot-*het*	fate
1189	loven-*vb*	praise
476	lucht-*de*	air, sky
159	luisteren-*vb*	listen
793	luitenant-*de*	lieutenant
614	lukken-*vb*	succeed
1027	lunch-*de*	lunch
1682	lunchen-*vb*	lunch
1891	lust-*de*	lust

M

1361	maagd-*de*	virgin
1559	maag-*de*	stomach
1691	maal-*de; het*	time; meal
1902	maaltijd-*de*	meal
387	maand-*de*	month
902	maan-*de*	moon
19	maar-*adv; con*	however, just; but
622	maat-*de*	size, buddy
2088	maatschappij-*de*	society
1136	machine-*de*	machine
658	macht-*de*	power
2265	machtig-*adj; adv*	powerful; powerfully
653	ma-*de*	mom
2342	maffia-*de*	mafia
1417	magie-*de*	magic
1798	magisch-*adj*	magic
2107	mail-*de*	mail
1060	majesteit-*de*	majesty
111	maken-*vb*	make
555	makkelijk-*adj; adv*	easy; easy
317	mama-*de*	mom
391	mam-*de*	mom
1668	mamma-*de*	mum
1274	manager-*de*	manager
76	man-*de*	man
265	manier-*de*	way, how
1697	mankeren-*vb*	lack, ail

1719	mannetje-*het*	small/little man
1543	marine-*de*	navy
2518	marinier-*de*	marine
1465	markt-*de*	market
1577	masker-*het*	mask
1554	materiaal-*het*	material
2255	mazzel-*de*	luck
1379	medelijden-*het*	compassion, pity
1097	medicijn-*het*	medicine
1393	medisch-*adj*	medical
2054	medium-*adj; het*	medium; medium
85	mee-*adv*	also, with
1819	meebrengen-*vb*	bring
1514	meedoen-*vb*	participate
1633	meegaan-*vb*	come
1776	meekomen-*vb*	come along with
1249	meemaken-*vb*	experience
826	meenemen-*vb*	take, bring
65	meer-*adj; adv; het*	more; more; lake
1558	meerdere-*de; adv*	superior; multiple
852	meestal-*adv*	usually
599	meester-*de*	master, teacher
477	meid-*de*	girl
214	meisje-*het*	girl
1839	mekaar-*prn*	each other
1522	melden-*vb*	report
1062	melk-*de*	milk
154	meneer-*de*	mister
500	menen-*verb*	mean
2234	menigte-*de*	crowd
1098	mening-*de*	opinion
487	men-*prn*	people, one
1191	menselijk-*adj*	human
1536	mensheid-*de*	humanity
96	mens-*het*	human
20	me-*prn*	me
1704	merken-*vb*	notice
862	mes-*het*	knife
350	meteen-*adv*	immediately
582	meter-*de*	meter
24	met-*prp; adv*	with; along with
2086	metro-*de*	metro
313	mevrouw-*de*	lady
412	mezelf-*prn*	myself
1599	middag-*de*	noon
2034	middel-*het*	waist, method
724	midden-*het; adj; prp*	middle; mid; amidst
1654	middernacht-*de*	midnight

1587	mijl-*de*	mile
867	mijnheer-*de*	sir, mister
26	mijn-*prn*	my, mine
56	mij-*prn*	me
1913	mijzelf-*prn*	myself
1384	militair-*adj; de*	military; soldier
1998	miljard-*nu*	billion
430	miljoen-*nu*	million
1342	min-*adj; adv*	poor; minus
496	minder-*adj; adv*	less; less, fewer
1386	minister-*de*	minister
2108	ministerie-*het*	ministry
1570	minstens-*adv*	at least
269	minuut-*de*	minute
326	mis-*adj; adv; de*	wrong, erroneous; wrong; mass
1052	misdaad-*de*	crime
90	misschien-*adv*	maybe
2358	misselijk-*adj*	nauseous
629	missen-*vb*	miss
824	missie-*de*	mission
935	mist-*de*	fog
2385	misverstand-*het*	misunderstanding
2315	mobiel-*adj*	mobile
2320	modder-*de*	mud, dirt
2493	mode-*de*	fashion
1644	model-*het*	model
2078	modern-*adj; adv*	modern; contemporary
597	moe-*adj*	tired
1043	moed-*de*	courage
151	moeder-*de*	mother
351	moeilijk-*adj*	difficult, tough
1842	moeilijkheid-*de*	difficulty
752	moeite-*de*	trouble, effort
2247	moeras-*het*	swamp
43	moeten-*vb; av*	must, need; should
390	mogelijk-*adj; adv*	possible, eventual; possibly
1467	mogelijkheid-*de*	possibility
112	mogen-*vb*	may, like
1442	momenteel-*adv*	currently, at the moment
274	moment-*het*	moment
367	mond-*de*	mouth
897	monster-*het*	sample, monster
158	mooi-*adj*	beautiful, pretty
528	moord-*de*	murder
652	moordenaar-*de*	killer, murderer
1870	morgenavond-*adv*	tomorrow
205	morgen-*de*	tomorrow, morning

1297	morgenochtend-*adv*	tomorrow morning
977	motor-*de*	engine
2361	muis-*de*	mouse
1904	munitie-*de*	ammunition
1725	museum-*het*	museum
709	muur-*de*	wall
486	muziek-*de*	music
2205	mysterie-*het*	mystery

N

1950	naaien-*vb; het*	sew; dressmaking
1301	naakt-*adj*	naked
181	naam-*de*	name
32	naar-*prp; adv; adj*	to, for; along; awful
464	naartoe-*adv*	there
601	naast-*adj; prp*	near; next to
314	nacht-*de*	night
1352	nachtmerrie-*de*	nightmare
651	nadat-*con*	after
957	nadenken-*vb*	reflect, think
2477	naderen-*vb*	approach
1688	namelijk-*adv*	namely
1859	namens-*prp*	on behalf of
161	na-*prp; adv*	after; post
1218	nat-*adj*	wet
2276	natie-*de*	nation
1493	nationaal-*adj*	national
1266	natuur-*de*	nature
1263	nauwelijks-*adv*	hardly
1408	nederlands-*adj; het*	Dutch; Dutch
922	neef-*de*	cousin
46	nee-*prt*	no
336	neer-*adv*	down
1040	neerschieten-*vb*	shoot
2172	negatief-*adj; het*	negative; negative
664	negen-*nu*	nine
1881	negeren-*vb*	ignore
834	nek-*de*	neck
146	nemen-*vb*	take
1786	nep-*adj*	fake
449	nergens-*adv*	nowhere
1039	nerveus-*adj*	nervous
2440	nest-*het*	nest
109	net-*adv; het; adj*	just; net; elegant
1353	netjes-*adj*	neat
2365	netwerk-*het*	network
733	neus-*de*	nose

1564	nicht-*de*	niece
139	niemand-*prn*	nobody
8	niet-*adv*	not
88	niets-*het; prn; adv*	nothing; nothing; none
499	nietwaar-*int*	is(n't) it
204	nieuw-*adj*	new, novel
1767	nieuwsgierig-*adj*	curious
382	nieuws-*het*	news, novelty
141	niks-*prn; adv*	nothing; none
1407	niveau-*het*	level
1443	noch-*con*	nor
101	nodig-*adj*	necessary, required
442	noemen-*vb*	call, mention
40	nog-*adv*	yet, still
495	nogal-*adv; adj*	rather; pretty
1335	nogmaals-*adv*	once again
1915	nood-*de*	need
83	nooit-*adv*	never, no way
2153	noord-*adj*	north
1168	noorden-*het*	north
489	normaal-*adj*	normal
81	nou-*adv*	now
2331	november-*de*	November
48	nu-*adv; con*	now; now
1667	nul-*het*	zero
335	nummer-*het*	number, digit
2087	nut-*het*	utility
2446	nuttig-*adj*	useful

O

1299	oceaan-*de*	ocean
1013	ochtend-*de*	morning
1390	oefenen-*vb*	practice
2040	oefening-*de*	exercise
58	of-*con*	or, whether
2481	offer-*het*	sacrifice
1110	officier-*de*	officer
1812	ofwel-*con*	or
1671	ogenblik-*het*	moment
124	oh-*int*	oh
1354	okee-*in*	okay
2311	olifant-*de*	elephant
699	oma-*de*	grandmother
118	omdat-*con*	because
1967	omdraaien-*verb*	turn around
1727	omgaan-*vb*	handle
1302	omgeving-*de*	surroundings
469	omhoog-*adv*	up
1101	omkeren-*vb*	turn

1429	omlaag-*adv*	down
31	om-*prp; adv*	to, for; about
1508	omstandigheid-*de*	circumstance
1843	onbekend-*adj*	unknown
2382	onbeleefd-*adj; adv*	rude; discourteously
1282	ondanks-*prp*	despite
190	onder-*adv; prp*	under, underneath; under
2066	onderdeel-*het*	part, component
1970	ondergoed-*het*	underwear
1980	onderhandelen-*vb*	negotiate
1841	ondertussen-*adv*	meanwhile
721	onderweg-*adv*	en route, on the way
1513	onderwerp-*het*	subject, topic
1116	onderzoeken-*vb*	examine
572	onderzoek-*het*	research, study
801	ongelooflijk-*adj*	incredible, unbelievable
565	ongeluk-*het*	accident
1922	ongelukkig-*adj*	unhappy; unfortunately
1438	ongerust-*adj*	anxious, worried
536	ongeveer-*adv*	about, approximately
2016	onlangs-*adv*	recently
907	onmiddellijk-*adj*	immediate
683	onmogelijk-*adj; adv*	impossible; impossibly
1048	onschuldig-*adj*	innocent
64	ons-*prn; het/de*	us; ounce
1566	onszelf-*prn*	ourselves
1004	ontbijt-*het*	breakfast
2499	ontbreken-*vb*	lack
933	ontdekken-*vb*	discover
1450	onthouden-*vb*	remember
2479	ontkennen-*vb*	deny
441	ontmoeten-*vb*	meet
1748	ontmoeting-*de*	encounter
2351	ontploffen-*vb*	explode
899	ontslaan-*vb*	dismiss, fire
1409	ontslag-*het*	dismissal
871	ontsnappen-*vb*	escape
1653	ontspannen-*vb*	relax
940	ontvangen-*vb*	receive
1532	ontvoeren-*vb*	kidnap
2287	ontwerpen-*vb*	design
2482	ontwikkelen-*vb*	develop
1556	ontzettend-*adj; adv*	tremendous; enormously
97	onze-*prn*	our
2433	onzichtbaar-*adj*	invisible

484	onzin-*de*	nonsense, rubbish
263	oog-*het*	eye
188	ooit-*adv*	ever
55	ook-*adv*	also, as well
490	oom-*de*	uncle
2184	oordeel-*het*	judgment
1026	oor-*het*	ear
371	oorlog-*de*	war
2335	oorzaak-*de*	cause
2459	oost-*adj*	east
1356	oosten-*het*	east
861	opa-*de*	grandpa
2244	opblazen-*vb*	blow
2012	opdagen-*vb*	turn up
967	opdracht-*de*	assignment
1061	opeens-*adv*	suddenly
230	open-*adj; adv*	open, overt; overtly
1883	openbaar-*adj; adv*	public; openly
1070	openen-*vb*	open
2429	opening-*de*	opening
980	operatie-*de*	operation
1601	opeten-*vb*	eat
2185	opgeblazen-*adj*	bloated
1332	opgeven-*vb*	quit, give up
1856	opgroeien-*vb*	grow up
1078	ophalen-*vb*	collect
1520	ophangen-*vb*	hang
794	ophouden-*vb*	stop
1820	opleiding-*de*	training
2461	opletten-*vb*	pay attention
1273	oplossen-*vb*	solve
1188	oplossing-*de*	solution
1796	opname-*de*	recording
1115	opnemen-*vb*	record, take
524	opnieuw-*adv*	again
1613	oppakken-*vb*	take up
2495	oppassen-*het; vb*	babysit; beware
15	op-*prp; adv; adj*	on, up, at; on, up; spent
2233	oproep-*de*	call
1773	opruimen-*vb*	tidy up
784	opschieten-*vb*	hurry
1380	opsluiten-*vb*	lock
1002	opstaan-*vb*	stand up, rise, get up
2508	opstand-*de*	rebellion
2266	optie-*de*	option
1512	optreden-*vb*	perform, appear
2515	opvallen-*vb*	notice
2190	opvoeden-*vb*	bring up
1242	opwinden-*vb*	excite, wind up
2225	opzetten-*vb*	put on

1034	opzij-*het*	aside
1460	opzoeken-*vb*	visit
234	orde-*de*	order, discipline
1765	organisatie-*de*	organization
259	oud-*adj*	old
402	ouder-*adj; de*	older, senior; parent
407	overal-*adv*	everywhere
2179	overdag-*adv*	in the daytime
2410	overdrijven-*vb*	exaggerate
1795	overeenkomst-*de*	agreement
2197	overeind-*adv*	upright
1890	overgeven-*vb*	hand over, vomit
1951	overheen-*adv*	across, over
1742	overheid-*de*	government
1749	overkant-*de*	other side
1135	overkomen-*vb*	happen, visit
1083	overleden-*adj*	deceased
884	overleven-*vb*	survive
2469	overlijden-*het; vb*	death; decease
2134	overnemen-*vb*	take over
57	over-*prp; adv*	about; over
2215	overstuur-*adj*	upset
1573	overtuigen-*vb*	convince
1679	overval-*de*	raid, robbery
1921	overvallen-*vb*	ambush, rob
1471	overwinning-*de*	victory

P

639	paard-*het*	horse
198	paar-*het*	couple
424	pa-*de*	dad
1001	pad-*het*	path
2264	pagina-*de*	page
1086	pak-*het*	suit, pack
1740	pakje-*het*	packet
305	pakken-*vb*	grab
1866	paleis-*het*	palace
2164	pan-*de*	pan
1146	paniek-*de*	panic
298	papa-*de*	dad
463	pap-*de*	dad
1012	papieren-*adj; de*	paper; papers
1181	papier-*het*	paper
1718	pappa-*de*	daddy
2065	paradijs-*het*	paradise
494	pardon-*het*	pardon, excuse me
872	park-*het*	park
1533	partij-*de*	party

751	partner-*de*	partner
251	pas-*adv; de*	just now; pass
1909	paspoort-*het*	passport
2064	passagier-*de*	passenger
932	passen-*vb*	suit, fit
1999	passie-*de*	passion
2377	pastoor-*de*	priest
2451	pater-*de*	father (priest)
1373	pauze-*de*	pause, break
1781	pech-*de*	bad luck
1592	pen-*de*	pen
1831	penis-*de*	penis
1487	pensioen-*het*	pension
509	perfect-*adj*	perfect
1938	periode-*de*	period
358	per-*prp*	by
1215	pers-*de*	press, media
1677	personeel-*het*	staff
523	persoon-*de*	person
813	persoonlijk-*adj*	personal
1729	pest-*de*	plague
2175	pet-*de*	cap
2000	piano-*de*	piano
275	pijn-*de*	pain
2055	pijnlijk-*adj; adv*	painful; painfully
2168	pijp-*de*	pipe
1208	pikken-*vb*	steal, peck, put up with
1344	pil-*de*	pill
1374	piloot-*de*	pilot
2018	pissen-*vb*	piss
540	pistool-*het*	pistol
1479	pizza-*de*	pizza
2072	plaat-*de*	panel, illustration, record
264	plaats-*de*	place, location
906	plaatsen-*vb*	place, plant, put
920	planeet-*de*	planet
306	plan-*het*	plan, scheme
1535	plannen-*vb*	plan
1981	plant-*de*	plant
1778	plas-*de*	puddle
2305	plastic-*het*	plastic
1780	plat-*adj*	flat
1528	plegen-*vb*	commit
354	plek-*de*	place, spot
462	plezier-*het*	fun
1364	plicht-*de*	duty
2318	plots-*adv; adj*	suddenly; sudden
1598	plotseling-*adv; adj*	suddenly; sudden
1713	podium-*het*	stage
1641	poging-*de*	attempt

2156	politieagent-*de*	policeman
239	politie-*de*	police
1286	politiek-*de*	politics
2525	politieman-*de*	policeman
2339	pols-*de*	wrist
1082	pond-*het*	pound
1449	poort-*de*	port
2279	poot-*de*	leg
1517	pop-*de*	doll
2106	populair-*adj*	popular
2371	porno-*de*	porn
2242	portemonnee-*de*	wallet
783	positie-*de*	position
2137	positief-*adj; het*	positive; positive
1064	post-*de*	post
1219	pot-*de*	crock, pot
418	prachtig-*adj; adv*	wonderful, magnificent
2456	praktisch-*adj*	practical
152	praten-*vb*	talk
247	precies-*adv; adj*	exactly, precise; exact
440	president-*de*	president
1318	prettig-*adj*	gratifying
1269	priester-*de*	priest
617	prijs-*de*	price, prize
297	prima-*adj;adv*	great, fine
969	prins-*de*	prince
888	prinses-*de*	princess
2431	privacy-*de*	privacy
249	proberen-*vb*	try, attempt
231	probleem-*het*	problem
2386	procedure-*de*	procedure
942	procent-*het*	percent
1202	proces-*het*	process, trial
1814	proef-*de*	test
1990	proeven-*vb*	taste
753	professor-*de*	professor
1031	programma-*het*	program
1169	project-*het*	project
1979	promotie-*de*	promotion
1470	proosten-*vb*	toast
1847	psychiater-*de*	psychiatrist
958	publiek-*het; adj*	audience; public
2394	puinhoop-*de*	mess
537	punt-*het*	point
2422	put-*de*	well
1699	puur-*adj*	pure

R

1127	raad-*de*	advice
750	raam-*het*	window

631	raar-*adj; adv*	strange; strangely
1254	race-*de*	race
649	raden-*vb*	guess
790	radio-*de*	radio
611	raken-*vb*	hit, touch
1907	raket-*de*	rocket
1486	ramp-*de*	disaster
2161	ranch-*de*	ranch
1744	rand-*de*	edge
1145	rapport-*het*	report
2049	ras-*het*	race, breed
1529	rat-*de*	rat
1584	reactie-*de*	reaction
1867	reageren-*vb*	react
2368	realiseren-*vb*	realize
1709	realiteit-*de*	reality
2472	recept-*het*	recipe
1220	rechercheur-*de*	detective
403	recht-*adj; adv; het*	right; right; right
1523	rechtbank-*de*	court
807	rechter-*adj; de*	right; judge
731	rechts-*adj*	right
2160	rechtstreeks-*adv; adj*	directly; direct
2378	rechtszaak-*de*	trial
2149	reclame-*de*	advertisement
2450	record-*het*	record
392	redden-*vb*	save, rescue
406	rede-*de*	reason, speech
1547	redelijk-*adj; adv*	reasonable; reasonably
1406	reden-*de*	reason
1894	reeds-*adv*	already
626	regel-*de*	rule
716	regelen-*vb*	arrange
1329	regen-*de*	rain
2141	regenen-*vb*	rain
840	regering-*de*	government
2271	regisseur-*de*	director
607	reis-*de*	travel
1197	reizen-*vb*	travel
1130	rekenen-*vb*	calculate, count
836	rekening-*de*	account, check
748	relatie-*de*	relation(ship)
624	rennen-*vb*	run
2401	rente-*de*	interest
1949	repareren-*vb*	repair
1571	reputatie-*de*	reputation
705	respect-*het*	respect
981	restaurant-*het*	restaurant
393	rest-*de*	rest, remainder

1877	resultaat-*het*	result
1974	revolutie-*de*	revolution
2146	revolver-*de*	revolver
1635	richten-*vb*	direct, aim
876	richting-*de*	direction
2099	ridder-*de; adj*	knight; cavalier
2229	riem-*de*	belt
2006	rijbewijs-*het*	driving license
609	rij-*de*	row
428	rijden-*vb*	ride, drive
657	rijk-*adj; het*	rich; empire
2444	rijzen-*vb*	rise
818	ring-*de*	ring
1088	risico-*het*	risk
1861	rit-*de*	ride
816	rivier-*de*	river
959	roepen-*vb*	call
968	roken-*vb*	smoke
914	rol-*de*	role
1813	rollen-*vb*	roll
2418	roman-*de*	novel
1714	romantisch-*adj*	romantic
1693	rommel-*de*	clutter
378	rond-*adv; adj*	around; round
1281	ronde-*de*	round
2504	rondje-*het*	round
2480	rondlopen-*vb*	walkabout
725	rood-*adj*	red
941	rook-*de*	smoke
2366	roos-*de*	rose
588	rot-*het; adj*	rot; rotten
1982	rots-*de*	rock
1707	route-*de*	route
1687	roze-*adj*	pink
594	rug-*de*	back
1030	ruiken-*vb*	smell
1674	ruilen-*vb*	exchange
1255	ruim-*adj*	spacious, amply
2329	ruimen-*vb*	clear
662	ruimte-*de*	space
1582	rus-*de*	Russian
1488	russisch-*adj; het*	Russian; Russian
372	rusten-*vb*	rest, lie
217	rustig-*adj; adv*	calm; quietly
878	ruziën-*vb*	argue, fight
2231	's ochtends-*adv*	in the morning

S

1267	saai-*adj*	dull, boring
2355	salaris-*het*	salary

224	samen-*adv*	together	1706	seizoen-*het*	season
1833	samenwerken-*vb; het*	co-operate; teamwork	615	seks-*de*	sex
			2067	seksueel-*adj*	sexual
1418	scène-*de*	scene	1229	senator-*de*	senator
1275	schade-*de*	damage	717	sergeant-*de*	sergeant
1542	schaduw-*de*	shadow	2209	serie-*de*	series
2194	schakel-*de*	link	526	serieus-*adj*	serious
1758	schamen-*vb*	be ashamed	2211	service-*de*	service
1608	schande-*de*	shame	1918	set-*de*	set
281	schat-*de*	treasure, honey	1008	sexy-*adj*	sexy
1277	schattig-*adj*	sweet, cute	745	sheriff-*de*	sheriff
2510	schedel-*de*	skull	1232	shirt-*het*	shirt
1343	scheiden-*vb*	separate	586	show-*de*	show
1892	scheiding-*de*	divorce	1375	sigaret-*de*	cigarette
613	schelen-*vb*	differ, care	1272	signaal-*het*	signal
2121	schema-*het*	scheme, schedule	886	simpel-*adj*	simple, basic
2155	scherm-*het*	screen	353	sinds-*adv; con*	since; since
1675	scherp-*adj*	sharp	1896	sindsdien-*adv*	since then
260	schieten-*vb*	shoot, fire	688	situatie-*de*	situation
2519	schijn-*de*	appearance	1946	slaaf-*de*	slave
1089	schijnen-*vb*	seem	557	slaan-*vb*	beat, hit
2379	schilderen-*vb*	paint	1360	slaapkamer-*de*	bedroom
1852	schilderij-*het*	painting	1057	slachtoffer-*het*	victim
2467	schild-*het*	shield	627	sla-*de*	lettuce
583	schip-*het*	ship	781	slag-*de*	battle, stroke
1324	schitteren-*vb*	shine	960	slagen-*vb*	succeed
700	schoen-*de*	shoe	1567	slang-*de*	hose, snake
270	school-*de*	school	340	slapen-*vb*	sleep
923	schoon-*adj*	clean	273	slecht-*adj; adv*	bad, evil; badly
1099	schoonheid-*de*	beauty	554	slechts-*adv*	only
1968	schoonmaken-*vb*	clean	677	sleutel-*de*	key
1741	schoppen-*vb*	kick	534	slim-*adj*	smart
1190	schot-*het*	shot	961	slot-*het*	lock
1858	schouder-*de*	shoulder	728	sluiten-*vb*	close
1958	schreeuw-*de*	scream	1294	smaken-*vb*	taste
1230	schreeuwen-*vb*	shout	1464	smeken-*vb*	beg
548	schrijven-*vb*	write	2367	smeren-*vb*	lubricate
1358	schrijver-*de*	writer	1383	smerig-*adj*	filthy
2313	schrik-*de*	scare	345	snappen-*vb*	understand, get
1290	schrikken-*vb*	start, jolt, scare	1580	sneeuw-*de*	snow
1750	schudden-*vb*	shake	186	snel-*adv; adj*	fast; quick
2476	schuilplaats-*de*	shelter	1326	snelheid-*de*	speed
398	schuld-*de*	debt, blame	1621	snijden-*vb; het*	cut; slicing
660	schuldig-*adj*	guilty	2133	snoep-*de*	candy
2252	schutter-*de*	shooter	1952	sociaal-*adj*	social
1926	schuur-*de*	barn, shed	1755	soep-*de*	soup
2497	scoren-*vb*	score	856	soldaat-*de*	soldier
625	seconde-*de*	second	544	sommige-*adj; prn*	some; some
2334	secretaresse-*de*	secretary			
2403	sectie-*de*	section	240	soms-*adv*	sometimes
2466	sector-*de*	sector	302	soort-*de*	kind

166	sorry-*int*	sorry
2522	sowieso-*adv*	definitely
2082	spaans-*adj*	Spanish
1940	Spanje-*het*	Spain
1746	spannend-*adj*	exciting
2019	spanning-*de*	tension, voltage, pressure
2375	sparen-*vb*	save
798	speciaal-*adj; adv*	special; especially
1774	speelgoed-*het*	toy
272	spelen-*vb*	play, game
1800	speler-*de*	player
467	spel-*het*	game
1459	spiegel-*de*	mirror
2501	spier-*de*	muscle
143	spijt-*de*	regret
2219	spijtig-*adj*	regrettable, unfortunate
1978	spion-*de*	spy
1862	spoedig-*adv; adj*	soon; early
982	spoor-*het*	track
1652	sport-*de*	sport
296	spreken-*vb*	speak
930	springen-*vb*	jump
547	spul-*het*	stuff
2419	staal-*het*	steel
148	staan-*vb*	stand
1722	staart-*de*	tail
261	stad-*de*	city
2245	staf-*de*	stave
2380	stam-*de*	tribe
1602	stand-*de*	position
456	stap-*de*	step, move
1118	stappen-*het; vb*	step, go, stride; night out
2296	star-*adj*	rigid
2023	staren-*vb*	stare
952	starten-*vb*	start
1186	station-*het*	station
2326	status-*de*	status
183	steeds-*adv*	always, still
1071	steen-*de*	stone
1081	steken-*vb*	put, poke, stab
619	stelen-*vb*	steal
352	stel-*het*	set, bunch, couple
538	stellen-*vb*	suppose, put
632	stem-*de*	vote, voice
1929	stemming-*de*	vote; mood
929	ster-*de*	star
584	sterk-*adj*	strong
373	sterven-*vb*	die
1311	steun-*de*	support
1895	steunen-*vb*	support
2024	stevig-*adv; adj*	firmly; firm
1370	stijl-*de*	style, steep
396	stil-*adj; adv*	quiet, still; quietly
1096	stilte-*de*	silence
1412	stinken-*vb*	stink
865	stoel-*de*	chair
2327	stoer-*adj*	tough, seasoned
1387	stof-*het*	substance, dust
1984	stok-*de*	stick
533	stom-*adj*	stupid
318	stoppen-*vb*	stop, cease
971	storen-*vb*	disturb
1187	storm-*de*	storm
2207	stout-*adj*	naughty
541	straat-*de*	street
1227	straf-*de; adj*	punishment; strong
2280	straffen-*vb*	punish
1837	strak-*adj; adv*	tight; tightly
416	straks-*adv*	soon, later
1065	strand-*het*	beach
2503	streng-*de; adj; adv*	strand; strict; strictly
962	strijd-*de*	fight, competition
1351	strijken-*vb*	iron
1213	stront-*de*	shit
1420	stroom-*de*	current, stream, electricity
1790	student-*de*	student
1346	studeren-*vb*	study
2046	studie-*de*	study
1788	studio-*de*	studio
385	stuk-*het; adj*	piece, part; broken
516	sturen-*vb*	send, steer
560	succes-*het*	success
1646	suiker-*de*	sugar
1056	sukkelen-*vb*	struggle
1228	super-*adj*	super, great
2309	symbool-*het*	symbol
859	systeem-*het*	system

T

1045	taak-*de*	task
1114	taal-*de*	language
1259	taart-*de*	cake
640	tafel-*de*	table
1161	talent-*het*	talent, gift
2321	tandarts-*de*	dentist
973	tand-*de*	tooth
1615	tank-*de*	tank
764	tante-*de*	aunt

1827	tape-*de*	tape	965	test-*de*	test
806	tas-*de*	bag	778	teveel-*het; adj*	excess; excess, too much
866	taxi-*de*	taxi	1054	tevreden-*adj*	satisfied
16	te-*adv; prp*	too, to; in	1666	theater-*het*	theater
429	team-*het*	team	1452	theorie-*de*	theory
2291	techniek-*de*	technique	2110	therapie-*de*	therapy
2081	technisch-*adj*	technical	219	thuis-*adv*	home
1930	technologie-*de*	technology	2171	ticket-*het*	ticket
2344	teen-*de*	toe	327	tien-*nu*	ten
1505	tegelijk-*adv*	at the same time	104	tijd-*de*	time
2473	tegelijkertijd-*adv*	at the same time	2169	tijdelijk-*adv; adj*	temporarily; temporary
1149	tegenhouden-*vb*	retain, hold	458	tijdens-*prp*	during
1211	tegenover-*prp*	opposite	2140	tijger-*de*	tiger
106	tegen-*prp; adv*	against	2139	timen-*vb*	time
2347	tegenstander-*de*	opponent	2098	tip-*de*	tip
1166	tegenwoordig-*adv; adj*	current; currently	1805	titel-*de*	title
			2053	tja-*interj*	well
1017	tekenen-*vb*	draw, sign	78	toch-*adv; con*	yet, so, right; nevertheless
685	teken-*het*	sign			
2454	tekort-*het*	deficit	1279	toegang-*de*	access
1732	tekst-*de*	text	1441	toegeven-*vb*	admit
410	telefoon-*de*	phone	542	toekomst-*de*	future
2333	telefoonnummer-*het*	telephone number	2236	toekomstig-*adj*	future
			107	toen-*con; adv*	when; then
1622	teleurstellen-*vb*	disappoint	163	toe-*prp; adv*	to; towards
1639	televisie-*de*	television	2428	toespraak-*de*	speech
1919	telkens-*adv*	constantly, again and again	2116	toestaan-*vb*	allow
			1561	toestand-*de*	state
1339	tellen-*vb*	count	2218	toestel-*het*	device
2007	tempel-*de*	temple	928	toestemming-*de*	permission
2303	temperatuur-*de*	temperature	1411	toeval-*het*	chance
2424	tempo-*het*	pace	1036	toevallig-*adj*	accidental
1975	ten minste-*adv*	at least	2132	tof-*adj*	great, amazing
553	tenminste-*adv*	at least	1028	toilet-*het*	toilet
1823	tenslotte-*adv*	finally	2127	ton-*de*	tonne
1106	tent-*de*	tent	2416	toneel-*het*	stage
722	tenzij-*con*	unless	1003	tonen-*vb*	show
1077	terecht-*adj;adv*	justified; back, found	1203	tong-*de*	tongue
2488	tering-*de*	typhus	1131	toon-*de*	tone
566	ter-*prp*	to	996	top-*de*	top, peak
1430	terrein-*het*	terrain	2356	topper-*de*	top class
1923	terrorist-*de*	terrorist	1716	toren-*de*	tower
84	terug-*adv*	back, again	891	totaal-*adj; het; adv*	total; total; totally
2362	terugbrengen-*vb*	bring back			
1614	teruggaan-*vb*	return	641	totdat-*con*	until
2490	teruggeven-*vb*	give back	93	tot-*prp; con*	to; until
1914	terugkeren-*vb*	return	1400	touw-*het*	rope
1066	terugkomen-*vb*	return	1900	tovenaar-*de*	wizard
1808	terugtrekken-*vb*	withdraw	1723	traan-*de*	tear
383	terwijl-*con*	while, whereas	2035	traditie-*de*	tradition
2312	testament-*het*	will	1619	trainen-*vb; het*	train; training

1527	training-*de*	workout, training
909	trap-*de*	stairs
2463	tred-*de*	pace
2359	treffen-*vb; het*	meet; encounter
693	trein-*de*	train
475	trek-*de*	pull
618	trekken-*vb; het*	pull; draft
2126	trekker-*de*	tractor
1964	triest-*adj*	sad
1058	troep-*de*	flock, pack, mess
2345	troon-*de*	throne
517	trots-*de; adj*	pride; proud
945	trouw-*de; adj*	faith; loyal
562	trouwens-*adv*	by the way
444	trouwen-*vb*	marry
1806	truc-*de*	trick
1051	truck-*de*	truck
2131	tuig-*het*	rig, harness, scum
1151	tuin-*de*	garden
1588	tunnel-*de*	tunnel
299	tussen-*prp*	between
532	tv-*abr*	TV
917	twaalf-*nu*	twelve
438	tweede-*nu*	second
2180	tweeling-*de*	twin
103	twee-*nu*	two
1102	twijfel-*de*	doubt
900	twintig-*nu*	twenty
1095	type-*het*	type
2425	typisch-*adj*	typical

U

1845	uitdaging-*de*	challenge
765	uiteindelijk-*adj; adv*	finally; sooner or later
1548	uiteraard-*adv*	naturally
2292	uiterlijk-*het*	appearance
1899	uitgaan-*vb*	go out
2003	uitgang-*de(m)*	exit
2487	uitkijken-*vb*	be careful
2001	uitkomen-*vb*	come
766	uitleggen-*vb*	explain
2157	uitmaken-*vb*	extinguish
1163	uitnodigen-*vb*	invite
1879	uitnodiging-*de*	invitation
52	uit-*prp; adv; adj*	from; out; off
2182	uitputten-*vb*	exhaust
2406	uitschakelen-*vb*	switch off
2158	uitstappen-*vb*	get off
1137	uitstekend-*adj*	excellent

2307	uitvinden-*vb*	figure out
2198	uitvoer-*de*	export
2370	uitvoeren-*vb*	execute
2047	uitweg-*de*	solution, way out
2512	uitzending-*adj; de*	broadcast; transmission
1738	uitzicht-*het*	view
1664	uitzien-*vb*	look
1243	uitzoeken-*vb*	sort, find out
2389	uniek-*adj*	unique
1510	uniform-*het*	uniform
1042	universiteit-*de*	university
1966	universum-*het*	universe
27	u-*prn*	you
160	uur-*het*	hour
105	uw-*prn*	your
2073	uzelf-*prn*	yourself

V

421	vaak-*adv*	often, regularly
1129	vaarwel-*het*	goodbye
127	vader-*de*	father
851	vakantie-*de*	holiday, vacation
1848	vak-*het*	section, compartment, profession
370	vallen-*vb*	fall, drop
1455	vals-*adj*	FALSE
427	vanaf-*prp*	from
243	vanavond-*adv*	tonight
209	vandaag-*adv*	today
404	vandaan-*prp*	from
2208	vandaar-*adv*	hence
1177	vandoor-*adv*	away
1079	vangen-*vb*	catch
1458	vanmiddag-*adv*	this afternoon
905	vanmorgen-*adv*	this morning
707	vannacht-*adv*	tonight
1546	vanochtend-*adv*	this morning
11	van-*prp*	of, from
665	vanuit-*prp*	from
2304	vanwaar-*adv*	from where
691	vanwege-*prp*	because of
1908	vanzelf-*adv*	self, by itself
2097	varen-*vb; het*	sail; fern, sailing
1341	varken-*het*	pig
1246	vasthouden-*vb*	hold
1828	vat-*het*	container, keg
443	vechten-*vb*	fight, battle
1961	vee-*het*	cattle
94	veel-*adv*	much, a lot

1988	veertig-*nu*	forty
384	veilig-*adj; adv*	safe, sure; safely
995	veiligheid-*de*	safety
1055	veld-*het*	field
369	vent-*de*	fellow, geezer, guy
360	ver-*adj; adv*	far, remote; far
451	veranderen-*vb*	change
1478	verandering-*de*	change
1035	verantwoordelijk-*adj*	responsible
1334	verantwoordelijkheid-*de*	responsibility
1304	verband-*het*	connection, bandage
1947	verbazen-*vb*	surprise
2289	verbazingwekkend-*adj*	astounding
1212	verbergen-*vb*	hide
2498	verbeteren-*vb*	improve
1499	verbinden-*vb*	link
1762	verbinding-*de*	connection
2294	verblijf-*het*	stay
1044	verboden-*adj*	forbidden
1231	verborgen-*adj*	hidden
1345	verbranden-*vb*	incinerate
1355	verdedigen-*vb*	defend
1476	verdediging-*de*	defense
1120	verdenken-*vb*	suspect
250	verder-*adj; adv*	further; moreover
1534	verderop-*adv*	further ahead
741	verdienen-*vb*	earn
1271	verdieping-*de*	floor
168	verdomme-*int*	damn
454	verdommen-*het*	refuse
800	verdorie-*interj*	shucks
2390	verdragen-*vb*	bear
1585	verdriet-*het*	grief
1956	verdrietig-*adj; adv*	sad; sadly
796	verdwijnen-*vb*	disappear
1521	verenigen-*vb*	unite
2447	vereren-*vb*	honor
2404	verf-*de*	paint
1195	vergadering-*de*	meeting
2221	vergelijken-*vb*	compare
304	vergeten-*vb*	forget
877	vergeven-*vb*	forgive
1268	vergissing-*de*	mistake
330	verhaal-*het*	story, redress
2405	verhouding-*de*	ratio
1381	verhuizen-*vb*	move
830	verjaardag-*de*	birthday
502	verkeerd-*adj; adv*	wrong; wrong
1965	verkeer-*het*	traffic
1864	verklaren-*vb*	explain
1019	verklaring-*de*	statement
2195	verknallen-*vb*	mess up
585	verkopen-*vb*	sell
1838	verkrachten-*vb*	rape
2083	verlangen-*het; vb*	desire; desire
529	verlaten-*vb; adj*	leave; abandoned
734	verleden-*het*	past
550	verliefd-*adj*	in love
448	verliezen-*het; vb*	loss; lose
1466	verloven-*vb*	commit, betroth
2506	vermaak-*het*	entertainment
2523	vermijden-*vb*	avoid
1321	vermist-*adj*	missing
2114	vermogen-*het*	power, ability
258	vermoorden-*vb*	murder, assassinate
972	vernietigen-*vb*	destroy
2044	veronderstellen-*vb*	assume
1948	verontschuldigen-*vb*	apologize
1804	veroordelen-*vb*	condemn
1889	veroorloven-*vb*	afford, permit
1468	veroorzaken-*vb*	cause
1959	verpesten-*vb*	spoil
1822	verplaatsen-*vb*	move
2183	verpleegster-*de*	nurse
2154	verplichten-*vb*	oblige
1957	verraad-*het*	betrayal
1192	verraden-*vb*	betray
1739	verrader-*de*	traitor
1660	verrassen-*vb*	surprise
811	verrassing-*de*	surprise
1928	verrotten-*vb*	rot
1821	vers-*adj*	fresh
2437	verschijnen-*vb*	appear
844	verschil-*het*	difference
963	verschrikkelijk-*adj; adv*	horrible; terrible
1659	verschuldigd-*adj*	indebted
2077	versie-*de*	version
2210	versieren-*vb*	decorate
1085	verslaan-*vb*	defeat
1312	verslagen-*adj*	defeated
1503	verslag-*het*	report
2105	verspillen-*vb*	waste
1939	verspreiden-*vb*	spread
1818	verstaan-*vb*	understand, hear

1124	verstand-*het*	intellect, sense
1698	verstandig-*adj*	wise
2085	versterking-*de*	reinforcement
1315	verstoppen-*vb*	hide
1050	vertalen-*vb*	translate
988	vertaling-*de*	translation
193	vertellen-*vb*	tell
535	vertrek-*het*	departure, room
1109	vertrekken-*vb*	leave
460	vertrouwen-*het; vb*	confidence, faith; trust
1472	vervangen-*vb*	substitute, replace
1320	vervelen-*vb*	bore
2269	vervloeken-*vb*	curse
2113	vervolgens-*adv*	then
497	verwachten-*vb*	expect
2348	verwarren-*vb*	confuse
1811	verwijderen-*vb*	remove
2222	verwoesten-*vb*	destroy
1779	verzamelen-*vb*	collect, gather
2324	verzekeren-*vb*	ensure
2060	verzekering-*de*	insurance
1661	verzet-*het*	resistance
2089	verzinnen-*vb*	invent, come up with
1366	verzoek-*het*	request
1647	vet-*het*	fat
648	via-*prp*	via
954	vieren-*vb*	celebrate
280	vier-*nu*	four
1539	vies-*adj; adv*	dirty; nastily
1708	Vietnam-*het*	Vietnam
769	vijand-*de*	enemy
1844	vijfde-*adj*	fifth
257	vijf-*nu*	five
1461	vijftien-*nu*	fifteen
1541	vijftig-*nu*	fifty
147	vinden-*vb*	find
1128	vinger-*de*	finger
1605	virus-*het*	virus
802	vis-*de*	fish
1853	vlag-*de*	flag
990	vlak-*adj; het; adv*	flat; surface; just
1695	vlakbij-*adv*	nearby
746	vlees-*het*	meat
1735	vleugel-*de*	wing
563	vliegen-*vb*	fly
549	vliegtuig-*het*	airplane
1234	vliegveld-*het*	airport
1705	vloek-*de*	curse
1174	vloer-*de*	floor
2485	vloot-*de*	fleet
659	vluchten-*vb*	flee
849	vlug-*adv; adj*	quickly; quick
2052	voeden-*vb*	feed
1154	voedsel-*het*	food
246	voelen-*vb*	feel
1157	voeren-*vb*	feed, pursue
2436	voertuig-*het*	vehicle
2031	voetbal-*de/het*	football (ball), football (sport)
777	voet-*de*	foot
1178	vogel-*de*	bird
337	vol-*adj; adv*	full, crowded; full
1648	voldoende-*adj; de*	satisfactory; sufficient
291	volgens-*adv*	according to
254	volgen-*vb*	follow, track
2285	volhouden-*vb*	hold on
770	volk-*het*	people, folk
1731	volkomen-*adv*	utterly
827	volledig-*adj; adv*	full; completely
1022	volwassen-*adj*	adult
666	vooral-*adv*	especially, above all
1403	voorbeeld-*het*	example
1576	voorbereiden-*vb*	prepare
333	voorbij-*adj; adv; prp*	gone; past; beyond
332	voordat-*prp; con*	prior to; ere
1624	voordeel-*het*	advantage
1752	voorgoed-*adv*	permanently
1292	voorkomen-*vb; het*	prevent; appearance
1553	voorlopig-*adj; adv*	temporary; for the time being
23	voor-*prp; adv; con*	for; before; ere
1389	voorstel-*het*	proposal
610	voorstellen-*vb*	propose
2346	voorstelling-*de*	performance
2033	voortaan-*adv*	henceforth
1557	voort-*adv*	on
2505	voortduren-*vb*	continue
286	vooruit-*adv*	forward, ahead
2111	vooruitgang-*de*	progress
2341	voorwaarts-*adj; adv*	forward; forward
432	voorzichtig-*adj; adv*	careful, cautious; carefully
2230	voorzien-*vb; adj*	provide; anticipate
1690	voorzitter-*de*	chairman
667	vorig-*adj*	last
1018	vorm-*de*	form

202	vraag-*de*	question
1885	vrachtwagen-*de*	truck
206	vragen-*vb*	ask
759	vrede-*de*	peace
491	vreemd-*adj; adv*	strange; strangely
2338	vreemdeling-*de*	stranger
1337	vrees-*de*	fear
574	vreselijk-*adj; adv*	terrible; terribly
2170	vreugde-*de*	joy
180	vriend-*de*	friend
1125	vriendelijk-*adj*	friendly, kind
397	vriendin-*de*	girlfriend
1596	vriendschap-*de*	friendship
319	vrij-*adj; adv*	free, clear; free
1123	Vrijdag-*de*	Friday
1897	vrijen-*vb*	have sex
885	vrijheid-*de*	freedom
2251	vrijlaten-*het; vb*	release; release
515	vroeger-*adv; adj*	earlier; former
1200	vrolijk-*adj*	cheerful, happy
130	vrouw-*de*	woman, wife
2039	vrouwelijk-*adj*	feminine, female
742	vuil-*het; adj; adv*	dirt; dirty; filthily
1876	vullen-*vb*	fill
1498	vuren-*vb*	fire
519	vuur-*het*	fire

W

2058	waanzin-*de*	madness
2220	waaraan-*adv*	whereat
47	waar-*adv; con; adj; de*	where; where; true; merchandise
1875	waarbij-*con; adv*	whereby; whereat
510	waard-*adj*	worth
1396	waarde-*de*	value
1463	waardeloos-*adj*	worthless
2101	waarderen-*vb*	appreciate
1280	waardoor-*con*	whereby
1314	waarheen-*adv*	where to
375	waarheid-*de*	truth
985	waarin-*adv*	wherein
939	waarmee-*adv*	with which
66	waarom-*adv; con*	why; why
819	waarop-*con; adv*	when; whereupon
975	waarover-*adv*	about which/what
368	waarschijnlijk-*adv; adj*	probably, presumably; likely
1511	waarschuwen-*vb*	warn
1581	waarschuwing-*de*	warning

908	waarvan-*adv*	of which, whose, where from
711	waarvoor-*adv*	for what
116	wachten-*vb*	wait
645	wagen-*de; vb*	car; risk
331	wakker-*adj*	awake
1506	walgelijk-*adj*	disgusting
1436	wandelen-*vb*	walk
2421	wang-*de*	cheek
1931	wanhopig-*adj*	desperate
189	wanneer-*adv; con*	when; when
210	want-*con; de*	because; mitten
2248	wapenen-*vb*	arm
453	wapen-*het*	weapon
690	warm-*adj*	warm
2448	warmte-*de*	heat
1399	wassen-*vb; adj*	wash; wax
10	wat-*con; prn; adv*	what; what; few
282	water-*het*	water
1483	wc-*de*	toilet
1256	wedden-*vb*	bet
643	wedstrijd-*de*	match, game
2453	weduwe-*de*	widow
301	week-*de; adj*	week; soft
831	weekend-*het*	weekend
100	weer-*het; adv*	weather; again
77	weg-*de; adv*	road; away, gone
1402	wegens-*prp*	due to, because of
723	weggaan-*vb*	go away, leave
2162	weghalen-*vb*	take away
2204	wegkomen-*vb*	escape
1893	weglopen-*vb*	walk away
593	wegwezen-*vb*	get out
1313	wei-*de*	whey
2143	weigeren-*vb*	refuse
570	weinig-*adj*	little, few
42	wel-*adv; adj; con*	well; alright; as many as
278	welk-*con; prn*	which; which
381	welkom-*int, adj*	welcome, appreciated
1428	wellicht-*adv*	perhaps
1474	welnee-*prt*	surely not
747	welterusten-*int*	sleep well
1372	wennen-*vb*	get used to
787	wens-*de*	wish
1244	wensen-*vb*	wish
12	we-*prn*	we
201	wereld-*de*	world
761	werkelijk-*adv; adj*	really; real
1868	werkelijkheid-*de*	reality

252	werken-*vb*	work
149	werk-*het*	work
1238	west-*de*	west
1173	westen-*het*	west
672	wet-*de*	law
1492	wetenschap-*de*	science
2300	wetenschapper-*de*	scientist
35	weten-*vb*	know
1010	wezen-*het; vb*	being; be
1350	whisky-*de*	whiskey
70	wie-*con; prn*	who; who
1759	wijf-*het*	hag
810	wijn-*de*	wine
102	wij-*prn*	we
1206	wijs-*adj; de*	wise; tune
2395	wijsheid-*de*	wisdom
992	wijten-*vb*	blame
1650	wijzen-*vb*	point
1245	wild-*adj; het*	wild; wildlife
41	willen-*vb*	want
823	wind-*de*	wind
2070	winden-*vb*	wrap
740	winkel-*de*	shop
2120	winkelen-*vb*	shop
1376	winnaar-*de*	winner
481	winnen-*vb*	win
1610	winst-*de*	profit
1504	winter-*de*	winter
2483	wiskunde-*de*	mathematics
2514	wisselen-*vb*	exchange
174	wissen-*vb*	wipe
689	wit-*adj*	white
2524	wodka-*de*	vodka
1651	woede-*de*	rage
1331	woestijn-*de*	desert
1445	wolf-*de*	wolf
2343	wolk-*de*	cloud
2475	wond-*de*	wound
986	wonder-*het*	wonder, miracle
580	wonen-*vb*	live
419	woord-*het*	word
95	worden-*vb*	will be, become
1016	wraak-*de*	revenge
2112	wreed-*adj*	cruel

Z

321	zaak-*de*	case, matter
2074	zaal-*de*	room
1530	zacht-*adj; adv*	soft; gently
895	zagen-*vb*	saw
579	zak-*de*	bag
1689	zand-*het*	sand
682	zee-*de*	sea
2057	zeep-*de*	soap
380	zeer-*adj; adv; het*	very, highly; very; sore
1645	zegen-*de;*	blessing
2232	zegenen-*vb*	bless
89	zeggen-*vb*	say
120	zeker-*adj; adv*	confident; sure
1927	zekerheid-*de*	certainty
2439	zelden-*adv*	rarely
846	zelfmoord-*de*	suicide
211	zelf-*prn*	self
216	zelfs-*adv*	even
2288	zender-*de*	transmitter
1815	zenuwachtig-*adj*	nervous
2079	zenuw-*de*	nerve
14	ze-*prn*	she, they
2500	zesde-*nu*	sixth
349	zes-*nu*	six
2511	zestien-*nu*	sixteen
245	zetten-*vb*	put, place
2352	zeuren-*vb*	whine
482	zeven-*nu*	seven
150	zich-*prn*	himself
478	zichzelf-*prn*	himself
473	ziek-*adj*	sick
527	ziekenhuis-*het*	hospital
1222	ziekte-*de*	disease
674	ziel-*de*	soul
1509	zielig-*adj*	pathetic
79	zien-*vb*	see, look
1678	zijde-*de*	side
5	zijn-*prn; vb*	his, its; be
125	zij-*prn; de*	she, they; side
425	zin-*de*	sentence
720	zingen-*vb*	sing
2412	zinloos-*adj*	pointless
108	zitten-*vb*	sit
39	zo-*adv; con;*	so, that; if
131	zoals-*adv; con; adj; prp*	as; as; such as; like
338	zodat-*con*	so that
663	zodra-*con*	once, as soon as
266	zoeken-*vb*	search
2151	zoenen-*vb*	kiss
2409	zogenaamd-*adv; adj*	supposed; allegedly
346	zoiets-*adj*	such a thing
1264	zojuist-*adv*	just (now)

591	zolang-*con*	as long as	1977	zowel-*adv*	both
512	zomaar-*adv*	just	1196	zuiden-*het*	south
974	zomer-*de*	summer	749	zulk-*adj*	such
1175	zondag-*de*	Sunday	60	zullen-*vb; av*	will; shall
692	zon-*de*	sun	483	zus-*de*	sister
1180	zonde-*de; adj*	sin; too bad	1771	zusje-*het*	little sister
179	zonder-*prp*	without	670	zuster-*de*	sister
1826	zone-*de*	zone	2119	zuurstof-*de*	oxygen
2489	zonsondergang-*de*	sunset	661	zwaar-*adj*	heavy
2349	zonsopgang-*de*	sunrise	1024	zwaard-*het*	sword
2122	zooi-*de*	mess	1172	zwak-*adj*	weak
229	zoon-*de*	son	857	zwanger-*adj*	pregnant
320	zorg-*de*	care, worry	543	zwart-*adj*	black
199	zorgen-*vb*	care, worry	2293	zweet-*het*	sweat
1994	zout-*adj; het*	salt; salt	1448	zwembad-*het*	swimming pool
300	zoveel-*adv*	so many, so much	1009	zwemmen-*vb*	swim
655	zover-*adv*	as far as	633	zweren-*verb*	swear
2187	zowat-*adv*	almost	1209	zwijgen-*vb*	keep silent

Contact, Further Reading and Resources

For more tools, tips & tricks visit our site www.mostusedwords.com. We publish various language learning resources. If you have a great idea you want to pitch us, please send an e-mail to info@mostusedwords.com.

Frequency Dictionaries

In this series:

Dutch Frequency Dictionary 1 – Essential Vocabulary – 2500 Most Common Dutch Words
Dutch Frequency Dictionary 2 – Intermediate Vocabulary – 2501-5000 Most Common Dutch Words
Dutch Frequency Dictionary 3 – Advanced Vocabulary – 5001-7500 Most Common Dutch Words
Dutch Frequency Dictionary 4 – Master Vocabulary – 7501-10000 Most Common Dutch Words

Our mission is to provide language learners worldwide with frequency dictionaries for every major and minor language. We are working hard to accomplish this goal. You can view our selection on https://store.mostusedwords.com/frequency-dictionaries

Bilingual books

We're creating a selection of parallel texts. We decided to rework timeless classics, such as Alice in Wonderland, Sherlock Holmes, Dracula, The Picture of Dorian Gray, etc.

Our books are paragraph aligned: on one side of the page you will find the English version of the story, and on the other side is the translation in the language you're learning.

To help you in your language learning journey, all our bilingual books come with a dictionary included, created for that particular book.

For more information, check https://store.mostusedwords.com/bilingual-books . Check back regularly for new books and languages.

Other language learning methods

You'll find reviews of other 3rd party language learning applications, software, audio courses, and apps. There are so many available, and some are (much) better than others.

Check out our reviews at www.mostusedwords.com/reviews.

Contact

If you have any questions, you can contact us through e-mail info@mostusedwords.com.

Made in the USA
Middletown, DE
10 October 2022

12447432R00124